Oscar Hammerstein's Manhattan Opera Company

Oscar Hammerstein's
MANHATTAN
OPERA
COMPANY

By John Frederick Cone

UNIVERSITY OF OKLAHOMA PRESS

NORMAN

The publication of this volume has been aided by a grant from
THE MIRIAM AND IRA D. WALLACH FOUNDATION

Manuscript microfilm copyright 1964 by John F. Cone. Book copyright
1966 by the University of Oklahoma Press, Publishing Division of the
University. Composed and printed at Norman, Oklahoma, U.S.A., by the
University of Oklahoma Press. First edition.

*To Miriam and Ira Wallach
and their son Kenneth*

Preface

In THE FOUR YEARS of the existence of New York's Manhattan Opera Company (1906–10), Oscar Hammerstein presented many operatic productions with outstanding casts and conductors. Irving Kolodin has called this institution "the most worrisome competition that the Metropolitan [Opera Company] had ever known—artistically, without question, even though the social lustre was silver and rhinestones, rather than gold and diamonds." However, although the Manhattan was such an important factor in American operatic history, there has never been, in all these years, a definitive account of Hammerstein's group.

To remedy this gap, I have maintained certain basic objectives: (1) to determine the status of opera in New York and Philadelphia in the years immediately preceding the founding of this company; (2) to establish Hammerstein's background in the production of grand opera and his plans for its presentation; (3) to evaluate the day-after criticisms and the extended criticisms of the artists and the productions; (4) to provide accurate annals of the performances with the casts and conductors; (5) to ascertain the relationship between the Manhattan and the Metropolitan Opera Company; and (6) to note the significance of the Manhattan as part of American operatic history.

John Frederick Cone

Scarsdale, New York
February 7, 1966

Acknowledgments

—◦✄❧✄◦—

Without the assistance of many persons, this history would never have been possible. In particular, the author is grateful to the archivists at the Victoria and Albert Museum, Covent Garden, Royal Academy of Music, Paris Opéra; Miss Bernice M. Armstead of the Fisk University Library; M. Jules Bazin of the Service du Secrétariat, Division des Bibliothèques, Montreal; Mr. Alexander P. Clark of the Princeton University Library; Mr. Richard G. Conried; Mrs. Jack Crawford of the Yale University Library; Mme Pauline Donalda; Mrs. Dorothy English of the Carnegie Library of Pittsburgh; Lynn Farnol Public Relations; Miss Geraldine Farrar; Miss Edith G. Firth of the Toronto Public Library; Mr. George Freedley; The Free Library of Philadelphia Newspaper Division; Miss Mary Garden; Mr. Robert P. Giddings of the Boston Public Library; Mrs. Lawrence Gilman; Miss Anne Gordon of the Press Department of the Metropolitan Opera Company; Mr. Theodore Hammerstein; Mr. William Hammerstein; Mrs. Elizabeth L. Hunter and Mr. Augustus M. Long of the Ottawa Public Library; Mr. Gilbert Kahn; Miss Ellen Kenny and Miss Norma Jean Lamb of the Buffalo and Erie County Public Library; Mrs. Catherine M. Kilcoyne of the Public Library of Cincinnati and Hamilton County; Mr. Irving Kolodin; Mrs. Bernice B. Larrabee of the Free Library of Philadelphia; Lauterstein and Lauterstein, Legal Counsel of the Metropolitan Opera Company; The Library of Congress; Mr. Horace Mather Lippincott; Mrs. Clarence Mackay; Maison Durand; Mrs. Mary Jane Matz; Mrs. Marguerite McAneny of the Princeton

University Library; The Metropolitan Opera Archives; The Metropolitan Opera Guild; Mr. Philip Miller; Miss Stella Murray, Mme Melba's pupil and friend, who was graciousness itself during a sojourn in London; The Museum of the City of New York; The New York Historical Society; New York Public Library Music Division; New York Public Library Newspaper Division; New York Public Library Theater Division; Mr. Sam Pearce; Mrs. John DeWitt Peltz; Mr. Harold Rosenthal; Mrs. John Barry Ryan; Mrs. May Davenport Seymour; Mr. Vincent Sheean; Mrs. Dorothy E. Simpson of the Hamilton Public Library, Hamilton, Canada; Mr. Marziale Sisca; Mrs. Emma Swift of the Rochester Public Library, Rochester, New York; The White Plains Public Library, White Plains, New York; Mrs. Helen D. Willard of the Harvard College Library; Mr. R. N. Williams, II, of The Historical Society of Pennsylvania, Philadelphia; Mr. Carl Van Vechten; Mme Alice Zeppilli.

I wish to thank Eyre and Spottiswoode (Publishers) Ltd., for permission to quote lengthy extracts from Nellie Melba's *Melodies and Memories*, published by Thornton Butterworth Ltd. in 1925.

Of especial help were Mr. Arthur Shimkin and Mr. Henry W. Simon of Simon and Schuster; Mrs. Jean Bowen Bloch and Dr. Sirvart Poladian of the Music Division of The New York Public Library; and Mrs. Alice Vitale of the Newspaper Division of The New York Public Library. Mrs. Bloch, Mrs. Mary W. Howard, and Mrs. Harriet Trilling Schwartz patiently read through the manuscript and deserve warmest gratitude for their abiding interest, as do Mr. Joseph M. Galvin, Mr. George F. Reed, Dr. Elbert Gross, and Mr. John C. Kemp, a colleague and an esteemed friend who assisted in gathering material concerning the Manhattan Opera Company.

Professors Fred C. Blanchard, James H. Hanscom, and William P. Sears, of New York University, devoted hours to reading and criticizing this history. To them I am indebted for their untiring efforts, patience, and encouragement.

Finally, I am deeply indebted to Mrs. Henriette Beal, who was of assistance in assembling the pictures and illustrations.

JOHN FREDERICK CONE

Contents

Illustrations

Oscar Hammerstein's Manhattan Opera Company

I

All Was But Prologue
———❦———

On February 23, 1906, Oscar Hammerstein fired the opening salvo of the greatest opera war in the history of the United States. Without stockholders, advisers, partners, a board of directors, or the patronage of the rich, he announced his intention to compete against New York's Metropolitan Opera Company in the fall by presenting opera on an unprecedented scale and with international stars at his new theater, the Manhattan Opera House, then being constructed on West Thirty-fourth Street, between Eighth and Ninth avenues. His object was great opera, not just grand opera.

Hammerstein proudly made known that the incomparable Edouard de Reszke would be a member of the company and that Jean de Reszke, the nonpareil of tenors, was more than likely to make some guest appearances. The basso was to receive $1,000 a performance; his brother, $3,500. Who the other luminaries were Hammerstein did not say except that they were eminent artists, worthy colleagues of the de Reszkes. The repertory of twenty-five Italian and French operas would comprise not only standard works but also such novelties as Charpentier's *Louise*, Bruneau's *L'Attaque du Moulin*, and Debussy's *Pelléas et Mélisande*. The chorus and orchestra were to be mostly Americans; the conductors, well-known Europeans. In short, Hammerstein's purpose was to revivify the presentation of opera in New York, which, he maintained, had deteriorated at the Metropolitan, and to make the United States more conscious of the great music dramas.[1] What had been amiss was to be redressed. He would lead the way out of the operatic desert.

No doubt many who read or heard of Hammerstein's venture were skeptical. Henry Edward Krehbiel, in *Chapters of Opera*, relates that some "looked upon his enterprise as quixotic, down to the very day of the opening of his house."[2] Few would deny that Hammerstein was an able man of the theater and that he was extraordinarily resourceful, usually accomplishing what he set out to do. The fact remained, however, that since New York already had the great Metropolitan Opera Company, it seemed foolhardy for any individual to found a second operatic organization of the first rank without the support of society. To compete against the Metropolitan appeared to be the height of the ridiculous. There was something else to remember: Hammerstein's past efforts in serious opera productions had not been enlivening. Still, some may have conceded that this time it might be different. After all, Hammerstein had accomplished the miraculous before in other fields of entertainment. Of greater significance, he had always welcomed challenges and had triumphed over seemingly insurmountable odds. It is likely that there were those who would say that his life thus far had been a testament to this very fact.

VAULTING AMBITION

As a youth in Berlin, Hammerstein had sedulously applied himself to school work and to the study of the piano, flute, and violin, as well as harmony and counterpoint. Not all of these efforts, however, were self-inspired. His father, a prosperous building contractor, was a martinet, determined that his son should become a man of erudition. In time the lad resented the Procrustean discipline, and after the death of his mother, he found his home life intolerable. One evening, when he was fifteen, he returned late from ice skating and his father, furious and unreasonable, hit him, hurting his forehead. Resenting this kind of chastisement, the boy slipped away later that night, sold his violin to a nearby pawnbroker, and, taking his meager savings, en-

[1] News item in the *New York American*, February 23, 1906.
[2] Henry Edward Krehbiel, *Chapters of Opera*, 363.

trained for Hamburg. There he found passage on a cattle boat bound for the United States, then, in 1863, in the midst of the Civil War.[3]

Arriving in New York almost penniless, Hammerstein found a job making cigars at two dollars a week. His industry and ambition were enormous and he received one wage raise after another. When not working, he studied English and attended the theater, his first New York theatrical experience apparently occurring in March, 1864, when he saw the Bryant Brothers' Minstrels at Mechanics' Hall.[4] Opera presentations at the Academy of Music also attracted him. It was there, according to his biographer Vincent Sheean, that he "first felt the strange longing to bring opera to performance himself."[5] In 1868, Hammerstein married a woman who shared many of his interests. From their union came five sons, but in 1876, his beloved wife died. Later he remarried and by his second wife had two daughters.

In the 1870's, Hammerstein was still employed in the cigar business and made many inventions which he patented and from which he derived considerable income, the first one being a mold that facilitated the manufacture of cigars. By now he was an apt student in English, and successfully published the *United States Tobacco Journal*, which he founded in 1874. As editor and publisher, he wrote everything in the paper, which was peddled to the men in the cigar business. Then, as his fortunes increased, he began to invest in real estate and to build apartments. Sheean speculates that Hammerstein's real motive in amassing money was to enable him to become a producer of opera.[6]

Hammerstein also composed music and wrote plays in German. He was encouraged in these efforts by his friend Adolph Neuendorff, a conductor of some standing. These two men often discussed the theater, especially opera and its production. In September, 1871, when Neuendorff got together a company to present a short season of German opera at the Stadt Theater, Hammerstein invested some money in the enterprise, wrote publicity for it, and helped in any way

[3] Vincent Sheean, *Oscar Hammerstein I*, 13–14.
[4] *Ibid.*, 23.
[5] *Ibid.*, 26.   [6] *Ibid.*, 39.

he could. From 1874–77, the two men were associated in the Germania Theatre, where some of Hammerstein's plays and music were presented. In this milieu he was happiest, for the theater was in his blood.

In the 1880's, Hammerstein devoted most of his time to real estate speculation, building, and to his inventions, although he retained his interest in theatrical affairs, even backing several plays. He crowned his building efforts at the end of the decade when, after constructing various apartment houses, as well as dwellings on 141st and 142nd streets, he built his first theater, the Harlem Opera House, on 125th Street, between Seventh and Eighth avenues. It opened on September 30, 1889. At first it was not a success, although Hammerstein had engaged star performers. His penchant for the best or nothing at all is indicated by some of the players and attractions: E. H. Sothern; Marie Wainwright; Boyd Putnam in *The Wife*; Tommy Russell in *Little Lord Fauntleroy*; Mme Modjeska and Edwin Booth in Shakespearean plays; Fanny Davenport in Sardou's *La Tosca*; Joseph Jefferson and W. J. Florence in *The Rivals*.[7]

In 1890, Hammerstein constructed another playhouse in Harlem, the Columbus Theatre, which opened with Margaret Mather and Otis Skinner in *Romeo and Juliet*. Several years later (1892), he built the first Manhattan Opera House, on West 34th Street. In July, 1893, he entered into partnership with Koster and Bial, turning over the Manhattan to variety shows. After approximately a year and a half, Hammerstein withdrew from this association and received in settlement $375,000 and a $300,000 mortgage on the building.[8] The enormous profit in this kind of theatrical entertainment is indicated by Hammerstein's having received approximately $150,000 during the partnership.

During this period (1893) Hammerstein accomplished a feat which contributed to his growing legend. James Huneker, in *Steeplejack*, related that he was at lunch one day at the Gilsey House with

[7] George C. D. Odell, *Annals of the New York Stage*, XIV, 307–309.
[8] Sheean, *Oscar Hammerstein I*, 82.

Hammerstein, Gustave Kerker, the composer of operettas, and other men interested in the theater. Kerker complained that it was difficult to write an operetta and that it required a great deal of time, at least two months. Hammerstein pooh-poohed the idea and declared that he could write the words and music for an operetta within forty-eight hours. Although his friends laughed, he was serious and bet a hundred dollars that it could be done, and Kerker accepted the challenge.

The men escorted Hammerstein to a room at the Gilsey House, where for the next forty-eight hours he labored over his composition, later called *The Kohinoor*. Although there were distractions (organ-grinders under the window, for one), Hammerstein continued to write and compose. At the end of the stated time he emerged triumphant with the completed work in his hands, which he subsequently produced. Huneker recalled the first performance, on October 30, 1893:

> ... That first night of *The Kohinoor* was a notorious one; also side-splitting. The audience, of the true Tenderloin variety, laughed themselves blue in the face. I remember that the opening chorus consumed a third of the first act. Oscar knew the art of camouflage before the word was invented. Two comic Jews, alternately for a half-hour sang: "Good morning, Mr. Morgenstern, Good morning, Mr. Isaacstein," while the orchestra shifted the harmonics so as to avoid too much monotony....[9]

Hammerstein next built the Olympia, on Broadway at 44th and 45th streets, much farther uptown than the theatrical district of the day. When completed in 1895, it was the largest theater in the city and housed variety acts, plays, European celebrities (Yvette Guilbert was one of the stars) and some of Hammerstein's own works, including the ballet *Marguerite* and the operetta *Santa Maria*. Although Hammerstein's successes had been dazzling, they proved to be ephemeral. In the next few years he suffered a series of financial reverses which resulted in his having to close the Olympia. Hammer-

[9] James Gibbons Huneker, *Steeplejack*, II, 63.

stein was bankrupt, the debacle being so complete that his biographer states he did not have money for food.[10] People said that he was finished, a has-been; but they did not know their man.

With some borrowed money and income from inventions, Hammerstein built still another theater, the Victoria, located at 42nd Street and 7th Avenue, which opened on March 2, 1899. All of this he accomplished nine months after losing the Olympia! It is no wonder that Broadway considered him a fantastic individual. Alan Dale wrote this of the opening:

> New York is a pretty good place to make a hit in. If there is a kinder, more appreciative and more encouraging public anywhere, tell me where it is. Oscar was the hero of the night. I don't believe that there was one speck of humanity present that didn't wish him Godspeed from the very base of the ventricles. They clamored for his speech before it came. The roars of approval must have been heard at the Battery. It was a red-letter night, with very red letters. The enthusiasm will cling to the house for many days to come.[11]

This theater was a gold mine, particularly when, in 1904, it became a vaudeville house. Sheean maintains that each year the profits were $200,000 and occasionally more.[12] With this source of revenue, Hammerstein could now indulge his ambition to be a producer of grand opera. Some people thought him mad, and believed that this endeavor would be his Waterloo, with good reason. Certainly his past independent ventures in operatic production had not revealed any exceptional ability, since they had mostly been mediocre.

EARLY OPERATIC VENTURES

Soon after the opening (September 30, 1889) of the Harlem Opera House, Hammerstein engaged the Emma Juch Grand Opera Company for a series of performances in English: *Faust* (November

[10] Sheean, *Oscar Hammerstein I*, 98.
[11] News item in the *New York American*, March 3, 1899.
[12] Sheean, *Oscar Hammerstein I*, 114.

4); *The Trumpeter of Säckingen* (November 5); *Mignon* (November 6); *The Bohemian Girl* (November 7); *Carmen* (November 8); *Maritana* (November 9 matinee) and *Der Freischütz* (November 9 evening).[13] Unfortunately the peripatetic troupe was neither an artistic nor a financial success. Although the critics admired Juch in the four roles in which she appeared: Marguerite, Mignon, Carmen, and Agathe (*Der Freischütz*), they were dissatisfied with her associates, who were lacking in the "gifts and training commensurate with even the moderate requirements of her repertory."[14] Much had been expected of Maria Decca, formerly a soprano with the Carl Rosa and Mapleson Opera Companies in England. However, her appearance as Philine in Thomas' *Mignon* was so disastrous that she relinquished her part in the following evening's production (*The Bohemian Girl*) to Laura Bellini, who consented to appear in order to make the performance possible even though she was not a regular member of the company. She, too, was unsatisfactory. In the lovely aria "I Dreamt I Dwelt in Marble Halls," Bellini, according to the *Times*, dreamed she resided in halls "half a tone lower than those occupied by the orchestra."[15] Often the stage had so many furnishings that the singers had little room to move about. This cluttering of the stage in *Faust* "would have been amusing had it not been pitiful that it should have been permitted to mar the charm of Miss Juch's tasteful and sympathetic singing."[16] The week had hardly been an auspicious beginning for one who aspired to be an impresario.

In March, 1890, Hammerstein was again involved in the production of opera. This time he was directly responsible for the presentations, personally assembling a company of notable artists as well as engaging the conductor, orchestra, and chorus, and arranging for the scenery and costumes. Having no engagement for his theater at the end of the month, Hammerstein contemplated a short season of opera with singers from the Metropolitan. With this purpose in mind, he

[13] Odell, *Annals of the New York Stage*, XIV, 308.

[14] *New-York Daily Tribune*, November 9, 1889.

[15] *The New-York Times*, November 8, 1889.

[16] *New-York Daily Tribune*, November 9, 1889.

arranged for an interview with Edmund Stanton, the Metropolitan's director, who rejected Hammerstein's offer. Years later Hammerstein recalled Stanton's impatience: " 'Some people think they can come here and take up my time with the most absurd schemes. I should think you would have more sense than to come here and talk such nonsense to me!' "[17] With these words ringing in his ears, Hammerstein was more determined than ever to have grand opera that spring.

He went at once to the Hotel Normandie for the purpose of explaining his project to the artist he had wanted all the time: Lilli Lehmann, who was about to conclude her fifth consecutive season at the Metropolitan. In Germany she had been a highly esteemed soprano at the Berlin Opera and one of Wagner's favorite singers (she was a Valkyrie and the Forest Bird in *Siegfried* at the first Bayreuth Festival). In the United States, Lehmann had grown in artistic stature and had become the leading soprano at the Metropolitan after making her debut there on November 25, 1885. Always a perfectionist, she never spared herself or her voice. Her pre-eminence in the Wagnerian repertory, her artistic integrity, and her magnificent voice made such an impression on the New York opera-going public of the day that for years afterwards all other singers of her roles were evaluated according to Lehmann's lofty standard.

When Hammerstein met this formidable soprano and her husband, Paul Kalisch, a tenor who was also at the Metropolitan, he told them of his plan and asked them to appear in his Harlem Opera House. To his great joy, they were understanding and agreed to sing under his auspices. Thus encouraged, Hammerstein then engaged other singers and a chorus, with Walter Damrosch to conduct the performances. Since there was no time to construct scenery, Hammerstein had to rush all over New York, trying to get warehouse sets, costumes, and various stage furnishings required to produce grand opera.[18] With all arrangements finally concluded, he was ready for the series of performances given March 25–29, 1890.

[17] "Hammerstein's Plans for Grand Opera," *The Theatre Magazine*, Vol. VI (April, 1906), *vii.*
[18] *Ibid.*

Lehmann's farewell at the Metropolitan that season was her performance as Brünnhilde in a matinee of *Siegfried* on March 22, three days before she was to appear for Hammerstein. That New York opera-goers held her in high esteem was evident; for after having given her and the other artists many curtain calls, they shouted for the soprano to appear alone. "Cries of 'Lehmann' filled the air so persistently and people remained so doggedly that the prima donna could not mistake the ovation which was given her."[19] After some twenty minutes she came before her admirers, bowing low and appearing deeply moved by their demonstration of admiration. All this boded well for the Hammerstein engagement.

Lehmann opened the week at the Harlem Opera House on March 25 in Bellini's *Norma*. She had first sung the title role of this opera at the Metropolitan for a benefit performance about a month before, on February 27, 1890, and had astounded music critics and the public, accustomed to her German dramatic roles, by her versatility and style. For a Wagnerian soprano to be able to command florid singing was, then as now, a veritable sensation. Lehmann always retained her love for the more ornamental aspects of song, and she enjoyed singing roles requiring elegance of finish and facile vocalization. Of her first Metropolitan Norma, the *Times* said that she "demonstrated that her voice possessed far more flexibility and that she had a greater command of the pure ornamentation of singing than any one suspected . . . ."[20] Dramatically, she was commanding, sincere, forceful, "possessed of that rare combination of traits and equipment which made it possible for her to delineate the divinity in womanhood and womanhood in divinity, the mingling of the unapproachable goddess and the melting pitying human being . . . ."[21] Her reception was overwhelming, with a crowded and enthusiastic audience that was eager to hear her in a part which combined dramatic and coloratura singing and which, according to Lehmann herself, was more

[19] *The* [New York] *Sun*, March 23, 1890.
[20] *The New-York Times*, February 28, 1890.
[21] W. J. Henderson, *The Art of Singing*, 360.

difficult than singing all three Brünnhildes.[22] It was a role and an opera very dear to her. Of *Norma*, she wrote that it "should be sung and acted with fanatical consecration, rendered by the chorus and orchestra, especially with artistic reverence, led with authority by the director, and, to every single eighth note, should be given the musical tribute that is its due."[23]

Whether Hammerstein's production was up to her standards, Lehmann does not say; in fact, she does not mention him at all in her autobiography, *My Path Through Life*. The audience at the Harlem Opera House, however, must have thought the presentation a very good one, for they were most enthusiastic and generous in their applause. Of this performance, *The New-York Times* reported that rarely "if ever has grand opera been heard before on this island in the same high latitude. Mr. Hammerstein's venture is necessarily experimental, but the size of the audience called out last evening demonstrated the wisdom of making it. The house was literally crowded, not a seat being vacant up stairs or down. It was, moreover, an audience accustomed to hearing grand opera. Evening dress prevailed, and many carriages stood at the doors."[24]

The rest of the week included performances in German of *Les Huguenots* (March 26 and 28); another *Norma* (March 27); and *Il Trovatore* (March 29). In addition to Lehmann (who sang only in *Norma*) and Kalisch, the other singers in the company were Ida Klein, Conrad Behrens, Sophie Traubmann, Sophie Wiesner, Julius Perotti, Theodore Reichmann, Felicie Kaschowska, Josef Arden, Louise Meisslinger, Helen von Dönhoff. By the end of the highly successful engagement, Hammerstein had made a good deal of money and had tasted the first fruits of success in the production of grand opera. According to the *Tribune*, it had been "a musical, a managerial and a social success, and the commendable enterprise of Mr. Hammerstein was recognized by the presence of large audiences at each

[22] Krehbiel, *Chapters of Opera*, 150.
[23] Lilli Lehmann, *My Path Through Life* (trans. Alice Benedict Seligman), 326.
[24] March 26, 1890.

performance."[25] This outcome must have been gratifying to Hammerstein, whose competition this very week provided a preview of the future. At the Metropolitan, Henry E. Abbey and Maurice Grau had been presenting a spring season of opera with Patti, Tamagno, Albani, and Nordica.

Seven months later (October, 1890), Hammerstein brought forward more operatic productions. For the official opening of the fall season of the Harlem Opera House, he advertised an attraction that was called Hammerstein's English Opera Company, under the musical direction of Gustav Hinrichs. With the success of the Lehmann engagement behind him, Hammerstein, no doubt, was eager to follow up this happy venture with another. He decided to present opera in English, even though he must have realized that many before had made the same endeavor without conspicuous success; indeed, his own experience with the Emma Juch Grand Opera Company was a graphic example. Hammerstein believed, however, "that cheap prices and good singing in our native language"[26] would make people more opera conscious. He clung tenaciously to this idea, for from this time all his other early ventures in opera were productions in English.

The season, which began on October 11 and ended November 1, included in the repertory *Ernani* (October 11, 14, 16, 17 matinee); *Faust* (October 13, 15, 17, 18 evening); *Mignon* (October 20, 22, 24, 25 matinee); *Il Trovatore* (October 21 and 23); *The Bohemian Girl* (October 25 evening); and *Masaniello* and *Carmen* in succession from October 27 through November 1. Among the members of the company were Sig. Tagliapietra, T. S. Guise, William H. Clark, Minnie Landes, Adele Strauss, Fannie Gonzales, Alexander Gorsky, Sig. Montegriffo, Baron Berthald, May Kessler, Frank Pearson, Louise Meisslinger, Charlotte Walker, Cora Collini.[27] Paradoxically, one of the very qualities Hammerstein deemed requisite for opera in the vernacular, "good singing in our native language," was not a strong feature of the group. The names of some of the performers

[25] News item in the *New-York Daily Tribune*, March 30, 1890.
[26] Huneker, *Steeplejack*, 61.
[27] Odell, *Annals of the New York Stage*, XIV, 588–89.

suggest that they might have had difficulty singing intelligible English, and comments in the contemporary publications confirm this suspicion. The music critic of the New York *Sun*, reviewing the first performance of *Ernani*, said that, except in the case of one of the singers, "no one could tell what was the purport of the arias."[28] Then, too, some of the principals did not have the vocal technique for the parts they essayed. The work of the chorus and orchestra, "more powerful than refined,"[29] was erratic; it was obvious that there had been insufficient rehearsals. A review in *Musical Courier* counseled the nascent impresario: "Mr. Hammerstein, you will have to do better if you expect either patronage or critical praise."[30]

Certain performances, however, were commended. Some encomiums went to *Faust*, which maintained a high level of performance. The production of *Carmen*, in particular, was considered a fine achievement: "The representation had many merits, and indeed it reached a very agreeable plane of general excellence."[31] The critic of the *Tribune* said that the singers, considered from a purely musical point of view, needed "not to shun comparison with many more ambitious performers in this city. The same might be said of the reading of the work on the part of Mr. Hinrichs. In fact, it needed little to make the representation in all respects admirable. It was certainly Mr. Hammerstein's finest achievement."[32] Nevertheless, although some of the performances received praise, too often in the critical comments there was a tone of condescension, indicating that the reviewers were using the kid-glove treatment. Finally, some of the music critics, obviously wanting to encourage Hammerstein, over-emphasized the importance of attending his performances. They were likely to include in their reviews such statements as the following one: "It is a happy thing for the population of the northerly part of this city that

[28] *The* [New York] *Sun*, October 12, 1890.
[29] *The New-York Times*, October 28, 1890.
[30] "The Raconteur," *Musical Courier*, Vol. XXI (October 15, 1890), 380.
[31] *The New-York Times*, October 30, 1890.
[32] *New-York Daily Tribune*, October 30, 1890.

Mr. Hammerstein's enterprise enables them to hear such works as this at prices no greater than those asked at the theatres. His undertaking is a courageous one, and deserves support."[33] Perhaps their attitude was that it was better to have opera in Harlem even if it was not of the highest quality than to have no opera at all.

Hammerstein's next connection with grand opera was a group known as the Metropolitan English Opera Company, which appeared from May 25 to June 13, 1891, in Harlem, at his Columbus Theatre, the second playhouse he had erected. It was several blocks east of the Harlem Opera House on 125th Street, between Lexington and Fourth avenues. Among the singers in this troupe were Payne Clarke, Otto Rathjens, E. W. Knight, Georgine von Januschowsky, Louise Meisslinger, Nina Bertini, Marie Freebat, E. H. Knight, Thomas Guise. Many of them had been with the Emma Juch Company, which had recently disbanded in St. Louis, and several had appeared with Hammerstein in his English Opera Company. Adolph Neuendorff was musical director. The repertory, similar to the one Juch's company had presented at the Harlem Opera House, consisted of *Rigoletto*, *Carmen*, *The Bohemian Girl*, *Il Trovatore*, *Maritana*, *Der Freischütz* (presented under the title of *The Freeshooter*), and *Faust*.[34]

As was true with Hammerstein's English Opera Company, the principal criticism of this troupe was that the English text was not clear. Of the singers' efforts, one critic said the company presented a travesty of grand opera; he called it "burlesquing in Harlem."[35] In no uncertain terms, the writer lamented that "this season we have to endure the remnants of the defunct Juch Company, Mr. Locke [the director] having left them in the lurch, and the prima donna being in Europe. Lord deliver us from such music!"[36]

Still, some of the singing and acting was meritorious. Georgine von Januschowsky, in particular, proved a mainstay of the company.

[33] *The New-York Times*, October 14, 1890.
[34] Odell, *Annals of the New York Stage*, XIV, 593–94.
[35] *Musical Courier*, Vol. XXII (June 3, 1891), 577.
[36] *Ibid.*

The critics also commended Neuendorff's conducting for its "firm and spirited beat."[37] Above all, what remained most impressive was the sincerity, earnestness, and efforts of all concerned. The members of the group did the best they could with their talents, performing at all times *con brio* if not always with finesse.

Although all these ventures had caused little stir in the operatic sea, Hammerstein's proposed production for October 1, 1891, created a tempest. He intended to be the first producer in New York of Mascagni's *Cavalleria Rusticana*, the sensation of the time and a fantastic world-success since its *première* in Rome on May 17, 1890. For this purpose, Hammerstein made a contract with Eduardo Sonzogno of Milan, publisher of the opera, which was dated August 25, 1891.[38] He was to have the exclusive right to the production of the work in German and English in the United States (H. E. Abbey had the privilege of presenting it in Italian). In turn, Hammerstein was "to pay Sonzogno $3,500 and eight per cent royalty."[39]

About the first of September, Hammerstein discovered that another New York producer, Rudolph Aronson, also intended to give the opera. In fact, much to Hammerstein's consternation, his rival emphatically stated that Mascagni had given him permission to do so. To ascertain the truth of this statement, Hammerstein cabled the composer, who replied on September 5 that he had " 'granted rights in all countries to [his] publisher, Sonzogno.' "[40] Questioned about who had given him the authority to produce the opera, Aronson replied evasively:

> "Never mind . . . I've got the right. That's my business. I've got the right, and I'll produce the opera."[41]

Hammerstein's only recourse was to seek a permanent injunction against Aronson and the New York Concert Company in order to prevent the production.

[37] *New-York Daily Tribune*, June 2, 1891.
[38] News item in *The New-York Times*, September 19, 1891.
[39] *Ibid.*, September 26, 1891.
[40] *Ibid.*, September 19, 1891.
[41] *Ibid.*

On September 25, Judge Ingraham, of the Supreme Court, heard Hammerstein's and Aronson's pleas. Hammerstein stated his case, claiming sole rights, while Aronson maintained that the opera was public property and that parts of it had already been published and were available to any buyer. After hearing both the plaintiff and defendant, the Judge did not act, deferring judgment.

In the meantime, Hammerstein rushed rehearsals, still hoping that he would be the first to present *Cavalleria Rusticana* in New York. Aronson, however, had the same idea. On the very afternoon of October 1, the date Hammerstein had announced for the *première*, Aronson had a so-called rehearsal at the Casino, which served the purpose of a professional performance. He sent complimentary tickets to the theaters; among the ones who responded were the Anton Seidls, De Wolf Hopper, Walter Damrosch, Mrs. Georgiana Drew Barrymore, and Miss Marie Tempest. In this way, even though the opera was not actually performed publicly, Aronson robbed Hammerstein of the honor of the New York *première*, for many musicians and lovers of opera had heard the day's most talked of music drama some three hours before Hammerstein's presentation at the Lenox Lyceum. In Aronson's production, staged by Heinrich Conried, Laura Bellini was Santuzza; Grace Golden, Lola; Helen von Dönhoff, Mama Lucia; Charles Bassett, Turiddu; and William Pruette, Alfio, with Gustave Kerker conducting.

In Hammerstein's cast that evening were Georgine von Januschowsky (Santuzza), Louise Pemberton-Hincks (Lola), Jenny Bohner (Mama Lucia), Payne Clarke (Turiddu), Hermann Gerold (Alfio), under the baton of Adolph Neuendorff. Since the Lenox Lyceum had not been constructed for opera, Hammerstein had had to improvise in order to make the performance at all possible. The situation was difficult, as there was no proscenium arch, no orchestra pit, and the acoustics were abominable.

Of the performance, the *New-York Daily Tribune* said:

> Mr. Hammerstein's first performance took place at the Lenox Lyceum in the evening. Everything about it samcked [*sic*] of an improvization except the singing of Madame Jan-

ouschowsky as Santuzza, Payne Clark as Turriddu, and the chorus, the playing of the orchestra and the conducting of Mr. Neuendorf. A canvas proscenium was hung up all awry in front of the platform which was made to do duty as a stage.... The orchestra, composed of some of the best musicians in New-York, sat in the audience-room with nothing separating it from the audience. The costumes represented all countries except Sicily, where the scene of the little play is laid. When Turriddu sang his drinking song the chorus regaled itself with supposititious Chianti, which it drank with Teutonic gusto from beer mugs. In the audience, which was numerous and contained many well-known musicians and music-lovers, sat Mr. Kerker, who had conducted the Casino performance in the afternoon, and Miss Helene von Doenhoeff, who had sung the part of Lucia .... The audience listened to four pieces of orchestral music which preceded the opera with impatience, and were stirred into great enthusiasm by the Easter chorus, the first air of Santuzza and Turriddu and by the Intermezzo. It was plain that the excerpts played so often by Mr. Seidl's orchestra at Brighton Beach and the Madison Square Garden had awakened a lively interest in the opera. The performance was marked by a number of comical mishaps, and the general effect was that of a concert in costume.[42]

The day following the *première*, Judge Ingraham made known his decision not to enjoin Aronson since there was no longer an exclusive right to the production of the opera because the libretto, piano, and vocal scores had already been published. All that remained unpublished were some parts of the orchestral accompaniment. Furthermore, since the opera had been produced earlier in the United States (in Philadelphia and in Chicago) " 'without the authority of the composer or his assignees,' "[43] he saw no reason why Aronson should not also have the right to produce the work.

[42] October 2, 1891.
[43] News item in *The New-York Times*, October 3, 1891.

Aronson subsequently presented the opera for fifty-five performances. Hammerstein was bitter about the experience and staged the work only a few times at the Harlem Opera House. Later he said that the opera "should have been called Cavalleria Busticana instead of Rusticana!"[44]

Before his plan to rival the Metropolitan developed, Hammerstein made one final effort at opera production, fifteen months after the *Cavalleria* sensation. At that time he was building another theater, the first Manhattan Opera House, which was located on West 34th Street, between Broadway and 7th Avenue, the site that the R. H. Macy store now occupies. Originally he had hoped to dedicate it by presenting opera in German. In a circular letter, dated May 30, 1891, he informed the New York public that he intended to present sixty performances of opera in German beginning in December, 1892, since the "recent strong and enthusiastic demonstrations in favor of opera in German [were] the incentive to [his] project."[45] He planned magnificent productions, but to make them feasible he needed advance subscriptions for the boxes, at $2,500 each for the season. Payment would not be asked until singers, conductors, and other personnel had been determined. What Hammerstein wanted, of course, was the assurance that he would have financial backing for the season. He requested that the subscription list be completed within ten days, hardly giving any would-be subscribers time to consider the proposal. *Musical Courier* posed several questions and made a pertinent comment:

> ... Where will Mr. Hammerstein get a competent conductor? Where are his artists? And, most important of all, where are the subscribers at $2500 a head for the boxes?
> This last is a very important question, Mr. Hammerstein.[46]

Not being successful in obtaining sufficient subscriptions, Ham-

[44] Rudolph Aronson, *Theatrical and Musical Memoirs*, 87.
[45] News item in the *New-York Daily Tribune*, May 31, 1891.
[46] "Hammersteiniana," *Musical Courier*, Vol. XXII (June 3, 1891), 578.

merstein had to content himself with more opera in English. His beautiful new theater had opened on November 18, 1892, with a company of actors that included Miss Bernard-Beere, who had been a success in London, Maurice Barrymore, and Guy Standing. Other attractions followed until finally, on January 24, 1893, Hammerstein again turned to the production of opera with what seemed a tremendous advantage: he had the field to himself. Since a fire at the Metropolitan, on August 27, 1892, had destroyed much of that building's auditorium and stage, there was no opera in the house until the fall of 1893. Hammerstein chose for his initial presentation a novelty, Moszkowski's *Boabdil*, which, when first performed in Berlin, on April 14, 1892, was only a *succès d'estime*.

The plot of this work is not unfamiliar in grand opera; it is the self-sacrifice of a woman who, to save her husband's life, dies in his stead. As produced by Hammerstein, the opera fell short of the display and pageantry which the libretto and score demanded; still, the *Times* said, it was "much better than some recently witnessed in the Metropolitan Opera House. To be sure, there were no great 'stars' in the cast, but there was a respectable general level of merit and an abundant sincerity of purpose . . . ."[47] In the list of principals were several who had appeared with Hammerstein in the past: Januschowsky, Conrad Behrens, Payne Clarke, Otto Rathjens. These singers as well as J. Bolze and Thea Dorri "acquitted themselves with no little credit."[48]

The music critic of the *New-York Daily Tribune*, on the other hand, was indignant:

> . . . That a quartet of Moors in the first act should be permitted to outrage the ears of the listeners, and a "serpentine" dancer, imported from some poverty-stricken concert-hall allowed to provoke smiles of derision in the second, were, however, unpardonable features of the representation and if the future of the opera and the entire enterprise was endangered thereby,

[47] *The New-York Times*, January 25, 1893.
[48] *Ibid*.

Mr. Hammerstein need not be at a loss where to lay the blame. There is a limit to the amiability even of an audience anxious to give opera in English a fair trial.[49]

The production of *Carmen* the following evening (January 25) was unfortunate, the tenor Durward Lely being ill and suffering from stage fright, with the chorus bungling various details. In the first act, when the captain of the dragoons gave orders to face right, some of the squad turned backstage, while others faced the audience. Finally, since the stage management was lax and the mechanical effects were weak, the production never really got off the ground. The whole performance showed that Bizet's opera had not been sufficiently rehearsed.

Rigoletto, The Bohemian Girl, Il Trovatore, and *Fidelio* were not especially good productions, though Januschowsky's Leonore (*Fidelio*) was a moving portrayal. The soprano revealed a "thorough comprehension of the dramatic significance of her role, and she sang with unfailing vigor."[50] Other singers in these operas were mediocre or worse, and they were overworked. The stage management was hopelessly inadequate; the presentations needed more rehearsals. Realizing that the season was a fiasco, Hammerstein concluded it with the evening performance of *Il Trovatore* on February 4. Instead of a series of performances of eleven weeks, which he had originally announced, he concluded the engagement at the end of a fortnight. Once again Hammerstein had not produced artistic opera; it was all inferior work. This time he came in for some sharp censure:

> . . . In view of the width and depth of the chasm which yawns between Mr. Hammerstein's promises and protestations and his achievements it is becoming season after season more diffi- cult to take him seriously . . . .[51]

Of the early operatic ventures, the only success that Hammerstein

[49] *New-York Daily Tribune,* January 25, 1893.
[50] *The New-York Times,* February 4, 1893.
[51] *New-York Daily Tribune,* February 5, 1893.

realized was the Lehmann engagement, while the other enterprises
had been financial and artistic failures. What had been palpably lacking was adequate staging, costuming, and settings; there had not been
sufficient rehearsals; and too many of the singers had lacked the vocal
ability to perform the roles assigned to them. Hammerstein's presentations had been, more often than not, slipshod, makeshift, and
mediocre.

In all these enterprises, even though the spirit had been willing,
insufficient finances had been a thorn in the flesh. Hammerstein's last
attempt at the Manhattan Opera House could have succeeded since
there was no season at the Metropolitan and New York was athirst
for opera; but he had not allowed himself enough time to plan his
season, and again he lacked the all-important funds.

A Golden Opportunity

Since there had been little success for Hammerstein in these inde-
pendent operatic enterprises (except for the Lehmann engagement),
it might have been assumed that he would not attempt further sallies
into the treacherous field. His family hoped that he would not do so,
but observed with growing trepidation that, beginning in 1904, he
played opera scores on the piano more often than usual and that opera
was a recurrent subject in conversation. Hammerstein finally confessed to several of his sons what they had already guessed: he intended to produce opera again.[52] He had his reasons for believing that
this was the propitious time.

Hammerstein believed that opera as given at the Metropolitan
Opera House was a disgrace and that Heinrich Conried, the director
since 1903, was incompetent, " ' not equal to the occasion.' "[53] According to Vincent Sheean, Conried aroused in Hammerstein a loathing
that was unusual for a man who was known not to hold grudges. The
exact reason for his antipathy to this former Austrian actor is not
known. What is certain is that during their association of many years

[52] Sheean, *Oscar Hammerstein I*, 119–20.

[53] News item in *The* [New York] *Globe and Commercial Advertiser*,
June 1, 1906.

before in the production of a German opus called *The Perjured Peasant* (Hammerstein backed the play while Conried acted in it), the two men quarreled irreconcilably, parting with bitter feelings towards each other.[54] Because of this active hostility towards Conried, Hammerstein's criticism of the Metropolitan might very well have been biased. Preceding seasons might explain whether his criticisms were valid or not.

After the financially disastrous inaugural season of 1883–84, the Metropolitan entered into one of the most artistic periods in its history. For the next seven seasons opera was presented in German, with the repertory dominated by the masterpieces of Wagner, magnificently interpreted by a group of artists whose selfless devotion to their art has been unique in the history of opera. Among the achievements of this epoch was the first presentation in the United States of the complete *Ring des Nibelungen, Tristan und Isolde,* and *Die Meistersinger.* By 1891, however, the directors, though satisfied with the financial results of German opera, desired a change. It was said that the list of operas was tedious, that the gloom of the auditorium, necessitated by the many dark scenes in Wagner, had become intolerable to society folk, who were unable to display jewels and other finery.[55]

The collaboration of Henry E. Abbey, Maurice Grau, and John B. Schoeffel in the season of 1891–92, which lasted until the death of Abbey in 1896, marked the beginning of another distinguished era at the opera house, a period remembered ever since for the phenomenal singers with the highest vocal ideals and artistic aims. Each one could easily have been the epitome of the art of singing: Jean and Edouard de Reszke, Victor Capoul, Jean Lassalle, Emma Albani, Emma Calvé, Emma Eames, Lilli Lehmann, Lillian Nordica, Pol Plançon, Nellie Melba, Victor Maurel, Francesco Tamagno. After Abbey's death in 1896, with the reorganization of the company and Maurice Grau's assuming the duties of director, other extraordinary artists were added to the already peerless roster: Ernestine Schumann-Heink, Johanna Gadski, Milka Ternina, Louise Homer,

[54] Sheean, *Oscar Hammerstein I,* 39.
[55] Krehbiel, *Chapters of Opera,* 210.

Ernest Van Dyck, Antonio Scotti, Charles Gilibert, Marcel Journet, and Marcella Sembrich, who returned to the company in the season of 1898–99, after an absence of fourteen years. It would seem that in the years 1891–1903 the Metropolitan had virtually all the great singers in the world.

Fortunate indeed were the New York opera-goers in those days! In the season of 1898–99, for instance, they could hear during the week of January 2, 1899, a *Don Giovanni* with Lehmann, Sembrich, Nordica, Edouard de Reszke, Maurel, Salignac; *Roméo et Juliette* with Suzanne Adams, Dufriche, Jean and Edouard de Reszke, Plançon; *Le Nozze di Figaro* with Eames, Sembrich, Edouard de Reszke, and Campanari; the Saturday matinee of *Tristan* with Lehmann, Jean and Edouard de Reszke, Brema, and Van Rooy. It was this particular occasion that Lehmann referred to years later as " 'the ideal *Tristan* performance' "[56] of her entire career. And, as W. J. Henderson remarked, Lehmann "had sung with all the Tristans from Niemann down."[57] The first opera of the following week, *Lohengrin,* included the de Reszkes, Nordica, Schumann-Heink, and Bispham. Two nights later *Faust* was heard with the de Reszkes and Melba. The next day the Metropolitan began the first American uncut Ring cycle. Such prodigality for these two weeks was not the exception but the rule. During this era, week after week and season after season, the casts at the opera house were exactly as the management advertised: ideal. Stars of the first magnitude with such vocal excellence and with such highly developed artistry have always been rare, but this era is truly unusual in operatic history. As Kolodin has said: "There have been, in each period of the Metropolitan, unusual artists; artists of fine voices, splendid presence, and superior intelligence. But there has been at no time so abundant a flow of them; so uncommon a succession of new personages, of individualities so strongly developed, who were yet so conscious of their obligations to the art which they served."[58]

[56] Henderson, *The Art of Singing,* 338.
[57] *Ibid.*
[58] Irving Kolodin, *The Metropolitan Opera 1883–1935,* 88.

Still, the productions at the Metropolitan were not always what they should have been. Criticism was rife. W. J. Henderson wrote in February, 1895:

> The best that can be said of the system under which our opera-house is conducted is that it has made us acquainted with some of the greatest singers the world has ever known . . . . But . . . [the] presentations have been marred by the presence of minor singers who threw a clamorous note of discord into the general harmony, by ballet-dancing which was little short of absurd, and by choral and orchestral work utterly out of place in so pretentious an establishment as the Metropolitan Opera-house . . . . Yet it would not be difficult to so improve the ballet, chorus, orchestra, and *mise en scène* that public taste would be educated to a higher standard. The next step would be the introduction of an enlightened system of stage management which would regard the opera as a lyric drama, and aim at a consistent, symmetrical treatment of the various elements which go to make up an operatic representation . . . .[59]

The paucity of new operas in the repertory also was lamented. Grau's policy was to produce few novelties since he believed that the public did not want them and that it was the star, not the opera, that drew. As a result, year after year he presented to his patrons those casts and operas which they liked and to which they were accustomed. So long as he had the matchless vocalists, he could well afford to continue giving few novelties, even though certain dissatisfied elements of the public might desire them. The only question was how long the splendiferous singers would last.

After the retirement of Grau, who was in bad health, at the end of the 1902–1903 season, Heinrich Conried was selected as director of the opera. He had had a great deal of experience in the theater but, like Grau, knew little about music or singing. Some found him high-handed. According to his biographer Montrose J. Moses, Conried

[59] "The Season of Grand Opera," *Harper's Weekly,* Vol. XXXIX (February 16, 1895), 159.

learned early in life at the Bremen Stadttheater that there was "no one . . . above him,"[60] and he thereafter adopted "an imperious manner which instilled confidence into those under him, but which gained for him many enemies."[61] In the United States he had been in charge of the Germania Theatre, the director of the German Thalia Theatre, a manager of operetta companies at the Casino (where he staged the *Cavalleria* production for Aronson), and, most important, the director of the Irving Place Theatre, a position which attracted a great deal of attention from the press and which was a very great artistic success. It was said that Metropolitan directors were impressed with his achievements in this theater, as well as with his assiduousness and business acumen.

Conried began his administration with many high artistic aims. What he desired, above all, was opera with emphasis on the ensemble, not on stars. He set about making improvements in the stage at the Metropolitan, equipping it with modern appliances, ordering new constructions and scenery for different productions, and refurbishing the auditorium in the warm and rich colors still associated with that house. In his first season, he introduced to the American public, after a long controversy, Wagner's *Parsifal*, the opera which the composer had requested be performed only at Bayreuth. Many objected to the Metropolitan's production of this work not only for the lack of respect to the wishes of the Wagner family but also for the commercialization of the enterprise. The production, however, was a phenomenal success, both artistically and financially. Of more importance to the history of the Metropolitan, Enrico Caruso made his debut with the company on November 23, 1903. Actually Grau had had the perspicacity to make a contract with the tenor; and after Conried succeeded to his post, he retained Caruso, who became so popular a matinee idol that the choice of repertory, more often than not, centered around him. Fortunate to have such a singer in addition to the other artists, Conried finished his first season as director with financial success, although there were those who questioned how stimulating it had been in the artistic sense.

[60] Montrose J. Moses, *The Life of Heinrich Conried*, 17.   [61] *Ibid.*

In the next season Conried's new production of *Die Meistersinger* was magnificent. Many other presentations were commendable, and Caruso loomed as a more important figure in the company. Still, there were criticisms. Conried's promise to present opera with more emphasis on ensemble had not been redeemed. "Stars" were still in the ascendant just as they had been in Grau's day, although now some of the brightest of these (the de Reszkes, Melba, Calvé, Schumann-Heink, Lehmann) had either retired or currently made infrequent appearances at the opera house. Deficiencies in various departments also provoked dissatisfaction. This season Conried reduced the number of men in the orchestra, making it impossible for a conductor to produce the effects the score demanded; however, as Aldrich sarcastically phrased it in the *Times*, the "reduction . . . saved the salaries of perhaps a score of players."[62] Again and again, a master hand was needed to conduct the orchestra. Although Alfred Hertz was acceptable and at times excellent, he had "not reached the heights of supreme mastership"[63]; Vigna was erratic, conducting some operas well and others poorly. Many of the minor singers were not at all acceptable. As a consequence, some productions were so inadequate that they would "scarcely do credit to a provincial German theatre."[64] The chorus did not escape censure, needing, in particular, stage direction. One of the comments was that it could not "stand in a semi-circle without crowding toward the centre of the stage and shutting off the star singers from the view of people on the sides of the auditorium."[65] The stage management was slipshod, for "there were . . . evidences of a lack of perfect understanding between the various forces engaged in the performance. Curtains would fail to open or to close at the proper moment, light effects were occasionally bungled, there were noise and apparent disorder during changes of scene, and inadver-

[62] Richard Aldrich, "Apropos of Close of Opera Season," *The New-York Times Theatre Section*, March 5, 1905, p. 6.

[63] *Ibid.*

[64] *Ibid.*

[65] W. J. Henderson, "Opera Season Reviewed," *The* [New York] *Sun Theatre Section*, March 5, 1905, p. 8

tencies of other sorts were more frequent than they should have been."[66] Henderson was much more critical, maintaining that never in the history of the house had the Nibelung dramas been performed "with more slips, accidents, blunders and unsatisfactory illusion. At times they were made ridiculous . . . ."[67] It was in this season that the bridge fell down in the first act of *Carmen*, catapulting a number of choristers onto the stage and injuring some of them. The production of Strauss's *Die Fledermaus* for the director's annual benefit caused much discontent among the critics, who objected to the interpolated concert in the ballroom scene with such artists as Nordica, Homer, Fremstad, Eames, Caruso, and Plançon. It seemed an indignity to their artistic stature. Many believed that Mammon indeed had entered into the halls of this temple of music.

In 1905–1906, criticisms of the productions at the Metropolitan mounted to such an extent that Conried published accounts at the close of the season to prove that the cost of presenting opera was higher than in his predecessor's day. Apparently he did so "to combat the idea that had gained wide acceptance, that the three seasons of Mr. Conried's control had 'cheapened' the opera."[68] This season he had added no new singers of the first rank, nor was there yet a conductor to infuse new life into the performances, which too often lacked luster. Also, careful and sufficient preparation for some of the productions was still needed. Too often, a lack of skill and outright negligence were in evidence. To propitiate the grumblers, Conried pointed out that he had little time to stage the " 'between thirty and forty' "[69] works of the reportory (he produced thirty-one works this season); that there was not always ample time for rehearsals, as too often the principals arrived late in the United States; and that the

[66] Lawrence Gilman, "What Heinrich Conried Has Done for Opera," *Harper's Weekly*, Vol. XLIX (April 15, 1905), 548.

[67] W. J. Henderson, "Opera Season Reviewed," *The* [New York] *Sun Theatre Section*, March 5, 1905, p. 8.

[68] Richard Aldrich, "Close of Another Year of Opera," *The New York Times Theatre Section*, March 18, 1906, p. 3.

[69] *Ibid.*

opera house itself was unsatisfactory, since there was a lack of space
for proper rehearsals. Aldrich, in the *Times*, said that these problems,
which were not new ones at the Metropolitan, could not "fully
account for all the deficiencies of the season."[70] Nor did Conried's
benefit performance (this time it was Strauss's *Zigeunerbaron*) escape
censure. Conried's stars appeared to sing at an interpolated concert;
and the price of admission was doubled. Many bitterly commented
that at the Metropolitan there was an increasing "tendency to elevate
money over art."[71]

Hammerstein was well aware of this criticism; but he noted that
regardless of the complaints, the Metropolitan enjoyed a tremendous
subscription and that opera itself seemed more popular than ever.
He observed the tremendous growth of the metropolis in the early
1900's and the corresponding effect on attendance at the Metropolitan. His view was that " 'the demand for grand opera in New York
[exceeded] the supply.' "[72]

There was no question that New York City was undergoing a
metamorphosis. On both the west and east sides, tremendous demoli-
tions were taking place to make way for the new Pennsylvania Rail-
road Terminal and Grand Central Station, while on the corner of
42nd Street and Fifth Avenue, the site of the old Croton Reservoir,
workmen were busily erecting the magnificent marble structure that
was to become The New York Public Library. To the west a sky-
scraper, the Times Building, was thrusting its bulk upward; for years
it was one of the tallest buildings in the world. To keep pace with the
growth, many new edifices were appearing on the side streets. Already, as part of this transformation, retail traders of Fifth Avenue
were crowding up as far north as Central Park. Along Riverside
Drive builders were constructing a residential district.

On October 27, 1904, the New York Subway, begun in 1900, was

[70] *Ibid.*

[71] "The Opera Season," *Musical America*, Vol. III (March 24,
1906), 8.

[72] News item in *The* [New York] *Globe and Commercial Advertiser*,
June 1, 1906.

opened from City Hall to West 145th Street; other branches of the underground subsequently appeared. Recently completed tunnels uniting Brooklyn, Long Island, and New Jersey with Manhattan were bringing thousands of people to the island. On the New York streets automobiles were a hazard, even though drivers were not legally permitted to exceed the ten miles an hour limit,[73] while arc lighting along the main thoroughfares was replacing gas lamps. Indeed, by the fall of 1906, the *New-York Daily Tribune* could boast that "New York is the electric city."[74] The "Great White Way," which at that time meant Broadway from 34th up to 46th Street, alone used approximately 40,000 globes for illuminated signs.[75] The *Tribune* proudly continued that New York thus consumed "four times the amount of electric current used by the greater city of London, and she far [outdistanced] all other cities of Europe or America...."[76]

The tremendous growth of the city was matched by the rise in population, which on Manhattan Island increased from 1,441,216 in 1890 to 2,331,542 in 1910.[77] In these same years the total population of New York City including the boroughs (Manhattan, Bronx, Brooklyn, Queens, and Richmond) was 2,507,414 in 1890 and 4,766,883 in 1910.[78] It was this factor, Hammerstein believed, that was primarily responsible for the boom the theatrical world had been enjoying. In the season of 1904–1905, for instance, all theaters had been jammed. Every show, good or poor, had had extraordinary attendance. The city seemed to be amusement mad. Hammerstein was distressed because there were not enough theaters or opera houses to supply the demand. Warming up to the subject dearest to him, he commented that although the city had over forty theaters, there was but one opera house, which, he noted, was always crowded, with

[73] Mark Sullivan, *The Turn of the Century, 1900–1904*, 501.

[74] News item in the *New-York Daily Tribune*, September 22, 1906.

[75] *Ibid.*

[76] *Ibid.*

[77] Henry Hanson (ed.), *The World Almanac and Book of Facts 1961*, 304.

[78] *Ibid.*

people standing. Since the demand for opera was great and the supply limited, the ever alert Hammerstein promised to rectify that unfortunate situation, and by doing so, he would aid in another way. He would create the competition that would result in better opera.

A further consideration in Hammerstein's plan to re-enter the operatic field was the new theater he had been slowly building on West 34th Street, between Eighth and Ninth avenues. Originally he had called it the Drury Lane Theater and said that it was to be used for melodramas and spectaculars, but his biographer surmises that from the beginning he had considered it for the production of grand opera.[79] However that may be, in 1902 Hammerstein enlisted the aid of one Herman Wronkow, whom he had commissioned to purchase a plot of land on West 34th Street, where for many years the Decker Brothers' piano factory had stood. Soon after acquiring the site, Hammerstein declared that he would erect there a coliseum, which would seat 4,800 people. Farther uptown, however, the showmen Thompson and Dundy, backed by wealthy investors, were erecting the immense Hippodrome on Sixth Avenue, whereupon Hammerstein, " 'not wanting to buck up against billionaires,' "[80] abandoned the partly built theater and advised his realtors that the property was for sale. Later deciding to retain it, he ordered construction resumed, even though at the time he thought he had been the hapless victim of ill fortune. He subsequently felt " 'that it was Destiny doing the right thing,' "[81] for, of course, the edifice was ideal for grand opera!

The most important factor in Hammerstein's decision to go into opera production, however, was that it was an obsession with him, a compulsion. He had not lost his interest in opera or his enthusiasm for the cause. In a self-revelatory mood, he confided to a reporter that it had always been his great passion: " 'Ever since I can remember I have had a fondness, I might say an insatiable appetite, for opera. Even after I had grown to manhood and had begun to enjoy

[79] Sheean, *Oscar Hammerstein I*, 119.

[80] Anna Steese Richardson, " 'I'm the Little Man,' Says Hammerstein, 'Who'll Provide Grand Opera for the Masses,' " *The* [New York] *World Theatre Section*, January 21, 1906, p. 2.

[81] *Ibid.*

the fruits of successful business ventures I still clung to opera.' "[82]
The love for opera possessed him and would not let him go. It was
his life. What it meant may be gauged from an article published in
the Philadelphia *North American* in 1908. Hammerstein wrote:

> Grand opera is, I truly believe, the most elevating influence
> upon modern society, after religion. From the earliest day it
> has ever been the most elegant of all forms of entertainment.
> This was true when grand opera was extremely crude, as com-
> pared with today, when it employs and unifies all the arts . . . .
>
> I sincerely believe that nothing will make better citizenship
> than familiarity with grand opera. It lifts one so out of the
> sordid affairs of life and makes material things seem so petty,
> so inconsequential, that it places one for the time being, at
> least, in a higher and better world . . . .
>
> Grand opera is more than music; it is more than drama; it
> is more than spectacle; it is more than a social function; it is
> more than a display of passion, whether subdued or fierce; it
> is more than a song or a tale of love; it is more than a series of
> pictures; it is all these things and more.
>
> It is the awakening of the soul to the sublime and the
> divine; and this, I believe, is the true mission of grand opera.[83]

Approaching sixty, Hammerstein cherished the hope that he
could realize his *idée fixe*, to be an impresario, and thus to accomplish
his life's purpose. And though he had at first considered presenting
grand opera at popular prices, the conviction grew on him that his
company would have to be analogous to the Metropolitan or nothing
at all. He was determined to succeed and to show New York fantastic
and great operatic productions. If he could not eclipse Conried's
efforts at the Metropolitan, he would abandon opera entirely.

[82] " 'Poverty, the Madhouse and Untimely Death Have Been the
Reward of Operatic Management,' " *The* [New York] *World Theatre
Section*, January 17, 1909, p. 2.

[83] Oscar Hammerstein, "The Mission of Grand Opera," *The* [Phil-
adelphia] *North American Grand Opera Edition*, November 17, 1908,
p. 1.

II

Second to None

WITH HIS SON Arthur in charge of the final stages of the construction of the opera house, Hammerstein set out for Europe on March 6, 1906, to recruit his company. Although there were many artists available to him, it soon became apparent that his task was more difficult than he had anticipated. When he tried to negotiate with music agents in Paris, he found these gentlemen cold to his offers. At first they had received him graciously, but in a few days' time he found them unwilling to be of assistance. Hammerstein did not hesitate to explain why: " 'Their demeanor reminded me of December icicles as they told me one by one that anything they might do in my interest would endanger their relations with the Metropolitan Grand Opera Company and that they could not afford to risk losing Mr. Conried's good will by entering into business relations with me.' "[1]

Hammerstein always maintained that the adversities he experienced in assembling his company were due to the machinations of Conried, who apparently was determined to quash the upstart. Whether the director of the Metropolitan was guilty of such actions is now impossible to say. In view of later developments, it is likely that Hammerstein had not exaggerated the situation, nor were his statements concerning it unfounded. Conried certainly had wasted no time in securing the production rights to Puccini's operas. Moses, his official biographer, said: "When the latter [Conried] heard of Hammer-

[1] "Monsieur Hammerstein Tells in Nobody's Words but His Own How He Engaged Songbird Melba," *The* [New York] *World Theatre Section*, May 6, 1906, p. 2.

stein's entrance into the operatic field, he hastened to secure exclusive rights to all of Puccini's scores for America."[2] Hammerstein's announcement that Jean de Reszke might appear with the Manhattan Opera Company may have inspired Conried to send the following telegram to Gabriel Astruc, the French music agent: "My offer for Jean was ten performances in six weeks, three thousand dollars each performance, with right to renew for ten more performances at the same terms. This is absolutely the highest salary possible. Would have to know at once. If I had known before, would not have engaged Rousselière and Soubeyran [two French tenors who made their debuts at the Metropolitan the same season the Manhattan opened]."[3] Conried also tried to engage Arturo Toscanini; but the maestro declined the offer, reluctant to work with a director he did not know.[4] Apparently the regular conductor of Italian operas at the Metropolitan, Arturo Vigna, would no longer suffice. It would indeed seem that Conried hoped to thwart his challenger in every possible way.

While in Paris, Hammerstein accomplished very little. He did confer with Edouard de Reszke concerning the forthcoming season, but he was not able to induce Jean de Reszke to return to the United States. Discouraged, Hammerstein went next to Milan, where he found that telegrams from Conried had preceded him and that music agents and singers were unwilling to negotiate. It would seem that the opposition was too strong, that he would not be able to engage artists of the first magnitude. Then, unexpectedly, Hammerstein found an ally, a French singing soubrette, Bianca Lescout, who had been in his production of *The Talisman* at the old Manhattan Opera House. In her after years, she apparently had acquired wealth and seemed to wield considerable influence in the Italian musical world. Knowing of Hammerstein's difficulties in Milan, she did all in her power to help him and furnished letters of introduction to important personages in Naples, Rome, Genoa, Venice, and Nice. To his surprise

[2] Moses, *The Life of Heinrich Conried*, 188–89.
[3] *Ibid.*, 201.
[4] Giulio Gatti-Casazza, *Memories of the Opera*, 144.

and satisfaction, agents and singers now received him cordially, ready and willing to assist in the gathering together of a company.[5]

His greatest good fortune at this time was the engagement of Cleofonte Campanini, a marvelously gifted conductor, who had just resigned from La Scala, dissatisfied with conditions at that opera house. He was not entirely unknown to the United States, having been an assistant conductor at the Metropolitan in the first season of 1883–84. In 1887–88 he had been associated with his brother, Italo Campanini, the famous tenor, in a short season of opera in New York that was financially disastrous. It was during this engagement that Campanini conducted the first New York performance of Verdi's *Otello*, with Francesco Marconi as the Moor, Antonio Galassi as Iago, and Eva Tetrazzini as Desdemona. In private life the soprano was his wife. Since then he had devoted his efforts to seasons of opera in the great European music centers, as well as in South America, constantly gaining authority and artistic stature. He had become a celebrated Italian maestro, one of the master conductors of the day.

MELBA, THE GREATEST OF THEM ALL

Having Campanini as the leading conductor promised much for the artistic quality of the new venture. Still lacking, however, was the pre-eminent star, an artist to be a counterattraction to the best the Metropolitan had to offer. There was but one, and Hammerstein resolved that he must have this luminary: Nellie Melba, the greatest singer in the world. With this purpose in mind, he returned to Paris, determined that if he could not secure her as a member of his company, he would give up the entire undertaking. How he persuaded her to be his leading prima donna is now a part of operatic legend. Both Hammerstein and Melba had their versions.

His has hitherto been ignored or unknown:

I got back to the Grand Hotel in Paris on a Sunday after-noon almost disheartened . . . . I had travelled to all the musical centres of Europe, hearing voices, visiting artists and

[5] "Monsieur Hammerstein Tells . . . How He Engaged Songbird Melba," *The* [New York] *World Theatre Section*, May 6, 1906, p. 2.

negotiating with agencies. Everywhere I had gone I found that hostile cablegrams had preceded me and an icy reception was awaiting me. But one by one I had gathered together artists who more than fulfilled my desires.

I say I had gathered them in, but technically I hadn't. In every contract was a punitive clause by which, with the payment of a forfeit, I could withdraw. I had made up my mind that if I couldn't get Mme. Melba I would be obliged to drop the whole grand opera undertaking.

It was make or break with me, and I decided there was no time like the present. So I got into fresh linen, brushed my travel-stained clothes, called a cab and at 6 in the evening headed for Mme. Melba's home in the Boulevard Malesherbes. I [*sic*] was a big project that I had on my hands, and I had reached the point where I had to trust to luck.

The house loomed up in the dusk big and beautiful. In answer to the bell a maid came to the door. She could not speak English and I didn't know much French, but I finally made her understand that I wanted to talk with Mme. Melba on a matter of business.

"Madame is entertaining at dinner to-night and I do not think she will be disturbed, but I will see," the maid replied as she left me standing in the dark, with my hat in my hand.

Three minutes later I heard a great rustling on the stairs and in came Mme. Melba with a great sweep and flourish.

"You are Mr. Hammerstein of New York—yes, I have heard of you—you want to give grand opera there—so New York is to have two companies?" she said in a quick, single sentence.

"And I have come to ask you to be my leading prima donna," I answered. "I"—

"It is impossible to talk of such a thing now. Why, I have guests at dinner. Come around to-morrow. Perhaps I will have an hour to talk with you then," Mme. Melba interrupted.

But I had made up my mind it must be now or never. "To-

morrow is impossible," I replied, "for I am going to Berlin.
I have a great list of artists, but my contracts are punitive and
I have made up my mind that without you I must give the
whole thing up."

"Ah, that would be unfortunate indeed," she cried. "You
must not do that."

"Then give me ten minutes and hear what I have to say,"
I answered.

Melba hesitated a moment and said, "But only ten minutes,
for my guests are waiting. I will excuse myself and return
directly."

Mme. Melba disappeared with another prodigious rattling
of skirts and a majestic sweep. I put down my hat and got
ready for the struggle of my life. Almost instantly she was
back again.

"Now," said she determinedly, "what do you want?"

I named the other singers I had engaged and gave a quick
outline of my plan. She quickly interrupted me with a gesture
and the remark, "I know all about that. See here."

Then she crossed the room to a desk and grabbed up a big
bundle of telegrams and cablegrams. "I have been annoyed to
death with despatches [sic]," she exclaimed. "My time is
open next season, and perhaps I would just as soon sing under
your management as any one else's, and so end the whole
matter."

I almost gasped, but caught myself in time. "And your
terms?" I asked.

She named the figures and conditions in a snappy, business
way.

"I am well-to-do," she concluded. "I need not sing unless
I want to—therefore I come high."

She certainly did come high! "Is this your final stipulation?" I asked.

"It is," replied Mme. Melba with a fidget and a look toward the stairway whence the sound of her guests could be
heard.

"Will you give me ten minutes to consider?" I asked.

"To-morrow morning will do," she answered.

"No, it must be to-night," I retorted, with determination.

"Very well," said she. "Take your own time."

It has always been my practice, when about to close an important deal, to take a walk around the block. So I bowed myself out into the Paris street. You can believe that before I had travelled half way around that big block my mind was made up. So I headed back toward Melba's house.

She came down again in a very few moments with a pleasant bow and stood waiting for me to speak.

"I accept," said I.

"Very good," said she, "and now I want to help you all I can to make this thing a great big success. Call on me for anything you wish, but come in to-morrow morning and we will sign the contracts."

It had all taken place quicker than I can tell it. But I had made up my mind to seal my bargain instanter.

"Take another minute and write me a line stating your acceptance," I pleaded.

Mme. Melba opened a little desk and scribbled a few words on a slip of paper . . . .

As she dropped the pen I picked it up and wrote her a reply in a couple of dozen words.

"That's settled," said I, and I still wonder if she noticed the exultant ring in my words.

"Not quite," she replied, dryly. "You know, Mr. Hammerstein," she went on, "I always require a guarantee, no matter for whom I sing—whether for Conried or Covent Garden, or"—

"Certainly," I answered. "How much must it be?"

"Twenty thousand dollars deposited wherever you desire— preferably in the Credit Lyonnaise," said she, without a quiver.

"Why not deposit it with you and avoid all the red tape of recording it?"

"That's asking too much," she exclaimed, with a surprised look, "but let it go until to-morrow. I must be getting back to my guests."

Two minutes later, less than half an hour after I had first driven to Mme. Melba's house, I was back in my cab and on my way to the Grand Hotel. The prospects of the Manhattan grand opera project had brightened into clear day in that brief time. For every disappointment and rebuff of the preceding six weeks I had been repaid a hundred fold.

Bright and early next morning I started for the bank, and had $20,000 changed into new, crisp thousand franc gold certificates. Then I drove back to Mme. Melba's house.

"You're early, Mr. Hammerstein!" she exclaimed, as she greeted me. "I thought you were starting for Berlin."

"Ah, I had more important business in Paris," I said. Then I laid on her desk twenty of those big scraps of paper that go for money in Paris.

She brushed the pile into a drawer of her desk without even counting it and turned the key.

"And now," said she, "we must work together, and I shall do all in my power for you. Last night you told me you could not get Renaud. You must get him, for he is the greatest baritone in France. Yes, you must—we must—get Renaud. I will get him for you. In three days you will receive word at your hotel to meet him and sign the contracts." . . .

Three days later, as Melba had promised, word came from Renaud that he had arrived in Paris, prepared to reopen the negotiations. A day before a note from Mme. Melba had informed me that we had secured him. How she contrived to do so I do not know.[6]

Hammerstein related his initial experience with the prima donna approximately a month after the event; Melba told her version years later in her autobiography *Melodies and Memories*, published in 1925. Apparently the soprano had decided that she would sing less

[6] *Ibid.*

during the season of 1906–1907, that she needed time for quiet and contemplation. At any event, Melba was in no mood to consider Hammerstein's proposal.

The diva wrote:

> One day, when I was in my flat in Paris, thinking what fun I was going to have in my coming season, Mr. Hammerstein called. I had an idea of what he wanted, and I wouldn't see him.
>
> Hammerstein went straight off to Mr. Maurice Grau, who, sad to say, was very ill at the time, and persuaded him to give him a letter to me. In view of the letter, I felt obliged to give him an appointment. But I kept on saying to myself: "I'm not going to America. I'm not going to America."
>
> When Hammerstein arrived, my first impression was of a determined man of Jewish persuasion, shortish, thin and dark, with piercing black eyes. He carried a top hat with a very wide brim in his hand, and he addressed me in a strong American accent.
>
> Hammerstein: "I'm out to do the big thing in opera. I am building the biggest and finest opera house in the world. And I can't do without you."
>
> Myself: "In what way do you want me to help you?"
>
> Hammerstein: "I want you to come and sing."
>
> Myself: "I'm very sorry, but I have no intention of going to New York next year."
>
> Hammerstein: "I can't do without you."
>
> Myself: "That's a great pity, because I'm not going."
>
> Hammerstein: "I shall give you fifteen hundred dollars a night."
>
> Myself: "Please don't discuss terms, Mr. Hammerstein, because I assure you that is useless."
>
> Hammerstein: "Oh, you'll come all right. (A pause.) What do you say to two thousand?"
>
> Myself: "If you offer me twenty thousand I shall still say the same thing."

Hammerstein: "It'll be the biggest thing you have done yet. Oscar Hammerstein says so."

Myself: "And Nellie Melba says 'No.' I have no intention of going. Good-morning, Mr. Hammerstein."

Had anyone else been so importunate, I should probably have been very angry. But there was a naïve determination about Mr. Hammerstein which appealed to my own character. He knew what he wanted, and did not hesitate to say so. We therefore parted good friends, and I regarded the matter as closed.

Not so Mr. Hammerstein. At intervals of six days during the next month he either called, wrote notes or telephoned, always prefacing his remarks by "Now that you have decided to come to America . . . ." I merely sat tight and set my lips. On one occasion, I remember, he obtained an entry into my rooms while I was in my bath. Not in the least deterred he came and battered at the door.

Hammerstein: "Are you coming to America?"

Myself (between splashes): "No!"

Hammerstein: "I'll give you two thousand five hundred a night."

Myself: "Not for ten times the money."

Hammerstein: "And you can sing as many nights as you like."

Myself: "Go away."

Shortly after that, Mr. Hammerstein decided on his Napoleonic *coup*. I had just breakfasted and was sitting down, reading *Le Figaro*, when he burst into my rooms in a great hurry.

Hammerstein: "It's all settled. You're to have three thousand dollars a night."

Myself: "But I've told you a hundred times———"

Hammerstein (interrupting): "Never mind about that. Three thousand dollars a night, and you open in *Traviata*."

Here, to my astonishment, he drew from his pocket a

bundle of thousand-franc notes and began scattering them over the floor like cards, until the carpet was littered with them. I was so surprised that I could say or do nothing, and before I could call him back, he had swept out of the room like a whirlwind, crying that he had to catch his train, and had no time to wait.

I picked up the notes, smiling quietly, and found that in all he had strewn my carpet with one hundred thousand francs. To-day it may not sound such a very vast sum, but then it meant four thousand pounds. And even nowadays one does not go strewing thousands of pounds on people's carpets.

I took the notes at the earliest possible opportunity to the Rothschild Bank, telling them that they were not mine, and that they must be kept safely until Mr. Hammerstein called for them.

However, he did not call for them. Instead, he called once again for me, in the early morning.

Hammerstein: "Well, and so you've made up your mind at last. Didn't Oscar Hammerstein say you would?"

Myself: "He did, and Oscar Hammerstein was wrong. As I've told you before, I am *not* going to America."

Hammerstein: "Oh yes, you are. You've got all my money."

Myself: "The money is in the bank. It has nothing to do with me."

Hammerstein: "Was there ever such a woman? Still, you'll come. Mark my words."[7]

It is difficult to say why Melba decided to appear at the Manhattan. Of course, Hammerstein had made the whole arrangement attractive financially, since she was to receive $3,000 a performance (an extraordinary sum in those days) as well as her traveling expenses. In addition, he had permitted her to arrange concerts outside New York whenever she was not singing at the Manhattan.[8] Still,

[7] Nellie Melba, *Melodies and Memories,* 236–39.
[8] Agnes G. Murphy, *Melba: A Biography,* 255–56.

money was not the sole inducement. Joseph Wechsberg, in *Red Plush and Black Velvet*, speculates that there was another consideration: "She knew that this time she was not just singing against another prima donna but against one of the world's great opera houses. It was an exciting challenge, the ideal challenge for the greatest living prima donna."[9] And Melba was a proud lady who loved the sense of power. The most persuasive factor, perhaps, was that at the Manhattan she knew she would be the prima donna *assoluta*, with all the attendant glory and authority that title bestowed. Melba herself said:

> If I had been one of the regular staff of the Metropolitan, I should have had to sing when and where they wanted. My rôles would have been dictated for me. I should have been at their beck and call. No artist gives her best under those conditions. I said to myself: "I am Melba. I shall sing when and where I like, and I shall sing in my own way." It may sound arrogant, but arrogance of that sort is not a bad way to get things done.[10]

Hammerstein was fortunate to secure Melba and Renaud as well as the other principal artists. Some critics considered his leading lyric tenor, Alessandro Bonci, who had not yet appeared in the United States, a greater singer than Caruso. One of the glories of La Scala, Bonci was an incomparable exponent of *bel canto*. In Brussels Hammerstein met and signed a contract with Charles Dalmorès, a young dramatic tenor whom Conried had wanted for the Metropolitan.[11] At first Dalmorès was not available, since he had accepted an engagement in Lisbon for four seasons; but when Hammerstein agreed to pay the forfeit of four thousand dollars, the tenor broke his contract.[12] Hammerstein also engaged Clotilde Bressler-Gianoli, a superb artist and a striking personality. The dramatic soprano of Giannina Russ,

[9] Page 319.
[10] *Melodies and Memories*, 243–44.
[11] Moses, *The Life of Heinrich Conried*, 213.
[12] "Monsieur Hammerstein Tells . . . How He Engaged Songbird Melba," *The* [New York] *World Theatre Section*, May 6, 1906, p. 2.

the lyric coloratura of Regina Pinkert, the contralto of Eleanora de Cisneros were all noteworthy, as were the sonorous bass of Vittorio Arimondi, the inimitable *basso buffo* of Charles Gilibert, and the rich baritone of Mario Ancona, who had appeared at the Metropolitan in Grau's regime. Hammerstein had every reason to be delighted with these singers and the others he and his agents were assembling for his company. He could return to the United States gratified by what he had accomplished. A broadside was in order. Thus, when he announced his plans in New York, on April 30, 1906, Hammerstein seized the moment to fire volleys at the inimical Metropolitan:

> "And now that I have called into life a new institution, opening up new avenues and new means for the elevation of musical tastes, I conclusively demonstrate with what I have already accomplished that this second home for grand opera is not to be second at all, but to be the first and foremost, not asking humbly for support and kind consideration, but forcing its acceptance and respect by its already predominating value . . . .
>
> In accessories, in surroundings that the great artists under my management are entitled to, I confess I will lack one thing—the provincialism which our operagoers have been forced to accustom themselves to."[13]

HAIL TO THE CONQUERING HERO!

When Hammerstein issued the official prospectus on June 11, 1906, he referred to the company in extraordinary terms: "In every respect the superiority of the Manhattan Grand Opera Company to the already existing grand opera is readily apparent."[14] He planned to select the repertory from thirty-four operas to be sung in Italian and French. Singers of the minor roles were competent artists who had gained experience in Italy and France. The chorus, recruited in New York as well as in Italy, numbered 100; the orchestra, 75. The stage manager was Charles Wilson, who had been with Colonel Mapleson

[13] News item in *The New York Times*, April 30, 1906.
[14] Manhattan Opera House Prospectus for 1906–1907 Season.

and had been a producer at the Alhambra in London. Mme E. S. Freisinger was in charge of making the costumes. Anna Marble was the press representative.

Subscription performances, which were to begin on November 19, were for Monday, Wednesday, Friday evenings, and Saturday matinees, for twenty weeks. Saturday evening performances were outside the regular subscription. The price for each box (there were forty-two of them) was $4,000 for the subscription of eighty performances. Scale of prices for single performances was $5.00 for each orchestra stall; $3.00, Dress Circle; $2.50, first three rows of the Balcony; $2.00 and $1.50, remaining rows of the Balcony; $1.50, first three rows of the Family Circle; and $1.00, remaining rows of the Family Circle.

From time to time Hammerstein made other announcements that fed public curiosity in the new venture. One that aroused much comment was the opening night opera: Bellini's *I Puritani*. Hammerstein had his reasons for selecting this particular work. The tenor's role is among the most difficult in all operatic literature, the *tessitura* being altitudinous. Since Bonci probably was the only vocalist in the world at the time who had the requisite style and range to sing the part, Hammerstein intended to demonstrate the quality of the new enterprise by introducing at once his star tenor. He had a further consideration: " 'I have been told that Bonci rarely makes his best impression on his first appearance—that it takes him some time to warm toward an audience and that he is much affected by the attitude of his audience toward him. That is the reason we have chosen *Puritani* for his début here. In that opera he has to begin working hard at the very beginning . . . . That won't give him time to think of his audience and will cause him to warm up to his work right from the beginning.' "[15]

Hammerstein also announced that there were innovations in the opera house itself. Although he intended to have boxes in the structure, they were to be an integral part of the architecture, not to dominate the auditorium as they did at the Metropolitan. His pur-

[15] "The Inauguration of the Manhattan Opera House," *The New York Herald Society and Drama Section*, October 21, 1906, p. 5.

pose was to minimize the social aspects of grand opera in the hope that people would come to hear Melba and Bonci, not to gaze at the box holders. What he was interested in was society with a small "s": " 'It is society in the broad sense that I hope to attract and to please. Society with a broad sense of music—a society that has increased enormously in the past ten or twelve years. It is my belief in the great and growing taste for music in New York that has led me to give it another opera-house.' "[16] Furthermore, the auditorium had been so constructed that the audience would be near to the stage, a design that created an intimacy between opera-goers and performers unknown in the vast reaches of the Metropolitan. There were to be no seats with a blocked or poor view of the stage. The comfort of all would be considered, rich and poor. Finally, in contrast to the darkness of the interiors of the European opera houses and the Metropolitan, the Manhattan was to be brightly illuminated with five thousand lights.[17]

The chorus, Hammerstein maintained, would be a marvel and an integral part of the ensemble, not discordant members of a performance shuffling off and on the stage. He selected many of these singers, who were of an amazingly high calibre, from New York voice studios. Just before the opening of the season Hammerstein augmented their number with experienced choristers from Italy.[18] Rehearsals began late in July and were held under the direction of Gaetano Merola, who years later founded the San Francisco Opera Company. After several weeks of intensive work, Hammerstein expressed his satisfaction with their progress. To a reporter from the *Herald* he said: " 'Look at them . . . note the different types. Do you not see that they are wholly different from an Italian chorus, in which every woman looks the same and every man seems to be built on the same lines and both men and women appear never to have learned more than

[16] News item in *The* [New York] *Evening World*, September 22, 1906.

[17] "The Inauguration of the Manhattan Opera House," *The New York Herald Society and Drama Section*, October 21, 1906, p. 5.

[18] "Building a Grand Opera Chorus from Native Material," *The New York Herald Magazine Section*, August 19, 1906, p. 2.

four gestures? Wait until you see these young men and women on the stage.' "[19]

Furthermore, Hammerstein intended to have some innovations in the stage settings. He laid great emphasis on the *mise-en-scène*, his idea of opera being that it should be acceptable and pleasurable not only for the magnificence of the vocal and orchestral work but also for the stage effects. He did not intend to minimize nor to economize one for the other. Since the costumes were all new, they, too, must blend into the picture and not be anachronistic; all must be aesthetically pleasing and historically accurate. What he purposed to do may be gleaned from a comment in the *Herald*: "The palace scene in *Don Giovanni* he is doing in white and blue, and as he has been obliged to provide entirely new costumes for his company he is making them tone in with the color schemes of the scenic settings."[20]

In the midst of these bright prospects, Hammerstein faced some grave problems. On July 25 he received a letter from George Maxwell, the American representative of Ricordi and Company, publishers of Puccini's operas. Maxwell stated that he had heard Hammerstein intended to produce some of the Italian composer's operas. He reminded Hammerstein that they were copyrighted and that there was a penalty if he tried to present them without Ricordi's permission. Later when Hammerstein heard that the Metropolitan had been granted the exclusive rights to their production in the United States, he was furious, at once suspecting Conried behind the arrangement; and when the situation was made public on August 26, he declared that he would not tolerate the inequity and that he would produce the Puccini operas.[21] And as Hammerstein pointed out, they had been played all over the world for years without any company's having an exclusive right to them. Why now, he thundered, should the Metropolitan have this monopoly? On October 19, Ricordi filed an action against Hammerstein to enjoin him from producing *La*

[19] *Ibid.*

[20] "The Inauguration of the Manhattan Opera House," *The New York Herald Society and Drama Section*, October 21, 1906, p. 5.

[21] News item in the *New-York Daily Tribune*, August 26, 1906.

Bohème, which he had been anxious to bring forward for Melba. For a time the situation looked ominous.

On November 11, Hammerstein announced that he had broken his contract with Edouard de Reszke. While in Paris in the spring, Hammerstein had heard the basso at a Mozart concert and was shocked by the deterioration of the once great voice. Before returning to New York, he had de Reszke promise that he would study in Paris during the summer with his brother to correct the vocal flaws; and although Hammerstein wrote and cabled to inquire about the condition of the voice, the basso never answered the communications. In time Hammerstein heard that the singer was on his estate near Warsaw, Poland, and that he had not trained with Jean. Again he wrote and reminded de Reszke that there was "a great deal at stake in making this venture into opera and that [he] could not afford to have any of [his] chief singers appear [at the Manhattan] unless they were in the best voice.' "[22] Finally, Hammerstein decided to break the contract, demanding the return of the $5,000 he had advanced. De Reszke believed that Hammerstein had treated him unfairly and had slandered him by the reports concerning his voice. He suspected that it was all part of an intrigue, confiding in a friend that Melba was the one who "had manoeuvred to have him released 'so she would have the stage to herself.' "[23] The fact remains, however, that he was not singing well. Even his brother Jean admitted this.[24]

Throughout the month of November members of the company arrived from Europe, ready to fulfill their engagements. The opening, however, originally announced for November 19, had to be advanced to December 3, since the house was not yet completed. Although many may have suspected the worst, Campanini had reassuring words for the enterprise: " 'Mr. Hammerstein has given me full power in making the productions at the Manhattan . . . and I can assure the New York public of an artistic success at his opera house. Never in my career have I seen a more perfect ensemble. Too often opera is given with a few stars and mediocre singers. In this case I can

[22] News item in *The New York Times,* November 12, 1906.
[23] Clara Leiser, *Jean de Reszke and the Great Days of Opera,* 309.
[24] *Ibid.,* 309–10.

Oscar Hammerstein, Impresario

The Manhattan Opera House, opened by Oscar Hammerstein on December 3, 1906, with Bellini's *I Puritani*, as it appeared while it was the home of the Manhattan Opera Company. Later additional stories were added.

The Philadelphia Opera House before its completion; it was opened on November 17, 1908, with Bizet's *Carmen*.

Oscar Hammerstein, Cleofonte Campanini (reading a note), and Jacques Coini (with pointed finger) on the set of Strauss's *Salome*.

say truthfully that we have all the elements to produce operas as they should be produced . . . .' "[25]

The Metropolitan Astir

Meanwhile, Conried announced that the Metropolitan would open its season on November 26, 1906, with a performance of Gounod's *Roméo et Juliette*, which was to be a vehicle for the debut of Geraldine Farrar, a young American soprano who had been the adored star of the Berlin Opera and a favorite of the royal family. There were to be new productions: Strauss's *Salome*, *Madama Butterfly*, *Manon Lescaut*, *La Damnation de Faust*, *Lakmé*, *L'Africaine*, and *Fedora*. Also the older house was to be honored by the presence of Puccini, who would supervise the production of his *Butterfly*. The Metropolitan, it would seem, was to give no quarter to the Manhattan; and though Conried protested that he had not made any unusual preparations for the coming season, it could not be denied that his solicitous efforts, artistically speaking, were rarely equalled at any other time during his tenure at the opera house.

To a representative of the press he said:

"I have not been urged to greater endeavor by the fact that there will be a rival in the field. I have gone ahead with only one idea, and that was to get the best. New York isn't satisfied with anything but the best . . . .

Prospects for a splendid season were never brighter. The fact that another opera-house is to be opened has not affected the Metropolitan Opera-House in the least. The subscription sale has opened larger than ever before."[26]

Conried, however, spoke too soon, for dark clouds gathered on the horizon. This season a series of unfortunate circumstances plagued the Metropolitan. The first of these concerned the company's star tenor. On November 16, while in the monkey house in Central

[25] News item in *The New York Times*, November 14, 1906.

[26] News item in *The* [New York] *Evening World*, September 22, 1906.

Park Zoo, Caruso purportedly annoyed a Mrs. Hannah Stanhope, who had him arrested, and, although the tenor protested his inno-cence, he was convicted of the charge. For a time Caruso's career seemed in jeopardy; but when he made his first appearance of the season, on November 28, in *La Bohème*, with the irreproachable Sembrich, he received a tumultuous welcome from his adoring public. New York had vindicated its hero. It was said, however, that Conried was the one who suffered the most from the scandal. A deterioration in his physical condition, brought about by a nervous breakdown, manifested itself, with the result that he had to limit his activities at the opera house.[27]

As the weeks passed, several of the new productions were not well received; but the worst calamity was the one and only public perform-ance of Strauss's *Salome*, which was so shocking to the New York sensibilities of the day that the directors of the Metropolitan re-quested Conried to withdraw the opera from the repertory. After several vain attempts to produce it again only as non-subscription performances, Conried had to accede to their wishes, even though it meant losing a great deal of money.[28] By the end of this turbulent season matters had altered considerably at the older house; it was even whispered that Conried's days there were numbered.

EXCITEMENT GALORE!

As the time approached for the opening of the Manhattan, many articles appeared in newspapers and periodicals describing the new edifice. The site measured on Thirty-fourth and Thirty-fifth streets was 125 feet; it was 200 feet deep. As for the structure itself, the house was 200 feet deep and 105 feet long on Thirty-fourth and Thirty-fifth streets. It was four stories in height, measuring 70 feet from the curb level to the highest point.[29] The original architect was William E. Mowbray, but later Hammerstein engaged the J. B.

[27] Moses, *The Life of Heinrich Conried*, 300.
[28] Irving Kolodin, *The Metropolitan Opera 1883–1935*, 116–19.
[29] "*Application for the Erection of a Theatre at 315 West 34th Street*," September 23, 1907.

McElfatrick and Son firm.[30] As for the exterior of the building, all decoration was on the Thirty-fourth Street side of the house. Here the façade was impressive with heavy stone pillars at the entrance and pilasters on the upper stories, rising to a pediment.

The interior was in the style of French architecture of Louis XIV. According to the original plans, the seating capacity of the orchestra was 1,373; the first, second, and third balconies each had 672 places. Included in these figures were the places in the proscenium boxes as well as the ones in the first tier. The total seating capacity of the house thus was 3,389.[31] This original plan, however, was modified. The figure generally given for the total seating capacity was 3,100,[32] with a stage that measured 75 feet deep and 100 feet wide. The proscenium opening was 47 feet wide and 53 feet high.[33]

The last weeks before the opening were difficult, hectic ones. In going up a stair in the opera house, Hammerstein became dizzy and fell. Though not seriously injured, he moved about with considerable difficulty for some time, a condition which created grave concern among those who knew him well. The orchestra rehearsals, which began on November 23, had to be held to such discordant sounds as the carpenters' and carpetlayers' hammers; nor was all bliss with Campanini and his men. Sam Franko relates in his autobiography that the conductor was dissatisfied with rehearsals. In particular, he disliked the concertmaster and refused to conduct unless another was secured. At this time Franko was free from any other engagements and accepted the position, much to Campanini's gratification.[34] A

[30] Although newspapers referred to the Manhattan as a $2,000,000 opera house, Hammerstein, according to George Blumenthal (and Arthur H. Menkin), in *My Sixty Years in Show Business* (p. 205), maintained that it was worth between seven and eight hundred thousand dollars.

[31] *"Application for the Erection of a Theatre . . . ,"* September 5, 1902.

[32] Sheean, *Oscar Hammerstein I*, 143.

[33] "Manhattan Opera House," *Architectural Record,* Vol. XXI (February, 1907), 148.

[34] Sam Franko, *Chords and Discords,* 110–11.

strike, which threatened to postpone the December 3 date, was called on November 26 by the carpenters and steam fitters.[35] Fortunately it ended several days later. Hammerstein had also had difficulty with members of the chorus. They demanded that they be paid for the rehearsals held three weeks before the opening. The impresario granted their request without comment.

Regardless of the tumult and confusion, Hammerstein maintained his equanimity. Somehow he found time for the hundreds of details to which only he could attend. Seemingly inexhaustible, he not only attended to countless demands on his time at the opera house but also found moments to have interviews and to receive many visitors, Camille Saint-Saëns being one visitor.[36] Escorted by Hammerstein, the French composer toured the new building and found it praiseworthy. Ruggiero Leoncavallo, who also was in the United States at this time, came to the house and expressed his admiration for what Hammerstein was accomplishing.[37]

All this publicity whetted public curiosity, which steadily mounted in the days preceding the opening of the house. On the eve of the first performance, Hammerstein wrote: " 'To the public of New York, to those who love the arts and to those who love effort and achievement of any sort, I dedicate the Manhattan Opera House.' "[38]

[35] News item in *The New York Times*, November 27, 1906.
[36] *Ibid.*, November 22, 1906.
[37] *Ibid.*, December 11, 1906.
[38] Oscar Hammerstein, "Waiting for the First Rap of the Baton," *The* [New York] *Evening Telegram Theatre Section*, December 1, 1906, p. 13.

III

The Opening of the Manhattan

—∘⊰⟨⟩⊱∘—

I N THE HISTORY of music, the inauguration of the Manhattan Opera House remains unique. Even up to several hours before patrons were admitted, workmen were placing the last of the seats; steam fitters were busy at work, so that the building would meet the requirements of the Fire Department; and painters were brushing on finishing touches. Later, some members of the audience were irate when they discovered that their apparel bore evidence of the fact that the paint was not dry. By six o'clock the police commissioner handed Hammerstein the license for the house.[1] The evening's edition of the *Tribune* had accurately stated the situation: "The last carpenter and carpet layer will no more than have slipped out the rear door when the first ticket holder walks in from 34th Street."[2]

By seven o'clock a crowd of hundreds of people, which extended to Eighth Avenue, stood about waiting in the wind-swept night to observe the arrival of the opera-goers. Across the street many curious spectators filled the windows of the boarding and apartment houses. When the box office opened, the supply of tickets for standing room was soon exhausted, approximately 750 persons having to be turned away.[3] Some of them may have been accosted by speculators who were asking for and getting as much as $15.00 for orchestra seats.[4] Excitement increased when the first-nighters began arriving. All of them

[1] News item in *The New York Herald*, December 4, 1906.
[2] News item in the *New-York Daily Tribune*, December 3, 1906.
[3] News item in *The New York Herald*, December 4, 1906.
[4] *Ibid.*

had to go to the 34th Street side of the house, since the entrance on 35th Street was not yet completed. As a result of this and the excited crowd, access to the opera house was difficult, ticket-holders virtually fighting to get through the enormous throng around the entrance. Members of the police force had all they could do to preserve even a semblance of order. After a time, cross-town streetcar lines were blocked. By eight o'clock, carriages, slowly threading their way through traffic, extended up Eighth Avenue to 42nd Street, and the congestion extended as far south as 23rd Street.[5] The *World* estimated that on this evening a total of 628 vehicles came to the house.[6] Everywhere hysteria and confusion reigned.

The crush inside seemed as great as it had been outside. The outer lobby was jammed. On the main floor, since every available space of standing room was occupied, those with orchestra seats had to jostle their way through the standees only to find themselves unable to proceed down the blocked aisles. This problem would have been avoided had the ushers known the seating plan, but they had not had sufficient time to familiarize themselves with it. Finally, by eight-thirty, a half-hour after the time announced for the opening,[7] the orchestra had taken its place; a moment later Campanini entered the pit. Lifting his baton, he led his men in the glorious strains of the National Anthem. When it was completed, the audience shouted and applauded. The Manhattan Opera House at last was launched on its inaugural season.

At the rise of the curtain there was applause from all parts of the crowded auditorium. People were still arriving but were being silenced by those who had come to hear the music rather than to be seen at a social function. By all accounts it was an audience that, on the whole, was filled with music lovers who were determined "that no one should mistake their mission. They had come to hear the singing of artists who had been got together regardless of expense from the ends of the earth, and they would brook no interruption. The slightest

[5] News item in the *New York American*, December 4, 1906.
[6] News item in *The* [New York] *World*, December 4, 1906.
[7] News item in *The* [New York] *Sun*, December 4, 1906.

utterance on the part of anyone was silenced immediately with a s-s-s-sh so imperative that it could not be mistaken. The opera was not to be employed, as society often uses it, as a vehicle for conversation."[8]

As each leading singer made his entrance, he was greeted with the utmost cordiality. When Ancona appeared, cries of " 'Viva, Bonci' " filled the house, some *aficionados* mistaking the baritone for the diminutive tenor.[9] Since *I Puritani* had not been performed in New York for over twenty years, opera-goers were unfamiliar with the work, and this kind of mistake was inevitable. Then, when Bonci did appear, the house was in an uproar. As Hammerstein had anticipated, the tenor was very nervous, but after a few tentative moments, he recovered his composure and went on to give a performance revealing superb vocal artistry and style.

After a number of recalls at the end of the first act, Bonci, Ancona, and Pinkert, a Polish coloratura appearing in the role of Elvira, rushed to Hammerstein, who had been sitting on an old chair at one side of the stage, and dragged him before the footlights to share in the tumultuous applause. Breaking away, Hammerstein made an effort to leave the stage by way of a door that would not open. The audience laughed good-naturedly, amused by the contretemps and Hammerstein's embarrassment.[10] Backstage, the singers and Campanini were delighted by their reception, Pinkert and Bonci declaring that they had rarely sung to a more appreciative audience. Hammerstein, in immaculate evening dress and white gloves, seemed as pleased as they, but, knowing New York theater-goers, remarked that " 'one must make allowances . . . for first night enthusiasm, and it remains to be seen whether the public will continue its support of the new opera house.' "[11] To a reporter from the *Herald*, he said, " 'Far from feeling the uplift and elation usually attendant on the successful launching of a big venture like this I am curiously apathetic. This

[8] News item in the *New York American*, December 4, 1906.

[9] News item in *The* [New York] *Sun*, December 4, 1906.

[10] News item in *The* [New York] *Evening World*, December 4, 1906.

[11] News item in *The New York Herald*, December 4, 1906.

is not the result of decayed interest, but rather attributable to the realization that my part of the work has been effected—the rest is for the music loving public to carry on or discard, according to their verdict.' ''[12]

During the intermission no doubt many members of the audience looked about to regard the huge main electrolier, which was fifteen feet in diameter and which dazzled them with its one thousand lamps;[13] to note the sculptured group of nine figures on the large shallow dome in the aureate ceiling as well as the mural, sixty by twenty feet, above the proscenium containing the portraits of more than one hundred eminent opera singers;[14] and to rejoice in the entire splendid auditorium, a cornucopia of warm reds, whites, and golds. The forty proscenium boxes as well as the fifteen loges in the Grand Tier were also a center of attention, but to identify the occupants was difficult, since it was Hammerstein's policy not to list the box holders in the Manhattan Opera House programmes, both on this occasion and at all later performances. Then, too, the auditorium had been designed so that the center of attention was the stage, not the boxes. As a result, "only those in the [proscenium] boxes and the orchestra stalls [could] see the occupants of the first tier. The space in the rear of each floor and many of the seats not forward of the arch [commanded] a splendid view of the stage, but not of the house."[15]

Nevertheless, among the prominent personages in the boxes, which were not all occupied, were Miss May Callender, Mr. and Mrs. Walter Damrosch, Dr. and Mrs. Holbrook Curtis, the J. H. Flaglers, the E. H. Weatherbees, Miss May Weatherbee, the Frederick C. Cornings, the Timothy Woodruffs, the Charles K. Hudsons. In box thirteen were Otto H. Kahn and Eliot Gregory, both directors of the Metropolitan. Though the Manhattan held these representa-

[12] *Ibid.*

[13] R. L. McC., "Taking Our Readers for a Glance Through New York's Brand-New Opera-House," *The* [New York] *World Theatre Section,* December 2, 1906, p. 2.

[14] *Ibid.*

[15] News item in *The New York Times,* December 4, 1906.

tives of New York society, they were hardly to be compared socially to those assembled the same evening at the Metropolitan, where Caruso, Sembrich, Homer, and Journet were appearing in a performance of *Marta*. In the boxes were the Vanderbilts, the Goulds, the Whitneys, the August Belmonts, the Charles B. Alexanders, the William D. Sloanes, the Goadby Lowes, Mrs. Ogden Goelet, and Mrs. Ogden Mills.

Social commentators were somewhat in a quandary. *Town Topics*, the journal of Society, said: "Society was there in force, but it was not of the kind one is likely to meet in the homes of New York families of the first magnitude. Still, Mr. Hammerstein should not feel discouraged on that account, for ... the first night at the Metropolitan, one October evening in 1883, did not rob the old Academy of Music of much of its social glory."[16] Time, however, had altered that situation; perhaps history would repeat itself. This same periodical further commented: "There was a rumor ... that Mr. and Mrs. Pembroke Jones had arrived at the Manhattan. Great was the craning of necks among those who hoped for the best, for until then the honor of being the most important personage present was divided among Mrs. Charlie Childs, who has an intimate acquaintance with Mrs. Hermann Oelrichs; Mrs. Dennis Brussell, who has the distinction of being a neighbor of the young Willie K. Vanderbilts, in West End avenue; Mrs. Timothy Woodruff, who was gorgeously dressed, and Mrs. Berry Wall, who presented an appearance as attractive as her husband's erstwhile sartorial display."[17]

On the matter of dress, *The New York Times* society reporter ruefully observed that although the auditorium was excellent for musical purposes, it was not at all well designed for the display of finery. Also, the opening night audience had "followed a go-as-you-please style of dressing."[18] Even some of the women in the orchestra stall were garbed in ordinary raiment, while others wore "the most gorgeous of highly colored or white dinner and evening gowns, wear-

[16] Vol. LVI (December 6, 1906), 5–6.

[17] *Ibid.*, 6.

[18] News item in *The New York Times*, December 4, 1906.

ing lofty aigrettes and quantities of pearls, diamonds, and other precious gems."[19] To be sure, the exquisitely gowned and bejeweled saved the evening for this reporter as well as for others who required their opera to be panoplied with the richest of clothes and ornaments.

At the end of the second act, which had gone very well indeed, Hammerstein again appeared on stage in one of many recalls, this time prepared to make a speech. When the house was quiet, he said:

" . . . Ladies and [g]entlemen, I am very much gratified. There is a sensation of pride and of fear (laughter). I can only say this is an effort to the furtherance of industry and music. I am compelled to add that I am the only one who has created this institution.

"I have had no assistance, financially or morally. The burden has all been on me and the responsibility is all mine. I have no board of directors, nobody to tell me what I should and should not do (laughter).

"I have concluded in my years of decline—for you can see I am already out of my boyhood days—that if I can aid with that which I have earned honestly—can aid the cause of music—it could be something I could look back upon with what you call pride.

"Many people endow libraries (Voice from the gallery, "One on Carnegie!") and hospitals; but I have yet to see one who has endowed opera. When the curtain falls tonight it is the beginning of a series of trials—nothing else.

"The ensemble which surrounds this institution is so large and is composed of so many celebrities of music that every opera for the next three or four weeks is experimental and depends for success or failure on this audience and this city." (Applause and cheers.)[20]

The evening's greatest outburst of applause for the artists occurred in the last act, after Bonci and Pinkert had sung the duet

[19] *Ibid.*

[20] News item in *The New York Herald*, December 4, 1906.

"*Vieni fra queste braccia.*" The house demanded an encore, but Campanini would not permit one,[21] thereby establishing at once his rule of no repetitions, a practice generally followed during his tenure with the company. At the Metropolitan, encores were the rule rather than the exception. The performance proceeded until just before midnight, when Campanini brought it to a triumphant conclusion.[22] The opening of the Manhattan Opera House had been an event long to be remembered in the annals of opera. For Hammerstein, it must have been a supreme moment of his life, for, all things considered, it was his evening—a dream become reality. Great must have been his satisfaction and joy.

Lucky Hammerstein!

The next day Hammerstein had even more cause to rejoice, since the reviews, on the whole, were most complimentary, critics lauding the male leading singers, the chorus, orchestra, stage management, and Campanini. Of the principals, Bonci had pleased the most with his elegant phrasing, excellent musicianship, and mellifluous voice, which had the "intrinsic beauty of an irreproachable pearl and [was] governed by a simply impeccable vocal art."[23] Some critics compared him to Caruso, even though such comparisons were invidious. Krehbiel maintained that in "nearly all the things which enter into the art of vocalization he is incomparably finer than his rival at the Metropolitan Opera House. His tones are impeccably pure, his command of breath perfect, his enunciation unrivalled by any singer now before the local public, his phrasing also, his sense of proportion, symmetry, repose, exquisite."[24] Although he did not have Caruso's luscious quality and huge sound, there was no question that Bonci's voice was a very beautiful organ, a magnificent one, and that in elegance of style he was superior to his rival. In him Hammerstein had an artist of the first rank. Ancona had improved since his days at the Metropol-

[21] *The New York Press,* December 4, 1906.
[22] News item in *The New York Times,* December 4, 1906.
[23] *The New York Press,* December 4, 1906.
[24] *New-York Daily Tribune,* December 4, 1906.

itan, his phrasing now being faultless and his voice "remarkably even and rich."[25] Arimondi was commended for the sumptuousness of his singing. Pinkert, however, was a disappointment. Even though she was a young woman, her voice sounded old and faded. In the cantabile passages the tones were unsteady; she excelled, however, in *fioriture*, her staccati being especially "clear, pure and bell like."[26] The chorus (and what a chorus!) was a revelation; New York had never heard anything like it at the Metropolitan. It was "one to rejoice the heart of the lover of opera; it [was] remarkably fresh and vigorous in its singing, with the freshness and vigor of youth."[27] The orchestra also was commended. Above all, however, the critics praised Campanini, whose authority, musicianship, and dynamism were readily apparent. It had been years since New York had known a conductor who made old-fashioned Italian opera a thrilling experience; Campanini "almost breathed into the music the spirit of interest, making the most of the climaxes and accompanying the singers with the deepest sympathetic feeling."[28]

Of the house itself, the *Tribune* remarked:

> Comments on the appearance of the opera house were, of course, the rule. Built, as it is, on the plan of a theatre, obviously the box holders are not generally visible except to those sitting well forward in the auditorium. This, from the point of view of opera for society's sake, is a distinct disadvantage. But the general scheme of the house as a theatre from which to watch the stage was commended, and the spacious red and cream interior, under its brilliant lights, was praised . . . . Of course, its location at present is a strange one; but what changes the Pennsylvania terminal will make in that part of town remains to be seen.[29]

[25] *The New York Herald*, December 4, 1906.
[26] *The* [New York] *Sun*, December 4, 1906.
[27] *The New York Times*, December 4, 1906.
[28] "At the Opera," *The Theatre Magazine*, Vol. VII (January, 1907), 9.
[29] News item in the *New-York Daily Tribune*, December 4, 1906.

The proximity of the audience to the stage contributed to an enjoyment of grand opera unknown in the vastness of the Metropolitan. Most important, music connoisseurs found the acoustics perfect. According to Pauline Donalda, one of the principal artists at the Manhattan this season, Hammerstein had used a sounding board to achieve this satisfying effect. She said: "The acoustics . . . at first were not good but they immediately had a sounding board installed and all went splendidly afterwards. This was done before the first performance."[30] However, the entrances to the house were lamentably insufficient, and there was very little space for promenading between the acts. The following season Hammerstein provided an additional entrance on 35th Street. The Manhattan remained, nonetheless, without adequate promenades.

[30] Letter to the author from Pauline Donalda, June 5, 1963.

IV

On with the Season

THE SECOND performance, on Wednesday, December 5, introduced
to New York another artist on whom Hammerstein counted much for
the success of the season: Maurice Renaud. In Europe this baritone
had appeared at the Théâtre de la Monnaie, Paris Opéra, and Covent
Garden, winning plaudits not only by his artistic singing but also
by his remarkable histrionic ability. His repertory included such parts
as Don Giovanni (some considered him the world's greatest interpreter of this role), Beckmesser, Wolfram, Athanaël, Méphistophélès
(Berlioz's *La Damnation de Faust*), Rigoletto, Scarpia, Hamlet,
Falstaff, Boniface (*Le Jongleur de Notre Dame*) and the three evil
geniuses in *Les Contes d'Hoffmann*. As an actor, he was compared to
Salvini,[1] and Sardou, seeing him as Scarpia in Monte Carlo, urged
him to act the role in Paris to Sarah Bernhardt's Tosca.[2] In Renaud,
Hammerstein had another consummate artist, one of the truly great
singing actors of all time. He had had difficulty inducing him to
appear with the company. It was only after much persuasion and
Melba's assistance that Renaud did accept a contract, which must have
been an extraordinary document, as it consisted of forty-eight pages
and included such a stipulation as a carriage for the baritone to and

[1] Abbie H. C. Finck, "Maurice Renaud," *The Century Illustrated
Monthly Magazine*, Vol. LXXVII (February, 1909), 614.

[2] Elsie Lathrop, " 'Each Time I Sing a Rôle I See New Possibilities
. . . ,' " *Musical America*, Vol. IX (December 26, 1908), 3.

from the opera house. Hammerstein said that nothing had been omitted.[3]

Hammerstein had wanted him to appear first as Don Giovanni; but Renaud, having arrived in New York very late (December 1), absolutely refused to undertake the role without more rehearsals.[4] *Rigoletto* was the subsequent choice for his debut, though the baritone would have preferred postponing it altogether, since he was suffering from severe hoarseness. Hammerstein, however, persuaded him to appear; and to put Renaud at ease, he promised to have an announcement made to the effect that he was singing under serious vocal difficulties. Hammerstein also promised the baritone that he would not have to perform again until his voice was in prime condition.

Critics praised Renaud for his artistry and acting but, under the circumstances, preferred not to render a complete evaluation of his voice. It was suggested by at least one critic that he should have postponed his debut until he was in full command of his vocal resources.[5] The New York *World* commented that Renaud "revealed a voice of great sweetness, especially in the more tender passages, but in the duet that closes the third act, when he cries for 'Vendetta! Tremenda vendetta!' his voice was lost between the screams of the cornets and the vocal gymnastics of Mlle. Pinkert, so that what should have been a duet became a soprano solo; the famous quartet in the last act became a trio, and the finale was cut out altogether."[6] Bonci was in splendid form, pouring out a wealth of golden tone. As for Pinkert, the opinion already expressed was confirmed; she was essentially a singer of florid music, very capable and winning in the execution of runs, staccati, and trills, but disappointing in phrases requiring cantabile. The audience was small, except for the upper part of the house,

[3] Charles Darnton, "Oscar Hammerstein Believes He Was Born for Grand Opera," *The* [New York] *Evening World Magazine Section*, December 15, 1906, p. 9.

[4] News item in *The New York Times*, December 3, 1906.

[5] *The* [New York] *Evening Post*, December 6, 1906.

[6] *The* [New York] *World*, December 6, 1906.

but it included some interesting musical personalities: Mr. and Mrs. Walter Damrosch, Geraldine Farrar, Mme Sembrich with her husband, Professor Stengel, Mr. and Mrs. Andreas Dippel, and, from a somewhat different musical echelon, the beauteous Lillian Russell. According to Hammerstein, the receipts for this performance were $1,823,[7] a figure somewhat higher than the fees Bonci and Renaud received for their contributions on this particular occasion. The same evening the Metropolitan held an enormous audience, participating in the American *première* of Giordano's *Fedora* with Caruso (Loris Ipanov), Lina Cavalieri (Fedora), Scotti (De Siriex), and Dufriche (Grech).

This performance of *Rigoletto* was just the beginning of a series of trials for the impresario. Aside from the temporary loss of Renaud, he was to know overwhelming financial problems. Before opening night the entire subscription for the season of twenty weeks was $52,600,[8] an amount that would barely cover expenses at the opera house for three weeks. Although *I Puritani* drew $11,000, the *combined* total of the receipts for the next six performances was approximately $10,000.[9] Hammerstein's nerves must have been on edge. It is not unlikely that he knew many moments of pessimism and heartbreaking despair, though he was optimistic and confident enough in his public comments. He did not expect, he said to the press, that his venture would be " 'an immediate financial success.' "[10] Ultimately, however, he would " 'see [his] way clear.' "[11]

On Friday, December 7, New York had the opportunity of seeing two operatic productions based on the Faust legend: Gounod's *Faust* at the Manhattan and Berlioz's *La Damnation de Faust* at the Metropolitan. On this evening Hammerstein introduced another distinguished singer, Charles Dalmorès, who was to be one of the most valuable members of the company this season and in the ones to follow. Originally he had studied the French horn, violin, and cello

---

[7] News item in *The New York Herald*, April 22, 1907.
[8] *Ibid.*
[9] *Ibid.*
[10] News item in *The New York Times*, December 10, 1906.
[11] *Ibid.*

in preparation for a musical career, and at twenty-three was a professor in the Musical Conservatoire at Lyons. Here another instructor heard Dalmorès singing and urged him to study voice seriously. In the season of 1899–1900, he made his first appearance in opera at the Théâtre des Arts, Rouen, and from there went on to greater successes at the Théâtre de la Monnaie and Covent Garden.[12] Like Renaud, Dalmorès had an extensive repertory that embraced Italian, French, and German operas. At his Manhattan debut, he sang beautifully, and critics praised his excellent stage presence, manly appearance, and fine acting. In the words of *The Evening World* he stood "easily in the foremost rank of the tenors who have sung in New York during the past decade."[13] The Marguerite, Pauline Donalda, a very attractive woman, was commended for her acting and clear, sweet voice. Melba had heard Donalda at Covent Garden, admired her voice and artistry, and urged Hammerstein to engage the young singer as the leading lyric soprano of the company.[14] Fortunately Hammerstein acted on Melba's suggestion. Of the new female artists he introduced this season, Donalda enjoyed the greatest success with the public for both her lovely appearance and her competent singing. Arimondi's Méphistophélès was strong vocally but somewhat weak dramatically; he played it along conventional lines. Seveilhac, Donalda's husband, was a satisfactory Valentin. The chorus and orchestra were again superb, with Campanini dominating the performance and infusing his spirit into all the proceedings. For the staging, scenery, and costuming, Hammerstein duplicated the version then being presented at the Paris Opéra, the keynote of the production being authenticity. The performance was sparsely attended; receipts were $1,630.[15]

The presentations at the end of the week were a Saturday matinee of *I Puritani*, with basically the same cast as at the *première*, and a

---

[12] Charles Dalmorès, "Well Known Singer Tells Story of Rise to Operatic Fame," *The New York Times Theatre Section*, December 29, 1907, p. 7.

[13] *The* [New York] *Evening World*, December 8, 1906.

[14] Letter to the author from Pauline Donalda, May 15, 1963.

[15] News item in *The New York Times*, April 22, 1907.

repetition of *Faust* in the evening, with Altchevsky replacing Dalmorès. Richard Aldrich, in *The New York Times*, commented that the performances this first week had been "remarkable in many respects; and in some [had offered] opportunities for enjoyment of an unusual kind."[16] Of the singers, he predicted that the success of the company would depend to a great extent on Bonci. The women were not good enough. Campanini had proved himself to be a conductor of "inexhaustible power and vitality . . . who . . . carried everything through with animation."[17] W. J. Henderson, of *The Sun*, also pointed out some interesting facts. According to him, Hammerstein had demonstrated that "most of the appalling obstacles in the way of giving acceptable ensemble in operatic performances in this town had no existence outside of the fine fancies of those who desired to find excuses. In his very first week Mr. Hammerstein showed us a good, if not uncommon, orchestra, competently directed; a chorus of attractive appearance and almost human intelligence in action, and minor singers capable of filling out the performance of important operas without thrusting upon the notice of the audience a contrast with the principal singers altogether too violent."[18]

In the second week Hammerstein brought forward *Don Giovanni* on Wednesday, December 12. Since Renaud's hoarseness persisted, Ancona replaced him as the dissolute Don and sang extremely well; yet his figure hardly suggested the romantic cavalier. As Donna Anna, Giannina Russ possessed the requisite style; but her voice was too explosive and unsteady. Arta, the Donna Elvira, was completely out of her element in this difficult part. Donalda's Zerlina afforded pleasure; and, of the women, she was the only one considered adequate in her assignment. Hermann Brag (Leporello) was "vocally lame."[19] The merits of the performance were Bonci's exquisite sing-

[16] "First Week of Opera by Mr. Hammerstein," *The New York Times Theatre Section*, December 9, 1906, p. 5.
[17] *Ibid.*
[18] "Opera and Opera Singers," *The* [New York] *Sun Theatre Section*, December 23, 1906, p. 6.
[19] *The* [New York] *Sun*, December 13, 1906.

ing and Campanini's magnificent interpretation of the score, his reading combining "continence with a delicately graded range of shading."[20] The entire production benefited by Renaud's presence when he assumed the title role for the first time at the Manhattan on Saturday, December 15. Though he still showed the effects of his illness, he triumphed as the result of his acting, artistry, and personal appearance. To many he was the Don incarnate with "every gesture and pose . . . charged with a significance appropriate to the part. There was not the slightest doubt that here was a man of noble lineage and an irresistible wooer—the embodiment of masculine blandishments."[21] He appeared again as the libertine on December 17 and January 16, the last performance of the opera this season.

ATTENDANCE GAINS

The first complete triumph for an opera occurred two nights after the initial *Don Giovanni*: the sensational, well-rounded presentation of *Carmen* (December 14), which simply bowled over the critics and "thrilled and startled"[22] the audience accustomed to the rather tame version at the Metropolitan. A triumph of ensemble, this *Carmen* was performed with so much spirit, vitality, and dash that its appeal was irresistible, creating an unforgettable impression. Because of the character of the auditorium and the marvelous acoustics, every action and nuance could be readily observed. The chorus, not a group of "vocal statues,"[23] and the orchestra were lauded to the skies. Campanini, never letting the action falter for a moment, molded all the forces under him and "brought out an infinity of detail in the score."[24] Fortunately, he had an ideal interpreter for the title role: Clotilde Bressler-Gianoli, an earthy, tempestuous Carmen. New York had seen her as the Seville cigarette girl in March, 1904, when she appeared at the Casino as a member of a company from New Orleans; but, at that time she had not made a profound impression. Now, how-

[20] *Ibid.*
[21] *The New York Press*, December 16, 1906.
[22] *New-York Daily Tribune*, December 15, 1906.
[23] *The* [New York] *Sun*, December 15, 1906.
[24] *The New York Times*, December 15, 1906.

ever, she took the city by storm. Her conception of the part was "an elemental, utterly frank, physical Carmen"[25] with "bodily movements as sinuous as her morals were loose,"[26] alluring in its "sheer wickedness and all the wiles and treacheries that wickedness suggests."[27] The keynote of her impersonation was the "essential commonness and sensuality of the creature."[28] Not an extraordinary vocalist, she made her voice subservient to the purposes of the drama. As Don José, Dalmorès, "resplendent in voice and gallant in action,"[29] presented an impassioned interpretation of the hapless dragoon, the victim of Carmen's wiles and charms. New York was beginning to recognize him as one of the finest French tenors heard in years. Ancona, the Toreador, sang with beautiful tone and gave a realistic portrayal, while Donalda was convincing and charming in the role of Micaëla.[30] In all, *Carmen* had a total of nineteen performances during the season; it was the most popular opera in the repertory and always good box office.

The extraordinary success of *Carmen* occurred at the end of Hammerstein's first fortnight in the new opera house. From that time on, larger and more enthusiastic audiences attended the performances, eager to see the well-integrated productions. When the public realized that the presentations were artistic and thrilling, then the company began to assume an importance in the musical life of the city which could no longer be ignored or denied. Hammerstein's explanation was simple: " 'The public will go anywhere if it can get what it wants .... You've got to deliver the goods.' "[31]

In the third week Hammerstein added two more operas to the repertory. The first of these was *Aïda*, presented on December 19,

[25] *The* [New York] *Sun*, December 15, 1906.

[26] *The* [New York] *Evening Telegram*, December 15, 1906.

[27] *The New York Times*, December 15, 1906.

[28] *Ibid.*

[29] *Ibid.*

[30] *Ibid.*

[31] Darnton, "Oscar Hammerstein Believes . . . ," *The* [New York] *Evening World Magazine Section*, December 15, 1906, p. 9.

1906, with Amadeo Bassi (Radames), whose singing had "tonal beauty and brilliancy of technique";[32] De Cisneros (Amneris), an imposing stage presence with a sumptuous voice; Russ (Aïda), always the sincere artist whose voice, alas, was not altogether pleasing; Ancona (Amonasro) and Arimondi (Ramfis), both vocally admirable. Like *Carmen*, *Aïda* was a triumph of ensemble; and for this Campanini deserved much praise. Walter Damrosch, present at the *première* and thrilled by what he had seen and heard, called Campanini the greatest Italian conductor in the world.[33] No doubt many others agreed with him. By all accounts, Campanini's reading of the score was memorable, exhilarating, and galvanizing with its "sheer rhythmical energy, stirring contrasts, significance of nuance and power of climax."[34] The production was impressive also from the spectacular and scenic point of view. Hammerstein had spared no expense. The *New York American* said: "Usually the long two-note trumpets [were] of brass; Mr. Hammerstein had them of silver. Ordinarily the Egyptian band, with its modern European instruments, [was] drafted from the orchestra; Mr. Hammerstein had a full and separate band, and, for sure, it gave a mighty blare of brass. Here, too, one saw the 400 Thebans and soldiers and priests and dancing girls, with a forest of plumed ensigns above and a rattle of armored feet below."[35] The impresario had been determined that his production of the Verdi masterpiece would not suffer in comparison to the Metropolitan's.

Apparently it did not, for it invariably attracted large audiences or sold-out houses; and when both the Manhattan and Metropolitan offered *Aïda* on Saturday evening, February 9, 1907, the Manhattan was filled to overflowing, whereas there were many unoccupied seats at the older house. Krehbiel relates that when a reporter revealed this fact to rapt listeners at the Manhattan, Campanini and members of the cast were so elated by the news that they joined hands and danced

---

[32] *The* [New York] *World,* December 20, 1906.
[33] *The* [New York] *Evening Telegram,* December 20, 1906.
[34] *The New York Press,* December 20, 1906.
[35] *New York American,* December 20, 1906.

in triumph about the stage.[36] Hammerstein had every reason to be proud of this exciting production, one of the most successful in the Manhattan repertory. It was heard twelve times this season, almost always with the same cast.

The second production of the third week was Donizetti's *Lucia di Lammermoor*, presented for the first time on December 21, 1906, with Pinkert (Lucia), Bonci (Edgardo), and Minolfi (Ashton). The soprano's singing of the florid passages pleased, her rendition of the lyric measures less so, since they were often marred by a slight tremolo. Bonci drew plaudits; and although nobody suggested that *Lucia* should be renamed *Edgardo*, it might as well have been, since Bonci received so much critical acclaim for his contribution to the evening that the chief role in the opera seemed to be the tenor's. Since Minolfi did not please, Hammerstein let him go after this performance. Tanara conducted, and therein lies a tale. On the previous evening Leandro Campanari, who was supposed to conduct the *première*, had had difficulty with the orchestra and singers, accusing them of forming a Camorra against him. They, in turn, had no confidence in his ability to lead them in this particular work, Bonci and Pinkert refusing outright to sing the way he directed them. To save the production, Hammerstein forced Campanari to resign and asked Tanara to conduct the opera.[37] It was a miracle that there had been any performance at all.

The repertory for the rest of December comprised repetitions of *Carmen*, *Faust*, *Rigoletto*, *Aïda*, and *Lucia*. Attendance steadily increased as New Yorkers realized, more and more, what Hammerstein was accomplishing.[38] Even in the first month it was obvious that the Manhattan was worthy of support and that the productions were sometimes of extraordinary excellence, seldom poor, and more often than not meritorious. Richard Aldrich, in *The New York Times*,

---

[36] Krehbiel, *Chapters of Opera*, 367.

[37] News item in *The* [New York] *Evening World*, December 24, 1906.

[38] W. J. Henderson, "New York the Greatest Opera City in the World," *The World's Work*, Vol. XVII (April, 1909), 11435.

maintained that already the company was a vital force in the city's musical life. Aldrich had liked the performances, observed the improvements, and believed in the Manhattan's future:

> What strikes the observer of the new opera house is the fact that there are intelligence, skill, and zeal at work in it continually to improve its results. But what also has impressed those who have followed the performances is that they are of an artistic merit quite worthy of the patronage of New York operagoers. It seems to be almost beyond question now that there is an operatic public in New York large enough and discriminating enough to support two opera houses of artistic merit.[39]

[39] "A New Opera House Worthy of Support," *The New York Times Theatre Section,* December 30, 1906, p. 5.

V

The Divine Diva

THE NEW YEAR began auspiciously, as it was now time for the long-awaited appearance of Madame Melba. Hammerstein announced that she would make her debut with the company on January 2, 1907. For months there had been rumors (Hammerstein claimed they had been inspired by Conried) that the diva would not appear at the Manhattan Opera House, that she had lost her voice, or that her health had been seriously impaired. From London, Melba denied these allegations and said that she would fulfill her promise to Hammerstein. She informed an American representative of the press that she actually was in *splendid* (!) vocal form.[1]

Melba's comments on the excellent condition of her voice were more than borne out by the criticisms of her appearances at Covent Garden during the fall season. In the opening night performance of *Rigoletto* (October 5), the London *Times* said that she was in "exquisite voice."[2] More praise followed; and when she appeared as Violetta in *La Traviata* (October 31, 1906), she triumphed "with even more than her usual success. Her singing in the brilliant music of the earlier scene was as faultless as was her delivery of the whole scene in the last act."[3] The tenor of the London reviews certainly did not indicate any diminution of Melba's powers.

Her return to New York was anticipated with the keenest pleasure, as the metropolis had not heard her in opera since December 16,

[1] News item in *The* [New York] *Morning Telegraph,* July 21, 1906.
[2] *The* [London] *Times,* October 6, 1906.
[3] *Ibid.,* November 3, 1906.

1904, when she appeared only once (as Mimi in *La Bohème*) at the Metropolitan. Although she was to have sung in opera four times that season, illness had forced her to cancel her engagements. Before that one appearance, she had been absent from the New York operatic scene for almost four years. It was greatly to be regretted that the city had been denied the pleasure of Melba's singing for what amounted to almost six years.

On December 19, 1906, the diva cabled Hammerstein that she would appear first as Violetta. She had wanted her initial performance to be in *La Bohème*; but since the dispute concerning the rights to Puccini's opera had not been settled, Melba had no further recourse than to select another role: Verdi's lady of the camellias. Anticipation was kept at fever pitch. It was widely reported that her costuming in the opera would be an innovation, that she would wear $2,500,000 worth of jewelry, and that among the magnificent gems was a five-strand necklace formerly in the collection of Marie Antoinette. Every word concerning the celebrated soprano was now so newsworthy that even a nondescript cable to Hammerstein, which she sent en route to New York, found its way into the papers: "Splendid passage. Feeling very well. Hope for season's success."[4]

At last divinity came to earth the morning of Sunday, December 30, 1906. Melba was in New York! Waiting to greet her were friends, admirers, the press, and Hammerstein. She set about at once to dispel the malicious rumors that had been circulated concerning her voice: " 'I have had a very pleasant trip . . . . My voice is said to be better than it has been for years. I expect that the season will be a great success. I have been singing at Covent Garden, and I come here not only in good voice, but in the best of health.' "[5] When photographers asked her to pose for pictures, she would not permit any to be taken, but after Hammerstein whispered some soothing words, she willingly consented. The interview over, Melba and her entourage went to her hotel, followed by the two detectives Hammerstein had provided to guard her person as well as her jewels and costumes. She

---

[4] News item in *The New York Times*, December 29, 1906.
[5] *Ibid.*, December 31, 1906.

granted other interviews soon after her arrival at the St. Regis. To a representative of *The New York Herald* she said: " 'I was tremendously struck with Mr. Hammerstein's pluck in organizing an opera company, when one was already playing in an established house here . . . . As a result I have entered into his plans most enthusiastically and have aided him gladly both with advice and with personal effort and persuasion in getting his company together.' "[6]

The following day Melba went to the Manhattan for the first time. In her autobiography *Melodies and Memories,* she records that when she arrived there, she found the opera house in the greatest ferment of excitement. She and others in the cast had to rehearse to the accompaniment of hammering, since extra chairs were being installed for the overflow audience at her initial appearance.[7] The Manhattan was anticipating a rousing, royal welcome for the acknowledged Queen of Song.

In the short time before her first appearance, the prima donna was to have little solitude. Her friends in the United States had warned her not to associate herself with the Manhattan, which they believed was a failure; now they visited her at her hotel, telling her that "society was talking of nothing else but the coming war"[8] and that the "first night promised to be one of the most remarkable in the whole history of the American stage."[9] No doubt Melba suffered some qualms; she admits that she wondered whether she would actually be able to carry off a great triumph that would redound to her glory as well as to the Manhattan's. She claimed that her accommodations at the St. Regis were not altogether pleasing. Was this nerves? The ringing of the telephone and the doorbell annoyed her to such an extent that she told her maid to remove the one from the receiver and to cover the other with padding. The very day of the performance, still not her usual composed self, Melba tried to take a nap in the afternoon, but not being able to relax, she went for a long

[6] News item in *The New York Herald,* December 31, 1906.
[7] Nellie Melba, *Melodies and Memories,* 242.
[8] *Ibid.*
[9] *Ibid.*

drive along the Hudson. Returning to the St. Regis, she felt ready for the ensuing fray, determined to sing gloriously.

An hour before the opera, people were being turned away from the packed lobby. There had not been such a crowd since opening night. Many members of society, pillars of the Metropolitan, were there, lured to the Manhattan by the siren sound of Melba's voice. When the diva arrived at the 35th Street entrance, Hammerstein was waiting for her and, according to the prima donna, "trembling with emotion."[10] He led her to the stage to hear the voices emanating from the full auditorium. Melba confessed that she, too, trembled, although she was not sure whether from excitement or fright. Hammerstein, she said, was convinced that he was going to triumph; and, Melba, like-minded, made a vow to herself that she would "sing as . . . never . . . before."[11]

At its best, the Melba voice, with its seamless scale, was of unparalleled beauty. The tones were equalized throughout the enormous range, extending from the lowest tone of B flat below the staff to F above high C.[12] Henderson, recalling the soprano's very first season in New York (1893–94), wrote that even then it was a voice "unique, impeccable, translucent, glittering . . . . There was nowhere a change in quality. And it had such astonishing power and brilliancy."[13] The word "silvery" was often used to describe it, but at this period of her career, critics had begun noting dramatic qualities and a warmth that had not been associated with her earlier singing. Her trill was phenomenal; her attack of a tone, miraculous; she gave the impression of singing with ease and restraint.[14] *Grove's Dictionary of Music and Musicians* notes that she used "her tone within rather than beyond its true limit of resonant power."[15] Possessed with such

[10] *Ibid.*

[11] *Ibid.*, 243.

[12] Eric Blom (ed.), *Grove's Dictionary of Music and Musicians* (fifth ed.), V, 660.

[13] W. J. Henderson, "A Dream of Two Singers," *The* [New York] *Sun Theatre Section*, January 6, 1907, p. 6.

[14] W.J. Henderson, *The Art of Singing*, 421.   [15] Blom (ed.), *ibid.*

technique, the diva was able to sing with ravishing beauty of voice for many years. Brilliant and musical staccati, mellifluent cantilena, impeccable phrasing, superb musicianship—all were facets of the divine Melba's singing and artistry. Before such perfection, criticism bends the knee.

The house burst into applause when Campanini entered the pit. From the wings, Melba saw familiar faces from the Metropolitan. At last came the moment for her entrance. When she appeared on stage, many in the audience did not recognize her in her blond wig; but in a moment the applause was tumultuous. Then there was silence. Melba began to sing, spinning one glorious tone after another; and she related that, though it may have been vanity on her part, in thirty seconds she "knew that [she] had won."[16] The *Herald* reported the next day that "the first few notes Mme. Melba sang more than confirmed recent London reports as to her particularly brilliant singing during the past season at Covent Garden, and the scene's succeeding numbers, the 'Ah for se [*sic*] lui' especially, which she sang seated . . . made it clear that she has never been in finer voice."[17]

At the end of the first act the house went wild and recalled Melba eleven times.[18] Twice she towed Hammerstein before the footlights to share in her overwhelming reception. Going to her dressing room, she was jubilant and said: " 'I am delighted, and as happy as a king.' "[19] The rest of the performance was just as exciting and electrifying; all of the singers "sang as if their very reputations were at stake, and Campanini led the orchestra as though his greatness was still in doubt—so much fervor marked the work of everyone."[20] When the opera was over, the audience remained, vociferously applauding and cheering Melba, her vis-à-vis, and Campanini. Then when the diva appeared with Hammerstein, "the enthusiasm of the audience passed all bounds, and for some minutes there was a deafen-

[16] Melba, *Melodies and Memories*, 243.
[17] *The New York Herald*, January 3, 1907.
[18] *The* [New York] *World*, January 3, 1907.
[19] Murphy, *Melba: A Biography*, 258.
[20] *The* [New York] *World*, January 3, 1907.

ing uproar, during which hundreds of people waved their handker-chiefs, and the younger members of the audience threw their floral buttonholes at her feet."[21] The next morning the *Tribune* posed a provocative question: "Does the great success of the evening mark a turning point in local operatic history?"[22]

Critics were lavish in their praise of the performance. The *Press* called it the "most satisfying representation of Verdi's work heard and seen here in years."[23] Of Melba's voice, Richard Aldrich, of the *Times*, said that it had "its old-time lusciousness and purity, its ex-quisite smoothness and fullness; it is poured out with all spontaneity and freedom, and in cantilena and in coloratura passages alike it is perfectly at her command. Such a voice is a gift such as is vouchsafed but rarely in a generation, and her art is so assisted by nature, by the perfect adjustment of all the organs concerned in the voice that, like Patti's, it seems almost as much a gift as the voice itself."[24] Her acting had improved, though she relied on her voice for most of her dra-matic effects. Renaud, the elder Germont, was also a revelation to the critics. He actually made the role sympathetic, dignified, sincere, transforming "a character so often represented in a manner at once sickly and artificial. It was the achievement of a remarkable artist."[25] Bassi (Alfredo) received mixed reviews. Campanini was superb, artis-tic to the smallest details, infusing everything with his enthusiasm.

The costuming also received much favorable comment. Melba had been anxious to do the opera in the style of the time in which it belonged: 1848. Usually it was presented in seventeenth-century *décor*, an anomaly that the diva did not countenance. At Covent Garden that fall season she had worn gowns of the correct period when she appeared in this opera. She brought them with her, and Mme Freisinger made all the other costumes for the production in one week. Richard Aldrich, in the *Times*, commented: "The old

[21] Murphy, *Melba: A Biography*, 258.
[22] *New-York Daily Tribune*, January 3, 1907.
[23] *The New York Press*, January 3, 1907.
[24] *The New York Times*, January 3, 1907.
[25] *Ibid.*

operagoer must have been somewhat startled; the young one views it with composure; and here is a straw, not very important in itself, that shows which way the wind blows now for dramatic verisimilitude, and how it has changed in the last half century."[26]

STAR DUST

Melba's presence gave a lustre to the company that it had not had before. Society, which had been very slow to attend performances at the new opera house, now flocked there. *Town Topics* noted that the "Manhattan is fast becoming a rendezvous of fashion, and it is to be regretted that the house does not possess more boxes"[27] and that whenever "Mme. Melba lets loose her golden notes, the Manhattan audience is sprinkled with social topliners and although carriage facilities are even more trying than at the [Metropolitan], these disadvantages are overlooked."[28] As the prima donna *assoluta*, she put the whole company on its mettle, with the result that performances, as a whole, seemed better than ever before. Melba, to be sure, was aware of what her presence meant at the opera house. She was especially cognizant of the inspiration she gave to the young American women in the chorus, many of whom had been eager to sing at the Manhattan simply because they would have the opportunity to observe firsthand the vocal method of the great diva. Melba said: " 'I have never known young women of the chorus to be more ladylike, more honest, more sincere, or more ambitious than the girls here at the Manhattan. It is a pleasure to feel their appreciation silently bestowed, and when, while singing, I glance toward the wings and see their attentive faces and realize that my every note is a guide to them in their musical path, you may be sure I sing my best.' "[29] No doubt many of the principals also benefited from her example; for, of

[26] Richard Aldrich, "*Traviata* at Last Properly Costumed," *The New York Times Theatre Section*, January 6, 1907, p. 5.

[27] Vol. LVII (January 17, 1907), 5.

[28] *Ibid.*, February 14, 1907, 5.

[29] Serious Students of Music in Manhattan Opera Chorus," *Musical America*, Vol. V (April 6, 1907), 14.

course, they, too, could learn from her, the greatest living exponent of *bel canto*.

After the initial performance in *Traviata*, Melba appeared four more times in January: another *La Traviata* on the nineteenth; *Rigoletto* on the eleventh and thirty-first; *Lucia di Lammermoor* on the twenty-eighth. The performance of *Rigoletto* (January 11) had a superlative cast; joining Melba were Bonci and Renaud, a combination that was second to no parallel trio at the Metropolitan. Again the house was sold out; the box office had been closed long before the curtain went up and speculators were reaping profits. Outside, crowds of people stood about watching the opera-goers; inside every available space was occupied. Hammerstein had to call the police to control the crush. Society was in force, faithfully in attendance for a Melba night. As for the performance, the *Times* said that it was "without question one of the best productions of *Rigoletto* that has been given in New York for many years."[30] Melba was peerless; Bonci amazed by adding "a volume of luscious tone which surprised his warmest admirers"[31] and Renaud "sang and acted with a power that carried all before him."[32] As for *Lucia*, both Melba and Bonci outdid themselves, the auditorium reverberating with their incomparable voices. The diva never spared herself in an effort to save her vocal resources for the difficulties of the mad scene, but "sang every note of the part with her full power."[33] It seemed as if the cascades of limpid tones were poured forth from an inexhaustible source.

[30] *The New York Times*, January 12, 1907.
[31] *Ibid.*
[32] *Ibid.*
[33] *New York American*, January 29, 1907.

VI

The Repertory Grows

IN THE SAME MONTH Hammerstein added five more operas to the repertory: *Il Trovatore* (January 1), *L'Elisir d'Amore* (January 5), *Les Huguenots* (January 18), *Il Barbiere di Siviglia* (January 21), and *La Sonnambula* (January 25). In the cast of *Il Trovatore* were Russ (Leonora), De Cisneros (Azucena), Dalmorès (Manrico), and Seveilhac (di Luna), under the baton of Tanara. Though De Cisneros and Dalmorès sang well, the production, as a whole, was not up to standard. Tanara did not have the orchestra firmly in control. The usually fine chorus disappointed, performing in a perfunctory manner. The presentation of *L'Elisir d'Amore* was excellent, with Pinkert (Adina), Trentini (Gianetta), Bonci (Nemorino), Seveilhac (Belcore), and Gilibert (Dulcamara), Campanini conducting. Although Bonci carried away the vocal laurels of the evening, Gilibert was the star of the production, his Dulcamara being irresistible. Altogether it was "one of the most delightful representations of *L'Elisir* ever heard in New York."[1] *Les Huguenots* was a creditable and, in some ways, a brilliant performance. In the cast were Pinkert (Marguerite), Russ (Valentine), De Cisneros (Urbain), Seveilhac (St. Bris), Ancona (Nevers), Bassi (Raoul), and Arimondi (Marcel), with Campanini conducting. Even though New York had heard the opera with some of the world's greatest voices, the production at the Manhattan was surprisingly good as the result of the general level of high quality. Of the singers, Ancona, Bassi, and Russ were particularly praised. One account said that Bassi and Russ's duet in the fourth act had "not been

[1] *The New York Press*, January 6, 1907.

so well given here since Nordica and Jean de Reszke were heard together in it."[2] The sets and costumes were appropriate and sumptuous. Rossini's *Il Barbiere di Siviglia* was a charming production, every member of the cast entering into the jocund mood of the piece. Among the principals were Bonci (Almaviva), Gilibert (Dr. Bartolo), Pinkert (Rosina), Ancona (Figaro), and Mugnoz (Don Basilio). Campanini conducted. The auditorium of the Manhattan was especially well adapted to operas of this genre, and every bit of stage business was not lost on the assemblage. Of the performance, the New York *World* said: "Seldom has the frothy musical charm of Rossini's opera . . . been so delightfully displayed to the public as it was last night . . . ."[3] In the cast of *La Sonnambula* were Pinkert as Adina, Bonci as Elvino, Mugnoz as Rodolfo, and Reschiglian, Tecchi, Trentini, Severina, with Tanara conducting. Although Pinkert and Bonci sang well, the opera itself was considered outworn, the *Times* referring to it "as dull, as lifeless, and as inane as anything that is kept upon the operatic stage at the present time."[4]

The season's first presentation of the "operatic twins," *Cavalleria Rusticana* and *I Pagliacci*, on February 1, 1907, was the occasion for another evening of great singing; for it marked the debut of Mario Sammarco, a brilliant young Italian baritone. He came to the Manhattan with an enviable reputation gained in leading opera houses in Italy, Spain, Portugal, Belgium, Russia, Poland, Austria, Germany, and England. Among the roles he had created were Worms in Franchetti's *Germania*, Cascart in Leoncavallo's *Zaza*, and Gérard in Giordano's *Andrea Chénier*.[5] As Tonio in *I Pagliacci*, Sammarco thrilled the Manhattan audience with his magnificent open-throat singing of the Prologue. At the end of it, enthusiasm ran riot, the audience rising to its feet, applauding and waving programmes and handkerchiefs. Campanini, however, would not permit a repetition. Critics found Sammarco's voice to be ringing, powerful, sonorous, and velvety; his

---

[2] *The* [New York] *Evening Post*, January 19, 1907.
[3] *The* [New York] *World*, January 22, 1907.
[4] *The New York Times*, January 26, 1907.
[5] Blom (ed.), *Grove's Dictionary of Music and Musicians*, VII, 395.

dramatic ability was far above the ordinary. According to the *Times*, he was "one of the best Italian baritones heard here in a considerable time."[6] The *Press* awarded him the highest accolade: "a Caruso among baritones."[7] During the season Sammarco was heard also in *Rigoletto* (February 14), *Lucia* (February 16), *La Traviata* (February 23), *Un Ballo in Maschera* (February 27), *La Bohème* (March 1), *Faust* (March 22), and *Aïda* (April 20).

Later in February Hammerstein added three more operas to the repertory: *Mignon* (February 7), *Dinorah* (February 20), and *Un Ballo in Maschera* (February 27). The Thomas work must have been a welcome change for Bressler-Gianoli, who by this time had appeared in *Carmen* nine times. She was admirable in her dramatic interpretation of the pathetic Mignon but deficient vocally. Bonci, Pinkert, and Arimondi were her chief associates. The opera itself, like *La Sonnambula*, no longer seemed to interest the public; it was merely "an interesting relic."[8] At the beginning of the performance Campanini had been thoroughly annoyed by noise on stage. Stopping the overture, he went backstage to remonstrate with the offenders. After that, he returned to the podium; and the work proceeded without any more interruptions. Meyerbeer's *Dinorah* was another opera that no longer pleased, the *Herald* calling it "a dead opera with a live goat."[9] Though it had been painstakingly prepared and there were many excellent features of the performance, it seemed dull and hopelessly old-fashioned. Pinkert sounded fine as the demented Dinorah, being encored for the "Shadow Song," but the "eccentricities of her style"[10] were more noticeable than at any of her other appearances. Perhaps her facial contortions were a part of her method to produce tones. Since the opera had been resurrected as a vehicle for her, naturally she was the center of interest, although the cast also included Altchevsky, Trentini, and Ancona. For Hammerstein's production of Verdi's

[6] *The New York Times*, February 2, 1907.
[7] *The New York Press*, February 2, 1907.
[8] *The* [New York] *Evening Post*, February 8, 1907.
[9] *The New York Herald*, February 21, 1907.
[10] *The New York Press*, February 21, 1907.

Un Ballo in Maschera, the setting was laid in Boston at the time of the Puritans. Campanini brought out unexpected beauties and subtleties in the score while Sammarco's Renato was superb. Krehbiel said that it was "as perfect a performance in its way as anything that has been heard in either house from a male singer this season."[11] Bassi, Russ, Zeppilli, and Arimondi were admirable in their parts. Hammerstein's insistence on the appropriateness of costumes and scenery drew forth comparisons with the production of the same opera at the Metropolitan during the 1902–1903 season. In an article in *The Forum*, Joseph Sohn recalled the "motley aggregations of costumes"[12] in the Metropolitan's presentation, some "suggesting Italian *marinari*, others French peasants, while the remainder might have been mistaken for frowzy Cossacks."[13] He also commented on Hammerstein's policy of filling the minor roles with competent singers and his emphasis on the dramatic element. "Everywhere a sense of aesthetic fitness prevailed. Arimondi and Mugnoz made us forget their cognomens Samuel and Tom; indeed, they were probably the most acceptable and dignified villains that ever appeared in [*Un Ballo*]. . . . The part of Oscar, the page, instead of being relegated to a person of minor ability, was assigned to Mlle. Zeppilli, who immediately upon her entrance captivated all hearts by her charming presence, her irresistibly graceful acting, and her fresh and not unpleasing voice."[14]

MELBA'S TRIUMPHS CONTINUE

This same month Melba appeared five times: *Faust* (February 8), *Rigoletto* (February 14 and 25), *Lucia* (February 16), and *La Traviata* (February 23). The performance of *Faust* on the eighth was the only occasion she appeared in this opera during her engagement. Krehbiel said that the audience "revelled in the outpouring of scintillant notes in the jewel song and were stirred to rapture by [her] invocation at the window."[15] The comment in the *Times*, though it

[11] *New-York Daily Tribune*, February 28, 1907.
[12] "Opera in New York," Vol. XXXVIII (April, 1907), 513.
[13] *Ibid.*
[14] *Ibid.*
[15] *New-York Daily Tribune*, February 9, 1907.

praised her singing, was not entirely kind: "Her impersonation has not at the present time attributes of girlishness nor of ingenuous pathos, for the years have told upon Mme. Melba's presence, as they have not been able to tell upon her voice."[16] Apparently before the performance Melba had been temperamental and imperious. Hammerstein, needless to say, was equal to any rebuff or demand, inured to the turmoils of the opera house. Walter Prichard Eaton, who interviewed him this evening, asked why he preferred to be an opera director rather than a captain of industry, a manufacturer of cigars. The answer was characteristic of the impresario. Eaton said:

> [Hammerstein] smiled, and his eyes squinted as they do when he doesn't wish you to know whether he's ironic or not, and he said, "Ah, but the tobacco business is prose, this is poetry—you know? It's more fun to make Melba sing than it is to make a cigar. Tonight, now, first she tells me it's too hot in her dressing-room; then it's too cold; then she wants me to ring up at eight, when there are only two people in the house, and I have to set my watch back and show her it's only seven-thirty—you know? You must handle these singers just so—it's an art—or else they'll go out on the stage and phrase like the devil. If you let 'em do that you'd have to admit people to your house on transfers—you know?"
>
> The scene was set by now, there was a sudden awareness of the people out front as the curtain hissed up its wires, a muscular chord from the orchestra, a "Sssh" for silence from the stage manager. Oscar spread out his palms. "You see, in my own house, too, they won't let me speak!" Presently Melba, prayer-book in hand, stole along behind the canvas frame that to the audience was a garden wall, paused for her music cue, and entered the gate. Then we heard her voice, luscious, perfectly phrased, and once more he spread out his palms, this time with another inflection. He tiptoed up to the window of Marguerite's house . . . and peeped out upon the stage. He patted the scenery affectionately as he did so. He was smiling

[16] *The New York Times,* February 9, 1907.

to himself when he came back to his chair, his hands behind
him, his head down . . . .[17]

This performance and the other Melba nights were gala affairs;
always there were tremendous crowds, excitement, and enthusiasm
with society out in force—the Vanderbilts, Goelets, Belmonts. Hammerstein had cause to rejoice for, in the words of *Town Topics*, the
"gold poured no more lavishly from her throat than it piled up in
the box-office."[18]

[17] "Oscar Hammerstein A Boy Who Never Grew Up," *The American Magazine*, Vol. LXIV (May, 1907), 32–34.

[18] Vol. LVII (January 24, 1907), 16.

VII

Cause La Bohème

THE PRODUCTION announced for March 1 received the greatest
fanfare of any presentation in the Manhattan repertory this opening
season. At one time, it had seemed well nigh impossible for Hammerstein to give the opera at all, for it was none other than Puccini's *La
Bohème*. After all the fuss, Ricordi and Company had not been
awarded an injunction to prevent the production.

The whole matter was long and involved. In an affidavit Hammerstein declared that before he went to Europe in March, 1906, he
had had a verbal agreement with George Maxwell, the American
representative of Ricordi, and that it had been agreed he might produce any Puccini opera except *Madama Butterfly* for $150 a perform-
ance, the same fee Conried paid. Hammerstein said that he had
conferred with Tito Ricordi in Milan regarding the production of
the Puccini operas and had sought his advice concerning the artists for
them. He then had gone ahead to invest many thousands of dollars
for scenery and costumes. It was not until July 25, 1906, that he
received a letter from Maxwell reminding him of the copyright. The
letter did not mention that the Metropolitan had been granted an
exclusive contract for the Puccini operas. Maxwell, on the other hand,
denied that there had been any verbal contract. He said that he had
seen Hammerstein the first time on March 5, 1906, the evening
before the impresario went to Europe to recruit his company, and that
when Hammerstein asked for a contract, he replied that he could not
grant one until he knew precisely who was to sing in the operas. He
declared that this was a policy of Ricordi and Company. Hammerstein

promised that ten days after arriving in Europe, he would advise him of the artists he intended to engage. Maxwell then stated that after this initial meeting he had not received a word from Hammerstein. In May he granted Conried the exclusive license and, upon hearing that Hammerstein intended to produce Puccini's operas, sent the letter of July 25. Since Hammerstein, however, had persisted in his efforts, Ricordi and Company filed the injunction, on October 19, to enjoin him from producing *La Bohème*.

Several months later, on January 3, 1907, Judge Townsend refused to grant the injunction. It was his opinion that " 'most of the assertions and counter assertions may be so harmonized as to show that even if said agreement was not originally made, Maxwell and Tito Ricordi, by their conversation and conduct led or permitted Hammerstein to make said contracts, and incur said expenses upon the faith of an understanding that a license would be given him to produce *La Boheme*, provided the usual conditions were complied with.' "[1] Furthermore, the Judge asserted that if Ricordi and Company wanted to grant Conried an exclusive contract, Hammerstein should have been notified of this action and in good time. He continued: " 'But although Maxwell states that he made the exclusive license to Conried in May he did not notify Hammerstein of that fact even so late as July 25, and the letter then written might fairly be interpreted merely as a notice of the complainants' copyrights.' "[2] For these reasons the court refused to grant the injunction " 'in view of the great hardship which would be imposed thereby on Hammerstein in view of the contracts made and expenses incurred on the faith of the situation produced or permitted by Maxwell and Ricordi as established by their own statements.' "[3]

On the following day, January 4, 1907, Ricordi and Company appealed the decision. Hammerstein, of course, was pleased by the court's ruling and said he had expected it in his favor all during the controversy. The Metropolitan, however, persisted in its prosecution

---

[1] *"Boheme* for Hammerstein," *Musical Courier*, Vol. LIV (January 9, 1907), 24.

[2] *Ibid.* [3] *Ibid.*, 23–24.

and after Melba had appeared four times in the opera, Hammerstein consented to the injunction on April 15, 1907. By then Ricordi's victory (or was it Conried's?) meant nothing. Hammerstein had successfully produced *La Bohème*, much to the delight of many opera-goers and Mme Melba.

It is interesting to speculate what Puccini thought of the situation. In the fall of 1906 Conried invited him to come to New York to supervise the productions of *Manon Lescaut* and *Madama Butterfly*, both new to the Metropolitan repertory. The fee which Conried proffered the composer was $8,000. Puccini accepted and arrived late on January 18, 1907, the same evening of the *Manon Lescaut première*. After the first act the audience applauded him vociferously while the orchestra greeted him with a fanfare.[4] In a letter to friend, he recalled the "great reception"[5] and the admirable portrayals of Cavalieri as Manon and of Caruso as Des Grieux.

In the weeks that followed, the Metropolitan repeatedly presented his operas, which, Puccini proudly noted, always drew enthusiastic crowds. Much was anticipated for the *Madama Butterfly première*, on February 11, with Farrar, Caruso, Scotti, and Homer. Puccini, however, was dissatisfied. In his opinion, Vigna, the conductor, was asinine; Farrar intractable; and Caruso indolent. He complained that he had had to supervise all of the stage setting.[6] Although the critics and public thought it one of the best productions given at the Metropolitan in some time, Puccini would not be placated; to him it "lacked the poetry which [he had] put into it."[7] Several weeks after the first performance, Puccini went back to Italy, no doubt happy to return to the idyllic pleasures of Torre del Lago.

During his American sojourn (January 18–February 26), Puccini refused to make any comments concerning the Metropolitan-Hammerstein dispute over *La Bohème*; and yet it was during this precise period that the wrangling was at the highest pitch. A man of discre-

---

[4] George R. Marek, *Puccini*, 239.
[5] Vincent Seligman, *Puccini Among Friends*, 116.
[6] *Ibid.*, 118.
[7] *Ibid.*, 119.

tion, he remained silent; even if he had wanted to voice his opinion on the affair, to do so would have placed him in an awkward position. He was the guest of the Metropolitan and the Ricordis' friend; he also would not want to offend Mme Melba and Campanini, artists whom he admired. As far as the public was concerned, however, his sympathies were entirely with the older house. At the time, Puccini and the Metropolitan seemed indissolubly linked. Perhaps this was the effect which Conried desired.

Although Hammerstein had the legal right to present the opera, he possessed no score; for the work had never been published. The Ricordis saw to it that he would not be able to obtain any of the manuscript copies, which were numbered and accounted for all over the world. Ultimately, however, Hammerstein did succeed in finding one: a copy that the Ricordis had considered too mutilated for use again. Agnes Murphy maintains that it had been used in the United States by the Del Conti Opera Company, a touring group from England.[8] The *New York Times* of March 2, 1907, said that Hammerstein had obtained a score that Clementine de Vere had used when she was touring the United States some years before. Campanini knew the opera so well that he was able to write in the missing parts. He refused, however, to conduct any of the public performances, apparently fearful of the Ricordis' ire. As the time approached for the first presentation of the work, some maintained that his refusal was due to a difference with Melba concerning her interpretation of the role of Mimi. He denied this and wanted it understood that he held the highest admiration for the prima donna both as a person and as an artist. In a letter to the editor of *The Evening Telegram*, he gave his ostensible reason for not conducting the opera: "The true reason why I am not directing *Boheme* is because I am very tired and am greatly occupied in directing rehearsals and performances, as you can see for yourself."[9] Fernando Tanara, one of his deputies, had the honor of leading the public performances, though Campanini had rehearsed the opera *in segreto*.

[8] *Melba: A Biography*, 269.
[9] Letter dated February 28, 1907, p. 8.

The night before the *première* of *La Bohème* at the Manhattan, the Metropolitan offered the same opera with Caruso, Cavalieri, Alten, Stracciari, and Journet in the authorized version. The older house hoped, no doubt, that the comparison would be in its favor. On the very afternoon of the performance, Maxwell issued the following statement: "Mr. Hammerstein's presentation of the opera *La Bohème* is without the authority and consent of the composer, Giacomo Puccini, or ourselves as owners of the copyright. It will be given with an unauthorized orchestration, and we would request all who attend the performance not to hold Signor Puccini as composer or ourselves responsible for it."[10] The natural reaction was that many thought Hammerstein's production would be inadequate. Even up to curtain time, the opposition was intense; for the lobby of the Manhattan was filled with detractors who harassed those going into the auditorium.[11]

In spite of the dire predictions, the evening was a triumph. Years later Melba recalled that it was "one of the best performances"[12] of this opera in which she had appeared during her entire career. No doubt keyed up by the occasion, she never spared herself, singing "with positive recklessness. At times her voice fairly flooded the auditorium."[13] According to the *Times*, she sang "more beautifully than she [had] done anything else this season in New York."[14] Her impersonation of the frail seamstress was touching, although her appearance hardly suggested a Latin Quarter grisette. Bonci surprised his most ardent admirers by the plenitude and fervor of his singing. Trentini, as Musetta, was a revelation. Earlier in the season she had appeared in such various secondary roles as Siébel in *Faust*, Berta in *Il Barbiere di Siviglia*, Frasquita in *Carmen* without any special distinction; but as the dashing vixen in Puccini's opera, she was a sensation. It was "a piece of work that [raised] this young person

[10] News item in *The* [New York] *Sun*, March 2, 1907.
[11] Murphy, *Melba: A Biography*, 269–70.
[12] Melba, *Melodies and Memories*, 245.
[13] *The* [New York] *Evening World*, March 2, 1907.
[14] *The New York Times*, March 2, 1907.

perceptibly in the estimation of the frequenters of the Manhattan. It [was] her most important contribution to the operatic history of that institution: a most vivacious and mirthful character sketch, full of the highest spirits and boisterous mischief, yet very intelligent and very well sung."[15] John McCormack considered her the ideal Musetta.[16] Sammarco (Marcello), Gilibert (Schaunard), and Arimondi (Colline) were entirely satisfactory. Gianoli-Galletti and Tecchi, who was Bonci's brother, rounded out the cast. The only adverse criticism was that the orchestra was frequently too loud, obliterating some of the singing of the principals.[17] All in all, it was a red-letter night for the Manhattan and a victory for Melba and Hammerstein.

[15] *Ibid.*, March 7, 1907.
[16] L. A. G. Strong, *John McCormack*, 138.
[17] *The* [New York] *Sun*, March 2, 1907.

VIII

Final Weeks of the Season

Two OTHER OPERAS were duly added to the repertory: *Fra Diavolo* (March 8) and *Marta* (March 23). Also, on Good Friday, March 29, the company presented Verdi's *Manzoni Requiem* with Russ, De Cisneros, Bassi, and Arimondi as soloists. Both *Fra Diavolo* and *Marta* enlisted the services of Bonci; and although the critics liked the productions, they were not popular successes. Under the baton of Campanini, *Fra Diavolo* was a sparkling and effervescent performance which "was carried off with a lightness of touch and precision of ensemble that were delightful, and of which none of the details were lost upon the listeners."[1] The principal roles were taken by Pinkert (Zerline), Bonci (Fra Diavolo), Gilibert (Milord). *Marta* was another charming production, both musically and scenically. The White Horse Inn of the third act inspired much comment, as it was an exact copy of an English inn. Charles Wilson, the stage director, had surpassed his previous efforts in the verisimilitude of the *mise-en-scène*. Bonci did not sing as was his wont, his tones lacking their accustomed mellowness. His voice was beginning to show the effect of his having sung so often during the season. Others in the cast were Donalda (Harriet), De Cisneros (Nancy), Arimondi (Plunkett), and Gianoli-Galletti (Tristan), Tanara conducting. The Verdi *Requiem*, preceded by Haydn's *Symphony No. 3*, was rendered in a devotional manner with the soloists, chorus, and orchestra obtaining "surprising results of sonority, precision, and contrast . . . ."[2]

[1] *The New York Times*, March 9, 1907.
[2] *Ibid.*, March 30, 1907.

Au Revoir, MME MELBA

On March 25, Melba made her farewell performance for the season in the fourth presentation of *La Bohème*. As on each previous occasion when this opera was performed (March 1, 6, 11), she was again the Mimi. This gala marked her fifteenth appearance with the company. Although originally having contracted to sing only ten performances, she had twice extended her stay so that she could be in additional presentations at the Manhattan, concertize in various cities, and make some recordings. Seats for her farewell were at a premium; it was reported that some orchestra stalls had gone for $30 each, or even more.[3] At the end of the opera, which had been a spirited performance, Melba sang the mad scene from *Lucia*. The audience responded by giving her perhaps the greatest ovation of the season. It remained cheering and applauding for some forty minutes as the beloved diva came before the footlights twenty-three times.[4] After a while Melba had the stagehands push a piano onto the stage, where, accompanying herself, she sang the air "Mattinata," apparently not considering this song anti-climactic to the mad scene. When she finished, the house was pandemonium all over again. Finally the lights were dimmed, and those still in the auditorium made their way outside, glorying in an unforgettable operatic evening.

Meantime caterers on stage were busily preparing for a supper party to be given in honor of the departing star. To join in the festivities, Hammerstein had invited all the principals and their husbands or wives, as well as some of Melba's friends. Thirty-five musicians entertained the guests as they dined with "Memories of the Manhattan Opera Season," composed by the impresario himself. The menu was apropos, for it included *suprême de volaille Hammerstein* and *pêche Melba*. In an expansive mood, Hammerstein extolled his guest of honor as a person and as a singer. And well he might! He had every reason to be proud of what she had accomplished and of what his company now meant to New York. No doubt he contemplated that the concluding weeks of the season should be highly successful, since

[3] Murphy, *Melba: A Biography*, 272.
[4] *Ibid.*, 274.

he had been able to engage another great star to add lustre to the Manhattan: the inimitable Emma Calvé. His opera house would not lack a prima donna. It is likely that he was sorry she had not come to the supper party, even though she had been invited. Perhaps Calvé realized it was best that the impresario not share his attentions with his two *prime donne*.[5] Even for a man of his known fortitude, such a combination might have been a hazardous undertaking.

Melba's final word about Hammerstein and her experiences with the company was made known on the eve of her departure for Europe:

> "I have never enjoyed any season in America so much as the one now closing. All through I have been in splendid health and spirits, and I shall never forget the kindness with which I have been received. The demands on my time have been so exacting that many courtesies must remain without direct acknowledgment.
>
> "I am proud to have been associated with Mr. Hammerstein in his launching of New York's new opera house. What courage Mr. Hammerstein has shown and what wonders he has done! I think there must be something in the conditions of American life to encourage him, for I know of no manager in any city of the world who, single-handed and under circumstances of such difficulty and competition, would have risked his fortune on opera.
>
> "His pluck appealed to me from the first, and I leave as I came, his loyal friend and admirer."[6]

Bonjour et Bienvenue, MME CALVÉ

Calvé was a welcome addition to the company. One of the most fascinating operatic personalities of the time, she combined, to a rare degree, a magnificent voice, temperament, magnetism, individuality. After a series of triumphs at many of the leading opera houses in the

[5] News item in *The* [New York] *Evening Telegram*, March 26, 1907.

[6] News item in *The New York Times*, April 1, 1907.

world, Calvé had made her impressive debut at the Metropolitan on November 29, 1893, as a tempestuous Santuzza in *Cavalleria Rusticana*. Her fiery impersonation of the Sicilian peasant awakened the New York public to the possibilities of this role, which hitherto had been interpreted at the Metropolitan by Emma Eames, too much the aristocrat for the part. Several weeks later Calvé eclipsed her previous efforts there when she appeared for the first time in *Carmen*, on December 20, 1893, with a cast that included Jean de Reszke (Don José), Lassalle (Escamillo), and Eames (Micaëla). From that time on, in the opinion of many, there was no other singer who was comparable to Calvé as Bizet's heroine; indeed, Carmen and Calvé became indissoluble. During the 1890's, she thrilled New York operagoers in a variety of roles and was one of Grau's most popular stars. In the early years of the new century, however, the soprano appeared less frequently at the Metropolitan. When she did, it was noted that she had become increasingly capricious in her operatic portrayals, a law unto herself. Still, Calvé possessed a magic which enthralled her audiences. Her last appearances at the Metropolitan had been in the 1903–1904 season. It was said at that time that the relationship between the stolid Conried and his volatile prima donna had been less than amiable.

Calvé made her debut at the Manhattan on March 27, 1907, two days after Melba's farewell, in the inevitable *Carmen*, with Dalmorès (Don José), Ancona (Escamillo), and Donalda (Micaëla), under the direction of Campanini. Calvé's presence at the opera house aroused much anticipation and interest; the *Tribune* reported that on this occasion 720 carriages came to the Manhattan, the record number of the season.[7] Although the soprano enjoyed a success with her audience, critics were not unanimous in praising her, some maintaining that she was very much the same great performer as of yore while others lamented her waning powers. According to the *Herald*, she had returned with "her powers unimpaired . . . [and was] the same woman of sinuous, serpentine grace and insinuating laughter; the same woman with the same wonderful arms and hands that speak

[7] *New-York Daily Tribune*, March 28, 1907.

with every motion; in a word the same Carmen."[8] There were those, however, who noted a deterioration in her singing. Too prodigal in the squandering of her vocal gold, Calvé no longer sang with her former beauty of tone but forced her voice so that the high tones were shrill. She dragged the tempo, altering rhythms "to suit her own unaccountable fancy"[9]; her acting, however, was not so capricious as it had been in her last seasons at the Metropolitan. Nevertheless, there was no question that Calvé remained a compelling, pervasive personality, an artist who exerted an undeniable fascination.

Calvé's first appearance as Santuzza in *Cavalleria Rusticana* was a matinee performance on March 30 with Dalmorès and Seveilhac. Again, she drew mixed critical comments for her singing and acting. However, her Anita in Massenet's *La Navarraise*, first presented on April 10, was enthusiastically received, this opera being more suited to her present powers. The role exposed "but little of her decadence as a singer, while it [gave] ample scope for the exercise of her ability as an actress."[10] It did much "to restore something of her former prestige."[11] Calvé's farewell performance was the nineteenth and final presentation of *Carmen* on April 20. During her engagement, she appeared nine times: five Carmens, two Santuzzas, and two Anitas.

That evening (April 20) the season concluded with a gala *Aïda*, in which Sammarco assumed the part of Amonasro for the first time at the Manhattan. It was a superb performance, a time for exhilaration, cheers, sentiment, and reminiscences. It was also an appropriate occasion for Hammerstein to make a speech. To the packed, demonstrative house, the impresario said:

> "I was not sure of my position when I stood on these boards five months ago, when I was starting an Opera House without the aid of society. I found soon after that there was no regular opera-going public, and I had to make one. In the first few weeks sometimes there was not over $1,500 a night in the

[8] *The New York Herald,* March 28, 1907.
[9] *The New York Press,* March 28, 1907.
[10] *The* [New York] *Sun,* April 11, 1907.
[11] *New-York Daily Tribune,* April 11, 1907.

house, but I convinced the people that I was doing the right thing by them, that I had no commercial aim in view, and I made a public which wanted to hear grand opera sung in the best manner.

"Other men would have been discouraged by the lack of support, but I was not. I went ahead and did the best I could, with the result that I am ending the season, with the balance on the profit side.

"I am going abroad in a few weeks to engage artists to sing here next year—"

Some one in the gallery shouted, "Mr. Campanini."

"Yes, Mr. Campanini is coming back. I want him most of all. I am going to spend all the money I have earned in an attempt to make this the most wonderful opera house in the world. Think of it, New York is the only city in the world which can support two opera houses of the first rank. The other one is certainly established [laughter], and this one is, too. [Applause.] And the people who come here come here for the opera. I want no others. I am not trying to establish a society clientele . . . . Ladies and gentlemen, I thank you for your support and hope to see you again next year."[12]

GOOD NEWS AND PLANS

On April 22, two days after the final performances, Hammerstein made known the receipts for the past twenty weeks; they were approximately $750,000.[13] According to Arthur Hammerstein, the net profit was $100,000.[14] With this sum and the loan of $400,000, with the opera house as security, the future looked very bright indeed from the financial standpoint. Hammerstein had obtained this loan from Frank Woolworth, the founder of the stores that bear his name and a patron of the Manhattan.[15] The same season the Metropolitan

[12] News item in *The New York Times,* April 21, 1907.

[13] *Ibid.,* April 22, 1907.

[14] Kolodin, *The Metropolitan Opera 1883–1935,* 121.

[15] Sheean, *Oscar Hammerstein I,* 173.

showed a loss for the first time in many years. The exact amount was $84,039, not an inconsiderable deficit.[16]

Hammerstein had every reason to be proud of the Manhattan's outstanding achievements, which were due, in a very large measure, to his own unremitting efforts. He had fulfilled his promise and presented a series of performances that had successfully rivalled and at times eclipsed the best efforts of the Metropolitan management. The older house, no doubt anticipating that Hammerstein's season would last for only a few performances, had preferred at first to ignore the challenge of the opera house down the street. The period of grand isolation, however, did not endure for long. The first head-on collision had been the production of *La Bohème*, from which the Metropolitan suffered a resounding defeat; but there had been other serious setbacks, the most notable one being the withdrawal of *Salome* from the older house's repertory after its one public performance, since it was considered too immoral for proper New Yorkers.

Then Conried tried to lure away some of the Manhattan's artists by offering them large fees. On February 26, 1907, articles appeared in the press concerning Bonci, who, it was said, was negotiating with the Metropolitan and who was likely to join that company next season. The following day Conried confirmed the engagement of the diminutive singer. It must have been galling to him to have his great tenor Caruso compared to Hammerstein's Bonci. Hammerstein, meantime, had not been caught napping. Several weeks before, he had signed a five years' contract with the magnificent tenor Giovanni Zenatello, a versatile, brilliant singer. On February 28 Hammerstein announced that he would not release Bonci from his contract and that he was well aware Conried also desired the services of others in the company: " 'It is very flattering to me to have Mr. Conried run after my singers, whom I have discovered for this country. He has tried to get Dalmorès and Bassi away from me, and I understand that an offer has been made to my conductor, Campanini, at a salary of $1,000 a week for a season of twenty weeks and a guarantee of four years. This all proves that Mr. Conried believes I know where to obtain

[16] Moses, *The Life of Heinrich Conried,* 219.

good artists and he does not, so he gets them from me.' "[17] Although these three artists remained loyal to the Manhattan, Bonci ultimately joined the Metropolitan after Hammerstein decided to release him. Had Hammerstein not let the tenor go, court proceedings might have dragged on interminably. In particular, clause S of his contract made an early settlement difficult:

> To decide all questions that may arise with regard to the present contract the undersigned [Hammerstein and Bonci] agree to accept the application of the Italian laws, the jurisdiction of the Italian judicial authorities, and the judicial authority of Florence, to which all questions must be referred and by which all must be judged.[18]

On April 26, 1907, it was announced that the law suit had been settled out of court and that Bonci would definitely appear with the Metropolitan Opera Company the next season.[19]

Hammerstein, of course, reciprocated in like fashion and raided his enemy's forces. Apparently he made several futile overtures to Caruso, who remained loyal to Conried at an advance in fees from $1,440 a performance to $2,000 each,[20] but Nordica and Schumann-Heink were delighted to sing at the new house. To secure Nordica, Hammerstein had engaged in a ruse, maintaining all the while that the star he really wanted was Eames. Somewhat later he divulged his tactics:

> "Nordica's engagement required some maneuvring. I knew the Other House had offered her a season of twenty-four appearances in New York and four in Philadelphia for next year, as against their offer for this year of only twelve performances. I made it appear that I was after Eames, and the Metropolitan closed with Eames in a hurry. Then I was sure

[17] News item in *The* [New York] *World*, February 28, 1907.
[18] News item in *The New York Times*, March 9, 1907.
[19] *Ibid.*, April 26, 1907.
[20] Kolodin, *The Metropolitan Opera 1883–1935*, 284.

Alessandro Bonci left the Manhattan at the end of the first season, in the spring of 1907. Enrico Caruso, the star of the Metropolitan, drew this cartoon to represent the event. Caruso shows himself and Conried, the Metropolitan's general director, awaiting Bonci's arrival, while Ba

Courtesy Library of Congress, from *Musical Courier*

chevsky, and Dalmorès, tenors at the Manhattan, look on. Zenatello,
mmerstein's replacement for Bonci, is shown at the extreme left, with
valet.

of Nordica, who didn't relish being second fiddle to Eames at the Metropolitan."[21]

In addition to these two luminaries, Hammerstein had Melba and Calvé. No doubt he had been annoyed by the criticisms of the company's lack of great female artists and was determined that never again would the Manhattan be without glorious *prime donne*. Another artist he said would appear next season was the glamorous Mary Garden; and though he did not have her under contract when he first made this announcement, the preliminary negotiations had been so satisfactory that Hammerstein had no doubt at all of acquiring her services. The roster of principal singers at the Manhattan for the season of 1907–1908 would not be overshadowed by the Metropolitan's.

The impresario's plans for the repertory were ambitious and somewhat startling. He was eager to present novelties, to familiarize New York with what was new in opera. One concrete expression of his interest was his announcement, on April 5, 1907, that Victor Herbert, beloved operetta composer, was to write an opera for the Manhattan.[22] What this opportunity meant to Herbert is patent in all his comments concerning Hammerstein, whom he praised " 'for making it possible that an opera by an American ... be produced. The activity, the enterprise which he has stimulated in the American operatic field, and the avenues of opportunity that he has opened to musicians of all sorts, are in striking contrast to the conditions and apathy and stagnation that have hitherto prevailed.' "[23] Hammerstein also announced that he would offer a $1,000 prize for the libretto, which he preferred to be written by an American.[24] What ultimately resulted was *Natoma*, Herbert's first grand opera. Later it was said that Hammerstein would also produce an opera to be written by Reginald de Koven, who intended to use Du Maurier's *Trilby* as the basis of the libretto.[25] It seemed that at long last American operatic composers would see their music dramas brought to production. *Musical America*

[21] News item in *The* [New York] *Evening Telegram*, March 15, 1907.

[22] News item in *The New York Times*, April 5, 1907.

[23] Unidentified clipping, New York, early April, 1907.

commented: " . . . Beyond the musical value which their [Herbert's and De Koven's] grand operas will undoubtedly possess, the production of these operas will have a still greater national value. It marks the beginning of a new epoch in American music. Oscar Hammerstein has opened the breach, and the composers will leap to the charge . . . ."[26]

Furthermore, Hammerstein maintained that he would produce some of the great operas from the contemporary French school, works that New York had not yet heard. He must have known that to continue with a repertory similar to the first season's, largely composed of bread-and-butter operas, would place the Manhattan quite beyond the pale of serious consideration. Casting about for something new, Hammerstein turned to such masterpieces as Charpentier's *Louise* and Debussy's *Pelléas et Mélisande*, which Conried had been offered but which he had rejected "with a contemptuous wave of his hand,"[27] preferring to present the familiar operas, the ones he thought the public wanted to hear. His failure to obtain the novelties was to be Hammerstein's golden opportunity. Of greater significance, the production of these works was to be the basis of the Manhattan's importance in American operatic history.

In presenting *opéra comique*, Hammerstein was, to say the least, extremely daring. For many years the tradition in New York had been that the public would not attend operatic novelties. Hammerstein was well aware that many held this opinion and that no less an impresario than Maurice Grau had publicly stated this; yet he wondered whether the lack of interest in new works would apply to the present time.[28] If he should succeed, then precedents would be useless.

[24] News item in *The New York Times,* April 5, 1907.

[25] J.B.C., "*Trilby* in Grand Opera Form Will Be Reginald De Koven's Next Task," *Musical America,* Vol. X (July 24, 1909), 3.

[26] "An Epoch for America," *Musical America,* Vol. X (July 24, 1909), 14.

[27] Gatti-Casazza, *Memories of the Opera,* 168.

[28] "The Manhattan Opera House Opens Its Season of 1907–08," *The New York Herald Society and Drama Section,* November 3, 1907, p. 12.

At any rate, since he could not produce Puccini and since another season with hackneyed operas would not sustain public interest for long, he had no other recourse than to include the modern French operas in the repertory.

IX

Enter Mary Garden

ONE OF THE singers Hammerstein needed for the venture into new fields and the one he had been interested in for some time was Mary Garden, then the reigning Queen of the Paris Opéra-Comique. Even before the opening season he had considered engaging her. While in Europe during the spring of 1906 to gather together his company, Hammerstein endeavored to see Garden and sent her his card at the time she was appearing in *Aphrodite* at the Comique. Disliking to receive anyone during a performance and not knowing who he was, she requested that he call on her the next day. According to *Mary Garden's Story*, published in 1951, Hammerstein did not pursue the matter further but returned to the United States without seeing her.[1] Some years before the publication of her autobiography, Garden gave a slightly different interpretation of her initial contact with Hammerstein. In June, 1930, she stated that when Hammerstein requested the interview, she sent back word that she had " 'no inclination to sing in America.' "[2] She waited to explain her objection, that the modern French operas were not performed in the United States; but she said she had no opportunity to see Hammerstein, as he had left for New York.

The conviction grew on Hammerstein, considering the series of performances for the second season, that he must have Garden as a member of the company if he intended to produce novelties from the

[1] Mary Garden and Louis Biancolli, *Mary Garden's Story*, 99.

[2] Mary Garden, "The Heights," *Ladies' Home Journal*, Vol. *XLVII* (June, 1930), 115.

modern French repertory. He confessed this to Herman Klein, the eminent vocal coach and friend of many great singers: " '[If] I could get Mary Garden at a reasonable figure I would do the new French operas in which she has made a hit, and take my chance of her making a success in New York.' "[3] Subsequently Gustave Schirmer acted in Hammerstein's behalf. At first Garden was reluctant, fearing that New York might not understand her art nor appreciate the operas in which she had gained her fame. After all, most of these music dramas were completely unknown in the United States. Would Americans accept her and *Thaïs, Louise, Pelléas et Mélisande?* Always the diplomat, Schirmer ultimately succeeded in persuading her to accept Hammerstein's offer.[4] It has been said that Monsieur Durand, the Paris publisher of many of the modern French operas, also was of assistance in persuading Garden to appear at the Manhattan.[5] It was strictly understood, however, that she was to appear in those operas which had been her greatest successes and that other French artists were to be in the casts with her, singers who possessed the requisite style for the modern French works. She wrote a letter to Hammerstein "relative to the company she would like to have around her,"[6] knowing very well that if the modern operas were to succeed, she would need the assistance of other artists who were thoroughly familiar with the French tradition. Fortunately Hammerstein understood and agreed. It was with great pleasure that he was able to announce that she would be a member of the company for the 1907–1908 season.

Like so many other singers, Garden had little in her background to suggest the genesis of an operatic career. She was born in Aberdeen, Scotland, on February 20, 1877; eight years later she and her family

[3] Herman Klein, *Unmusical New York,* 72–73.

[4] Mary Garden, "My Life," *Hearst's International,* Vol. XLV (February, 1924), 152.

[5] Klein, *Unmusical New York,* 73.

[6] "Changes Planned at the Manhattan," *Musical America,* Vol. V (March 23, 1907), 13.

came to the United States, making their home for a time in Brooklyn, later moving to Chicopee, Massachusetts, finally settling in Chicago. There, at the age of sixteen, Garden began studying voice with Mrs. Robinson Duff, who, recognizing the young girl's potential, encouraged her to consider music as a career. As Mrs. Duff became more and more pleased by her protégée's good work and progress, she recommended to Garden's parents that their daughter go to Paris for further study. Mr. Garden was hesitant, as he did not have the funds for this expensive undertaking. In time, however, Mrs. Duff was able to elicit financial aid from the David Mayers, wealthy Chicago patrons of the arts.

In Paris, Garden spent considerable time looking about for a suitable teacher, one in whom she would have the utmost confidence. She studied briefly with Mme Mathilde Marchesi (the teacher of Melba, Eames, Frances Saville, Suzanne Adams, Frances Alda) and subsequently with Trabadello, Lucien Fugère, and Jules Chevalier. After approximately a year and one-half, Garden's sponsors suddenly withdrew their support. With little income, Garden was in a desperate plight, uncertain what to do. Good luck, however, had not deserted her. According to *Mary Garden's Story*, one day while walking in the Bois de Boulogne, she encountered by chance the beautiful American soprano Sybil Sanderson, for whom Massenet had written *Thaïs*. Garden, knowing her slightly, did not speak; but Sanderson, recognizing the dejected operatic aspirant, stopped and called to her. Garden, quite beside herself, told of her troubles, whereupon Sanderson, mourning the death of her husband and disconsolate, invited her to live in her sumptuous apartment on the Champs-Élysées.[7] This chance meeting was a turning point in Garden's life.

Sanderson, acquainted with many important musical personages, introduced Garden to Albert Carré, the director of the Opéra-Comique, who seems to have liked the young singer from the beginning and to have recognized instinctively her musical creativity. He permitted her to attend rehearsals at the opera house, sent her tickets

[7] Garden and Biancolli, 22–23.

for the performances and, when she evinced interest in *Louise*, then being prepared for its world *première* (February 2, 1900), gave her a score of it to study. Since this opera appealed to her strongly, she worked on it for weeks, also seeing it as often as possible. After a time Carré offered her a contract with the Opéra-Comique effective beginning in October, 1900.[8] Then the unexpected occurred.

The morning of April 10, 1900 (Garden, in her autobiography, mistakenly recalled the date as April 13, 1900),[9] Carré asked Garden to come at once to the opera house. Mlle Rioton, the original Louise, was to sing in the Charpentier opera that evening; but since she was ill, Carré wanted Garden on hand just in case Rioton was not able to finish the performance. By 7:30 Garden had taken her place in an orchestra seat. The opera seemed to go well, but after the second act, Garden was summoned back stage. Rioton was unable to continue; and Garden, without a rehearsal, took her place. What she did is now not only a memorable part of musical history but also a legend. Unknown, Garden walked out on the stage before an extremely critical audience and, rising to the occasion, succeeded in turning the evening into a complete triumph for herself. Years later Carré said that on this April night, Garden " . . . chanta le grand air de *Louise*, ce terrible casse-cou, avec une telle assurance, une voix si pure et un sentiment si juste que, de toutes parts . . . s' élevèrent, pendant plusieurs minutes, de bruyantes acclamations."[10]

After this unforgettable debut Garden sang *Louise* many times, confirming the excellent impression she had first made. Then Carré gave her other roles to study and to perform. In time her vaulting ambition was to be known as a *créatice*; for she preferred to appear not in standard works but in the new operas, thereby creating her own traditions.[11] The modern music dramas thrilled her; even her limited experience as a public performer had convinced her that "there [was]

[8] *Ibid.*, 28.
[9] Le Figaro, April 11, 1900.
[10] Albert Carré, *Souvenirs de Théâtre*, 256.
[11] Garden, "My Life," *Hearst's International*, Vol. XLV (February, 1924), 73.

no reason in the world why modern grand opera should not come nearer expressing the essentials and realities of life than [had] been the case heretofore."[12]

In her development as an artist, Garden was fortunate to have Carré as her director, since he did not try to make her conform to the conventional in opera but encouraged her in her individualism. Garden maintained that she had never taken any acting lessons but that Carré "saw in [her] what he thought to be dramatic talent, and he brought it out. He did not teach [her] to act . . . . [She] simply needed direction."[13] Fearful that she might overdo her characterization, Garden was reassured by Carré, who told her: " 'Mademoiselle . . . you were born with an instinct that will always protect you from going too far. Go to what you think is the limit, then exaggerate and you will still be within the boundary line.' "[14]

As her musical and histrionic abilities developed and her unique talent for characterization unfolded, Garden was able to portray an amazing variety of operatic roles during her first seasons at the Opéra-Comique. Three months after her debut she created the role of Marie in Lucien Lambert's *La Marseillaise*. On February 19, 1901, she took a leading part in another new opera, Gabriel Pierné's *La Fille de Tabarin*, and was praised for her beautiful voice and moving portrayal: "la voix est jolie et fort bien conduite, les attitudes et le jeu sont d'une rare sincérité."[15] As Massenet's Manon, a role which she assumed for the first time on September 21, 1901, Garden impressed in the Cours-la-Reine scene. She was infinitely charming, while in the Saint-Sulpice scene she was vociferously acclaimed for the power of her acting: "elle a su se montrer vibrante et pleine de passion au tableau de Saint-Sulpice. Le public lui a prodigué les plus chaleureux

---

[12] *Ibid.*, January, 1924, 130.

[13] Mary Garden, "The Opera Singer and the Public," *The American Magazine*, Vol. LXXVIII (August, 1914), 31.

[14] Garden, "The Heights," *Ladies' Home Journal*, Vol. XLVII (June, 1930), 115.

[15] Edmond Stoullig, *Les Annales du Théâtre et de la Musique*, XXVII, 97.

applaudissements."[16] As a result of her success in this opera, Covent Garden was eager to have her. She agreed to make her debut there the summer of 1902.[17]

Garden's next role was to be permanently associated with her name: Mélisande in Claude Debussy's *Pelléas et Mélisande*, based on the play by Maurice Maeterlinck. Carré was particularly insistent that Garden be Mélisande, although Maeterlinck wanted his "wife," Georgette Leblanc, in this role and maintained that Debussy had agreed that she should have it. The composer, however, once he heard Garden sing his music, was adamant and would not have anyone else as Mélisande. The ensuing Debussy-Maeterlinck feud scandalized Paris. To prevent the production, the playwright went to court and when that failed, he remained petulant and antagonistic. On April 14, 1902, approximately two weeks before the *première*, *Le Figaro* published a letter from him in which he emphatically and unequivocally stated that he hoped the presentation would be a failure.[18] Ultimately the work triumphed, even though the dramatist had apparently done all he could to prevent its production. In time, he forgave Carré; but it was said that he could never forgive Debussy.[19]

When Garden first heard the opera, she was ineffably moved by the subtle beauty of the music and its mood, which created within her all kinds of emotions. The cast had assembled in the apartment of André Messager, the leading conductor at the Opéra-Comique, to go over the opera with Debussy, who played the score and sang the different parts. At the beginning the artists seemed indifferent; gradually, however, its manifold beauties began to exert a singular power and charm; in time, the cast was overcome with emotion; and, at the end, Mélisande's death scene, Garden and Mme Messager left the room, both sobbing uncontrollably.[20]

Later, when Garden rehearsed the part with Debussy, he was

---

[16] *Le Figaro*, September 22, 1901.
[17] Garden and Biancolli, *Mary Garden's Story*, 47–48.
[18] Victor I. Seroff, *Debussy Musician of France*, 195.
[19] *Ibid.*, 196.
[20] Garden and Biancolli, *Mary Garden's Story*, 62.

amazed by her understanding of the character of Mélisande, the perfection of her interpretation, the suitability of her voice and personality for the role. He confessed he had " 'nothing, absolutely nothing, to tell her.' "[21] It seemed that she *was* Mélisande; in an uncanny way, he had before him the physical manifestation of the Mélisande in his dreams. Now after working on the opera from 1892–1902, Debussy had in Mary Garden the ideal interpreter. In her score, he wrote: " 'In the future others may sing Mélisande, but you alone will remain the woman and the artist I had hardly dared hope for.' "[22]

The work was rehearsed for almost four months; Debussy met with the artists for forty-one rehearsals, lavishing infinite care on the opera, so that it would be perfection itself.[23] Finally, on April 26, 1902, the dress rehearsal was held; but, to the dismay of those intimately concerned with the production, it was mocked and derided, the performance constantly being interrupted by comments and interjections. Perhaps a printed "program," which ridiculed the work and which had been sold outside the opera house, contributed to the unseemly conduct. Four days later, April 30, at the official *première* the audience was better behaved; but the opera was not received enthusiastically. Ultimately, however, the tide turned; and Debussy's *Pelléas et Mélisande* was recognized as a masterpiece.

Regardless of the merits of the opera, the beauty of Garden's Mélisande was evident from the beginning. On the day following the official *première*, Eugène d'Harcourt, in *Le Figaro*, did not praise Debussy's work, calling it a "curiosité"; but he did laud Garden for her portrayal and beautiful voice: "Mlle Mary Garden a tiré du rôle de Mélisande le meilleur parti possible. La voix est fort jolie . . . ."[24] Edmond Stoullig, in *Les Annales du Théâtre et de la Musique*, praised Garden's Mélisande for its poetic evocation and intangibility: "l'idéale Mélisande aux cheveux d'or, petite princesse de légende,

[21] *Ibid.*, 63.
[22] Henry T. Finck, "Mary Garden," *The Century Illustrated Monthly Magazine*, Vol. LXXVI (May, 1908), 150.
[23] Seroff, *Debussy Musician of France*, 192.
[24] *Le Figaro*, May 1, 1902.

amoureuse et mystique, nous donnant merveilleusement en toute sa personne la sensation de l'irréel."[25] In time, many considered this part Garden's greatest creation.

On July 3, 1902, the soprano made her debut at Covent Garden, singing the title role in Massenet's *Manon*. The music critic in the London *Times* praised her excellent stage presence, grace, marvelous play of facial expression, and voice, "flexible and admirably used."[26] It was not just one attribute of her artistry that predominated; it was the "rare combination of all . . . that made her success so complete."[27] The critic commented that he could not remember "so triumphantly successful a first appearance at Covent-garden"[28] and predicted that she would go very far in her career. On July 14 Garden created the role of Princess Osra in Herbert Bunning's *La Princesse Osra*, she and Maréchal valiantly trying to save an inconsequential opera by singing and acting "with the utmost spirit, so much so, indeed, that to them fell most of the applause at the end of the second and third acts."[29]

A year later when Garden returned to London, she appeared in *Roméo et Juliette*, *Manon*, and *Faust* but, unfortunately, did not do herself justice. As she relates in *Mary Garden's Story*, she was not in good voice for her re-entrance as Juliette (June 6, 1903) since she was suffering from laryngitis.[30] She went on with the performance, however, and acted with "such charm and sincere conviction"[31] that the vocal difficulties seem to have been forgiven her, the critic of *Pall Mall Gazette* commenting that there were "moments of real brilliance."[32] Garden herself admitted that because of her indisposition she could not take the high tones. The London *Times* said: "Her execution of florid passages, though very neat, [was] not always quite

---

[25] Vol. XXVIII, 110.

[26] July 5, 1902.

[27] *Ibid.*

[28] *Ibid.*

[29] *Ibid.*, July 15, 1902.

[30] Garden and Biancolli, 48.

[31] *The* [London] *Times*, June 10, 1903.　　　　[32] June 8, 1903.

to be depended upon; the top note of the cadenza in the valse was omitted . . . ."[33] At a later performance, as Marguerite in Gounod's *Faust*, Garden redeemed herself. She was a vision of loveliness, "slender, agile, unsophisticated, and thoughtless—it was in her thoughtlessness that her originality lay—she . . . made the part far more rational than is usual, proving, indeed, that the fall of Marguerite was surely the most natural thing in the world . . . . Her singing was sweet and pleasant, though not over-distinguished by strength . . . ."[34]

From 1903 to July, 1907, Garden was the star in many highly interesting productions at the Opéra-Comique. She impressed as Violetta in Verdi's *La Traviata*, in which she first appeared on February 12, 1903. Her versatility amazed the Parisians—the Louise, Manon, Mélisande of yesterday, and now the endearing Violetta! James Huneker saw her in this role and said that the "singing was superlative . . . . It was, however, the conception and acting that intrigued [him]. Originality stamped both. The death scene was of unusual poignancy; evidently the young American had been spying upon Bernhardt and Duse."[35] On December 23, 1903, Garden created the title role in Xavier Leroux's *La Reine Fiammette* and was "l'idéale interprète d'Orlanda, l'étoile radieuse dont l'éclatant succès a déjà rempli tout Paris."[36] She was admired for her portrayal of the title role in Saint-Saëns' *Hélène* and the boy Chérubin in Massenet's opera of the same name. As Chrysis in Camille Erlanger's *Aphrodite*, which she created March 27, 1906, Garden had another of her great triumphs. Dressed in Grecian costumes, she was a magnificent figure, classic and alluring. Gabriel Fauré said, in *Le Figaro*, that it was not possible to be more beautiful, more seductive, nor more affecting than she was in this part.[37] Carl Van Vechten commented that in the prison

---

[33] *The* [London] *Times*, June 10, 1903.
[34] [London] *Pall Mall Gazette*, July 16, 1903.
[35] James Gibbons Huneker, *Bedouins*, 13.
[36] Stoullig, *Les Annales* . . . , XXIX, 144–45.
[37] *Le Figaro*, March 28, 1906.

scene "she attained heights of tragic acting which [he did] not think . . . she [had] surpassed elsewhere."[38]

Her interpretation of the name part in Massenet's *Thaïs* was another one of her best achievements. When she sang it for the first time at Aix-les-Bains, King George I of Greece complimented her highly and foresaw a brilliant success for her in this part. Garden said that his conversation so impressed her that when she considered the role for her debut at the Manhattan Opera House, she decided that it would be as Thaïs.[39] The vogue of this opera dated from the time she and Maurice Renaud assumed the principal parts.

An Ideal Interpreter

Garden's career had been built, to a very great extent, on her successes in the modern repertory. She preferred operas that were new, for she enjoyed creating, not just following the tried and true. Furthermore, she believed in placing emphasis on the interpretation of roles, not just the singing of them. Vocal beauty might be sacrificed for dramatic truth, but her artistic credo would not have it otherwise. It is not unlikely that Garden sincerely believed that to be a true operatic artist, a singer must forget his beautiful voice and think only of what the text and music demanded. In opera such a performer is always part of the picture; he does not rush to the footlights for high C, as many singers did and still do, nor ignore the action on stage while he is not singing. Instead, Garden maintained that the real operatic artist works to become one with the character he portrays and to be an integral part of the ensemble. In this respect, Chaliapin, who also made his New York debut this season, was like Garden; for he, too, disliked operatic performances in which singers "moved majestically through the operas, uttering exquisite notes with technical perfection, but . . . lifeless and mechanical as a marionette-show."[40] Modern opera placed new demands on the artist. Voice alone would

[38] Carl Van Vechten, *Interpreters and Interpretations*, 73.

[39] Garden and Biancolli, *Mary Garden's Story*, 46.

[40] Feodor Chaliapin, *Man and Mask* (trans. by Phyllis Mégroz), 81.

not suffice. The question remained, however, whether New York would accept Garden with her new French operas. Perhaps they were too ultra-Parisian and ultra-modern. Hammerstein, nevertheless, was willing to take the risk. Once decided, he could not turn back; he had crossed his operatic Rubicon.

Before Hammerstein arrived in Paris (May, 1907), he had confirmed the terms of the contract with Garden by cable. Shortly after they met, this unusual artist and he discussed *Pelléas et Mélisande*. She urged him to see it at the Opéra-Comique before deciding whether he wished to buy the production rights for the United States. He saw it and, as she had hoped, was enthusiastic; but she made it clear that she would not sing it at the Manhattan unless other French artists with the requisite style also were in the cast.[41] Hammerstein's answer was to go out and engage three other singers who had been in the original production: Jean Périer, Hector Dufranne, and Jeanne Gerville-Réache. Then, too, he had the scenery painted in Paris by the artist who had done the original sets. New York was to see a *Pelléas et Mélisande* that was virtually the same as the Paris production.

Garden now was ready to sign the contract; and Hammerstein, in merry sport, suggested they do so in the palace at Fontainebleau. On the way, an unforeseen accident occurred when a wheel of their chauffeur-driven limousine came off. Both Garden and Hammerstein were thrown into a field of poppies; and there, instead of in the palace, they signed the contract.[42] From the beginning it would seem the two got along famously.

[41] Garden and Biancolli, *Mary Garden's Story*, 100–101.
[42] *Ibid.*, 101–102.

X

New Operatic Horizons

—◦•◦⊰❦⊱◦•◦—

AFTER RETURNING to New York in July, 1907, Hammerstein
made repeated visits to Philadelphia, looking for an opera house site.
His purpose was to enlarge his scope of operation, to extend his sphere
of influence. It was all part of the challenge to the Metropolitan, of
the dream of a chain of opera houses throughout the United States;
and the initial object in the scheme of aggrandizement was to be Philadelphia, where for years the Metropolitan had given performances
during the season (usually one a week) at the Academy of Music,
with a guarantee of $7,000 each. Hammerstein had several reasons
for considering the Quaker City as the first step in this master plan.
Traditionally the metropolis had a fondness for and an interest in
grand opera; its proximity to New York made a concurrent season
with the Manhattan feasible; and he had been told that some wealthy
Philadelphians would assist materially in a grand opera enterprise.

In 1898 a number of leading citizens, dissatisfied with conditions
at the Academy of Music, decided to join together "to promote the
building of an opera house that should conform to modern condi-
tions...."[1] Among these were George H. Frazier, W. W. Frazier,
Alfred C. Harrison, C. Hartman Kuhn, Andrew Wheeler, Jr.,
Thomas De Witt Cuyler, J. Dundes Lippincot, Craige Lippincot,
E. T. Stotesbury, Alexander Van Rensselaer, George W. C. Drexel,
P. A. B. Widener, George D. Widener, Bradley H. Warburton,

[1] G. Heide Norris, "New Opera House Makes This a Socially United
City and Center of Art," *The* [Philadelphia] *North American Grand
Opera Edition,* November 17, 1908, p. 1.

Edward Morrell. Although the venerable Academy of Music, which opened in 1857, had been the home of fashionable opera for many years, these men were of the opinion that it no longer sufficed, the dissatisfaction being due to the inadequate seating accommodations, the antiquated auditorium, and the obsolete stage. Or was it the limited number of boxes? The opera house project, however, never really got under way, as the Spanish-American War intervened. Afterwards, although there were occasional discussions concerning the plan, nothing definite transpired.

One of the leading citizens Hammerstein knew in the city was Thomas B. Wanamaker, who had been a member of the original group seeking to better opera conditions and who introduced him to G. Heide Norris, a Philadelphia attorney and an opera enthusiast. At their first interview, sometime in the summer of 1907, Hammerstein proposed to Norris that "if Philadelphians should build an opera house and turn it over to him he would give the opera and turn over to the builders whatever net profits might ensue."[2] Norris' opinion was that such a plan would not be acceptable to the members of the committee. Undismayed, Hammerstein held tenaciously to the idea of constructing an opera house and devoted a great deal of time looking about for an appropriate site. It is not unlikely that he decided to take the initiative himself, thereby hoping to build up a feeling of confidence in the Philadelphians and thus to persuade them to enlist in the venture. At the moment, the paramount problem was the excessive price of choice locations.

Meanwhile, there had been persistent rumors concerning the enterprise. Hammerstein finally confirmed them on August 13, 1907, when he announced that he would construct an opera house " 'worthy of the name and of this great city,' "[3] that he hoped to have it ready by the fall of 1908, and that then Philadelphia would be not an

[2] "How Impresario Was Led to Build Opera House Here," *The* [Philadelphia] *North American Grand Opera Edition,* November 17, 1908, p. 8.

[3] News item in *The* [Philadelphia] *Evening Telegraph,* August 13, 1907.

operatic follower but an operatic leader. Hammerstein also declared that " 'the only solution of the problem, the only way possible for Philadelphia to have adequate opera, opera of the best, [was] to have its own company, and that [he purposed] to give it.' "[4]

When Philadelphians heard, on September 7, that Hammerstein had paid $150,000 for the old Harrah property on Broad and Poplar Streets as his choice of the site, they were incredulous; for, as far as society was concerned, the location was unsuitable. To them, it seemed as far distant as Pittsburgh. According to John Curtis, local historian, much of this attitude emanated from a joke "which had its basis in a snobbish remark once made by a Society dame that 'there was no Society north of Market Street.' The region to many was really a sort of howling wilderness . . . ."[5] Social wiseacres said that the Main Line would never go to such a place; and when people told Hammerstein of this prejudice, he thought it all nonsense, his attitude being, as in New York, that opera patrons will go anywhere if they can hear great music.

Hammerstein took title to the property on the first of October. Also, on that day, he issued a public statement in which, among many remarks, he denied rumors to the effect that he had backers and that his building an opera house on the north side was part of a real estate scheme which would affect the value of property in that area. Of greater importance, he made it clear that he would not go ahead with the construction unless he had the positive assurance that he would have the support of people of wealth. He wanted "the best elements of Philadelphia, those that [appreciated his] efforts and [were] willing to assist in the elevation of all classes in the name of grand opera, to come forward and subscribe to the boxes of the house to be erected for the period of two years."[6] The appeal was to their standard of

[4] John Curtis, "One Hundred Years of Grand Opera in Philadelphia" (unpublished MS, The Historical Society of Pennsylvania), III, Sec. 2, pp. 473–74.

[5] Ibid., 509.

[6] News item in The [Philadelphia] North American, October 2, 1907.

noblesse oblige. He stipulated that he must have the assurance by November 1 and that there be subscribers for the thirty boxes for two years, each at $5,000 a year. In other words, what he required was a guarantee of $300,000. The payment of the $5,000 for the first season was to be made after the edifice was completed.

Although it would seem that Hammerstein's proposal was equitable enough and that he was offering the city a magnificent opportunity, Philadelphia, on the whole, did not respond, whereupon it was again announced that unless there were the required thirty box subscriptions, Hammerstein would abandon the enterprise and sell the Harrah property. Meanwhile, Norris and his associates, who had rallied around the impresario, made every effort to enlist the support of society leaders; but too often they were met by apathy, the principal reason being that there had been a slight recession and people feared a financial depression. Perhaps the real explanation was that Philadelphians already had enough opera at the Academy of Music and were content with the Metropolitan presentations. Nevertheless, on October 22, Norris, as chairman, and eight other prominent Philadelphians sent out letters to 400 leading citizens, outlining Hammerstein's plans, stating the necessity of the subscriptions for the thirty boxes, and expressing the hope that the " 'cultured and wealthy people . . . [would], for the love of music and for the commercial and educational welfare of the city, subscribe in order to secure this opera house . . . .' "[7] Unfortunately the response was not heartening. By the first of November, the date of Hammerstein's deadline, there were but sixteen box subscriptions. The impresario stated, however, that if the committee obtained four more, he would build the opera house, even though it was not the number he had first proposed. He advanced the deadline to November 15. Though the members of the committee worked feverishly, they were unsuccessful in obtaining the required number but, for a time, cherished the belief that Hammerstein would build anyway.

After a long, ominous silence it was announced on December 18, 1907, that the impresario had abandoned the grand opera enterprise

[7] News item in the Philadelphia *Public Ledger*, October 23, 1907.

in Philadelphia and that the property was to be sold.[8] At this time he was in the midst of the seventh week of his second season at the Manhattan Opera House, a season which even then was in peril; it seemed destined to be a financial disaster.

[8] News item in *The* [Philadelphia] *Evening Telegraph,* December 18, 1907.

XI

The Second Season Begins

H AMMERSTEIN made a number of important announcements
prior to the opening of the second season of the Manhattan Opera
House. In the prospectus for 1907–1908, he proposed to produce
eight musical dramas never heard before in the United States, to
bring forward ten productions new to the opera house repertory, and
to revive fourteen operas from the first season. He had enlarged the
orchestra to eighty-two " 'local musicians and . . . players from Berlin,
Paris, Vienna and St. Petersburg' "[1] and the chorus to eighty men
(fifty of these were from Europe) and sixty women, all from the
United States. He had engaged a new ballet and a *première danseuse*,
Anita Malinverni, as well as a new stage director, Jacques Coini, who
had gained an enviable reputation during his years of experience in
various European opera houses. William J. Guard was the new press
representative of the company. Of the greatest importance, his roster
of principal singers included such stars as Melba, Nordica, Calvé,
Garden, Bressler-Gianoli, Schumann-Heink, Gerville- Réache, Zenatello, Dalmorès, Périer, Renaud, Sammarco, Ancona, Gilibert, Arimondi. After the unprecedented success of the inaugural season,
Hammerstein intended that the forthcoming series of performances
should be epochal.

He also made known that the Manhattan had undergone some
renovations. An entrance had been made on 35th Street to accom-

[1] "The Manhattan Opera House Opens Its Season of 1907–'08,"
The New York Herald Society and Drama Section, November 3, 1907,
p. 12.

modate the regular subscribers and to relieve the congestion on the 34th Street side of the house. A newly decorated hallway, which was at a side of the stage, now led to the proscenium and Grand Tier boxes. There was also additional space in the main lobby made possible by placing the stairways to the balcony, which had been on either side of the foyer, inside the auditorium to the right and left of the entrance. Great brick walls, sixty feet high, had been constructed in the adjoining alleys to eliminate the draughts, which had been a cause for complaints the opening season. Seats in the second balcony had been changed, so that there was more space between chairs. Two thousand lights had been added to the stage lighting, and a costume department had been installed in the opera house. Hammerstein said that he had spent $40,000 on these improvements.[2]

The subscription list was six times larger than at the beginning of the opening season; in early November, 1907, Hammerstein maintained that it was approximately $300,000.[3] The eight box subscribers of the initial season had increased to twenty-eight,[4] some of whose names the impresario did not hesitate to divulge, although he never listed them in the Manhattan programmes. Among the box holders were Clarence Mackay, E. H. Titus, Edwin H. Weatherbee, Issac Guggenheim, F. Lancaster, Robert Graves, Frank Woolworth, Commodore Frederick F. G. Bourne, Mrs. Samuel Untermyer, Senator William H. Reynolds, Mrs. Rutherford Stuyvesant, James Gayley, Daniel G. Reid, Frank Tilford, William T. Bull, Judge E. H. Gary, William E. Corey, William E. Reis, H. G. Campbell, W. B. Dickson.[5]

The Opening and First Weeks

The second season began on November 4, 1907, with Ponchielli's *La Gioconda*. Reminiscent of the opening almost a year before, carriages arrived early, and all available standing room was quickly and

[2] *Ibid.*
[3] *Ibid.*
[4] *Ibid.*
[5] *Ibid.*

completely sold out. So many standees had been admitted, in fact, that it was difficult to promenade during the three intermissions. In general, however, there was less confusion in the auditorium than at the first opening night. Some thought the improvement was due to the innovation of employing only women ushers, efficient and chic in their black-and-white uniforms. Although a very great number of social celebrities were present, the cynosure of most eyes was Mrs. Clarence Mackay's guest—Consuelo, Duchess of Marlborough. It was noted that Her Grace, the former Consuelo Vanderbilt, had arrived in the middle of the first act and that later she was joined by her brother William K. Vanderbilt, Jr. Another much observed and admired box occupant was Mary Garden, who was accompanied by her father and sister. There were also the Paul Cravaths, Mrs. Rutherford Stuyvesant, the Joseph Pulitzers, the Edwin H. Weatherbees, Mrs. James Griswold, Frank Woolworth, Mrs. James B. Eustis, the Courtlandt Schuyler Van Rensselaers. It was, all in all, a far more fashionable and cosmopolitan first-night audience than the one of the first season.

Still, most of the vast assembly had come to listen to music, not to acclaim society, "and if further proof of that fact had been needed the promptness with which every untimely outburst of applause was suppressed by 'hushes' would have supplied it."[6] For this reason, society's increased interest was looked upon with trepidation in some quarters. The following day *The Evening Post* said: "The social element was much more prominent than last year, and it is to be hoped it will not become too prominent, as it might tempt the manager from the path of artistic rectitude. So far he has worked for art, and for art alone, regardless of expense, and for this reason and because of his daring and pluck, he deserves complete success."[7] The hope was that the Manhattan might not become like the Metropolitan, an institution for the classes, not for the masses.

As for the opera itself, the *Times* thought that "it had been prepared in such a way that the several elements—solo singers, orchestra,

[6] News item in *The New York Press,* November 5, 1907.
[7] News item in *The* [New York]*Evening Post,* November 5, 1907.

chorus, ballet—cooperated with admirable effect."[8] Nordica, an old favorite, was welcomed, though, unfortunately, she was not in her best form. However, "her dramatic intelligence and her experience in her art were with her and assisted her in keeping her impersonation upon a good level."[9] Zenatello, making his debut, was a sensation with his superb, powerful tenor voice, singing with "brilliant, pealing and thoroughly musical"[10] upper tones and commanding a style "the finish of which [would] win for him admirers among the friends of Bonci as well as the friends of Caruso."[11] Other principals (De Cisneros as Laura, Gerville-Réache as La Cieca, and Ancona as Barnaba) sang beautifully, though Didur (Alvise), also making his debut on this occasion, was "somewhat disappointing, his voice being unsteady to a noticable [sic] degree."[12] The orchestra was much improved; Campanini, as always, conducted with precision, bite, fervor, and dramatic contrast. Reginald de Koven commented that the chorus sang "remarkably well, with good body of tone, and unusually good intonation; indeed, a better chorus has not been heard on the New York operatic stage."[13] The ballet was excellent as was Malinverni, the leading ballerina. The settings elicited praise except for a perverse moon that "fairly serpentined across a truly beautiful sky."[14] The opening was, in short, an artistic representation, an auspicious beginning.

The second performance, a matinee the following day, November 5, was a revival of the first season's greatest success, *Carmen*, with Bressler-Gianoli as the earthy cigarette girl. Some critics considered the opera better than the year before, a circumstance no doubt attributable to the improved orchestra, since the cast was very much the same. Dalmorès, once again the Don José, was warmly praised for

[8] *The New York Times*, November 5, 1907.
[9] *The* [New York] *Sun*, November 5, 1907.
[10] *Ibid.*
[11] *New-York Daily Tribune*, November 5, 1907.
[12] *The New York Herald*, November 5, 1907.
[13] *The* [New York] *World*, November 5, 1907.
[14] *The New York Press*, November 5, 1907.

"a well nigh faultless impersonation, both vocally and dramatically"[15]; Zeppilli, the Micaëla, pleased; Crabbé (Escamillo) drew mixed reviews, most critics considering him a conventional singer. The opera was repeated at the Saturday matinee, November 9.

On November 6, Hammerstein introduced Berlioz's *La Damnation de Faust*, which was not a novelty to New York, as it had been performed at the Metropolitan the previous season without much marked success, even though the cast had included Farrar, Rousselière, and Plançon. It had not seemed dramatic enough for opera presentation; of course, Berlioz had never intended the composition to be a music drama. Several reasons were advanced for Hammerstein's production: he had the scenery and stage mechanism prepared for the 1906–1907 season; and, more important, he had Renaud, whose magnificent portrayal of Méphistophélès was one of the finest operatic impersonations ever seen in New York.[16] Krehbiel wrote glowingly of it: "With due respect to M. Plançon . . . Mephistopheles [*sic*] never had adequate presentation here until last night. M. Renaud's appearance was as startling as the orchestral explosion to which he entered. A new conception of a figure which had long been thought to have become hopelessly conventionalized—a lean, cadaverous, hollow-eyed, long-taloned devil; a spirit that seemed to have all but consumed its fleshly tenement . . . a mournful, contemplative devil, wistful only for his victim."[17] Jeanne Jomelli, the Marguerite, who was also a former member of the Metropolitan, was an adequate performer whose singing, however, lacked color. As Faust, Dalmorès outdid himself. The presiding genius was the indefatigable Campanini, whose reading of the score was a joy to all. In general, the critics preferred Hammerstein's production of this opera to Conried's, one pundit remarking that "the entire musical element [was] infused with a finer intelligence that that to which [New York had been] accustomed by last year's representations."[18]

[15] *The* [New York] *World,* November 6, 1907.
[16] *The* [New York] *Evening Post,* November 7, 1907.
[17] *New-York Daily Tribune,* November 7, 1907.
[18] *Ibid.*

At the Saturday evening performance of *Il Trovatore*, on November 9, Carlo Albani made his debut as Manrico, with Jomelli (Leonora), De Cisneros (Azucena), and Fossetta (Di Luna). The tenor's voice was extremely disappointing, not being free and having a "liberal vibrato."[19] He sang in the same opera only one other time. On December 18 it was announced that he was not well and would not appear again at the Manhattan. Meantime, the performance of *Ernani* had been postponed, as he was to have sung the title role. When the opera was produced on December 11, Bassi replaced him. On December 20, *The New York Times* reported that Albani was appearing with the San Carlo Opera Company in Boston,[20] whereupon Hammerstein then sued the singer for breach of contract. The sheriff's officer made the arrest during a performance of *Il Trovatore*, a presentation which he permitted to continue provided that he might follow the tenor about on the stage. Incensed, the audience hissed the constable every time he appeared behind the footlights. It must have been quite an evening seeing Manrico, in his costumes of the fifteenth century, pour his heart out in song while at his elbow constantly hovered the officer, in Edwardian apparel, fearful that the artist might escape.[21]

The second week consisted of repetitions of *Carmen* on Wednesday and Saturday evenings and *La Gioconda* on the Saturday matinee, with *Aïda* on Monday and the *première* of *Les Contes d'Hoffmann* on Friday, November 15. In *Aïda* were Nordica, Zenatello, De Cisneros, Ancona, Arimondi, under the baton of Campanini. On paper the cast looked ideal. Unfortunately, however, the once superb Nordica showed a sad deterioration as the Egyptian slave, dramatically and vocally failing to sustain a high level. Some feared that she would not get through the performance. Also, she did not wear the proper make-up or costumes for the part, the *Press* protesting that she had "the pink and white complexion of an Anglo-Saxon instead of the tawny skin of an African, and [wore] costumes inappropriate

[19] *The* [New York] *Sun,* November 10, 1907.
[20] News item in *The New York Times,* December 20, 1907.
[21] *Ibid.,* December 27, 1907.

and unbecoming to a degree that [was] laughable."[22] Zenatello impressed by the power, richness, and dramatic qualities of his voice. Superb in the ensemble, he was at his best in declamation and full-throated singing but somewhat lacking in softer passages. De Cisneros, too, aroused enthusiasm by the power and richness of her voice and commanding stage presence. Ancona, as always, was lauded for his beautiful singing.

The high light of the second week and the opera that was the first great success of the season was Offenbach's *Les Contes d'Hoffmann*, which had been last produced in New York on October 16, 1882, and was, therefore, a revival and a novelty.[23] Since the work had been all but forgotten, its impact was sensational, the beautiful score, interesting libretto, and production arousing much comment. It was said that Maurice Grau had wanted to present it at the Metropolitan but felt that the vastness of the auditorium was not suitable for this *opéra fantastique*. Of the singers in Hammerstein's presentation, Renaud was the one who impressed by his amazing versatility and consummate artistry, performing all three baritone roles of Coppelius, Dapertutto, and Dr. Miracle. Each part he essayed was "perfect down to its smallest detail,"[24] and his singing had "uncommon finesse."[25] Dalmorès reaped his full share of praise, especially since he had undertaken the role of Hoffmann on very short notice, replacing Leon Cazauran, who was indisposed. Zeppilli (Olympia), Jomelli (Giulietta), and Francisca (Antonia) were the women Hoffmann adored. Of the three, the critics preferred Zeppilli, who was "the living image of a large doll, as expressionless, as automatic in movement, and her singing had all the passion and dexterity of a music-box—all being just as it should be."[26] Gilibert (Spalanzani and Crespel) and Crabbé (Lindorf and Schlemil) contributed much to the success of this spirited and attractive production. Fortunately for Hammerstein, this opera was a money-maker, good for endless repeti-

[22] *The New York Press*, November 12, 1907.

[23] *New-York Daily Tribune*, November 16, 1907.

[24] *The* [New York] *Sun*, November 16, 1907.

[25] *Ibid.*   [26] *The New York Times*, November 16, 1907.

tions. Hammerstein, in the words of the *Herald*, had "dived into the operatic oyster bed and [had] come to the surface with a tuneful pearl."[27] As Sheean remarks in the impresario's biography, it had been available to any producer for many years; but Hammerstein had had the perspicacity to include it in his repertory.[28] He must have been grateful to his daughter Stella, who had introduced it to him at a performance in London the previous spring.[29]

In the third week, Hammerstein presented *Les Contes d'Hoffmann* on Monday and Friday with the same cast as at the *première* except that Trentini replaced Francisca as Antonia. The opera for Saturday evening was another *Trovatore*. Nordica appeared twice as Aïda on Wednesday and at the Saturday matinee, on November 23. This latter performance was her last one at the Manhattan. By then, she had sung six times: three Giocondas and three Aïdas.

According to Sheean, the impresario was convinced at this time that Nordica was a liability, since she was not singing well and was no longer a box-office attraction.[30] Sometime later Hammerstein confessed that he was losing money at an alarming rate during these weeks.[31] If he were to fulfill the terms of Nordica's contract (30 performances at $1,750 each), he stood to lose a great deal more. To put the situation bluntly, she was an expensive commodity, one he could well do without. Another factor in his thinking was that since he was no longer interested in producing German opera, for which he had engaged Nordica in the first place, there seemed little reason to retain her. At any rate, Hammerstein was determined to get rid of the prima donna and began a "systematic campaign to induce her to break her contract."[32]

[27] *The New York Herald*, November 16, 1907.

[28] Sheean, *Oscar Hammerstein I*, 219.

[29] "Lure of the Footlights as Felt by a Manager's Daughter," *The New York Times Magazine Section*, May 31, 1908, p. 6.

[30] *Oscar Hammerstein I*, 216–17.

[31] "New York's $2,000,000 Season of Grand Opera," *The New York Times Magazine Section*, March 29, 1908, p. 4.

[32] Sheean, *Oscar Hammerstein I*, 217.

Knowing that she disliked tobacco fumes and that she had requested no smoking back stage, even before the season began, Hammerstein made it a point to puff on cigars in her presence and on stage during intermissions. And, to be sure, he was never without one while sitting in the wings. Campanini and others also seem to have been participants in the plot. The climax came at that final matinee of *Aïda*, when Hammerstein devised a total attack with Campanini, Coini, and "an army of stage carpenters, [creating] an atmosphere so thick, so noxious to [Nordica], that she very nearly failed to get through the opera. The last *entr'acte* was extended to a smoky half hour, and an apology had to be made to the audience."[33] Afterwards Nordica walked out, retiring to her estate at Ardsley-on-Hudson. Hammerstein then conceived of a plan to present her in a series of performances at cheaper prices and on non-subscription nights. He did not hesitate to tell why he was doing so. In a letter to Nordica, dated November 29, 1907, Hammerstein wrote:

"I want to inform you that I am preparing a series of operas containing your repertoire for every Tuesday and Thursday at popular prices, in which I want you to sing. The receipts derived from your appearances in the higher priced performances are so small that I am compelled to take this step."[34]

On December 15 it was officially announced that the soprano had left the company. Sheean suggests that Hammerstein may have made her some compensation for the remaining performances in her contract.[35] No financial arrangement, however, would be adequate for the indignities which Nordica had suffered. The whole episode was unfortunate and inexcusable on the part of the impresario. Surely there was a way to come to some kind of amicable understanding and thus to avoid such unpleasantness. Her biographer, Ira Glackens, maintained, however, that Nordica did not dwell on this cir-

---

[33] Herman Klein, *Great Women-Singers of My Time*, 126–27.
[34] News item in *The New York Times*, December 15, 1907.
[35] *Oscar Hammerstein I*, 217.

cumstance but immediately occupied herself with operatic and concert engagements.[36]

Thaïs Incarnate

The Monday performance of November 25, 1907, was one that made operatic history in the United States; for on that evening not only did Hammerstein present the American *première* of Massenet's *Thaïs*, but he also introduced a very great and controversial singer, a prima donna destined to become a household word: Mary Garden. Actually the first performance had been scheduled for November 22. On that day, however, Garden, ill with the grippe, informed Hammerstein that it was impossible for her to sing. She went to the piano and tried to produce some tones for the stunned and disappointed impresario, but it was obvious that she could not possibly appear. Hammerstein realized that there was nothing that could be done until Garden recovered and that he would have to arrange for another production as quickly as possible. He decided to present again *Les Contes d'Hoffmann* and offered to refund money to anyone who held tickets for *Thaïs* and who did not care to attend the Offenbach work. When patrons came to the Manhattan that evening, expecting to see Garden in the new opera, they were told of the change in program. Most of them accepted it philosophically and did not request their money back. Three evenings later Garden made her debut with the company, even though she had not yet completely recovered from her malady.

In the reviews for the *première* of *Thaïs*, on November 25, 1907, critics did not especially like the opera itself, considering it uninspired, although they did concede that there were some fine moments and that it was theatrically effective. The *Herald* thought it "for the most part colorless and saccharine."[37] Henderson, in the *Sun*, referred to the opera as a "highly finished piece of stagecraft by a skilled workman equipped with a good technic and a special feeling for

[36] *Yankee Diva*, 235.
[37] *The New York Herald*, November 26, 1907.

theatrical expression."[38] De Koven liked it better than the other Massenet operas which had been produced in New York City (*Manon, Werther, La Navarraise*), finding in the work "a deeper sentiment, a greater sincerity, a more inward feeling of humanity, a greater organic unity, and, more than this, a broader and more recognizable personal expression of thought . . . ."[39]

As for the principal singers, Renaud and Dalmorès were superb in their parts. Krehbiel's opinion was that Renaud's impersonation of Athanaël was the "notable artistic achievement of the evening,"[40] while Henderson thought it "consistent, convincing and pathetic."[41] In every way, he triumphantly depicted the fall of a holy man beset by tormenting conflicts deep within. *The Evening Post* critic said: "In the early scenes he was every inch the saint—stern, impulsive for his cause, fanatical in pursuance of his purpose. Every movement of those marvellously beautiful and soulful eyes was eloquent of spirituality. Even more impressive was the conflict of emotions in the scenes with Thaïs. One needed no book nor spoken words to realize the gradual change of the saint to the sinner in thought, the triumph of the man over the monk."[42] Dalmorès performed yeoman service; for, once again, he replaced Cazauran. As was his wont, he sang with great beauty of tone and brought the dignity of his splendid physique to the role of Nicias.

As for Mary Garden, critics considered her, above all, an extraordinary personality. There was no question that from the moment she came on stage, bursting upon the audience in an unforgettable entrance, Garden seemed Thaïs incarnate with her beautiful arms and neck, golden hair, jeweled diadem. As she scattered roses, she was every inch a magnetic, fascinating figure. Head held high, she looked irresistible, arresting, seductive. The *Press* described it this

[38] *The* [New York] *Sun*, November 26, 1907.
[39] *The* [New York] *World*, November 26, 1907.
[40] *New-York Daily Tribune*, November 26, 1907.
[41] *The* [New York] *Sun*, November 26, 1907.
[42] *The* [New York] *Evening Post*, November 26, 1907.

way: "Every motion of her sinuous body was visible through the thin, rose-colored drapery, which clung to limbs and torso with studied persistency. When she took breath the action of her diaphragm swayed her yielding form in wave-like undulations. At moments it seemed as if this creature of supple frame, slender as a sapling, pliant as a willow, wore only the garb of Eve as she moved along the boards with the stride of a tigress and the tortuousness of a serpent."[43] Critics also agreed that she was a consummate actress, impressing all by her ability to portray successfully the varying emotions of a self-willed pagan, as well as those of a renunciatory Christian. Her conception of the character was perfect even to the most minute details. The reviewer in the *Times* commented that as a forceful dramatic artist, "she [created] the deepest impression. She [had] . . . a swift litheness and graceful activity upon the stage, an incessant play of plastic pose, a rich suggestiveness of facial expression. [He considered her] an actress of the true vein, and her denotement of the changing phases of emotion through which she [passed were] clear, incisive, and subtle. There [was] an unceasing intensity and poignancy in her dramatic style."[44]

Although the critics found her physically alluring and dramatically arresting, they disagreed on her voice, not an unalloyed joy. On the whole, they did not praise her, nor did they tear her to pieces as legend has it. Garden, in *Mary Garden's Story*, said that the critics "pulled [her] to pieces . . . ."[45] Yet several days after her debut she commented that they had been "lovely"[46] to her personally, though she regretted that they had not liked nor understood the opera itself. Was this a sop to Cerberus? Unfortunately, however, for a good part of the performance, her voice had not been free. Interviewed after the second act, Garden was quoted as saying: " 'I am still suffering from the cold I caught at rehearsal last week, but after the first act I

[43] *The New York Press*, November 26, 1907.
[44] *The New York Times*, November 26, 1907.
[45] Garden and Biancolli, 109.
[46] "Miss Mary Garden Talks about Her American Operatic Debut," *The New York Herald Society and Drama Section*, December 1, 1907, p. 12.

felt my voice warming up. My nervousness left me and I felt as though, instead of making my debut in America, I had been singing here for several seasons.' "[47]

Henderson, in the *Sun*, Krehbiel, in the *Tribune*, Aldrich, in the *Times*, did not find her voice fresh or sensuous; they heard an acidulous quality as well as strident tones in the upper notes. They thought that she had "little in her song to entitle her to high rank upon the operatic stage."[48] The critics of the *Herald* and *Evening Post* were somewhat moderate and said that her singing improved after the first act, while there were those who lauded her for the entire performance, especially commenting upon her dramatic quality, passionate intensity of utterance, and emotional realism. De Koven, who praised her highly, said that she sang with "style, finish, artistic perception and conviction."[49] Charles Henry Meltzer, of the *New York American*, thought her voice "pure and curiously penetrating, but of exquisite quality. It [went] straight to the heart, as well as to the ear, of the listener . . . ."[50] The critic of the *Press* remarked that there was "a penetrating poignancy in this voice which [carried] home even when it [ruffled] the ear. Behind the voice, behind the musical impulse, there [was] an intensity of feeling, a temperamental verve and fiery energy exceedingly disturbing to the emotions. There [was] little beauty in this voice; but it [had] a pungent flavor not to be avoided."[51]

Admired for her personality, artistry, and histrionic ability, Garden was, it is true, less captivating in song. The soprano herself realized this. In an interview held several days after her debut,[52] she said: " 'I know full well that I have not a great voice, and I do not make any claim to such heights. I am not a Melba or a Calvé and do not

[47] *The New York Herald,* November 26, 1907.
[48] *New-York Daily Tribune,* November 26, 1907.
[49] *The* [New York] *World,* November 26, 1907.
[50] *New York American,* November 26, 1907.
[51] *The New York Press,* November 26, 1907.
[52] "Miss Mary Garden Talks about Her American Operatic Debut," *The New York Herald Society and Drama Section,* December 1, 1907, p. 12.

expect to be compared with such singers.' " What she hoped for was that critics would accept her for her over-all interpretations, not just for her voice: " 'It is by an art quite different from that of other opera singers that I have found my way, and I want to be judged not alone by my singing or my acting or my stage appearance, but by these combined into one art that is entirely different from all the rest.' "[53]

Perhaps if Garden had had a Melba-like voice, she might never have developed into the truly great dramatic artist and singer she was. After all, there is much to be said for those able to make the workmanship surpass the material. What is significant, however, is that Garden was one of the few singers of her era who impressed by an over-all ability, not merely by perfect tones. Van Vechten, perhaps, came closest to the truth of the impact of Mary Garden on New York opera-goers:

> The fact of the matter is that when Mary Garden . . . came to New York only a few of us were ready to receive her at anywhere near her true worth. In a field where mediocrity and brainlessness, lack of theatrical instinct and vocal insipidity are fairly the rule her dominant personality, her unerring search for novelty of expression, the very completeness of her dramatic and vocal pictures, annoyed the philistines, the professors, and the academicians. They had been accustomed to taking their opera quietly with their after-dinner coffee and, on the whole, they preferred it that way . . . . But what was not so evident at first was the absolute fitness of this voice and her method of using it for the dramatic style of the artist and for the artistic demands of the works in which she appeared. Thoroughly musical . . . Garden . . . often puzzled her critical hearers by singing *Faust* in one vocal style and *Thaïs* in another.[54]

The second *Thaïs* (November 30) was very lightly attended; in

[53] *Ibid.*

[54] Carl Van Vechten, *The Merry-Go-Round*, 116–17.

fact, Hammerstein told Garden that there was not " 'enough money in the house to pay the light bill.' "[55] Then, inexplicably, the third and fourth performances attracted larger houses. French opera seemed to be triumphing as it steadily gained public support, and there was anticipation for the next novelty—Charpentier's *Louise.* Hammerstein had intended to present this work on December 20, but when Garden had an attack of bronchitis and influenza, he had to cancel the performance until the twenty-seventh. Once more, however, he had to postpone the *première,* as the prima donna had not yet recovered. It was not until early in the new year that New York heard *Louise* for the first time and with a cast that probably could not have been duplicated anywhere else in the world.

REVIVALS

Meanwhile, Garden did not appear with the company from December 13 until January 3. What this meant was that Hammerstein had to rely on the staples from the repertory of the first season and on repetitions of the ever-popular *Les Contes d'Hoffmann.* He had revived *Faust,* sung in Italian, on November 28, with Zenatello (Faust), Zeppilli (Marguerite), Didur (Méphistophélès), Crabbé (Valentin), Giaconia (Siébel), Campanini conducting. Zenatello's voice was not ideally suited for Faust, although in moments of dramatic outbursts, he was capable of passages of "almost super-Carusoan vocal beauty."[56] Zeppilli was somewhat out of her element, and was unable to use her voice to its greatest effect. Didur, singing better than in *La Gioconda,* revealed hitherto unsuspected beauties in his sonorous and expressive bass. At a later performance of *Faust,* on December 21, Adelina Agostinelli made her debut with the company and proved herself to be a serviceable soprano. On December 9 *La Navarraise* and *I Pagliacci* were heard for the first time this season. In the Massenet opera, Gerville-Réache assumed Calvé's role, and, even though unable to efface the memory of the French soprano in this part, she was superb in her portrayal of the unhappy Anita, per-

[55] Sheean, *Oscar Hammerstein I,* 222.
[56] *The* [New York] *Evening Post,* November 29, 1907.

forming with "realism and unusual dramatic power."[57] Sammarco made his seasonal re-entry in the Leoncavallo opera, winning, as usual, plaudits for his magnificent singing; Bassi (Canio) poured forth ringing high notes, influencing De Koven to declare that he had not heard more wonderful declamations since De Lucia sang the role;[58] and Zeppilli was an effective Nedda. On December 11 Hammerstein presented Bassi, Ancona, and Russ in *Ernani*, which was not at all well received and only had this one performance. Revivals of *Rigoletto*, on December 20, with Sammarco, Bassi, and Zeppilli and *Un Ballo in Maschera*, on December 27, with Zenatello, Sammarco, Russ, De Cisneros, and Zeppilli were the operas substituted for the two postponed dates of the *Louise première*.

On December 28 Hammerstein added another opera to the repertory: *Don Giovanni*, a production that almost did not get on the boards. On the afternoon of the twenty-seventh, members of the orchestra refused to rehearse any longer, tired from the many extra hours devoted to preparations for the revivals. Campanini was furious, threatening to walk out of the house, never to conduct again at the Manhattan. Only after Hammerstein had placated him and the orchestra were rehearsals resumed. The presentation of *Don Giovanni*, on the following evening, was commendable. Renaud, as always, was wonderful in his unique characterization; Russ (Donna Anna), Jomelli (Donna Elvira), and Zeppilli (Zerlina) were merely acceptable; Gilibert (Masetto) was the "very embodiment of the word bumpkin";[59] Didur (Leporello) at last justified "the distinctly enviable reputation which he [enjoyed] in Europe";[60] Cazauran (Don Ottavio) was the weakest member of the cast, singing in a manner that inspired one savant to suggest he "experiment with other callings."[61]

[57] *Ibid.*, December 10, 1907.
[58] *The* [New York] *World*, December 10, 1907.
[59] *The* [New York] *Evening Post*, December 30, 1907.
[60] *New York American*, December 29, 1907.
[61] *The* [New York] *Sun*, December 29, 1907.

MANAGERIAL IRE

That nerves were frayed was evident from the rebellion of the orchestra and Campanini's threat to leave the company. Hammerstein himself began to show signs of the tremendous strain he was under. Poor attendance at the performances, patrons' complaints regarding the repetitions of operas, necessitated by Garden's illness and the small repertory, and the various pressures from within the house no doubt prompted him to write a circular letter to the Manhattan subscribers on December 22. In what virtually was a pronunciamento, Hammerstein referred to the repetitions of operas, which he maintained were necessary if the public ever was to be receptive to the new. He reminded his subscribers that he was alone in his enterprise, competing against the Metropolitan, which enjoyed the patronage of the rich, and a very large subscription. He said that, even though expenses at the Manhattan were very high, he intended to go on presenting opera and great singers without economizing. He hoped that New York would never again be in the position of having but one opera house, which he noted was now in a " 'less jocular position . . . .' "[62] Such a monopoly would " 'result in retrogression of the art and bring the opera lovers into a position of servility to those who remain willing to distribute musical alms . . . .' "[63] Still, if more support from the public were not forthcoming, he maintained that he would have to curtail the season or take the company to other cities; and though he did not want to be " 'patronized' " or " 'helped along,' " he felt that he was " 'entitled and [had] a right to demand as great a support as [was] accorded to any other institution.' "[64]

Hammerstein may have written this letter in a moment of pique, for he knew better than to expect gratitude from the public, invariably fickle and ungrateful, which goes where it can get what it wants in entertainment. Henderson, in the *Sun*, remarked: "No one can scold, coax, cajole reason or lecture it into liking, disliking or giving even passing attention to anything. Critics may preach, press agents

[62] Letter in *The New York Times*, December 23, 1907, p. 1.
[63] *Ibid.*
[64] *Ibid.*

rhapsodize and managers scold; but the opera public pays no attention to any of them."[65] Charles Henry Meltzer seconded Henderson's sentiments: "Despite [Hammerstein's] enterprise—despite, if you will, the altruism which he assures us has prompted him throughout his efforts to produce opera—we cannot admit that we *owe* him the financial recognition which he *demands* of us."[66] Conried, very contented with his large subscription at the Metropolitan, adopted a superior attitude and, indirectly referring to Hammerstein's letter and his efforts to popularize operatic novelties, commented that an impresario " 'cannot force the public to like certain operas any more than you can force it to like certain dishes. Both are matters of taste. Knowing that the opera impresario has but to give the public what he thinks it will like, not what he thinks it ought to hear, I have tried to do the former, and I am perfectly satisfied with the manner in which the public has supported my efforts.' "[67]

Regardless of the criticisms, Hammerstein maintained that the missive had been effective; for, soon thereafter, the company enjoyed enormous patronage. Perhaps it was not so much the efficacy of the letter as it was the return of Mary Garden and the debut of a fabulous singer, a coloratura soprano who aroused a fantastic degree of hysteria in the New York public: Luisa Tetrazzini.

Charpentier's Paris

The *première* of *Louise* on Friday, January 3, 1908, was an unequivocal dramatic and musical triumph as well as "an epoch at the Manhattan."[68] The opera itself was highly praised, although there had been those who had feared it would not be a success in the United States, supposing the American public as unable to understand

[65] W. J. Henderson, "The Record of the Year," *The* [New York] *Sun Theatre Section*, December 29, 1907, p. 8.

[66] "The Operatic Outlook," *New York American Drama and Society Section*, December 29, 1907, p. 3.

[67] "Mr. Heinrich Conried Says the Most Highly Educated Opera Audiences in the World Are Right Here in New York," *The New York Herald Society and Drama Section*, January 5, 1908, p. 12.

[68] *New York American*, January 4, 1908.

its "intense Parisianism."[69] The verdict of the opera-goers, however, was emphatic. The applause after the first and second acts was enthusiastic; after the third it was tumultuous; and, at the end of the performance, the house greeted the artists with "rapturous plaudits."[70] Aldrich, in the *Times*, said that it was "a remarkable work; a work . . . penetrated by the intense sincerity of the author, testifying to his efforts to disregard what he views as the conventionalities of lyrical drama and of hitherto accepted aesthetics of that art, to enter into the realities of life as he sees them."[71] The modernity, humanity, and reality of the characters appealed to many who were unaccustomed to opera plots related to contemporary realism. To have plain working people as the subject of a grand opera was a revelation. Krehbiel, however, although he liked the performance, was unhappy with the subject of free love and filial disloyalty: "idealism outraged, sacred things ridiculed, high conceptions of beauty and duty dragged into the gutter . . . ."[72] Regardless of such adverse opinion, public curiosity concerning the work remained unabated, and large, appreciative audiences attended the remaining ten performances during this season.

As for the singers, the principals were inimitable in their roles. Garden, who had completely immersed herself in the part of the Parisian grisette, sang well, even though she was not entirely free of the effects of her illness. While, in general, she was greatly admired for her portrayal, there were a few critics who felt that her Louise was somewhat artificial and disingenuous. Dalmorès was excellent as Julien; Bressler-Gianoli (the Mother) "searched with profound insight the depths of the role and gave a representation exquisite in all details";[73] and Gilibert was superb as the Father, some considering his characterization one of the greatest portraitures on the opera stage.

---

[69] W. J. Henderson, "Walter Damrosch on the French *Tristan et Yseult*," *The* [New York] *Sun Theatre Section*, December 15, 1907, p. 8.

[70] *The* [New York] *Evening Post*, January 4, 1908.

[71] *The New York Times*, January 4, 1908.

[72] *New-York Daily Tribune*, January 4, 1908.

[73] *The New York Press*, January 4, 1908.

French opera had scored another triumph. One result was that the audience at the Manhattan Opera House slowly but surely began to change. To a great extent, heretofore it had been boisterous, one that applauded and loved the old-fashioned Italian operas. To be sure, Melba in the opening season attracted a different type, since she was a great favorite of the *haut monde*. The productions of *Les Contes d'Hoffmann*, *Thaïs*, and *Louise*, however, introduced new patrons to the house, individuals of refinement and musical culture, as well as those theater-goers who thought it "smart" to know of the new operas.[74]

[74] W. J. Henderson, "Mr. Hammerstein's Season," *The* [New York] *Sun Theatre Section*, March 29, 1908, p. 8.

XII

Tetrazzini

SOON AFTER the *Louise première*, the Manhattan was the scene of one of the most brilliant debuts ever recorded in New York's music history. The phenomenal singer was Luisa Tetrazzini, who triumphed by her captivating personality, dramatic ability, and magnificence of voice. A vast and fashionable audience thronged to greet her, curious, excited, anticipatory, determined to make of this an extraordinary event. The moment she appeared on the stage that memorable evening the house exploded in "a fusillade of welcome"[1] and, at the end of the first act, heaped "such applause upon her as [was] rarely given in [New York] to artists who [had] thoroughly established their right through their achievements to the highest place on the roll of great artists."[2] The rest of the performance was as exciting and momentous. Such an occasion is the genesis of operatic legends.

ACCLAIMED IN LONDON

At this time Tetrazzini was in her late thirties, and although she had been singing for years in various parts of the world (Italy, Spain, Portugal, Russia, South America, and Mexico), she had never created much of a stir on the operatic scene until the fall of 1907. She might, however, have gained earlier recognition in New York. After her

[1] Richard Aldrich, "Tetrazzini's Reception Almost Unparalleled in New York's Operatic History . . . ," *The New York Times Theatre Section,* January 19, 1908, p. 4.
[2] *Ibid.*

success at the Tivoli Opera House in San Francisco during the 1904–1905 season, laudatory reports concerning her singing and art reached New York. Conried arranged for a contract but, not being sure of her abilities, subsequently allowed it to lapse. Hammerstein also wanted Tetrazzini and, when he announced the members of his company for the initial season, included her name as one of his leading sopranos. It was said later, however, that the singer had been evasive and that Hammerstein had lost interest in her when she asked for exclusive roles, $1,000 a night, and other considerations.[3] The impresario probably never again gave Tetrazzini a second thought until she had made her fabulous debut at Covent Garden, after which critics acclaimed her as "the greatest new singer that [had] burst upon the musical world for an age."[4] The usually reserved English quite lost their heads and hearts to the wondrous artist. Hammerstein could not ignore this and determined to engage her.

Tetrazzini's debut in London almost had not occurred. According to her autobiography *My Life of Song*, Campanini, who was married to her sister Eva, recommended her to Harry V. Higgins, the director of Covent Garden, early in 1907. What the impresario offered was a contract for ten performances at £120 each. Tetrazzini, who "literally jumped and sang for joy,"[5] accepted and at once began preparing for this all-important engagement. For a time, however, it seemed that she would not appear there after all. Since the fall season in London had not been financially successful, Higgins wrote to Tetrazzini, suggesting she postpone her debut until 1908; but, not willing to be put off, the soprano insisted that he honor the contract they had made. Ultimately Higgins decided to go ahead with the original agreement. After her fantastic success he quipped that "the maximum effort he had made to secure [her] for London was to *offer* [*her*] £300 to keep away."[6]

At her debut as Violetta in *La Traviata*, on November 2, 1907,

[3] "Hammerstein Loses Luise Tetrazzini," *Musical America*, Vol. IV (August 18, 1906), 1.

[4] News item in *The New York Herald*, November 10, 1907.

[5] Luisa Tetrazzini, *My Life of Song*, 176.

[6] *Ibid.*, 175.

Tetrazzini simply overwhelmed the Covent Garden audience, creating a hysteria unusual for London opera-goers. Critics at once recognized her as a very great singer as well as an actress of no mean ability. What was especially noteworthy and commented upon was the emotional warmth and color of the voice, qualities that brought tears to the eyes. Her "sympathetic"[7] singing, brilliant staccati, *fioriture*, ascending and descending scales, trills, double swells—all evoked the wildest enthusiasm. Of her histrionic ability, the London *Times* said that her "consistent conception of the character . . . [gave] it a genuine dramatic significance."[8] Subsequent performances at Covent Garden were gala affairs. Of her appearance in *Lucia*, the music critic of the London *Times*, praising her highly, remarked that her singing was "a true example of the *bel canto*" and that it was "most gratifying to think that the traditions of that art [would] be handed on for a few years longer."[9] So boundless was the public's interest in Tetrazzini that Higgins arranged for her to appear in four concerts at the opera house in order to accommodate those eager to hear the new star. After her second concert, on December 7, 1907, the London *Times* said that "the Mad Scene from *Lucia* was interrupted by so much applause that a good many of the hearers thought the singer was obliging with an encore when she was only finishing the song. In this, and in the 'Air de [sic] Clochettes' from *Lakmé*, the agility and certainty of the *fioriture*, and the power of the high E, came up to expectations . . . ."[10] The crowd for this occasion was unprecedented, probably the most immense audience ever assembled at Covent Garden, "for the space usually filled by the orchestra had been boarded over, and there were in all 25 rows of stalls, while the removal of so many boxes gave room for a far greater number of seats in the open balconies so contrived."[11] In London a new Queen of Song had begun her reign.

Tetrazzini had proved to be what every opera manager prays for:

[7] [London] *Pall Mall Gazette*, November 4, 1907.
[8] November 4, 1907.
[9] November 16, 1907.
[10] December 9, 1907.   [11] *Ibid.*

every performance in which she sang was sold out in a matter of hours. Such a singer is a rarity and a godsend to any opera company. And such a singer Hammerstein determined to have at the Manhattan. On November 11, 1907, *The New York Times* reported that Tetrazzini had just closed a contract by cable with Hammerstein for three seasons, beginning in November, 1908; but, eager to present her before then, Hammerstein would not be put off and urged her to make her debut at the Manhattan following her London engagement. Perhaps she would duplicate her Covent Garden triumphs at his opera house. Then, too, he needed her to replace Melba, who, unable to come to the United States, had canceled her engagement. On November 30, 1907, Pietro Brignoli, Hammerstein's personal representative, sailed for Europe to persuade Tetrazzini to journey to America for the current season. After he had successfully concluded the necessary arrangements, it was announced that Tetrazzini would make her debut at the Manhattan in January, 1908.

HYSTERIA IN NEW YORK

Having read the dispatches from London, New York was anxious to hear for itself, a fact demonstrated by the immense advance sale of tickets. On January 11, 1908, Hammerstein said that for her first appearance he had already received $25,000 in mail orders alone. Since the capacity of the Manhattan was $11,500, he had been obliged to return thousands of dollars.[12] What is more, the house had been completely sold out for her next four performances. No doubt there were moments when Hammerstein wondered whether Tetrazzini would live up to all the expectations and the advance publicity. Would she be an overwhelming success in New York? Since he had never heard her sing, he could not possibly know what kind of artist she was or whether she possessed a magnificent voice. Other singers with great European reputations had failed dismally in the New World. Chaliapin at the Metropolitan was a conspicuous example of that fact this very season. Whether Tetrazzini's engagement would be an unqualified success was a chance which he would have to take.

[12] News item in *The New York Times*, January 12, 1908.

Hammerstein need not have worried. Tetrazzini's debut, on January 15, 1908, in *La Traviata* was one of the great nights of the Manhattan Opera Company. The diva's triumph was overwhelming, complete. When she first appeared on stage, the house, packed to the walls, greeted her with "faint applause,"[13] waiting to hear her in song. Tetrazzini seemed restrained, not singing the "Libiamo" in full voice. People who had eagerly anticipated her appearance looked disappointed. Soon, however, they were enraptured, for when the soprano began the "Ah, fors' è lui," the house was flooded with the glorious, golden tones of an incomparable voice. She sang the aria with aplomb, unusual ease and beauty, dramatic feeling and emotional power, ending on a high C, which she "swelled and diminished . . . with evenness and precision."[14] The "Sempre libera" was brilliant, the upper tones being of extraordinary volume, the scales delivered with fluency and fire, the final E flat above high C produced "with so great an ease and freedom that persons possessed of the sense of abolute [*sic*] pitch almost doubted their senses."[15] Singing that magnificent note, Tetrazzini bent to gather up the long train of her gown and proceeded to walk offstage, all the while affecting the utmost insouciance and all the while holding onto that phenomenal E flat until she disappeared from view. Her tour de force brought down the house.

Called before the curtain twelve times at the end of this act,[16] Tetrazzini, tossing kisses, radiated happiness as she acknowledged the torrential applause and the shower of flowers thrown from many boxes. *The World* described the scene this way:

> . . . Tetrazzini brought both hands to her lips and tossed kisses to the parquet, flung them toward the boxes and raised her eyes toward the galleries. Those occupying seats nearest the stage heard her rippling laughter. She was happy as a

[13] *The* [New York] *World,* January 16, 1908.
[14] *The New York Times,* January 16, 1908.
[15] *The New York Press,* January 16, 1908.
[16] *The* [New York] *World,* January 16, 1908.

child. She caught up the flowers which lay around her. She snatched her handkerchief from her bodice and waved a response which would have done credit to a Chautauqua miss.[17]

Among those who paid homage to the new star were other opera singers. From the Metropolitan, Geraldine Farrar said that she had rarely seen " 'so much enthusiasm in the theatre' " and that the debut " 'was certainly a success in every sense of the word,' "[18] while Mary Garden, it was observed at the end of this act, applauded with such vigor that she split her gloves.[19] Regular patrons of the Metropolitan and society fashionables, including the Cornelius Vanderbilts, the younger W. K. Vanderbilts, the Clarence H. Mackays, Mrs. Frank Jay Gould, the Charles Astor Bristeds, were also generous in their praise and applause. Altogether it was a cyclonic demonstration "for which it would be difficult to find a parallel in the operatic annals of New York."[20]

The rest of the evening saw no diminution of enthusiasm. Tetrazzini's sympathetic singing with the elder Germont was touching, further revealing the emotional power of her voice as well as her ability as an actress; and, in the last act, the soprano, by no means a thin person, "preserved the illusion and pathos of the scene in spite of her unconsumptive figure."[21] Bassi (Alfredo), the same tenor Hammerstein had cast for Melba's debut approximately a year before, thrilled with his "opulent outpouring of voice";[22] and Ancona (Germont), "dignified and touching,"[23] sang with "great nobility and beauty of style."[24] Under the master, Campanini, the performance had been vital, compelling, unforgettable.

[17] *Ibid.*

[18] News item in *The New York Times*, January 16, 1908.

[19] News item in *The* [New York] *World*, January 16, 1908.

[20] Aldrich, "Tetrazzini's Reception Almost Unparalleled in New York's Operatic History . . . ," *The New York Times Theatre Section,* January 19, 1908, p. 4.

[21] *The* [New York] *World*, January 16, 1908.

[22] *The New York Times*, January 16, 1908.

[23] *Ibid.*   [24] *Ibid.*

The following day critics praised the new singer lavishly, although there were certain reservations. What some pundits decried was the fact that although Tetrazzini's voice was efflorescent and powerful in the upper register, the lower tones occasionally sounded thin and worn, almost colorless and unmusical.[25] A few thought her cantilena was not even at all times. Such comments, however, were in the minority. The general consensus of opinion was that her voice was one of the most beautiful in the world and that she was a sensation with her vocal pyrotechnics, dramatic warmth, and artistry.[26] What was noted, above all, was that Tetrazzini, unlike most coloraturas, sang the role of Violetta not for mere vocal display but for musical significance. Krehbiel commented that:

> ... The secret [of her great success] lay in the combination of beautiful singing, as such, and acting. Not acting in the sense of attitude, motion and facial expression, although these were all admirable, but in the dramatic feeling which imbued the singing—the dramatic color which shifted with kaleidoscopic swiftness from phrase to phrase, filling it with the blood of the play. The voice, weak and pallid in its lower register, had a dozen shades of meaning nevertheless, and as it soared upward it took on strength and glitter, though it lost in emotional force as it gained in sensual charm.[27]

Hammerstein had every reason to be gratified by Tetrazzini's success and the accolades from the public and press. He anticipated an even greater triumph for her when she appeared in *Lucia*, since she would have more opportunity to use coloratura in the Donizetti opera than in *La Traviata*. As for Tetrazzini, the soprano seemed overwhelmed by the reception, and looked forward eagerly to her next appearances. All of this must have been unpleasant reading for Conried, who had had an option on her and let her go, and for the directors of the Metropolitan, who must have known that the prestige

[25] *The* [New York] *Sun,* January 16, 1908.
[26] *The* [New York] *World,* January 16, 1908.
[27] *New-York Daily Tribune,* January 16, 1908.

of that company had suffered by their inability to secure Tetrazzini. Soon changes would take place there; perhaps the new star's presence at the Manhattan had more than a little effect on the rejuvenation.

Tetrazzini's first appearance as Lucia occurred on January 20, with a cast that included Zenatello (Edgardo), Sammarco (Ashton), and Arimondi (Raimondo), under the baton of Campanini. Hammerstein had accurately predicted that the coloratura would surpass her previous efforts; for she sang gloriously, rejoicing the hearts of all those who reveled in great singing and vocal filigree. Pitts Sanborn said that "the voice [was] so fresh, the upper range [was] so strong, so brilliant, and so richly colored, and the coloratura [was] often delivered with such enchanting ease that it [was] not in flesh and blood to listen unmoved."[28] Her "Spargi d'amaro pianto" was enthralling with its "leaps, runs, staccati, double swells from piano to forte twice repeated, and a finish on the high E flat."[29] Intensely emotional and effulgent, the voice dazzled and almost overwhelmed as she "seized high notes in midair with surety and lightness of touch and flung them at her auditors with a force and directness that at times smote the ear too powerfully."[30]

On January 29 Tetrazzini appeared as Gilda in *Rigoletto*, with Renaud as the Jester, Bassi as the Duke, and DeCisneros as Maddalena. Some thought this role unsuitable to her abilities, as it offered her few opportunities to indulge in the ornaments of coloratura. Her "Caro Nome," however, was encored, cheered to the echo for its limpidity and brilliance. Of her rendition of the aria, the *Press* said: "She produced a few beautiful messa di voce effects; she gave a scintillant chromatic scale; she seized with astonishing precision purity and clearness of tone two or three high notes in mezza voce; she obtained a pretty trill on middle D sharp and E; she sang what might be called a slow trill . . . on high B and C sharp."[31] Renaud's imper-

[28] *The* [New York] *Globe and Commercial Advertiser*, January 21, 1908.
[29] *The* [New York] *Sun*, January 21, 1908.
[30] *The New York Press*, January 21, 1908.
[31] *Ibid.*, January 30, 1908.

sonation had not lost any of its puissance, polish, humanity, and he sang with a great plenitude of voice.

Later in the season the prima donna appeared in *Dinorah* and *Crispino e la Comare*. On February 26 Hammerstein revived the Meyerbeer opera as a vehicle for her talents. Although the work itself was not liked any more than the year before, when Pinkert appeared as Dinorah, Tetrazzini's magnificent voice and bravura made it more tolerable. On March 6 Hammerstein resuscitated the Ricci brothers' *Crispino e la Comare*, one of Patti's favorite operas which had not been heard in New York for many years. Tetrazzini had a marvelous time as a comedienne, acting with vivacity and humor, keeping the house in "continual laughter."[32] She sang gloriously, decorating the melodies with pyrotechnical wonders, and ended the opera with a performance of Sir Julius Benedict's variations on the "Carnival of Venice." Sammarco and Gianoli-Galletti shared the honors.

This season Tetrazzini was the luminous star in twenty-one performances: five *Traviatas*, eight *Lucias*, three *Rigolettos*, one *Dinorah*, three *Crispinos*. She also sang in a mixed bill on March 28. Every time she was announced, New York flocked to hear her; and though some might have questioned the importance of her appearances artistically, there was no question of the sheer joy she gave to thousands by the beauty of her voice. At any rate, the city had another prima donna of the first rank to adore and a strong case of Tetrazzinitis. Krehbiel, in *Chapters of Opera*, said: "[Tetrazzini] was rapturously acclaimed by the public and a portion of the press. It is useless to discuss the phenomenon. The whims of the populace are as unquestioning and as irresponsible as the fury of the elements."[33] There was no gainsaying that the public liked Tetrazzini. To them, she was not just another star; she was a meteor. And she remained so. Not many singers have this destiny.

MEANWHILE, SCHUMANN-HEINK AND A *Première*

The sensational debut and subsequent appearances of Tetrazzini

[32] *The* [New York] *Evening Post*, March 7, 1908.
[33] Pages 392–93.

and the growing popularity of *Thaïs* and *Louise*, so ably interpreted by Garden and her colleagues, tended to overshadow other attractions at the opera house. On January 27, 1908, Ernestine Schumann-Heink made her only appearance with the company as Azucena in *Il Trovatore*, with Russ (Leonora), Zenatello (Manrico), Sammarco (di Luna), and Arimondi (Ferrando), Parelli conducting. The beloved contralto sang in German, while the others in the cast performed in Italian. Although Schumann-Heink had sung the role more than three hundred times, this was her first American appearance as Azucena.[34] The voice with its glorious organ-like tones was still marvelous, opulent, plangent. She made of the gypsy the central figure, enacting the character "with deadly earnestness, not to say a ferocity, that introduced a new note among the more conventional doings of her Italian companions in the cast."[35] It is not unlikely that the reason for her singing but this once at the Manhattan was that since Hammerstein had abandoned the production of German opera, he had no further plans for the contralto in the works he was producing. Perhaps he made some kind of financial settlement for the remainder of her contract.

The American *première* of Giordano's *Siberia* was on February 5, with Zenatello, replacing the indisposed Bassi; Agostinelli; Trentini; Sammarco; Crabbé. Thus far, New York had heard but two operas by this composer: *Andrea Chénier* at the Academy of Music in 1896 and *Fedora* at the Metropolitan this very season. Lawrence Gilman thought that this work was "the best and the most promising demonstration of Giordano's talents" and that the strength of the music "[lay] in the truly impressive manner in which it [intensified] and [underscored] the more dramatic moments in the action."[36] Krehbiel, however, considered Giordano's melody mediocre, primarily objecting to the superficiality and banality of a number of the musical

[34] *The New York Press*, January 28, 1908.
[35] *The New York Times*, January 28, 1908.
[36] Lawrence Gilman, "Giordano's *Siberia*," *Harper's Weekly*, Vol. LII (February 22, 1908), 25.

episodes.[37] What was especially significant was that Hammerstein had aroused enough interest in novelties to be reasonably sure of their being patronized, even though he did not have an all-star cast for this particular new work.[38]

[37] Krehbiel, *Chapters of Opera,* 402.

[38] W. J. Henderson, "Mr. Hammerstein's Production of *Siberia,*" *The* [New York] *Sun Theatre Section,* February 9, 1908, p. 8.

XIII

A Great Modern Opera

FINALLY, on Wednesday, February 19, 1908, Hammerstein brought forward the long awaited *première* of Debussy's *Pelléas et Mélisande*, an opera which many thought New York would not understand or accept. Some anticipated that the audience would leave after the first act, bored and mystified by the unusual musical score, while others maintained that, although it might be disliked at first, it would ultimately triumph in New York as it had in Paris. Hammerstein probably did not know what to expect. Since he said that he never anticipated making any money with it,[1] he must have felt that it would be, at best, a *succès d'estime*. Garden also did not know what would happen and said so ten days before the *première* in an interview with Carl Van Vechten, then with *The New York Times*:

"It took us four years to establish *Pelléas et Mélisande* in the répertoire of the Opéra-Comique. At first the public listened with disfavour or indecision, and performances could only be given once in two weeks. As a contrast I might mention the immediate success of *Aphrodite*, which I sang three or four times a week until fifty representations had been achieved, without appearing in another rôle. *Pelléas* was a different matter. The mystic beauty of the poet's mood and the revolutionary procedures of the musician were not calculated to touch the great public at once. Indeed, we had to teach our audiences to enjoy it. Americans who, I am told, are

[1] "New York's $2,000,000 Season of Grand Opera," *The New York Times Magazine Section*, March 29, 1908, p. 4.

fond of Maeterlinck, may appreciate its very manifest beauty at first hearing, but they didn't in Paris. At the early representations, individuals whistled and made cat-calls. One night three young men in the first row of the orchestra whistled through an entire scene. I don't believe those young men will ever forget the way I looked at them .... But after each performance it was the same: the applause drowned out the hisses. The balconies and galleries were the first to catch the spirit of the piece, and gradually it grew in public favour, and became a success, that is, comparatively speaking. *Pelléas et Mélisande*, like many another work of true beauty, appeals to a limited public and, consequently, the number of performances has always been limited, and perhaps always will be. I do not anticipate that it will crowd from popular favour such operas as *Werther*, *La Vie de Bohème* and *Carmen*, each of which is included in practically every week's répertoire at the Opéra-Comique.

"We interpreters of Debussy's lyric drama were naturally very proud, because we felt that we were assisting in the making of musical history . . . ."[2]

At the Manhattan the audience did not interrupt the *première* with any disturbances; on the contrary, the large house watched and listened to the opera with rapt attention. The earlier acts were followed by a "respectful titter of applause";[3] but when Campanini entered the pit just before the beginning of the fourth act, he was roundly applauded; and at the end of the performance there was a "sincere demonstration of approval,"[4] the artists being called before the curtain many times. De Koven commented that the applause, however, was more for the singers than for the opera itself: "The attitude of the large audience was one of rather amazed, respectful and intelligent attention, of courteous and hearty appreciation of the re-

[2] Van Vechten, *Interpreters and Interpretations*, 76–78.
[3] *New-York Daily Tribune*, February 20, 1908.
[4] *The New York Herald*, February 20, 1908.

markable work of the artists, rather than of spontaneous enthusiasm for the work itself, though the applause was ample."[5]

CRITICS DIVIDE ON MERITS OF THE OPERA

As for the opera, the critics were divided. Some refrained from giving a definite opinion: "The work deserves repeated hearing; it is too unusual, too curious, too original in plan and execution for hasty judgement."[6] Krehbiel heard little beauty in the score, disliking the "combinations of tones that sting and blister and pain and outrage the ear,"[7] while the critic of *The Evening World* declared that the opera was "decadent."[8] Henderson was bored by the first two acts, "deadly dull, monotonous, wearisome."[9] Gilman, however, was among those who liked it; in his opinion, the opera "[contained] page upon page of miraculous, of almost insupportable beauty, a beauty that is utterly individual in impulse. No music written for the stage since the death of Wagner . . . is comparable to this."[10] It is likely that the critic of the *Herald* accurately stated the situation: "It is a work that is entirely dependent upon the mood it exerts. If you are a musician of the old school your ears will probably be outraged by this composition, for there is no limit to the composer's daring; and if you are just an ordinarily happy mortal you will either fall completely under the spell of the work or you will be bored. But, whatever happens, the fact is not to be gainsaid that *Pelléas and Mélisande* is enormously clever, the product of a thinking brain; and it is, above all, something new in music."[11]

ARTISTS AND PRODUCTION LAUDED

Nothing that Garden had done before so impressed the New York critics as her Mélisande, wistful, elusive, otherworldly. She was

[5] *The* [New York] *World,* February 20, 1908.
[6] *The New York Press,* February 20, 1908.
[7] *New-York Daily Tribune,* February 20, 1908.
[8] *The* [New York] *Evening World,* February 20, 1908.
[9] *The* [New York] *Sun,* February 20, 1908.
[10] Lawrence Gilman, "Concerning an Epoch-Making Score," *Harper's Weekly,* Vol. LII (March 21, 1908), 25.
[11] *The New York Herald,* February 20, 1908.

poetry itself. Her gowns, long golden hair,[12] gestures, and repose created an indelible impression. As Mélisande, Garden was the personification of youth, an enchanted and enchanting princess, the quintessence of tenderness and femininity. Richard Aldrich, in the *Times*, wrote:

> ... Miss Garden made ... a new disclosure of her art and of the power of her dramatic personality. She is the dreamy, wistful maiden, wandering, uncertain, unhappy; and her denotement of the veiled and mysterious character is of much beauty and plastic grace. In places, as in the difficult scene with the wounded Golaud, and in the scene in which he does her violence, she rises to a height of tragic power that ought to put her among the greatest of lyric actresses. It was difficult to believe this statuesque mediaeval maiden was of the same stuff as Thais, as Louise. Melisande adds many cubits to Miss Garden's artistic stature.[13]

The beauty of her impersonation so impressed De Koven that he called her "one of the great dramatic artists of her day."[14] Critics also praised the other three principals from the original Paris cast: Jean Périer (Pelléas), admired less for his singing than his acting, was inimitable in his role; as Golaud, Hector Dufranne sang superbly and "triumphed over the very repugnance of the character which he was portraying";[15] Jeanne Gerville-Réache (Geneviève) made her impersonation of Pelléas' mother a moving portrayal, one in harmony with the whole. Crabbé (Physician) and Sigrist (Little Yniold) were acceptable; only Arimondi (Ärkel) seemed wholly miscast.

Campanini conducted the difficult work understandingly and masterfully, his interpretation creating a profound impression. In

[12] "The Longest Wig in the World," *The* [New York] *World Magazine Section*, February 16, 1908, p. 5.

[13] *The New York Times*, February 20, 1908.

[14] *The* [New York] *World*, February 20, 1908.

[15] *The* [New York] *Evening Telegram*, February 20, 1908.

The New York Times, Richard Aldrich wrote that the conductor had found "the innermost secret of this most elusive of all music" and that never had "the commanding genius of this great artist so completely established itself as in this achievement."[16]

The production itself was "by far the most elaborate and artistically satisfying achievement in the history of the Manhattan Opera House. Hammerstein ... provided eight settings, each finely effective in color and design and delightfully suited to the poetic scheme of the music-drama."[17] The sets, copies of the original Opéra-Comique production, were beautiful, a perfect background for the poetic work. The only defect was that the lighting was frequently too bright for scenes that should have been dim.[18]

In this general praise, Hammerstein was not forgotten. Many of the critics lauded him for his managerial fortitude in producing a work that was a milestone in the annals of music but that might be a failure financially. It would seem that Hammerstein had only art, not pecuniary considerations, in mind. The impresario, however, may have had another compelling reason to produce the opera. In a speech at the very end of the performance, after the singers, Campanini, and Coini had acknowledged much applause, Hammerstein said to the full house:

> "If a work of such sublime poetry and musical grandeur meets with your approbation and receives your support, it places New York at the head of cities of musical culture throughout the world. As for myself, I have had but one object in presenting the opera—to endear myself to you and perpetuate myself in your memory."[19]

In France, Debussy read of the historic *première* and its cordial reception. Grateful for what Hammerstein had done, he sent him a letter expressing his pleasure in the great success, which he main-

[16] February 20, 1908.
[17] *The New York Press*, February 20, 1908.
[18] *The New York Times*, February 20, 1908.
[19] *Ibid.*

tained aided " 'the cause of French music.' "[20] He also wrote to Campanini:

> "The newspapers of New York have said—the fact is so unusual as to be remarked—that you have displayed the skill of a master in directing *Pelleas et Melisande*. I know personally that it is not enough to be a good orchestral director to succeed in this respect. The orchestration of *Pelleas* is a frail piece of architecture, which supports the work and expresses its feeling. It is therefore the artist as well as the orchestral director that I hasten to congratulate and to thank for his precious collaboration. I hope to have the opportunity of shaking your hand with the gratitude I feel toward you here—so far away."[21]

The first performance of *Pelléas et Mélisande* occurred in the sixteenth week of the season. In the remaining weeks, the repertory leaned heavily on the Tetrazzini operas and the productions of *Louise* and *Pelléas*, which received seven representations in all. Some variety to this bill of fare was offered on March 13, when Calvé returned as Carmen, the role in which she had become a fetish. As in the previous season, she did not sing too well nor impersonate the Sevillian gypsy with quite the old abandon. Nevertheless, she still fascinated by her personality and temperament. Her impersonation, regardless of its exaggeration and self-consciousness, retained "that note of meridional and exotic passion, of willful depravity and sensuous allurement that makes itself felt and that exerts its attraction."[22] Calvé was also heard in this part on March 16 and 21.

[20] Letter in *The New York Times*, March 21, 1908, p. 9.
[21] Letter in *The New York Times*, March 19, 1908, p. 7.
[22] *The New York Times*, March 14, 1908.

XIV

Hammerstein Triumphant

I N THE last two weeks of March, the company presented two performances at the Philadelphia Academy of Music in response to a formal invitation from several prominent citizens of that town. This was the first time the Manhattan appeared outside of New York. G. Heide Norris, C. Hartman Kuhn, and Andrew Wheeler, who had been interested in Hammerstein's projected opera house, were the ones most responsible for this enterprise. In extending the invitation, these gentlemen had several considerations in mind. They thought that once Hammerstein saw for himself the enthusiasm of a Philadelphia audience, he would then realize that the opera-goers there were not the apathetic individuals he thought them to be; they were also eager to have Philadelphia see the quality of the company's productions and singers, in this way hoping to create subscribers for future appearances of the Manhattan; and, finally, they wanted to persuade Hammerstein to return for a series of ten Thursday matinees during the 1908–1909 season, with each performance guaranteed at $7,000. As a compliment to them and the others who had wanted Philadelphians to know the Hammerstein brand of opera, the impresario agreed to present *Lucia* at a matinee, on March 19, and *Louise* the evening of March 26.[1]

The announcement of the performances aroused tremendous interest. On March 13, the first day of the advance sale, practically

[1] "How Impresario Was Led to Build Opera House Here," *The* [Philadelphia] *North American Grand Opera Edition*, November 17, 1908, p. 8.

every box and seat was sold. On the following day more than five hundred mail orders had to be returned, while hundreds were told at the box office that there were absolutely no seats left. When the first opera was given, an enormous crowd was turned away, with people almost fighting for admission to the standing room area.[2] Hammerstein could not help but be impressed by this and by the overwhelming critical and popular reception accorded the company.

The Philadelphians who saw *Lucia* were ecstatic over Tetrazzini, Zenatello, and Sammarco. The coloratura especially endeared herself for her kind attention to an invalid authoress, Mrs. Caspar Wister, a seventy-eight-year-old lady who had been unable to attend opera for twenty-five years. A director of the Academy, who had secured her a place in one of the proscenium boxes, told Tetrazzini of the supreme effort Mrs. Wister had made to attend the performance. After the Mad Scene the diva, deeply moved by her reception and the presence of the septuagenarian, went over to the stage box and kissed the elderly lady's hands. Of this gesture, the *Press* said: "The spectacle of the great prima donna . . . paying this spontaneous tribute to one who [represented] Philadelphia in the fullest sense of the word was one of the most moving episodes ever seen on the Academy stage."[3]

Philadelphians enjoyed the magnificent attire of the singers, the work of the chorus, the beautiful playing of the orchestra and the conducting of Campanini, who enkindled the entire performance with his musical fire and inspiration. Philadelphians were also impressed by the *mise-en-scène*. According to Curtis, local historian, the massive scenery, so different from the sets used for years at the Academy, made a profound impression on those who observed that it was gotten onto the stage "only with the greatest difficulty."[4] The performance had been a true occasion.

A week later, when Hammerstein presented *Louise*, Garden

[2] News item in *The* [Philadelphia] *Press*, March 20, 1908.

[3] *Ibid.*

[4] John Curtis, "One Hundred Years of Grand Opera in Philadelphia" (unpublished MS, The Historical Society of Pennsylvania), III, Sec. 2, p. 503.

scored a personal triumph, though the opera itself puzzled the audience, used to "its traditional opera as to its family gatherings in the boxes and its antiquated scenery."[5] The modernity shocked; people gasped when they saw the fluffy ruffles, the coat suits, mushroom hats, and a chorus that was "the apotheosis of pompadour, the tan pump, and, the jumper blouse!"[6] The greatest surprise of the evening, however, came at the end of the third act, when Hammerstein appeared before the curtain, prepared to make a speech:

> "I thank you for the reception you have given me. I decided to produce two operas in Philadelphia, one of the old school and one of the new. Both seem to have given you pleasure. After the welcome you accorded me I feel that you really want me here. (Applause)
>
> "Last Fall I purchased ground at Broad and Poplar Street for the purpose of erecting an opera house. The financial crisis and other matters, however, finally made the undertaking seem doubtful. I reluctantly withdrew.
>
> "But what you've shown me last week and to-night has changed my resolution. On Tuesday there were submitted to me the plans of the greatest palace of music ever designed for this or any other city of America. Next week I'll break ground. (Long applause) . . . My Philadelphia opera house will be opened on November 15, 1908."[7]

The audience jumped to its feet, madly cheering and applauding.

Several days later Hammerstein elaborated on his plans. Always hoping to democratize grand opera, he maintained that the new edifice would have accommodations equally comfortable for both the rich and the poor; the gallery was to be as luxurious as the ground floor and not a "place where you find sanded floors and spittoons."[8] Perhaps one of the auditoriums he had in mind was the Philadelphia Academy of Music, where, even today, the topmost balcony still has

[5] News item in *The* [Philadelphia] *Press*, March 27, 1908.
[6] *Ibid.*
[7] *Ibid.*   [8] *Ibid.*, March 28, 1908.

Mme Mazarin (foreground) as she appeared in the title role of *Elektra*, when Strauss's work was given its American *première* at the Manhattan Opera House on February 1, 1910. She is shown at the beginning of her dance of joy after the avenging of her father's death. Mlle Baron, as Chrysothemis, is on the far left.

Nellie Melba as Violetta in *La Traviata*, the role of her debut with the
Manhattan on January 2, 1907.

Luisa Tetrazzini—one of Hammerstein's greatest stars.

Courtesy of the City of New York

Three tenors of the Manhattan: John McCormack (upper left), Charles Dalmorès (upper right), and Alessandro Bonci (below).

Mario Sammarco as Rigoletto (upper left), Giovanni Zenatello as Otello
(upper right), and Maurice Renaud as Hérode in
Massenet's *Hérodiade* (below).

The cast of the American *première* of *Pelléas et Mélisande*: Mary Garden
as Mélisande (left); Jean Périer as Pelléas (right); Jeanne
Gerville-Réache as Genéviève (facing page, left); and Hector
Dufranne as Golaud (facing page, right).

The artists shown on these two pages were in both the world *première* of
Debussy's opera, *Pelléas et Mélisande,* and the American *première*
of February 19, 1908, at the Manhattan Opera House.

Mary Garden in three roles she made famous: Thaïs (left), the Juggler (upper right), and Salome (lower right).

wooden benches. As for his announcement that he would open on November 15, he admitted that this would not be possible, since that date fell on a Sunday. Now the opening would be "around" that time.[9] His son Arthur, who had planned to go to Europe for a well-deserved holiday, was to be in charge of the construction, which, the impresario avouched, would begin at once.

GALA ENDING

On March 27, the evening after the performance of *Louise* in Philadelphia, Hammerstein staged Giordano's *Andrea Chénier* at the Manhattan as a benefit honoring Campanini. The work had not been heard in New York since 1896, when it was first given at the old Academy of Music. On the whole, the performance was meritorious, some critics believing that the opera should be in the repertory permanently. The cast included the conductor's wife, Eva Tetrazzini-Campanini, who had been in retirement for a number of years. As Maddalena, she proved herself a serious artist with a good voice of "decidedly pleasing"[10] quality; Sammarco, the Gérard at the world *première* and at this performance, impressed by his dramatic impersonation; and Bassi (Andrea Chénier) sang "with an opulence and [acted] with a fervor that carried the house by storm."[11] At the end of the second act Campanini, whom Hammerstein called the "greatest conductor in the world,"[12] received many gifts from the artists and friends. After this one performance the opera was dropped from the Manhattan repertory. To have produced it for just this one time seems foolhardy and extreme in operatic prodigality.

The season came to an end the following evening, March 28, in a program of scenes and acts from five operas; and though prices had been raised, all places had been taken a week before. The gala began with Tetrazzini and Bassi in the first act of *La Traviata* and proceeded with Zenatello, Sammarco, and Agostinelli in the first act of

[9] News item in *The Philadelphia Inquirer*, March 28, 1908.
[10] *The* [New York] *Sun*, March 28, 1908.
[11] *The* [New York] *Evening World*, March 28, 1908.
[12] *The* [New York] *Sun*, March 28, 1908.

I Pagliacci; then Garden, Dalmorès, Zeppilli, and Arimondi appeared in the Garden Scene from *Faust*. Garden simply amazed the critics, for "she acted . . . with . . . much individual charm and sang the music, including the jewel song, for the most part . . . brilliantly."[13] After this scene Jacques Coini, the stage manager, presented Hammerstein with a silver loving cup from the singers and Campanini. The performance continued with Tetrazzini in the Mad Scene from *Lucia* and concluded with Russ, De Cisneros, Bassi, Ancona, and Arimondi in the Triumphal Scene from *Aïda*. It seemed an appropriate finale for a most brilliant evening and season. Hammerstein could very well rejoice in the company's achievements, which inspired confidence in his roseate views and plans for the future. To a representative of the press he said: " 'I shall not stop. I shall go ahead. I have already ordered 60,000 yards of canvas to be shipped from Belfast, and scenic painters will get busy early in the Summer . . . . I shall go further even in the way of new and expensive productions than I have this year . . . .' "[14]

In the second season, Hammerstein presented twenty-one weeks of opera, one week longer than he had originally announced. Since he had had to repeat some operas on subscription nights, he added the additional week and, in a magnanimous gesture, gave his subscribers the privilege of attending the extra performances at no cost. He might very well have been generous; for, according to Arthur Hammerstein, the season ended with a huge profit: $250,000.[15] The Metropolitan, on the other hand, had a loss for the second consecutive year, the deficit being $95,806.[16]

THE METROPOLITAN—NO LONGER INVULNERABLE

While Hammerstein had produced many novelties, which were the important musical events of the season, Conried had brought for-

[13] *The* [New York] *Evening Post*, March 30, 1908.
[14] "New York's $2,000,000 Season of Grand Opera," *The New York Times Magazine Section*, March 29, 1908, p. 4.
[15] Kolodin, *The Metropolitan Opera 1883–1935*, 128.
[16] Sheean, *Oscar Hammerstein I*, 243.

ward only one new opera: Cilèa's *Adriana Lecouvreur*, with Caruso, Cavalieri, Scotti, and Journet. Apparently Conried was content to rely primarily on the ability of his star tenor to generate public interest in the presentations at the Metropolitan. In fact, Caruso was heard more often this season (he sang in 51 of the 122 performances) than at any other time in his New York career;[17] and when he was not singing, Conried offered another great Italian tenor, Bonci, who first appeared at the older house on November 22, in *Rigoletto*, with Sembrich, Stracciari, and Journet. Although there had been some concern that his singing would not be heard to advantage in the vast auditorium, it was readily apparent that his voice sounded as beautiful in the new surroundings as it had at the Manhattan.

Of the new singers whom Conried introduced, there was not one, save Bonci, who was an overwhelming success with the critics and public. Chaliapin had come to the Metropolitan with an enviable European reputation behind him; but American critics found his portrayals crude and, at times, offensive, his realism and individuality being too pronounced for the rarefied tastes of the time. Chaliapin resented the criticism and lack of understanding he encountered in New York. Farrar recalled that he "dissolved in a huge Russian pout all winter"[18] and would not be placated. Years later (1922) when he returned, his genius was recognized at long last; and it was at this time that he received the critical and public acclaim lacking in his initial season.

The most important new personality at the older house was the distinguished Gustav Mahler, who conducted memorable performances of *Tristan und Isolde*, *Don Giovanni*, *Siegfried*, *Die Walküre*, and *Fidelio*. His outstanding contribution to the season was his reading of the Beethoven opera, an incandescent interpretation. *Tristan* with Fremstad was marvelous. After one performance of this music drama, on March 12, 1909, Mahler declared that in all his musical experience he had never known another analogous to it.[19] His work

[17] Kolodin, *The Metropolitan Opera, 1883-1935*, 123.
[18] Geraldine Farrar, *Such Sweet Compulsion*, 111.
[19] Alma Mahler, *Gustav Mahler* (trans. by Basil Creighton), 119.

at the Metropolitan, however, was not always this inspirational, for the stars could be lax about rehearsals.[20] Years later Farrar recalled that Chaliapin, in particular, had been guilty of not being attentive at the sessions for *Don Giovanni* and that the other singers had done all they could to keep the peace.[21] Still, Mahler found his work congenial, a pleasant change from the myriad problems of the Vienna Opera.[22] In him the Metropolitan had an artist of the first magnitude.

Apparently Conried, suffering from poor health, was doing all that he could to meet Hammerstein's opposition; but the overwhelming success of the new French operas, which at one time had been available to him, and the sensation of Tetrazzini, whom he had failed to secure, were annoying to the directors of the older house. According to the minutes of the Metropolitan Opera for 1908–1929 in the Metropolitan archives, members of the Board of Directors sent Conried a letter in which they stated that he had erred in these acts of omission as well as in other ways and that too often he had followed a course of action contrary to the advice and wishes of the board. They believed that the prestige of the Metropolitan had lessened as the result of Hammerstein's activities, an eclipse which they decreed must end. For sometime there had been rumors that Conried was to be replaced, speculations which were confirmed on February 12, 1908, when it was officially announced that Conried's tenure with the company would be completed at the end of the season. In his place the directors appointed Giulio Gatti-Casazza, who had been the impresario of La Scala. It was also announced that Arturo Toscanini, the chief conductor at that opera house, would be with the Metropolitan next season. Andreas Dippel, one of the leading tenors at the Metropolitan since 1898, was appointed administrative director to work with Gatti-Casazza, who was unaware of his associate until he arrived from Europe in May, 1908.[23] What resulted was a dual-directorship

[20] Charles Henry Meltzer, "Smart Singers and Others," *New York American Drama and Society Section*, January 12, 1908, p. 4.

[21] Farrar, *Such Sweet Compulsion*, 111.

[22] Mahler, *Gustav Mahler* (trans. by Basil Creighton), 117.

[23] Gatti-Casazza, *Memories of the Opera*, 155.

that created confusion in policy and internal dissensions until Dippel resigned in 1910.

Gatti-Casazza recalled that he first met Otto H. Kahn, President of the Board of Directors of the Metropolitan, in July, 1907, and that, at their initial meeting in Paris, he had told Kahn he would be interested in the position of general director, should Conried retire.[24] Gatti-Casazza had earlier been somewhat undecided whether to consider the post; but Toscanini, displeased with some of the conditions at La Scala, urged him to negotiate with the Metropolitan. The conductor himself, whom Conried had wanted to engage in 1903 and again in 1906,[25] was willing to go to New York if his friend Gatti-Casazza became the manager of the opera house. Soon after the new year of 1908, negotiations began in earnest between the Metropolitan and Gatti-Casazza and Toscanini. Rawlins Cottenet, who was the secretary of the Metropolitan Opera Board, conferred with the two men in Milan and finally signed them to three-year contracts.[26]

The new directorship caused dismay in the ranks of the leading singers at the Metropolitan, fearful of the inevitable changes that would result. It would seem a golden opportunity for Hammerstein to make raids into the enemy territory. This very season Conried had tried to secure Gilibert and Dalmorès, but Hammerstein would not let them go. Reciprocity being the order of the day, Hammerstein made overtures to two of the Metropolitan's most brilliant stars: Caruso and Farrar. Rumors persisted that he was offering the tenor enormous fees to sing at the Manhattan; and it was reported that Caruso was at the new opera house more often than in the past, visiting backstage and conferring with Hammerstein. According to Vincent Sheean, however, it was not until next season that serious efforts were made to engage the tenor.[27] As for Farrar, the soprano was not at all sure that she would renew her contract with the Metropolitan unless the new directors accepted her terms.[28] After a rather pro-

---

[24] *Ibid.*, 146–47.   [25] Howard Taubman, *The Maestro*, 112.

[26] Gatti-Casazza, *Memories of the Opera*, 148.

[27] Sheean, *Oscar Hammerstein I*, 280–81.

[28] Farrar, *Such Sweet Compulsion*, 114–16.

longed period of negotiations she had her way and signed a new agreement. Meanwhile, Hammerstein wanted her at the Manhattan. Why she rejected his offer is revealed in a letter: "Needless to say, that despite some brilliant offerings and notable artists in the Hammerstein company, one would not consider breaking a contract, first of all, nor the somewhat insecure future of the second organization. Tradition of the Metropolitan would be a choice, at all times."[29]

Whether the new order at the older house would exert a potent influence remained to be seen. It would require time, patience, and familiarity with the New York terrain. Meanwhile, Hammerstein and the Manhattan seemed more entrenched than ever before. New York knew what to expect of Hammerstein, but Gatti-Casazza and Toscanini were unknown quantities.

[29] Letter to the author from Geraldine Farrar, April 20, 1961.

XV

The Philadelphia Opera House

—◦◦❖{}❖◦◦—

O**N** A**PRIL** 1, 1908, Hammerstein sailed for Europe to recruit additional singers for the two opera houses and to arrange for new productions in the repertory. During his absence his son Arthur supervised the construction of the Philadelphia Opera House, an awesome task, since he had but a little over seven months for the entire undertaking. The razing of the Harrah mansion began at noon on March 30. With several friends and associates about him and over a thousand spectators, Arthur loosened the first brick while the crowd cheered; then, after he broke a bottle of champagne to signal the beginning of the work, the demolition of the property began in earnest. Several days later, watching the laborers loading wagons with earth, Arthur confessed that he felt some qualms as he realized more and more the enormity of the enterprise; for it was "the biggest job of the kind ever undertaken. Not only that, [he] was to do it in at least one year less time than anything like it had ever been done before . . . . [It] was not only to be so much larger than other opera houses, but it was to include a lot of new ideas in theater construction."[1] He was fortunate that his assistants had been foremen for other theaters Hammerstein had built, and work went on with startling rapidity. Months later Arthur related what took place:

> I really can't tell how many yards of earth we excavated,

[1] Arthur Hammerstein, "Builder Tells How the Speed Record Was Made," *The* [Philadelphia] *North American Grand Opera Edition,* November 17, 1908, p. 9.

but we dug a hole 240 x 160 feet and 18 feet deep, and at the same time took down the old house, which contained more than 2,000,000 bricks. We began to put in the concrete footings for the foundations on June 1.

Meanwhile, I had bought the materials, and, with the exception of the steel, bought everything here in Philadelphia. I was forced to go outside for the steel and get it from seven different mills . . . . I had to buy nearly 7,000,000 [hard-pressed bricks] before I got through, and besides that I had the 2,000,000 old bricks that I got out of the Harrah mansion. There was also an immense amount of marble in the old house, which I utilized.

We used almost 20,000 tons of structural steel, metallic lathing and iron work in the house . . . . I haven't the figures at hand as to the amount of crushed stone, rubble and concrete, but it was enormous, for I have built the house as nearly absolutely fireproof in every detail as is possible. I do not believe there is another building of corresponding size in the country wherein there is so little lumber or other inflammable material.[2]

At the end of May the elder Hammerstein returned from Europe, and when he came to Philadelphia on June 1, he expressed his delight with what his son had accomplished. On June 24, the first steel pillar of the opera house was erected, and the following day Oscar Hammerstein laid the cornerstone in a brief ceremony witnessed by approximately five hundred interested persons. Inside it was placed a copper box containing photographs of Campanini, Melba, Tetrazzini, Garden, Calvé, Eva Tetrazzini-Campanini, Zenatello, Dalmorès, Sammarco, Renaud, and Oscar himself.[3] Also included in the box were phonograph records of all these singers,

[2] *Ibid.*

[3] S.E.E., "Cornerstone Laid in Philadelphia," *Musical America*, Vol. VIII (July 4, 1908), 5.

excepting Mme Campanini, and a paper, signed by the impresario, with these words:

> "Philadelphia Opera House erected by Oscar Hammerstein, of New York. Ground broken by Arthur Hammerstein, his son, on March 28, 1908; cornerstone laid June 25, 1908. The opera house to be opened to the public November 17, 1908."[4]

Steel construction went ahead rapidly, although not in the order customarily used in the building of a theater. Usually after the steel of the stage is put in, the steel in the auditorium is tied to it. In order to expedite the work, Arthur reversed this procedure. By August 10 the building had been completed except for the roof; but by the twenty-fifth it, too, had been constructed. The opera house was far ahead of schedule. Arthur was so elated by the amazing progress that on September 1 he invited a number of prominent Philadelphians to an alfresco supper on the newly completed roof. John Curtis recalled that stairs "had been hastily improvised through the rooms between the auditorium and outer walls and temporary, though strong railings in some open sections prevented one from taking an ignominious and probably fatal tumble to the street. Another railing had been placed around the roof far enough to act as an effective safeguard, and arc lights made the lofty and unique dining room brilliant. For music an up-to-date phonograph had been installed and Grand Opera records of famous singers provided."[5] The guests enjoyed a gargantuan repast washed down with many bottles of champagne. Curtis remembered that "corks popped with the frequency of machine gun fire, while the bubbles flowed and sparkled and exhilerated."[6]

[4] News item in the Philadelphia *Public Ledger*, June 26, 1908.

[5] John Curtis, "One Hundred Years of Grand Opera in Philadelphia" (unpublished MS, The Historical Society of Pennsylvania), III, Sec. 2, p. 521.

[6] *Ibid.*, 522.

Of the many other details in the construction of the edifice, Arthur said that he made some changes in the original plans, "the most notable being the creation of the great promenade over the lobby. It was a daring thing to do under the circumstances, because it required some changes in the steel structural work, the addition of some columns and so on, but it worked out with . . . success . . . ."[7] The stage had been made section by section in New York, and two sculptors, five modelers, and twenty-five casters made the plaster casts for the decorations of the interior.

Hammerstein Harangues Philadelphia

Meanwhile, the elder Hammerstein threatened that Philadelphia might not have its opera house after all. Before the subscription sale opened, on June 23, he stated flatly that if Philadelphians were not willing to subscribe to the projected season, he would devote the structure to other theatrical attractions. Appealing to civic pride, he hoped that this would not be necessary and that the new building would be considered "a public institution, conducted and supported by the community at large, impressive in its exterior and dignified in its beauty within."[8] The series of performances was to comprise twenty weeks, with four performances a week (Tuesday, Thursday, Saturday evenings and a Saturday matinee), prices for each, exclusive of the boxes, being five dollars to one dollar.

All places in the house were open to the general public except for the twenty-eight Grand Tier boxes, which were reserved for "representative Philadelphia families" approved by a committee composed of G. Heide Norris, who was the chairman; C. Hartman Kuhn; Francis E. Bond; Alexander Van Rensselaer; Andrew Wheeler, Jr.; and five society ladies whose names remained anonymous. Since Hammerstein was unacquainted with many prominent Philadel-

[7] Arthur Hammerstein, "Builder Tells How . . . ," *The* [Philadelphia] *North American Grand Opera Edition*, November 17, 1908, p. 9.

[8] News item in the Philadelphia *Public Ledger*, June 21, 1908.

phians, he left the details of selection to this committee. In a statement to the press, Norris made it clear that not everyone was eligible:

> "We want opera in Philadelphia . . . but we do not want the best seats in the house to go to every one who applies just because he has enough money to buy them. We want the seats in the grand tier to go to representative Philadelphia families who have a right to them. This method of selection may cause heartburnings in certain quarters, but there is nothing else to do. The boxes in the horseshoe will be select, and those who fill them will have to pass the social and financial eligibility tests which will be made by our committee and the ladies."[9]

On June 26 it was stated that the subscriptions amounted to $100,000. People, however, were slow in subscribing to the boxes and the orchestra stalls, the ostensible reason being that society and the wealthy were abroad or out of town during the summer. Hammerstein said that he was shocked by society's apathy and disappointed that some of the socially prominent people who had promised their support had not come forth with any tangible evidence of interest:

> " . . . I cannot find the slightest excuse for it; the town is full of mercantile and professional representations; your great clubs and societies certainly are not wholly deserted, depleted as they may be to a certain extent during the hot weather. The presidents and directors of your great banks and corporations have not deserted their institutions. Evidently this, for a great city, most important of all undertakings, the creation and maintenance of a permanent home for grand opera, a pride to the residents, an attraction to those intending to make Philadelphia their home, the increase in values in real estate, an instructive creation, a powerful factor in improving the morals, seems to awaken as much interest with the class just mentioned as the predicted extinction of sardines."[10]

[9] *Ibid.*, July 21, 1908.   [10] *Ibid.*, July 24, 1908.

On August 18 he made his final appeal, an ultimatum in a circular letter sent to 20,000 citizens urging them to indicate whether or not they would support the enterprise; otherwise, the structure would be devoted to dramatic presentations. Heeding this warning, Philadelphia became such a beehive of activity that by the end of the month Hammerstein was able to announce that since the advance sale was approximately $250,000, he would definitely present a season of grand opera. He also made known that the resident company would include 150 in the chorus, 80 in the orchestra, and 50 in the ballet. One galaxy of stars would appear at both his opera houses. For gala performances he intended to double the forces by employing the chorus, orchestra, and ballet of the New York house. Opening night was to be the first of these spectacular occasions. Giuseppe Sturani was to be the chief conductor in Philadelphia, though Campanini would conduct at certain performances.[11]

The following weeks saw no diminution of enthusiasm. Of paramount importance to certain elements in the city, society publicly endorsed the enterprise. Seeing the names of those who had subscribed, Hammerstein commented that he was delighted to have the support of such distinguished families.[12] *The North American* also contributed to the mounting interest in the approaching season. On September 13, 1908, the newspaper announced that on that day it was beginning a contest, which extended up to and included November 3, to give away sixty prizes to 278 of the best orchestra seats in the house for the opening season. The first prize was two seats for every Saturday evening performance; the second, two seats for fifteen Saturday evenings; the other awards were for correspondingly fewer tickets. After individuals expressed their willingness to become contestants, their names were published; friends and interested persons sent in coupons (one was printed in each issue of the paper); those collecting the most votes would be awarded the stalls. The coupons in the daily news were worth one point; the ones in the Sunday paper, five. The response was amazing! In two days' time almost one hun-

[11] News item in *The Philadelphia Inquirer*, August 29, 1908.
[12] News item in the Philadelphia *Public Ledger*, September 12, 1908.

dred persons had entered as contestants; and as the votes began to be close, the names and the number of votes for each contestant were published, so that there was intense rivalry. Circular letters were sent out on behalf of some candidates; various members of organizations and employees in shops and factories collaborated so that one of their number might be among the winners. Before the end of the first fortnight there were 1,174 contestants, the total number of votes being 261,000. Professor Adam Geibel, a Philadelphia blind musician, took an early lead; and when the awards were announced on November 15, he was ahead with a total of 134,239 votes. In the fifty-nine days of the contest readers from all over the United States and several foreign countries had sent in 3,594,350 coupons for 1,915 contestants—an average of 60,902 coupons each day or 2,538 an hour.[13] The value of this kind of publicity must have been enormous. It would seem that Philadelphia was opera mad.

At Last, the Completed Edifice

By the middle of October, 1908, the opera house was almost finished on the outside. The exterior was in the general style of the Louis XIV period. On Broad Street the frontage was 240 feet and on Poplar Street 160 feet. From the sidewalk to the elaborate cornice, the height was 75 feet; the roof above the stage, the highest part of the building, was 120 feet. Constructed of cream-colored brick, terra cotta and marble, the edifice was noble in its proportions, the façades being relieved by balconies and arched windows. At the main lobby on Poplar Street a huge marquee was placed above the five pairs of double doors. A porte-cochere protected the box holders who entered from Broad or Carlisle streets.

Inside, work went ahead rapidly; and, like the auditorium of the Manhattan, the focal point of the building was the stage, not the parterre boxes. Hammerstein maintained that a modern opera house should be so constructed that all opera-goers, regardless of their places in the house, must have an unbroken view of the stage. In a

[13] News item in *The* [Philadelphia] *North American*, November 15, 1908.

statement to the press, he said: " 'No opera house that I build will be subsidized for the rich. That is why I limited the number of [Grand Tier] boxes to twenty-eight. I believe that the architecture of the European houses represents deterioration, not growth. I wanted ours to express growth, and I believe it does.' "[14] The seating capacity was 4,200, with a ground floor accommodating 1,800 persons, a balcony of 2,000 places, and fifty-six Grand Tier and proscenium boxes.[15] The auditorium, dignified and handsome, was in the style of the Louis XVI period. The walls were of deep Tuscan red, relieved by handsome white fresco work; the proscenium arch, 52 feet wide and 40 feet high, was lavishly decorated in gold and red; at the top of it were two figures holding the coat of arms of Pennsylvania in their outstretched hands. The stage was 120 feet wide, 70 feet deep, and 90 feet to the gridiron. The ceiling was splendidly decorated in red and gold; a great canvas by Chmeilewski was in the center of the sounding board. At either side of the stage were the proscenium boxes decorated with moulded fronts. The Grand Tier boxes were suspended from the one balcony, which was sustained by massive columns of Pavanazza marble. Altogether there was 10,000 square feet of marble in columns, pilasters, and decorative balustrades. Ample space had been provided for promenades, one being behind the boxes for the pleasure of society and a *salle de promenade*, which was 140 feet long and 45 feet wide at the most narrow part, for all of the patrons.[16]

[14] "His Double Opera Life," *The* [New York] *Sun Magazine Section,* October 25, 1908, p. 2.
[15] News item in *The* [Philadelphia] *North American,* November 15, 1908.
[16] News item in *The Philadelphia Record,* November 15, 1908.

XVI

A New Opera Season—Peace for a Time

—◦◦❖◗❖◗◦◦—

HAMMERSTEIN seemed to have every reason to look forward with confidence to his third season in New York and the opening one in Philadelphia. In the 1908–1909 prospectus, he promised his New York patrons several interesting new singers, productions, revivals, in a season of twenty weeks, regular performances again being on Monday, Wednesday, Friday and Saturday evenings, with a Saturday matinee. Prices were unchanged except that Hammerstein abandoned the popular prices for Saturday evenings. He was especially pleased that he would bring forward productions of *Le Jongleur de Notre Dame* for Garden and Renaud; *Otello* for Melba, Zenatello, and Sammarco; and Strauss's *Salome* for Garden. Puccini's music would be in the repertory, as negotiations with Ricordi had been resumed in the spring of 1908. With the new directorate at the Metropolitan, it seemed likely that a more cooperative spirit would exist in New York's opera world. Hammerstein was explicit on this point. Discussing singers' salaries, he said: " 'And in the matter of artists' salaries I believe that the establishing of more friendly relations between the two opera houses would do away with the practice of having the artist use the one management as a wedge to jack up the offers of the other. Such a feeling of entente cordiale is now beginning to take root, with the new management of the Metropolitan Opera House in force and with the realization of the present ridiculously high salaries and the hopelessly extravagant cost of giving grand opera.' "[1] Of the

[1] "New York Opera Season Begins," *The New York Herald Society and Drama Section*, November 8, 1908, p. 9.

greatest importance, Hammerstein had an advance subscription in New York of $425,000, a sum more than eight times the amount of the initial season.[2]

The new dual directorate at the Metropolitan also promised an unusually brilliant season, which began on November 16 with *Aïda*, sung by Destinn, Homer, Caruso, and Scotti, with Toscanini conducting. For the first time, the company employed two separate choruses (one for the Italian-French repertory and the other for the German operas) as well as two separate orchestras of 135 players under three of the greatest conductors in the world: Toscanini, Mahler, Hertz.[3] Of the new singers, Destinn, Amato, Didur (who had left Hammerstein at the end of the last season), Frances Alda, and Herbert Witherspoon made favorable impressions in the roles they assumed and went on to enjoy outstanding careers in that opera house. A number of the productions had new settings; for when Gatti-Casazza first saw some of the antiquated sets, he was shocked and immediately set about rectifying that situation.[4] The repertory included an interesting group of novelties: Puccini's first opera, *Le Villi*; Catalani's *La Wally*; D'Albert's *Tiefland*; Smetana's *Die Verkaufte Braut*. Apparently Gatti did not intend to rely on the conventional works. During the summer he had devoted considerable time to securing rights to any new operas by Debussy, Charpentier, and Puccini.[5] It would seem that the older house was determined to regain its vitality and former brilliance, somewhat dimmed by the Manhattan's luster.

A GALA OPENING AT THE MANHATTAN

The Manhattan's third season opened on Monday, November 9, 1908, with Maria Labia, Zenatello, and Renaud in a fiery performance of *Tosca*, with Campanini conducting. It was a memorable evening, and the audience responded with enthusiastic demonstrations of approval. Labia, a member of an aristocratic Italian family and a

[2] *Ibid.*
[3] Kolodin, *The Metropolitan Opera, 1883–1935*, 140–42.
[4] Gatti-Casazza, *Memories of the Opera*, 156.
[5] *Ibid.*, 156–58.

favorite in Berlin, was an admirable Floria Tosca, although she did not efface the memory of Ternina or Eames. Her voice, not large in volume, was best in its medium register, the tones having much color; but the top notes seemed hard and somewhat constricted. As an actress, she displayed more ability and temperament than was usual on the opera stage. What was least satisfying was her costuming.[6] Zenatello, as Mario Cavaradossi, gave lavishly of his glorious voice, although a bit more subtlety in the use of it would have been desirable. For many, Renaud's Scarpia was the outstanding artistic achievement of the performance, his impersonation being "free from every melodramatic element in action, finely eloquent in its diction . . . ."[7] Campanini's reading of the score was lucid, sympathetic, masterful. The audience was brilliant; but, like the opening nights of the first two seasons, it was primarily there for the music. *Town Topics* noted, however, that there was no doubt that the *première* had brought to the Manhattan "the most fashionable assemblage it [had] yet known, [and] that [Hammerstein] could have filled again as many boxes with additional members of smart society. The many fashionables who sat in orchestra chairs were proof of that, as was the wire-pulling, which began weeks and even months ago, to secure what boxes the comparatively small house contains, while the fine gowns and splendid jewels worn on this occasion might well serve to diminish the lustre of the Metropolitan's coming *première*."[8] Among the well-known persons were the Berry Belmonts and August Belmont; the Clarence Mackays, who had Lord and Lady Northcliffe as their guests; the George Goulds; Baron and Baroness Hengelmuller; Mrs. Jack Gardner; Miss Anne Morgan; Miss Beatrice Mills; Mrs. E. H. Weatherbee; and from the Metropolitan directorate, the Otto H. Kahns and the Andreas Dippels, who were Hammerstein's guests! *Town Topics* said: "Otto Kahn had made the mistake of asking a party before he knew for a certainty whether or not he could secure accommodations, and then found he could not,

[6] *The* [New York] *Sun,* November 10, 1908.
[7] *New-York Daily Tribune,* November 10, 1908.
[8] Vol. LX (November 12, 1908), 3.

but Oscar himself came to the rescue and showed that he had no hard feelings against the directors of the rival house by giving his own box to Mr. Kahn . . . ."[9]

Mary Garden effected her re-entry in *Thaïs* at the second performance, November 11, and, as ever, was dramatically persuasive and forceful with her compelling impersonation of the Alexandrian courtesan who becomes a saint. Her voice, to some, seemed fuller in the medium register, while the higher tones had lost much of the strident quality that heretofore had marred her efforts. Other critics did not perceive any change, ruefully noting that perhaps it was "asking too much to demand an aural feast from one who so [ravished] the senses through the optic nerve."[10] There was no question that her singing was always eloquent, abounding in nuances that illuminated the meaning of the text. Renaud's impersonation of Athanaël allowed him every opportunity to reveal the different facets of his art. In his voice, facial expressions, gestures—in everything, he was the complete artist. Dalmorès, as he always did, impressed in the role of Nicias by his mien and voice. Félix Vieuille made his debut as Palemon on this occasion. According to *The New York Press*, his voice was "large, robust and resonant, a sturdy, manly organ, though lacking something, perhaps, in mellowness."[11] Of the audience at this performance, *Town Topics* noted that society was present in large numbers, Wednesday having been designated the fashionable night at the Manhattan.[12]

On Friday, November 13, Hammerstein introduced an opera that was virtually a novelty in New York: Saint-Saëns' *Samson et Dalila*. As an oratorio, it had been heard occasionally in the metropolis; but its one dramatic presentation at the Metropolitan on February 8, 1895, with Mantelli, Tamagno, Campanari, and Plançon had not created much of an impression. Hammerstein's production, however, amazed those who had thought the work not suited as an opera.

[9] *Ibid.*
[10] *The New York Press*, November 12, 1908.
[11] *Ibid.*
[12] Vol. LX (December 31, 1908), 5.

With an excellent cast, superb chorus, fine ballet, and effective *mise-en-scène*, it was a success and became a staple of the Manhattan repertory. Although Gerville-Réache, the Dalila, had appeared in various roles at the Manhattan, she had never sung so well before, nor had she made such an excellent impression as an artist. Her impersonation of the temptress had allure, warmth, and seduction; she sang with taste and authority. Philip Hale, Boston music critic, ranked her interpretation with such other supreme operatic portrayals as Calvé's earlier Carmen, Ternina's Isolde, Jean de Reszke's Roméo, Fernando de Lucia's Canio, and Victor Maurel's Iago. As Samson, Dalmorès added another superb characterization to his repertory and again impressed by his diction, vigor, personal appearance, and magnificent voice. *The Evening World* said he was "a virile, passionate, fighting man, inflamed with patriotism and with the fear of God in his heart. He [sang] lustily, without losing anything of the purity and lusciousness of his voice. By turns he [sounded] the note of the prophet, the revolutionist, the enslaved lover, the despairing captive and the glorified avenger."[13] Both Vieuille as the Old Hebrew and Dufranne as the High Priest were admirable in their respective roles. The *première danseuse*, Odette Valéry, twisting a long live snake about her arms and neck, was fascinating in her Oriental dance during the last act. The opera came to its overpowering climax when the columns of the temple, which were fifty feet high and built in sections, toppled over the sinful Philistines.

Tetrazzini's appearance this first week occurred on Saturday evening, November 14, in Rossini's ever delightful *Il Barbiere di Siviglia*, a sparkling, vivacious production. In the season before, she had revealed her ability as an ingratiating comedienne in *Crispino e la Comare*. It was no surprise, therefore, that she would be enchanting as the piquant Rosina. As for her singing, her voice seemed better than ever, the range more equalized, the tones thrilling in their clarity and brilliance. She embellished Rossini's lovely music "most liberally with all those ornaments with which she [was] most skilful. She sang all kinds of staccato leaps and progressions, chromatic scales

[13] *The* [New York] *Evening World*, November 14, 1908.

upward and downward, swells on high notes and soaring tones at the ends of airs."[14] In the lesson scene she interpolated Proch's "Air and Variations" as well as the "Bell Song" from *Lakmé*. The soprano's marvelous vocal condition promised much for the season's first *Lucia*, Wednesday, November 18. The rest of the cast for the Rossini opera was excellent except for the tenor, Angelo Parola (Almaviva), who had a voice too light for the opera house. Andrés de Segurola, making his debut as Don Basilio, at once won favor with his fine voice, artistry, and acting. Sammarco's Figaro was capital, and, as always, he sang well, though the part required more than usual lightness. Gilibert as Bartolo was inimitable, a great artist whose genius made even a small part memorable.

PLACE OF WONDERS

All during this first week of opera at the Manhattan, hundreds of workmen were busy day and night in the Philadelphia house, hammering, sawing, painting, and cleaning. Scaffolding remained in the auditorium. It did not seem possible that the building would be completed on time. Even as late as the night before the opening, plasterers, laborers, artisans, carpenters, masons, decorators, and painters were still at work. By four o'clock the afternoon of the *première*, only half the orchestra seats were in place.[15] However, when the public was admitted that evening, the house was ready. John Curtis recalled that "the cleaners with their brooms and mops were going out the back way as the audience began to enter by the front."[16] Nevertheless, Hammerstein, routing his detractors, had accomplished what he promised: Philadelphia had the opera house. And all had been brought to pass since the demolition of the old Harrah mansion on March 30! It is not surprising that there were those who referred to the miracle as Aladdin's palace.

The Philadelphia Opera House opened on Tuesday, November

[14] *The* [New York] *Sun*, November 15, 1908.
[15] John Curtis, "One Hundred Years of Grand Opera in Philadelphia" (unpublished MS, The Historical Society of Pennsylvania), III, Sec. 2, p. 531.
[16] *Ibid.*, 532.

17, 1908, with Labia, Dalmorès, De Segurola, Zeppilli in Bizet's *Carmen*. Never had the city seen anything like it. An estimated total of 1,800 vehicles wound their way to the opera house, choking the main avenues. On Broad Street seven rows of automobiles and carriages, extending from curb to curb, made it impossible for any other traffic to proceed northward. Mounted policemen galloped about the jumble, trying to keep the vehicles moving. It was virtually impossible. According to the *Public Ledger*, the situation was chaotic as the "[h]orses reared, plunged, pressed forward, automobiles twisted and skimmed under the noses of frightened steeds, the seven lines wove into each other, turned, twisted out, came back . . . ."[17] Many caught in this mass became exasperated and decided to go on foot, only to find that they had to press their way through the hundreds of people standing about the entrances of the house, gazing upon the splendors of society and the magnificent new structure itself, which was ablaze with light. Once inside, patrons were assisted by ushers, footmen, and uniformed maids, who knew the seating arrangement to perfection. Hammerstein had not forgotten the inconveniences of the opening night at the Manhattan Opera House almost two years before and had drilled these personnel so that there would not be an analogous situation.

The auditorium was imposing, "transplendent with light and the glint of golden carvings that [stood] out boldly against wide walls of crimson."[18] Patrons, no doubt, looked about with pleasure and awe at these new surroundings. They also must have given much attention to the boxes; and to assist them, Hammerstein had included a list of box holders in the programmes, an unheard of practice in his New York house.

It is interesting to recall the members of society occupying boxes at the opening night ritual. In box 15 were C. Hartman Kuhn, J. Gardner Cassatt, Thomas Leaming, Dr. Joseph Leidy. Also present were Mrs. Charles W. Henry, Samuel F. Huston, Dr. George Woodward in Box 17; Dr. S. Lewis Fiegler in 19; Mrs. J. Dundas

[17] News item in the Philadelphia *Public Ledger*, November 18, 1908.

[18] News item in *The* [Philadelphia] *North American*, November 18, 1908.

Lippincott in 21; Richard Y. Cook, George H. Earle, George H. Frazier, James L. Sullivan in 23; Alexander Van Rensselaer, Robert K. Cassatt, Drexel Paul in 27; Isaac H. Clothier, Jr. in 29; George D. Widener in 31; Theodore W. Cramp in 33; George W. Norris, Robert W. Lesley, Edward B. Smith, William Hinckle Smith in 35; J. N. Pew in 20; William Disston in 22. Other boxes held Alexander B. Coxe, Charles E. Coxe, Henry B. Coxe, William T. Wright, R. W. Meirs, Mrs. J. J. Alter, Mrs. H. P. Sauers, C. Howard Clark, Jr., Rodman E. Griscom, Mrs. Henry Pratt McKean, Joseph B. Townsend, George W. Elkins, Edgar Scott, Frederick Thurston Mason, Mrs. Francis L. Potts.

Not only was Philadelphia society in the audience, but almost every principal member of the company attended the opening, Garden and Tetrazzini perhaps being the most observed among them. The city was officially represented by Mayor Reyburn; the state, by Governor Stuart, who had journeyed from Harrisburg for this historic occasion. The house greeted both dignitaries with thunderous applause, *The North American* rhapsodizing that as they took their places "every light in the immense auditorium flared its finest and the cupids on the boxfronts looked as if they might soar away for very gladness ...."[19] In short, it was a gala evening, one long to be remembered.

At 8:30, fifteen minutes after the scheduled time, Campanini entered the pit and was greeted by prolonged applause. After bowing to his wife, who was in a proscenium box, he lifted his baton and led the augmented orchestra (160 members) in the "Star-Spangled Banner." When it was completed, the audience of approximately 5,000 people applauded and cheered.[20] Immediately afterward the performance got underway and was in progress until 12:20. It was something of a revelation to Philadelphia, for never before had the city seen such an excellent production of *Carmen*. The *Public Ledger* said that "it was the general perfection of detail, the combined beauties of lyricism, of orchestration, of mise-en-scene, that removed the

[19] *Ibid.*

[20] News item in *The* [Philadelphia] *Press*, November 18, 1908.

Hammerstein *Carmen* quite beyond the pale of precedent."[21] The crowd scenes were impressive with many supernumeraries and the huge, magnificent choruses of both the New York and Philadelphia houses. These performers amazed the first-night audience, singing with brilliance and verve and moving about on the stage naturally, instead of seeming like the wooden automatons of the traditional opera company. Labia was a most attractive Carmen pictorially but disappointing dramatically. Her interpretation of the tempestuous Spanish gypsy was tame, lacking seduction, diablerie, wantonness. Dalmorès (Don José) and Zeppilli (Micaëla) were highly praised; and De Segurola (Escamillo), encored for his second act aria, sang with authority and ardor. Campanini seemed inspired. Throughout the entire performance the audience gave rapt attention to all the proceedings on stage; and when it was over, they did not rush to leave immediately but remained in their seats for a moment, "gazing round about them at the brilliant house, then slowly preparing themselves, made their way to the street."[22]

All during the opera Hammerstein remained at stage left, sitting in his old chair which had been brought from New York. He was immensely pleased by the performance and by the comments of the singers, who told him that the acoustics were perfect and that the house itself was magnificent. Others congratulated him, the press noting, in particular, the visit of Otto H. Kahn and Andreas Dippel, who were in Philadelphia with the Metropolitan. Once again these two gentlemen from the rival company honored Hammerstein by their presence at another opening. It would seem indeed that at last peace reigned between the two houses and that a new day had dawned on the opera world. According to *The Philadelphia Inquirer*, Kahn said to Hammerstein:

"Mr. Hammerstein, you are a genius . . . . For years I have been watching you, and every day that passes my admiration for you increased.

[21] Philadelphia *Public Ledger*, November 18, 1908.
[22] News item in *The* [Philadelphia] *Press*, November 18, 1908.

"The house is magnificent. No one but you could have built it in the incredible short time. I doubted, at first, that you could do it. But then I knew that Oscar Hammerstein was back of the project, and I jotted down in a notebook that the Philadelphia Opera House would be completed on time.

"I think the house is one of the greatest in the world and I most heartily congratulate you. It is a great achievement in your wondrous career!"[23]

The audience had its opportunity at the end of the second act. During one of the many recalls, Hammerstein appeared on the stage; and the assemblage, shouting and applauding, rose to its feet in respect to him who had made it all possible. When the tumult subsided, Hammerstein made a brief speech:

"I wasn't embarrassed at the prospect of building this house, but I am embarrassed now. Under ordinary circumstances one would feel hilarious on an occasion such as this, but while I am gratified at your applause, I cannot help harboring a feeling of sadness when I wonder whether this house will remain the home of grand opera for years to come.

It is for you to decide and it is for you to make it the greatest opera house of the world. I have done my part. I promised, and I have fulfilled. I have not come here as a shopkeeper or a producer of operas, wholesale or retail. I have come to ask your aid in promoting great music, which is like misfortune since it makes us all akin.

When some months ago I was asked to come here and show the difference between real grand opera and attempts at grand opera, I was pleased, but I never hoped for such satisfaction as is mine tonight. Take me as a friend and not as a merchant, and when at the end of this season I have artistically completed what I intend to do, call me out again and tell me you are satisfied."[24]

[23] News item in *The Philadelphia Inquirer*, November 18, 1908.
[24] News item in the Philadelphia *Public Ledger*, November 18, 1908.

At the end of these remarks, several members of the chorus raised Hammerstein onto their shoulders, much to his discomfort, while the company and audience applauded and roared their approval. It must have been another supreme moment in the impresario's life.

The very same evening the Metropolitan opened its season at the Academy of Music with Caruso and Sembrich in *La Bohème*. During the summer the auditorium had been renovated. For years it had been neglected, but Hammerstein's challenge galvanized the directors of the venerable structure into action. Freshly painted walls, new seats, attractive box draperies and refurbished scenery contributed to the pleasure of the patrons and to the resplendence of the occasion. There was also a new smoking room which was only for men. Though there was the rival attraction uptown, each box in the double horseshoe was filled with representative Philadelphians; and every seat as well as standing space was occupied. The Academy seemed as impregnable as ever with members of the old families in force, ostensibly oblivious to the new house; however, after the second act many of the boxholders, having heard an exceptionally spirited performance, left the Academy to complete the evening at the new temple of music. Their social prestige was not to be in jeopardy.

For the second presentation at the new house, which was more brilliant socially than the *première*, Hammerstein brought forward *Samson et Dalila* with Gerville-Réache and Dalmorès, under the baton of Sturani. Philadelphia had never seen the work in operatic form, though the local choral society had presented it in concert style in 1906. Society, not having to divide its allegiance, was present in greater numbers than at the opening night performance. Women looked superb in their Parisian toilettes, which, "with their Directoire and Empire tones, gave a note of Old Worldliness to the scene resembling a salon of the Napoleonic era";[25] their escorts were worthy complements to this elegance. Also in the audience were approximately four hundred clergymen who had accepted Hammerstein's

[25] News item in *The* [Philadelphia] *Evening Bulletin*, November 20, 1908.

invitation to be his guests.[26] Since there had already been adverse criticisms against the proposed production of *Salome*, Hammerstein was eager to have the men of cloth see for themselves that an operatic version of a Biblical episode need not be sacrilegious. He succeeded in his purpose. The following day the ministers, impressed by what they had seen and heard, said that they had found nothing offensive in the work. It had been a beautiful experience. Hammerstein concluded that since there had been no objections to *Samson et Dalila*, he could not see why there should be any protest against Strauss's *Salome*. It is significant that he did not extend the clergymen an invitation to see this opera. Their comments might have made interesting reading. The second performance, however, was highly successful from every viewpoint. Conservative Philadelphia had reason to be proud of the new house. A social commentator in the *Press* wrote:

> To one who had been at the Academy Tuesday there came insistently throughout the promenade a challenge of comparison. And then came the baffling consciousness that here was no ground for comparison after all, but, instead, for contrast. Here was no possibility of saying "This is better than that," or "this is weak where that is strong." Here was only difference—a difference that fascinated, that made the Academy seem dearer than ever, the Opera House more beautiful, more magnificent, more satisfying, than one could have hoped.[27]

Hammerstein concluded the first week in Philadelphia on Saturday, November 21, with Tetrazzini in *Il Barbiere di Siviglia* at the matinee and Labia, Zenatello, and Sammarco in *Tosca* that evening. As usual at a Tetrazzini performance the crowd was immense; approximately fifty policemen attempted to preserve order. The prima donna was in marvelous voice. After singing the "Bell Song" as an encore in the Lesson Scene, she concurred in the opinion of her col-

[26] News item in *The* [Philadelphia] *North American*, November 20, 1908.

[27] News item in *The* [Philadelphia] *Press*, November 20, 1908.

leagues: the acoustics of the auditorium were perfect.[28] Tetrazzini said that this aria was the most difficult one in her repertory; yet singing it in the new house had been easy. As Tosca, Labia impressed the Philadelphians more than she had as Carmen. Zenatello won instant favor, singing with fervor and pealing tones; critics thought that Sammarco's interpretation of the evil chief of the Roman police, however, was not the equal in finish to the exponent of Scarpia with whom Philadelphia was more familiar: Antonio Scotti.[29] Hammerstein, at any rate, must have been gratified by the financial record of this first week in Philadelphia; the presentations had brought in $31,919 at the box office.[30]

The performance of *Thaïs* with the regular cast on Tuesday, November 24, was the notable feature of the second week at the new house, which also offered *Lucia* with Tetrazzini, Taccani, and Polese on Thursday; a repetition of *Samson et Dalila* at the Saturday matinee; and *Les Huguenots* that evening. The Meyerbeer opera had been revived at the Manhattan Opera House on November 20 without the stellar cast this work requires. Of the singers, Zenatello, Sammarco, and De Segurola were the most admired in their respective roles. These operas pleased the Philadelphia critics who were impressed by the stars, the stage pictures, the orchestra, and the chorus. What created the most profound effect, however, was the ensemble. The Philadelphia *Press* said:

> It is this combination that is the special gift of Mr. Hammerstein to Philadelphia. What has been done in the last ten years for the contemporary stage and for the frothiest of musical comedies in the way of unsurpassed presentation, he has done for opera. Each scene at the Philadelphia Opera House is an object lesson in all that is excellent in stage management, and the beauty of it enhances the value of the music and the

---

[28] News item in *The* [Philadelphia] *North American*, November 22, 1908.

[29] *The* [Philadelphia] *Evening Bulletin*, November 23, 1908.

[30] News item in the Philadelphia *Public Ledger*, January 7, 1909.

singing and the action to an unusual degree. If there should be any shortcomings on the part of the singers, at least there is everything in their surroundings, as Mr. Hammerstein mounts his operas, that should encourage them to do their level best.[31]

What Hammerstein had accomplished in opera production was beginning to sink in; and Philadelphia, according to Curtis, was at the impresario's feet.[32]

A "Miracle" Opera, Several Debuts, and Melba's Return

Meanwhile, in New York, the company was rehearsing for the American *première* of Massenet's "miracle" opera, *Le Jongleur de Notre Dame*. The cast was of more than usual interest. Although the role of the Juggler had heretofore been assumed by a tenor, Hammerstein assigned the part to Mary Garden. According to her, the inspiration for this innovation had come not from the impresario but from Maurice Renaud,[33] the creator of the role of Boniface at the opera's world *première* in 1902. Fortunately Hammerstein acted on the suggestion, for Garden was marvelous, adding another triumphant characterization, a veritable tour de force, to a gallery of memorable creations. New York opera-goers who had already been amazed by her versatility in such roles as Thaïs, Louise, and Mélisande were now to admire her anew for her superlative interpretation of Jean, Our Lady's Juggler.

Of the many parts in which she appeared, Garden seems to have had a marked preference for the poor Juggler. She confessed that it was difficult to sing,[34] since the tones had to be colored in a way that suggested a boy's voice before it changes; yet she found that this lad, whose only offerings to the Virgin were his Juggler's tricks, was one of the most rewarding roles in her varied repertory. The purists, no

[31] News item in *The* [Philadelphia] *Press*, November 25, 1908.

[32] Curtis, "One Hundred Years . . . " (unpublished MS, The Historical Society of Pennsylvania), III, Sec. 2, p. 535.

[33] Garden and Biancolli, *Mary Garden's Story*, 131.

[34] *Ibid.*, 132.

doubt, were distraught at such transvestitism; but the critics, on the whole, and the public liked the novelty. Massenet, however, did not. The composer expressed admiration for Garden's success in the opera but confessed that he was "somewhat bewildered . . . at seeing the monk discard his frock after the performance and resume an elegant costume from the Rue de la Paix."[35] Massenet's remarks are tempered; but the English translator of his memoirs, H. Villiers Barnett, relates that the composer was indignant, "simply furious."[36] For this reason, it seems strange that there has been any question about whether or not Massenet changed the score from tenor to soprano in order to accommodate Garden. At the time of the American *première*, De Koven stated explicitly that Garden sang it exactly as written and that there was no alteration made in the music allotted to her.[37] Irving Kolodin, however, says that the role had been adapted for Garden;[38] and others have commented on Massenet's modifying the part for the soprano.[39] Years later Garden, the center of this controversy, told Sheean that she had sung it precisely as Massenet had written it.[40] And, after all, she is the one who should know.

The first American performance of *Le Jongleur de Notre Dame* was at the Manhattan Opera House on Friday, November 27, 1908, with Garden as the Juggler, Renaud as Boniface, Dufranne as the Prior, Vallès as Monk Poet, De Segurola as the Monk Painter, Vieuille as the Monk Sculptor, Crabbé as the Monk Musician, and Gherkier, Zuro, and Pieruci. Campanini conducted. Critics declared that even though there were few moments of inspired writing in the score, Massenet's music was, at all times, melodious and charming. It was a refreshing, delightful, heart-warming work. Henderson, in the New York *Sun*, said: "The necessary summary is that it will please

---

[35] Jules Massenet, *My Recollections* (trans. by H. Villiers Barnett), 237–38.
[36] *Ibid.*, 238.
[37] *The* [New York] *World*, November 28, 1908.
[38] Kolodin, *The Metropolitan Opera 1883–1935*, 147.
[39] Wallace Brockway and Herbert Weinstock, *The Opera*, 438.
[40] Sheean, *Oscar Hammerstein I*, 263.

most operagoers without exciting the town and that it provides a most suitable medium for the display of Miss Garden's gifts."[41] De Koven thought that the entire opera revealed "evidence of its composer's wonderful knowledge and power of expression of telling dramatic effect" and that the "instrumentation [was] varied and full of color; beautifully clear and balanced . . . ."[42]

As for the singers, De Koven wrote that Garden "certainly made a fascinating boy in figure and mien, graceful, artless and wholly natural and unaffected, while her action was characterized by a sweetness and sympathy with underlying touches of sly humor which gave charm and constant variety to her impersonation."[43] The climax of her performance was the offering of the Juggler's art to the Virgin; then, as before, her whole action was spontaneous and affecting. For Garden it must have been a moment of exalted spiritual ecstasy. Her singing was eloquent; Pitts Sanborn, of the *Globe*, thought that her voice had "probably never sounded so free, so round, so steady."[44] Other critics concurred with this viewpoint, although a few still detected a shrillness in the upper tones. Renaud also enjoyed a great success. When he first appeared on stage riding astride a donkey, the audience did not seem to recognize him; for his make-up (and he was a past master in this art!) was superb. As the jolly friar, he held flowers for the Madonna, while vegetables bulged from his baskets at the sides of the animal. Throughout the opera his singing was artistic; and his rendition of the aria *"Légende de la Sauge,"* memorable. The other principals were meritorious. In fact, different critics commented that nowhere else in the world were there such fine male voices in one cast.

The production was beautifully mounted, with an excellent chorus and orchestra. Campanini once again demonstrated his extraordinary ability to conduct a French opera with complete mastery and

[41] November 28, 1908.
[42] *The* [New York] *World*, November 28, 1908.
[43] *Ibid.*
[44] *The* [New York] *Globe and Commercial Advertiser*, November 28, 1908.

understanding. He was at the podium for the seven other performances of the work at the Manhattan during the season. He also
conducted three of the six presentations of the opera in Philadelphia,
where it was heard the first time on December 3. The Quaker City
was as charmed as New York: *The North American* praised the
"[e]xquisite music, singing actors of profound intelligence and the
very ultimate in stagecraft . . . ."[45]

The beginning of December saw several interesting debuts at
the Manhattan Opera House. The first was Jeanne Espinasse, who
appeared as Nedda, on December 4, in the season's initial *I Pagliacci*,
which was paired with *Cavalleria Rusticana*. The critic of the *Herald*
thought she had a "light, pleasing voice that [rang] true and brilliantly."[46] The following evening Florencio Constantino, the superb
Spanish tenor, made his New York debut with the company in *Rigoletto*. Philadelphia had already heard him as the philandering Duke
on December 1. To the New York critics, he was the lyric tenor the
company had so sorely needed since Bonci's departure; his voice with
its exquisite tone, lusciousness, and brilliance was a perfect comple-
ment to Tetrazzini's. Pitts Sanborn thought that Constantino possessed "an agreeable stage presence, a beautiful voice, facility in song
and action, and abundant verve."[47] The other leading singers, Tetrazzini and Sammarco, were in excellent form. Of the soprano, Sanborn, like many critics, noted that this season her singing was far more
beautiful than before: "The crudities and inequalities that marred
much of her singing a year go were scarcely in evidence Saturday.
Instead there was an attention to the finer things of vocal style that
one hardly dared look for then, and far from losing brilliancy in gaining refinement, her singing seemed, if possible, more brilliant than
ever. 'Caro Nome' she sang exceedingly well, closing it with a dazzling display of bravura. Applauded to the echo, she sang the aria a
second time even better, with a more appealing delicacy, a more

[45] *The* [Philadelphia] *North American*, December 4, 1908.
[46] *The New York Herald*, December 5, 1908.
[47] *The* [New York] *Globe and Commercial Advertiser*, December
7, 1908.

enchanting finesse, and she had an entire new set of vocal ornaments for the close."[48] Campanini's rule of no repeats was held in abeyance; there were four encores on this occasion. The same hysteria was evident when these principals appeared in the season's initial *La Traviata* on December 12. Hammerstein was indeed fortunate in these three extraordinary artists, true exponents of *bel canto*.

Melba's return had been eagerly anticipated. She reappeared on Monday, December 14, 1908, in *La Bohème*, with a superlative cast that included Zenatello, Trentini, Gilibert, De Segurola, Sammarco, Gianoli-Galletti, a group of singers perhaps impossible to duplicate in any other opera company in the world. When the beloved soprano first appeared on stage, the house, filled to capacity, burst into wild applause, at once leaving no doubt whatsoever of the esteem and affection which the Manhattan opera-goers held for her. After the tumult subsided, she began to sing somewhat tentatively, apparently overexcited or nervous; but as the performance continued, Melba was her magical self, the perfect artist and vocalist, glorifying Puccini's music with her phenomenal voice. Always singing without a trace of effort, she sustained tones that were sumptuous, velvety, smooth. It was still a voice of ineluctable loveliness, although perhaps not quite so crystalline as in the past. Whatever it may have lost, however, was compensated for by a more profound eloquence in her singing, a deeper artistry, and more attention to the dramatic requirements of the role. Henderson observed that "what it has lost in silver it has gained in gold. It is still youthful and a warmer, more winning, more touching voice to-day than it ever was before; and better than all, it is backed by a more beautiful sincerity and a more rounded musicianship."[49] Of course, the diva did not look the part, as she had gained in weight and in years; but the exquisite voice and flawless musicianship carried all before her. The others in the cast, inspired by her presence, gave a rousing performance, wholeheartedly entering into the spirit of the occasion.

Several days later, on December 17, Hammerstein presented

[48] *Ibid.*
[49] *The*]New York] *Sun,* December 15, 1908.

Bohème in Philadelphia with virtually the same cast. What made Melba's return particularly significant was that she was appearing as Mimi, a part which she had first essayed on a stage in Philadelphia. That had occurred almost ten years before, December 30, 1898.[50] Her last appearance in opera there had been in 1904. For these reasons, Philadelphians were eager to pay homage to the long-absent diva; Melba, in turn, was anxious to sing for them and to appear in the new opera house. Before the opening of the season, she had written a brief message, printed in the November 17, 1908, issue of *The North American*:

> Mr. Hammerstein is a wonderful genius in opera. He has done so much for opera, and against such odds to begin with, that it makes me believe that impresarios, like singers, are born and not made. I am glad to be one who will assist in the inauguration of his great enterprise in Philadelphia, for I am certain that it will prove a most important factor in the making of the history of music in America.[51]

The evening was a triumph. The entire house was sold out. It was reported that there were more carriages in line than at any other time since the opening. The *Press* observed that the performance was the signal "for a gathering of 'everyone in town,' the like of which is usually known only on 'opening nights.' With the possible exception of the stupendous 'first night' last month, the opera last evening was beyond question the most brilliant social event of the Winter season."[52] On stage there was tremendous excitement, Melba having a glamour and prestige unrivaled in the opera world. For a time, however, there were some doubts whether or not she would sing, since she had been suffering from a slight throat ailment. Ordinarily, under these circumstances, she would not have appeared; but, as she

---

[50] *The* [Philadelphia] *Press*, December 18, 1908.

[51] Nellie Melba, "Singers Born, Not Made, Says Melba," *The* [Philadelphia] *North American Grand Opera Edition*, November 17, 1908, p. 1.

[52] News item in *The* [Philadelphia] *Press*, December 18, 1908.

said, " 'That wizard [Hammerstein] can make me do almost anything.' "[53] She had no reason to regret her decision to go on with the performance, for she was in perfect voice. Melba also seems to have been in excellent spirits. Coming offstage at the end of the first act, she said to Hammerstein, sitting in his usual place, with the ubiquitous cigar in his mouth: " 'I have never sung in such a house. It is simply delightful. All one has to do is to open one's mouth, and the house does the rest. You are a wonder. But how dare you smoke in my presence, you beast?' " Hammerstein, understanding the soprano very well, assumed an air of abject humility, which achieved its desired effect. Bursting into laughter, Melba said: " 'Oh, smoke away, you old fraud!' "[54]

Later in the evening Hammerstein joined the crowd in the promenade, an unusual action for him. When he came backstage, he remarked:

"Well, Philadelphia society is doing its full share in making this the house beautiful. What an audience. I tell you that you can't see anything like it in Europe. Such magnificence of wardrobe, such beauty, such refinement. It is glorious, and to see it makes me happy. But it is mighty expensive happiness. I pay Melba $3,000, Zenatello $1200, and royalties for the opera $250. There is about $5000 for those three items. Tonight costs me a lot of money more than the receipts. Still I am happy."[55]

The only new role in which Melba appeared was as Desdemona in Verdi's *Otello*, first presented at the Manhattan Opera House on Friday, December 25, 1908. The opera had not been given at the Metropolitan for six years, the artists at that time being Eames, Alvarez and Scotti. Hammerstein's production of this masterpiece was superb. According to De Koven, there was "a fervid sweep of

[53] "Oscar Inspects Operas from His Seat in Wings," *The* [Philadelphia] *North American Theatre Section*, December 20, 1908, p. 8.
[54] *Ibid.*
[55] *Ibid.*

passionate intensity that fairly whirled one along in a rush of varied emotions and made the atmosphere seem even overcharged with a vibrant force that was electrical."[56] Although Melba's impersonation was attractive and artistic, her singing was somewhat disappointing; for in her efforts to make her voice more dramatic, she lost some quality in her tones. However, in the last act her singing of the "Salce! Salce!" and "Ave Maria" was ravishing to the ears.[57] Zenatello, as the Moor, found the role congenial to his robust style; in fact, he had never appeared to greater advantage and scored a triumph with his passionate singing, emotional feeling, and dramatic ardor. As Iago, Sammarco was vocally magnificent, but he left something to be desired histrionically. Even so, what an evening this must have been! Zenatello's thrilling "Esultate!," Sammarco's intense singing of the "Credo," Zenatello's impassioned outburst of "Ora e per sempre addio," the two men's voices blending in the duet at the end of the second act, and Melba's angelic singing in the last act—all were treasured, ineffable moments in an overwhelming performance. Krehbiel, comparing the novelties at the Manhattan and this production of *Otello* to the new presentations at the Metropolitan this season as well as the one before, remarked: "As any one of Mr. Hammerstein's new productions last season made *Adriana Lecouvreur* and *Fedora* sink into insignificance, so *Otello* this season is likely to wipe out all memories of *Le Villi* and *Tiefland*."[58]

Too soon came the time for Melba to say farewell. Her final appearance in Philadelphia was at the Saturday matinee of January 9 in *La Traviata*. She had been heard there but two other times with the company, both being in *La Bohème*. Since the patrons who held subscriptions for Saturday evenings had not had an opportunity to hear her, Hammerstein invited them to attend the afternoon performance as his guests. Any lingering doubts as to the condition of her voice were set at rest. She sang more brilliantly than at her other

[56] *The* [New York] *World,* December 26, 1908.

[57] *The* [New York] *Globe and Commercial Advertiser,* December 26, 1908.

[58] *New-York Daily Tribune,* December 26, 1908.

appearances in the house, which was filled to its capacity. The music critic of the *Press* said: "From her very first utterance there was evidence of her splendid form, and all through the performance she not only sang with remarkable volume, but with all her old purity of tone in the whole range of her voice and with great brilliancy. Moreover, as if in an effort to give her audience more than it might naturally demand of the greatest florid singer of her time, Tetrazzini not excepted, a number of the arias were sung in a diminished tone, pure gold drawn to the finest thread, with a pathetic delicacy of shading that gave the sentiment of the words a double meaning."[59] At all times her singing demonstrated that she remained the prima donna *assoluta* whose star was still fixed in the firmament.

On January 11 Melba bid adieu to New York in *Rigoletto*, with an all-star cast: Renaud, Constantino, Gilibert, and Arimondi. It was the largest house of the season. Again the soprano was in excellent voice, "her tones having all their old-time lusciousness, rounded beauty, and freshness."[60] The audience seemed reluctant to let the singers go; and at the end the tributes to Melba were for her not only as an artist but also as a woman. Flowers, numerous recalls, cheers, her Australian countrymen's cries of the bushmen's "Coo-e-e!"—all must have lingered long in her memory. In the four weeks Melba was with the company she appeared in ten performances. In New York she sang in three *Bohème*s, three *Otello*s and one *Rigoletto*, while in Philadelphia she was seen in *La Bohème* two times and in *La Traviata* once.

During Melba's engagement Hammerstein revived three operas in New York: *Les Contes d'Hoffmann* (December 16), *Pelléas et Mélisande* (January 6), and *Crispino e la Comare* (January 9), while *Il Trovatore* re-entered the repertory in Philadelphia on December 19. The excellence of the Offenbach work was due primarily to the presence of the superb male singers: Renaud, Dalmorès, Gilibert, Daddi, and Gianoli-Galletti. On the distaff side, Hammerstein offered Zeppilli (Olympia), Espinasse (Giulietta), and the

[59] *The* [Philadelphia] *Press*, January 10, 1909.
[60] *The* [New York] *Evening Post*, January 12, 1909.

inimitable Trentini (Antonia). The cast in the Debussy opera was different from that of the preceding season. Dalmorès replaced Périer as Pelléas; Vieuille was cast as Ärkel; and Trentini, replacing Sigrist, was Little Yniold. Usually successful in the roles he essayed, Dalmorès, too vital a figure, seemed woefully miscast as the dreamy, shadowy legendary creature. *The Sun* said that he was not at all familiar with the style of the opera, that he seemed uncomfortable in the part.[61] Vieuille, the original Ärkel in Paris, was superb, even magnificent in this role, which had never been adequately interpreted by Arimondi. He "brought out the really noble music, as well as the sympathy and tenderness of the old king for all his suffering children."[62] According to De Koven, the performance, with Garden as the poetic Mélisande, still remained "vocally, scenically, dramatically and orchestrally the most complete and artistic ever seen in New York."[63] The opera was performed four times at the Manhattan Opera House this season and once in Philadelphia, where it was not a success and where the "great audience heard with bewildered ears . . . ."[64] The Ricci brothers' delightful *Crispino e la Comare* was another warhorse for Tetrazzini, who afforded much pleasure with her singing; and Gianoli-Galletti was excellent in the *buffo* part of the cobbler. At Philadelphia, Verdi's *Il Trovatore* with Agostinelli (Leonora), Doria (Azucena), Zenatello (Manrico), and Fossetta (di Luna) was not a distinguished performance, although Zenatello thrilled the audience by his ringing high tones.

[61] *The* [New York] *Sun,* January 7, 1909.
[62] *The* [New York] *Evening World,* January 7, 1909.
[63] *The* [New York] *World,* January 10, 1909.
[64] *The* [Philadelphia] *North American,* February 10, 1909.

XVII

Grave Problems, but Ultimate Victory

O STENSIBLY Hammerstein had every reason to rejoice, the season thus far having been unusually brilliant. The company had been liberally supported in both New York and Philadelphia. For the first seven weeks, the box office receipts in the Philadelphia house alone totaled $191,391.[1] Since there were four presentations a week, approximately $6,835 was the average intake for each performance during this period. The actual receipts were as follows:

Week November 17	$31,919
Week November 24	27,808
Week December 1	25,692
Week December 8	26,629
Week December 15	26,977
Week December 22	24,702
Week December 29	27,664[2]

Hammerstein considered these sums " 'phenomenal when the infancy of the great work [was] taken into consideration' "[3] and said that they indicated that " 'Philadelphia [could] support an opera house of its own.' "[4] Citizens of Baltimore, which had heretofore been a Metropolitan Opera satellite, had been clamoring for some appearances of the Manhattan at their Lyric Theatre. Amenable to the

[1] News item in the Philadelphia *Public Ledger*, January 7, 1909.
[2] *Ibid.*
[3] News item in *The* [Philadelphia] *Press*, January 7, 1909.
[4] *Ibid.*

pleas, Hammerstein scheduled one performance each of *Lucia* and *La Traviata* for early January, 1909, with the ever-popular Tetrazzini starring in both operas. This further excursion into Metropolitan territory must have sent chills down the spines of the directors at the older house. All things considered, the Manhattan appeared to be second to none in prestige and power, the future auguring of continued success. It seemed that Hammerstein was steering his ship of opera on a steady keel, apparently getting safely to port. Nevertheless, for some time, the impresario had seen the storm gathering on the horizon and had realized that a major crisis loomed ahead unless he could obtain additional funds to satisfy financial demands. The maintenance of two opera houses was becoming increasingly onerous.

In May, 1910, Arthur Hammerstein revealed the expenses of the 1909–1910 season.[5] No doubt those figures were comparable to the expenditures for the opera performances in New York and Philadelphia during the 1908–1909 season. Arthur said that in 1909–1910 it had cost his father approximately $55,000 a week to maintain both houses and that the total expenditures for a season of twenty weeks in the two metropolises required about $1,100,000. Of this amount, the leading artists received $500,000. In the season of 1909–1910 Hammerstein paid Tetrazzini $1,500 a performance and guaranteed her forty performances; Garden received $1,400 each performance and contracted for at least twenty engagements, although she sang many more than these; Gerville-Réache received $436.50 for each performance; Renaud, $1,000; Sammarco, $1,000; and Dalmorès, $600. Each week Gilibert was paid $750; Dufranne, $700; Crabbé, $360. The Manhattan orchestra of 85 men cost $6,000 a week. For certain operas Hammerstein had to hire more instrumentalists, adding even more expense. Campanini had received $1,000 per week. Arthur continued:

"The men in the orchestra had to give us a two-hour

[5] Sylvester Rawling, "What Opera Singers Really Are Paid Told Frankly by Arthur Hammerstein," *The* [New York] *Evening World*, May 7, 1910, p. 4.

rehearsal every day without extra charge, but for special rehearsals . . . they had to be paid from $1 an hour up, according to their wages. If on Sunday we tried to rehearse anything but the evening concert that meant more extra pay, too.

"Our chorus cost us $2,500 a week. The salaries ranged from $20 to $30 for each individual. Then there was the ballet at $700 a week and the stage band at $650 a week. The stage hands cost $3,000 a week. For our four storage warehouses, in which we kept the scenery, we paid $1,000 a month, and for shifting scenery our expenditure was $1,000 a week. Then there was the expense of what is called 'the front of the house,' clerks, ushers, doormen, etc., $2,500 a week. Add to this $30,000 a season for the return passage from Europe of principals and chorus . . . ."[6]

For the right to produce *Salome* and *Elektra*, Hammerstein had to pay $500 a performance for the former opera and $800 a performance for the latter, provided that he presented each of them six times a season. Hammerstein paid 3,000 francs each for *Thaïs*, *Louise*, *Le Jongleur*, *Sapho*, *Grisélidis*, and *Hérodiade* before he was allowed to include any one of them in a season's repertory. Each time he presented one of these he paid an additional 500 francs. As for *Pelléas et Mélisande*, $400 was required for the right to produce it in any season as well as $100 for every presentation at the opera house. The terms for *Samson et Dalila* were $100 a performance.[7]

In constructing the Philadelphia Opera House, Hammerstein not only invested much capital but borrowed $200,000 from the Philadelphia Northern Trust Company, mortgaging the ground on which the new opera house stood and providing a collateral mortgage on the Manhattan Opera House.[8] What he desired was a loan of $400,000 so that the obligation on the New York house would be released and so that he would have some additional working capital.

[6] *Ibid.*

[7] *Metropolitan Opera Company* v. *Oscar Hammerstein and Arthur Hammerstein*, File No. 18094–1913 (1914), p. 43.

[8] *The* [Philadelphia] *Press*, January 7, 1909.

Hammerstein explained the situation to G. Heide Norris, his staunch supporter and counsel, and asked his assistance in obtaining the money, offering as collateral a mortgage on the Philadelphia house. Norris agreed, began a subscription, and soon had $250,000 pledged. The only difficulty was that the gentlemen who were willing to advance this sum looked upon it as a business arrangement and asked for additional security on the loan—namely, a mortgage on the Manhattan Opera House. Hammerstein was incensed, and absolutely refused to do as they wished. He could not understand why the new house, which he claimed had cost $1,250,000,[9] was not sufficient security. The financiers maintained, however, that the property was worth its full value only as long as it was devoted to opera. If this were abandoned, its worth would diminish, for the structure would not be a source for much revenue if it were used for other purposes. Angered by their business proposition, Hammerstein would accept neither this argument nor the loan on such terms.

The public first heard of the impresario's plight on December 31, 1908, when Hammerstein announced in New York that since he had experienced difficulties in securing a loan without encumbering the Manhattan, he either would close the Philadelphia Opera House in three weeks or continue giving performances there, but with inferior casts. When this message reached Philadelphia, Norris retorted that all would be satisfactorily arranged, adding that Hammerstein's statement was "premature."[10] The impresario was also reassured by P. A. B. Widener, who told Hammerstein that the money would be forthcoming and that if he so desired, he might have $750,000 as a loan.[11] What angered Hammerstein, however, was that the terms proposed still included the Manhattan as collateral.

[9] Curtis, in "One Hundred Years of Grand Opera in Philadelphia" (III, Sec. 2, p. 535), maintained that Philadelphia builders thought the structure worth approximately $800,000. One of Hammerstein's associates, George Blumenthal, in *My Sixty Years in Show Business*, said (p. 116) that the opera house had cost Hammerstein $600,000.

[10] News item in the Philadelphia *Public Ledger*, January 1, 1909.
[11] News item in *The New York Times*, January 2, 1909.

On January 5, Hammerstein, losing his temper, alienated Norris in a tumultuous scene in the latter's Philadelphia office.[12] In a prepared statement to the press, Hammerstein said: " 'An altercation took place between myself and Mr. G. Heide Norris yesterday referring to the proposed mortgage of $400,000 on my opera house. In his attempt to obtain the result he had evidently forgotten my telegraphic instructions not to offer my Manhattan Opera House in New York as security. When he informed me that the subscriptions to the proposed mortgage . . . were based on the supposition that the Manhattan Opera House would serve as additional security, I severed my connection with him.' "[13] According to Norris, however, Hammerstein had originally given him permission to use the Manhattan as collateral but later, after the $250,000 had been pledged, changed his mind.[14] Disgusted, the Opera Committee, composed of Norris, C. Hartman Kuhn, Francis E. Bond, Andrew Wheeler, and Alexander Van Rensselaer, announced on January 7 that the money for the loan would not be exacted. It was widely believed that the services of these gentlemen would be withdrawn, Norris already having stated that under no circumstances would he any longer serve as Hammerstein's counsel. Hammerstein then tried to obtain the loan from the Philadelphia Land Title and Trust Company but, again, was informed that the money would be his only if he provided additional security.[15] Still unwilling to encumber the Manhattan, Hammerstein therewith declared that he was abandoning Philadelphia, the last performance at the new house being on January 23.[16]

The announcement was a sensation! Hammerstein adherents were immediately up in arms. Philadelphia would again be merely an operatic tributary of the Metropolitan! At this time the music critic of the *Public Ledger*, reviewing the performance of *Rigoletto*, on January 7, expressed the sentiments of many: "The great quartet

[12] News item in *The* [Philadelphia] *Press*, January 7, 1909.
[13] News item in the Philadelphia *Public Ledger*, January 7, 1909.
[14] *Ibid.*
[15] *Ibid.*
[16] *Ibid.*, January 8, 1909.

in the last act . . . came as the climax of a memorable evening—and when next year the Philadelphia Opera House is given over to negro minstrels and performing dogs, clog dancing and 'comedy sketches,' it will be a mournful satisfaction to recall that for a few weeks of one winter grand opera was given here on a scale not surpassed, and scarcely rivaled, elsewhere in the world."[17] Philadelphians sent letters to Hammerstein, urging him to reconsider the decision. The impresario was something of a civic project by now, and citizens did not want him to be lost to the city!

Among those who publicly expressed the desire to see him remain was his devoted friend Nellie Melba. At her farewell performance in Philadelphia, which occurred the day after Hammerstein announced his withdrawal from the city, the diva invited reporters to come to her dressing room at the end of the matinee, Saturday, January 9, 1909, as she desired to make a statement. Surrounded by friends and admirers, Melba took the initiative in the interview. She said to the representatives of the press:

"Now, boys—for we are all boys and girls today—I must interview you. Tell me what I can say that will help to save this glorious place to Philadelphia? Oh, it would be such a disgrace to have it closed, such a disgrace, not only to Philadelphia and to America, but to the whole world. It would seem like a death-blow to opera to me. It must not be, it must not be . . . .

Mr. Hammerstein is such an operatic genius, the greatest the world ever had. You mustn't let him get away from you. He will prove the glory of the city yet, if you only will not let him leave it. Oh, but it would be such a disgrace! I am so happy over the way you have shown that you liked me this afternoon that almost nothing could make me feel sad; but I would feel very, very sad if I thought that I would never sing in this superb house again."[18]

[17] *Ibid.*

[18] News item in *The* [Philadelphia] *North American*, January 10, 1909.

Addressing one of the members of the Box Committee, she urged him not to be annoyed by Hammerstein's eccentricities but to remember only his fine qualities. The gallant gentleman responded that his utmost desire was that the season would continue, promising the diva he would do everything possible for that result. Again appealing to the reporters to do all they could via the press, Melba hoped that before she left for Europe in four days' time, the issue would be settled and the season saved. Mrs. John Reyburn, the mayor's wife, assured Melba that a way would be found. The diva's final word was a peremptory command:

> "... Tell the people of Philadelphia that Melba says it would be a disgrace for them to sit idly by and see the splendid opera house closed. Tell them that I expect greater things of them, individually and collectively ...."[19]

Meanwhile, Norris, overlooking his personal feelings toward Hammerstein, sent a letter signed by Andrew Wheeler, C. Hartman Kuhn, and himself to one of the eminent magnates in the city, urging immediate help in the deplorable situation. The message was succinct; in substance it asked the financier whether he would " 'not, as a public-spirited citizen, consent to act at this time and take such measures as may be most expedient to secure the necessary funds, either by general subscription or otherwise.' "[20] The citizen responded. On January 13 Hammerstein obtained his loan from Edward T. Stotesbury, who personally took the $400,000 mortgage with only the Philadelphia Opera House as security.[21] This man of wealth was a member of Drexel and Company and associated with the banking house of J. Pierpont Morgan and Company. Rumor had it that he was acting for the interests of the directors of the Metropolitan in their efforts to eliminate Hammerstein from the field. This, however, has not been proved.

Stotesbury maintained that he had loaned the sum solely for the

---

[19] News item in *The Philadelphia Inquirer*, January 10, 1909.

[20] News item in the Philadelphia *Public Ledger*, January 11, 1909.

[21] *Ibid.*, January 14, 1909.

best interests of Philadelphia, seeking no encomium or commercial gain. He was well aware of what the opera house meant to the musical life of the city and what Hammerstein was trying to do. In a public statement, on January 14, he said:

> "I took the mortgage personally . . . and in doing so I believed I was acting for the best interests of Philadelphia. In fact, I am sure I was doing so. I had no commercial motive whatever in taking the mortgage. It is a splendid thing for any city to have available such superb productions as Mr. Hammerstein has been giving, and it would have been a great pity to see them discontinued. I was not seeking any praise whatever when I agreed to let Mr. Hammerstein have the money, with no other security than the Philadelphia Opera House. I only wanted to do what I could for Philadelphia."[22]

Another reason for his altruism may have been the impresario himself. It was known that he "favored those who made something out of themselves"[23] and that he "demanded that those who asked his friendship and support should prove themselves worthy of it."[24] It was obvious that Hammerstein had certainly "made something" of himself and was worthy.

Perhaps Melba also played a part. Apparently she and Stotesbury had been friends for years, enjoying a pleasant camaraderie. One anecdote will suffice. Months before, she had bet him a new hat that Hammerstein would have the opera house ready by November 17, 1908. When the season began on time, he had to pay the diva $200.[25] After her seasonal farewell performance in Philadelphia and her interview with the press (January 9), she went to the Stotesburys' home for a supper party. Some of the conversation may have con-

[22] *Ibid.*, January 15, 1909.
[23] Horace Mather Lippincott, "Edward T. Stotesbury" (paper read at the Old York Road Historical Association, Jenkintown, Pennsylvania, November 19, 1941), p. 23.
[24] *Ibid.*
[25] *Ibid.*, 10.

cerned the fate of the opera house. At any event, before leaving for Europe, Melba may have heard that the loan had been effected. Providentially, she left on the same day Hammerstein received his $400,000.

Hammerstein was jubilant. To the audience at the Philadelphia house for the performance of *Otello*, on January 14, he confessed that he was overjoyed by the happy outcome and that had he been compelled to leave the city, " 'the spectacle would have haunted [him] like a spectre for the rest of [his] life.' "[26] Once again peace reigned. Another crisis surmounted, Hammerstein, it would seem, could now devote his full attention to the sensational opera announced for the latter part of the month: Richard Strauss's *Salome*. For a time, however, the production seemed in peril.

THE CAVALIERI-GARDEN FEUD

On January 19, nine days before the *première* of this much-discussed work, Hammerstein announced the forthcoming debut of Lina Cavalieri, formerly a soprano at the Metropolitan and reputed to be one of the world's most beautiful women. As a singer, she was generally praised more for her pulchritude than for her voice. In Europe, Cavalieri had been an admired beauty, a favorite of the aristocracy. Among her many admirers was Prince Bariatinsky, the Grand Duke Alexis of Russia, whose fortune she had helped decimate.[27] As a grand opera star, she had appeared in Portugal, Italy, and England. At the Metropolitan she sang a number of roles, making her debut there in *Fedora*, with Caruso and Scotti, on December 5, 1906. At the time it was said that a young man of society, the son of a Metropolitan director, was infatuated with her and that his parents were firmly opposed to any attachment with the beauteous singer. For this reason she was not re-engaged at the end of the 1907–1908 season.[28] It would seem that New York opera-goers would behold her no more. Now, however, Cavalieri was to be a star

[26] News item in the Philadelphia *Public Ledger*, January 15, 1909.

[27] Harvey O'Connor, *The Astors*, 308.

[28] Kolodin, *The Metropolitan Opera 1883–1935*, 166.

at the Manhattan. Sheean, in his biography of Oscar Hammerstein, maintains that the impresario contracted for a limited number of performances as another strategic move in the feud with the older house. He knew that her presence at the Manhattan would be a great annoyance to those members of the Metropolitan Opera directorate who had been instrumental in not having her re-engaged.[29] Perhaps this was so. Hammerstein was, however, more cooperative with the older house this season and indulged in fewer public denunciations of that institution.

Regardless of the Metropolitan, Cavalieri's presence at the Manhattan was displeasing to Mary Garden; for Hammerstein had decreed that Cavalieri was to appear as Thaïs, one of Garden's favorite roles, a part she regarded as her own. Hammerstein's professed reason for doing so was that Garden needed to husband her strength for the all-important *Salome première*.[30] Amazed, Garden retorted that he had not thought of her health before when she had made and kept all the many engagements at both the Manhattan and Philadelphia opera houses. According to the irate soprano, the real reason why he wanted Cavalieri to appear in *Thaïs* was that he was governed by requests "from certain powerful sources."[31] She was furious. Even some forty years later she could be extremely emotional when she recalled the incident.[32]

On the afternoon of January 18 Hammerstein informed Garden that Cavalieri would have the title role in the Massenet opera, regardless of whose pride was hurt. Indignant, Garden flamed that the day he announced another singer as Thaïs, that day she would leave the company. She was determined not to let any Italian prima donna interpret a part that was hers and that she had introduced to the United States. Hammerstein, angered by Garden's attitude, went ahead and made the announcement, whereupon Garden promptly

[29] Sheean, *Oscar Hammerstein I*, 266–67.

[30] News item in *The* [New York] *World*, January 21, 1909.

[31] Mary Garden, "The Heights," *Ladies' Home Journal*, Vol. 47 (June, 1930), 118.

[32] Garden and Biancolli, *Mary Garden's Story*, 119–21.

sent in her resignation and consulted her lawyer, Samuel Untermyer.
The impresario was dumbfounded; but, in due course, Garden promised to return, provided that Hammerstein acceded to her wishes.
What she demanded was an exclusive right to all the parts she had
created and would create while appearing with the company. In one
of the missives to him she was bluntly explicit, writing in the style of
a Portia:

> ". . . It is of course understood that *Salome*, as well as any
> operas hereafter produced by you in any opera house or
> theatre under your management or in which you are the con-
> trolling spirit, and which you produce for the first time in this
> country, and in which I take part, are included in our present
> arrangement, and that as to all such operas as well as those
> mentioned in our old contract and *The Juggler*, you are not
> to produce or permit the production of any such operas during
> the term of our agreement, or any renewal term, unless I sing
> and play the roles in such operas created by me. You are not
> to substitute any one in any role without my express consent
> given in writing over my own signature."[33]

Hammerstein, having little choice, agreed and signed Garden to a
new contract. For the rest of the season she appeared in all the roles
associated with her except for the *Thaïs* of March 27, 1909, at the
Philadelphia Opera House. Being indisposed, she was replaced by
Espinasse. Philadelphia then was the only city in the United States
that had heard the Massenet opera without Garden.

A lurid aftermath of the *cause célèbre* was a heated dispute between Hammerstein and *The New York Press*, which had published
a malicious article referring to him as the "King of Press Agents."
The daily said that Hammerstein had contrived the entire quarrel
between the two prima donnas to gain publicity and that he had also
originated a report that he was being considered for the directorship
of the Metropolitan. Ill will between Hammerstein and the *Press*

[33] News item in *The* [New York] *World*, January 23, 1909.

had been brewing for some time, as the impresario had charged that the reviews of the paper's music critic were prejudicial and that the articles concerning him and the Manhattan were, more often than not, unfair. He ordered the critic barred from the opera house, canceled his advertising contract with the paper, and ended the relationship by writing a scathing letter to the editor in which he stated the low opinion he held of the brand of journalism that the *Press* endorsed. Several enraged reporters who thought Hammerstein had insulted them in the letter waited outside the Hotel Knickerbocker on the night of January 23 and, when he appeared, assaulted him, knocking him down to the pavement. Police intervened before Hammerstein was seriously hurt and took two of the attackers off to jail.[34] Hammerstein countered with a libel suit, which finally ended in his being awarded a settlement. Throughout the entire ordeal, public sentiment sided with the impresario, New York theatrical managers providing tangible evidence of this fact when they withdrew their advertisements from the *Press*.

Cavalieri made her debut on Monday, January 25, in *Tosca*, with Zenatello (Cavaradossi), Sammarco (Scarpia), and Gilibert (Sacristan), with Campanini conducting. The house was large, though not packed. Much of the audience's sympathetic interest in and enthusiasm for the prima donna may have been due, in part, to the genteel way she had conducted herself during the Garden-Hammerstein imbroglio. At the height of it she had written the impresario a letter, requesting him to withdraw the role of Thaïs from the operas in which she was to appear.[35] Her graciousness under the circumstances was exemplary. Critics remarked that as Tosca she was heard and seen to far greater advantage in the newer house than in the huge auditorium of the Metropolitan. She sang with intense emotional feeling and, generally, was histrionically effective. Meltzer, in the *American*, thought she was "more plausible, and more satisfying, as the singer than that greater and more tragic artist, Ternina, chiefly

[34] News item in *The New York Times*, January 24, 1909.
[35] News item in *The* [New York] *World*, January 22, 1909.

because she [was] less compassed [sic] and more human, in the expression of her feeling. . . ."[36] Of course her beauty, jewels, and sumptuous raiment added substantially to the excitement of the occasion. The other role in which New York heard her was as Mimi in *La Bohème*, on February 6, with Constantino (Rodolfo), Zeppilli (Musetta), Sammarco (Marcello), De Segurola (Colline), Fossetta (Schaunard). In Philadelphia she appeared in *Faust* and *Tosca*. For some inexplicable reason, Hammerstein chose not to present the perennial favorite, *Faust*, in New York this season. Philadelphia, however, heard it three times. As Marguerite, Cavalieri, who sang the role in Italian, was less successful than as Tosca and Mimi, although she won all hearts by her exquisite appearance. At her last performance in Philadelphia, on February 2, she left an indelible impression. According to the *Public Ledger*, Cavalieri, as Tosca, "added to her gowns one of the most gorgeous collections of diamonds that was ever seen outside of royal circles." In addition to "the Bonaparte tiara and double filets on her head, three strands of solitaires and picked pearls in cluster around her neck, and a huge stomacher, she wore square rubies on her fingers that blazed to the gallery."[37] She appeared six times with three performances each in New York and Philadelphia.

Aн, *Salome!*

The most eagerly anticipated opera this season (it had certainly been the most publicized!) was the production of Richard Strauss's *Salome*, which was first presented at the Manhattan Opera House on Thursday, January 28, 1909, and which was sung in French. New Yorkers remembered that when this work was given at the Metropolitan two years before, it had created a storm of protest and that it had been dropped from the repertory after one public performance. The Board of Directors, considering the subject matter objectionable, would not sanction further presentations of the work. It was said that J. P. Morgan had been prominent among those who had protested

[36] *New York American*, January 26, 1909.
[37] Philadelphia *Public Ledger*, February 3, 1909.

against any additional performances.[38] This speculation has since proved to be true. In a letter to Strauss, Otto Kahn explicitly stated that religious worthies had influenced Morgan to follow this course.[39] Though Conried tried to obtain permission to give the opera again, his pleas were to no avail. Approximately one week after the American *première*, it was withdrawn from the Metropolitan's repertory. This unusual episode had been the talk of the town. Undoubtedly there were those who wondered whether Hammerstein's production would meet a similar fate.

Aside from the opera itself, Mary Garden's assumption of the title role created much interest. Olive Fremstad had sung the part at the Metropolitan; and even though she was an extraordinary artist and a great singer, in appearance she hardly suggested a fifteen-year-old Judaean princess. Garden, pictorially and histrionically, seemed more nearly ideal. Ever since Hammerstein had asked her to assume the role, she had worked unremittingly on the part, finding it extremely demanding.[40] All during the previous summer in Paris, she prepared for it with her accompanist, Bartholemy. At the same time, she rehearsed the Dance of the Seven Veils with the *première danseuse* of the Paris Opéra. At the Metropolitan, Fremstad had retired to the side of the stage while a ballerina performed before the salacious Herod; but Garden insisted on doing the dance. Strauss himself had inspired Garden to take this action, for he had confided to her that a singer should be able to do it, since he had allowed a rest of ten minutes. Carl Van Vechten, then a reporter for *The New York Times*, attended one of Garden's terpsichorean rehearsals. His observations, wired to the United States, were duly reported in the press. From time to time, newspapers and journals also included descriptions of Garden's costume and her views on the interpretation of the role. All of this advance publicity whetted the public's curiosity.

At the opera house preparations for the production, which cost an

[38] Kolodin, *The Metropolitan Opera* 1883–1935, 117–19.
[39] "Kahn, Morgan, and *Salome*," *Saturday Review*, Vol. XLVII (May 30, 1964), 60.
[40] Garden and Biancolli, *Mary Garden's Story*, 125–26.

unprecedented $40,000, went on apace. Campanini, knowing full well the task before him, had held a prodigious number of rehearsals since December 3; there were eighteen sessions alone for separate parts of the orchestra, which had been augmented to 117 members, before the first general rehearsal. Strauss himself had counseled Campanini to follow this schedule. In the beginning the musicians were bewildered by the complexities of the score; rehearsals, therefore, were long and strenuous, and nerves frayed. For over three months Coini and his staff had been at work on the scenery and staging. Having seen productions of the opera in Berlin, Paris, Brussels, and Amsterdam, Coini intended to incorporate the best features of each. The scenery was designed to harmonize with principles of Assyrian architecture; nothing in it was to be anachronistic. All must be perfect for this long-awaited opera.[41]

Salome was, without doubt, the greatest success of the season; and even though the prices at this non-subscription performance ranged from $2.50 in the Family Circle to $10 in the orchestra (boxes were $30, $50, and $100), the house held an enormous audience. Some of the fashionables were the Ogden Mills, the Clarence Mackays, Rawlins Cottenet, Mrs. William K. Vanderbilt, Jr., the Otto H. Kahns. Announced to begin at nine o'clock, the performance did not get under way until twenty-five minutes past the scheduled time. The following day the press reported that throughout the next hour and a half the vast assemblage sat spellbound, watching a fascinating portrayal and a fascinating opera.

Adorned with a short tunic decorated with gems coruscating in the stage lights, Garden swept on stage trailing a long orange mantle which had been thrown over one bare arm and shoulder. She moved restlessly about, a willful, unrestrained adolescent. Then she heard the voice of Christ's disciple. Imperiously she commanded that John the Baptist be brought to her. Seeing the Prophet, Garden, as Salome, revealed her depraved desire for him; but although she pleaded and enticed, she was spurned by the ascetic in chains. After he was taken

[41] "Production of *Salome* Is a Costly Work," Philadelphia *Public Ledger Magazine Section*, January 24, 1909, p. 5.

back to the dungeon, Garden, crawling across the stage to the cistern, seemed like a predaceous animal deprived of its victim, a deadly creature that would not be denied. Lying prone on the grating of the well, she tried to see the object of her infatuation, unsated in her mad desire. When the Tetrarch entered, she ignored his attentions, still brooding over her unrequited demand that the Prophet let her kiss his mouth. She had but one thought: diabolic revenge. She would possess him, living or dead. Consenting to dance for Herod after he had promised a boon, she was triumphant, knowing that he would have to grant her wish. At the end of the dance, which was beautifully performed, she was implacable, blood-curdling in her demand for the Prophet's head. It was after Herod reluctantly consented that Garden smiled for the first and only time in the opera. In the concluding scene, she groveled over the decapitated head while singing an enraptured apostrophe. At last she kissed his mouth in a paroxysm of passion, the final act in an episode which had out-Heroded Herod and which even he had found so repellent that he commanded his soldiers to kill the princess at once. With shields, they crushed the infamous one to death.

When the curtain closed, the audience sat for a moment as if stunned; then the applause, at first intermittent, gathered in intensity, the artists being called out repeatedly. At the sixth curtain call Hammerstein and Coini joined the singers and were enthusiastically acclaimed. But the evening truly was Mary Garden's and hers alone. Some thought that with this role she had reached the apogee of her career.

The New York critics, in general, praised the performance, even though they did not care for the opera itself. De Koven, in the *World*, commented: "A sewer is certainly a necessity of our everyday life, but the fact of its existence does not also create the necessity for us to bend over its reeking filth to inhale its mephitic vapors."[42] Yet he conceded that *Salome* was musically "so monumental in its orchestral features that [it] . . . must either mark the beginning of a new musical era, or else be one of those sporadic manifestations of sensa-

[42] *The* [New York] *World*, January 29, 1909.

tional and considered eccentricity which will disappear as soon as the novelty has worn off."[43] Krehbiel, who had made so many mordant comments when the work was first presented at the Metropolitan, still objected to the tones and climaxes which "threatened to split the ears of the listeners."[44] The critic of *The Evening Post* thought the opera "a hideous nightmare, this wedding of a diseased libretto to a diseased score, in which the gospel of musical ugliness and perverseness is preached almost without interruption." He conceded, however, that there were two exceptions to the ugliness: Jokanaan's theme and the final pages of the score, which he declared were like "a soothing balm to one who has been impaled on a cactus bush for an hour and a half."[45] Strauss, however, had the last word on music critics; for, in his opinion, "all really great works, however new and unusual in form they may be, can regard hostile criticism with unconcern, just as they can dispense with laudatory criticism."[46]

Garden's characterization was praised to the skies; her singing, less so. Although Henderson admired her impersonation, he said that "*Salome* with Mary Garden as the heroine [was] a dance with commentary, for the plain truth must be admitted that Miss Garden [could not] sing a phrase of Strauss's music."[47] Rawling, in *The Evening World*, and De Koven, in *The World*, commented on the strange and unusual fascination of Garden's interpretation of the role. Krehbiel, usually not inclined to be generous in praise of Garden, wrote: "Miss Garden has realized a conception of incarnate bestiality which has so much power that it is a dreadful thing to contemplate. She has developed the stages from a wilful maiden to a human hyena, with wonderful skill and variety of phrase, and she has mastered all the agencies of expression. There is a terrible intensity in her acting,

[43] *Ibid.*

[44] *New-York Daily Tribune,* January 29, 1909.

[45] *The* [New York] *Evening Post,* January 29, 1909.

[46] Richard Strauss, "*Salome's* Composer on the Duties of Music Critics," *New York American Drama and Society Section,* March 28, 1909, p. 5.

[47] *The* [New York] *Sun,* January 29, 1909.

especially in the awful climax of the play, an intensity which, coupled with the music of the orchestra, is absolutely nerve racking to persons susceptible to music. Her dance is remarkable for its grace and voluptuous charm.... Through it all she is a vision of loveliness, and if the opera has a place in the repertory it will be due wholly to this feature."[48] Dalmorès, the neurotic Herod, gave "a lifelike picture of the royal voluptuary";[49] Dufranne, the Prophet, sang and acted impressively, his impersonation being "truly noble";[50] Doria was the able Herodias. Others in the cast were Vallès (Narraboth); Severina (Page); De Segurola and Malfatti (Two Nazarenes); Sellav, Venturini, Montanari, Daddi, Collin (Five Jews); Crabbé and De Grazia (Two Soldiers); Fossetta (Cappadocian); and Tancredi (Slave). Campanini conducted. The opera was heard thirteen times this season, ten performances being in New York and three in Philadelphia.

Meanwhile, loud were the rumblings of those set against the production of *Salome*. Many opera-goers inveighed against it, while clergymen thundered their vituperations from the pulpits and damned it in the press. Criticism in New York, however, was tame compared to the hue and cry in Philadelphia. When the opera was announced for February 11, many ministers and their parishioners demanded that it be prohibited. Columns of protests from the clergy as well as from the laity filled the local papers. Six ministerial associations, representing the Methodist, Episcopalian, Presbyterian, Reformed, Lutheran, and Congregational churches, denounced it as " 'indecent, immoral, demoralizing, a perversion of Scripture' "; it " '[pandered] under the guise of high art to the lowest passions of human nature.' "[51] Archbishop P. J. Ryan and the Federation of Catholic Societies were opposed. The Archbishop pontificated: " 'From all that I have heard of *Salome*, I believe its presentation here is calculated to demoralize the people, especially the youth of

[48] *New-York Daily Tribune*, January 29, 1909.
[49] *The* [New York] *World*, January 29, 1909.
[50] *New-York Daily Tribune*, January 29, 1909.
[51] News item in the Philadelphia *Public Ledger*, February 9, 1909.

the city, and I greatly desire that it be discountenanced and repressed if possible. Such action will be in harmony with the high moral character which this city has borne since the days of William Penn.' "[52] The Christian League, the W.C.T.U., the Delaware Branch of the Philadelphia Christian Endeavor Union, and other religious as well as lay organizations duly joined the opposition, ranting and railing and raving and roaring against the production of *Salome*. In short, Philadelphia blazed with philippics.

On the other hand, there were those who defended the production. One of these individuals, John H. Ingham, a prominent and respected citizen, stated that to deny *Salome* a representation would be " 'a gross reflection on the intelligence and civilization of this community, unless far better and more plausible reasons are given than those founded on a more or less dense ignorance of the contents and scope of the work in question.' "[53]

Ultimately a delegation of well-meaning souls called on Mayor Reyburn, requesting him to stop the performance; but His Honor refused to interfere, since he said that there was no legal reason to prevent it. He cited the fact that *Salome* had been given in Europe without protests, that Hammerstein intended to present only one performance, and that he did not believe in setting a precedent in this kind of liberty of action.[54] He would not condemn the opera without first seeing it. The Mayor promised, however, that he would be present at the performance and that if it were as objectionable as people said, he would not permit a repetition, even though Hammerstein might want to give it again.

In the meantime, people almost fought to obtain tickets, the box office having been sold out for days. Hammerstein, nevertheless, was not too sure that he would be permitted to produce *Salome* and was ready to substitute *Le Jongleur de Notre Dame*, which was the antithesis of Strauss's work in its religious overtones. In a speech after the

[52] *Ibid.*, February 7, 1909.

[53] News item in *The* [Philadelphia] *Evening Bulletin*, February 11, 1909.

[54] News item in the Philadelphia *Public Ledger*, February 11, 1909.

second act of *Pelléas et Mélisande* two nights before the Philadelphia *première*, he said, in part, that he intended to keep his agreement with his patrons as to the productions he had promised, that anyone who did not wish to attend might have his money refunded, and that there would be only one performance of *Salome* unless the public demanded a repetition and the clergy approved it.[55] The following evening at the Bellevue- Stratford Hotel, Mayor Reyburn, speaking at a testimonial banquet in Hammerstein's honor, reiterated his decision not to deter the presentation, which he said promised to be " 'still greater than any productions that have ever been given.' "[56] His speech was received with thunderous applause and a standing ovation. Hammerstein, it seemed, would not have to substitute *Le Jongleur de Notre Dame*.

According to the *Public Ledger*, the first performance of *Salome* in Philadelphia, on February 11, 1909, was "the most extraordinary operatic occasion in the history of the city."[57] Enormous crowds were both outside and inside the house; police had all they could do to preserve order with the mass of people milling about at the various entrances and the congested traffic. Space for standing room, which had gone on sale at seven, was soon exhausted, while 2,000 disappointed people waited in vain for admission to the performance. As nine o'clock approached, the enormous house filled rapidly. Society arrived early, eager to see who was present. The *Public Ledger* said: "From the amount of craning of necks in the forward parquet seats it might have been supposed that royalty was expected, and on every side was heard some sort of a comment as various social celebrities put in their appearance."[58] When the opera began at twenty minutes past the announced time of nine, every available space was taken except for four Grand Tier boxes, leased by patrons who opposed the produc-

[55] News item in *The* [Philadelphia] *Evening Bulletin*, February 10, 1909.

[56] News item in *The* [Philadelphia] *North American*, February 11, 1909.

[57] News item in the Philadelphia *Public Ledger*, February 12, 1909.

[58] *Ibid.*

tion. During the performance the audience listened and watched the same cast as at the New York *première* and at the end rose to its feet, clapping and cheering. Altogether there were fourteen curtain calls.

Contrary to what some had anticipated, the audience was not horrified by the spectacle. The *Public Ledger* said that nobody "left the house at crucial moments, no women fainted nor men cried hoarsely 'Enough enough!' as the head of the Baptist was handed up from the cistern's depths, as might have been expected, judging from what many have said and written of late . . . ."[59] Some of the box holders publicly praised the performance, P. A. B. Widener, for one, confiding that he had found nothing objectionable. The Mayor also enjoyed it but thought that some additional draperies in the Dance of the Seven Veils might be efficacious, since they " 'would add to its beauty and remove some of the grounds for objections . . . .' "[60] Music critics and musicians, on the whole, lauded the score but disliked the libretto. William R. Lester, in *The North American*, wrote: "Neither dramatic genius nor musicianly inspiration could avail to cloak the hideous moral deformity and sinister, demoniac suggestion of this one-act music drama—an inspiration that might have proceeded from the dread seventh circle of Dante's Inferno."[61]

When Hammerstein presented the opera a second time, on February 16, the house again was crowded, hundreds not being able to obtain admission. In the Grand Tier, however, there were more absentees than at the *première*; for nine box holders stayed away in protest. The third and last performance of *Salome* was on March 1. Since the Saturday matinee and evening subscribers had not seen the opera, Hammerstein permitted them to exchange their seats for this final presentation of the controversial work, thus fulfilling his obligations to them. Perturbations and protests not having abated, the impresario then withdrew *Salome* from the repertory of the Philadelphia house, thereby propitiating the " 'dissension among the estab-

[59] *Ibid.*

[60] News item in *The* [Philadelphia] *Evening Bulletin*, February 12, 1909.

[61] *The* [Philadelphia] *North American*, February 12, 1909.

lished clientele of the Opera House . . . .' "[62] In New York Hammerstein commented: " 'It has been my experience . . . that people often want to be informed about certain matters that perhaps they think they ought not to know about. Under these circumstances it makes a very bad impression to be the informer. So although I might have continued to have large houses with *Salome* in Philadelphia, I preferred not to take the risk of being the man that taught Philadelphia anything it thinks it ought not to know.' "[63]

More Revivals

In February Hammerstein added four operas to the repertory. On the tenth of the month he brought forth *Aïda* at the Manhattan with Agostinelli (Aïda), Doria (Amneris), Zenatello (Radames), and Sammarco (Amonasro). Two operas not heard since the first season, *La Sonnambula* and *I Puritani*, were revived at the New York house, on February 13 and 26 respectively, for Tetrazzini, who in the first named opera "displayed captivating lingerie and high notes and . . . walked in her sleep with admirable decorum."[64] Parola, her associate, was "pale and ineffective,"[65] while Trentini, a termagant in the opera, "could not well look otherwise than as an innocent child."[66] In *I Puritani* Constantino was the mellifluous Lord Arthur, whose "beautiful voice and really exquisite style pleaded quite as eloquently for the opera as did the art of Mr. Bonci two years ago . . . ."[67] On the nineteenth Hammerstein presented *Louise* at the Manhattan with Garden, Dalmorès, Doria, and Gilibert. After the extreme modernity of *Salome* and *Pelléas et Mélisande*, the Charpentier opera seemed a balm to the ear.

In March Hammerstein revived two more operas and introduced a new production. On the sixth, he presented *Un Ballo in Maschera* at the Philadelphia house with Agostinelli (Amelia), Zenatello (Ric-

[62] News item in the Philadelphia *Public Ledger*, February 18, 1909.
[63] News item in *The* [New York] *Sun*, February 21, 1909.
[64] *The* [New York] *Sun*, February 14, 1909.
[65] *The* [New York] *World*, February 14, 1909.
[66] *New-York Daily Tribune*, February 14, 1909.
[67] *Ibid.*, February 27, 1909.

cardo), Aldrich (Ulrica), Sammarco (Renato), Trentini (Oscar), Arimondi (Sam), and De Grazia (Tom), under the direction of Sturani. This opera, like *Faust*, was heard only in Philadelphia during the season. It was a handsome production, the same one New York had already seen; and from all accounts it was an effective presentation. Zenatello performed "at his best"[68]; Sammarco was "handsome and dignified"[69]; Agostinelli sang with "facility and brilliancy, her tones being firm, true and of crystalline clearness . . . ."[70] *La Navarraise* was revived for Gerville-Réache on March 20 at the Manhattan, sharing the matinee with *I Pagliacci* (Labia, Zenatello, and Sammarco). The final new production of the season was the American *première* of Jan Blockx's *La Princesse d'Auberge*, given for the first time at the Manhattan on March 10, with Labia (Rita), Gerville-Réache (Katelyne), Zeppilli (Reinilde), Vallès (Merlyn), Crabbé (Marcus), Gilibert (Bluts) and Dufranne (Rabo). Campanini conducted. The opera, sumptuously mounted, made no great impression, although the carnival scene at the end of the second act was such a success that it had to be repeated. The music, which Henderson said was "deficient in characterization,"[71] was neither expressive nor eloquent; and the libretto lacked any emotional content. De Koven maintained that there was "practically only one situation in the piece, that of the duel scene in the last act, and this was so inevitable from the start that its effect was largely discounted. All the characters are sketchily drawn, being tenuous, invertebrate, and elusive in substance . . . ."[72] Hammerstein presented the opera three times and only in New York; today it is virtually forgotten.

CAMPANINI LEAVES THE COMPANY

Three weeks before the end of the New York season Campanini issued a statement, on March 8, that his association with the company

[68] *The* [Philadelphia] *Evening Bulletin,* March 8, 1909.
[69] *Ibid.*
[70] *Ibid.*
[71] *The* [New York] *Sun,* March 11, 1909.
[72] Reginald de Koven, "New Flemish Opera . . . ," *The* [New York] *World Theatre Section,* March 14, 1909, p. 3.

would terminate at the end of the spring tour to Boston.[73] Although it had been announced on January 28 that the conductor had signed a new contract and would remain with the Manhattan for the next five years, he and Hammerstein were not able to agree on terms; and the impresario decided to part with the one person who had been, above all, a tower of strength during the three lustrous seasons of the young opera company.

Hammerstein maintained that it was not a question of salary and that their personal relations were as cordial as ever, and would always be so. According to the impresario, much of the disagreement resulted from the Garden-Cavalieri episode. The soprano's remarks concerning the ability of an Italian singer to interpret French roles properly had intimidated some members of the company who resented her aspersions.[74] Since then, relations between the French and Italian artists had not been amiable. Desiring to restore concord, Hammerstein had insisted on certain points; one of these had to do with casting. In the contract he had had with Campanini, the conductor was to be consulted as to the artists who would appear in the casts. Hammerstein no longer would agree to this. He did not intend to have his opera house "exclusively a school for Italian singers."[75] He intended to produce more French opera next season and to promote young Americans in minor roles. Since Campanini and he could not agree on these and other policies, the time had come for a change; and to replace him, Hammerstein engaged four conductors, retaining the services of Marcel Charlier and Giuseppe Sturani.

At the time, Campanini said that his reason for leaving the company was that there was not an agreement on policies. Later, however, after returning to Europe, he was more explicit.

" . . . The one and only true reason for my rupture with Mr. Hammerstein was this: He wanted to be the despot of the Manhattan, and acted as such. His only aim was to please a

[73] News item in *The New York Times*, March 9, 1909.

[74] News item in the *New-York Daily Tribune*, March 9, 1909.

[75] "Hammerstein Happy at Big Success Here," *The* [Philadelphia] *North American Drama Section*, March 14, 1909, p. 7.

well-known prima donna and give an absolute preponderance
to the French opera. He spent fabulous amounts for it in
sceneries and in all kinds of accessories, especially for *Pelleas
and Mélisande,* and at the same time entirely neglected in a
most deplorable way the Italian performances.

Now, I love and admire the French répertoire in a superlative way, but I could not help suffering nor help a feeling
of humiliation in my artistic dignity at such an evident
injustice."[76]

Sheean, in his biography of Oscar Hammerstein, sheds further
light on the situation. Apparently Campanini's feelings were very
much involved in Hammerstein's ungallant treatment of two of the
Manhattan's staunchest admirers: Mr. and Mrs. Clarence Mackay.
Fully cognizant of and appreciating the impresario's efforts, these
socially prominent and wealthy patrons of the opera had elected to
be benefactors of the company. After the *première* of *Thaïs* (November 25, 1907) Mr. Mackay told Arthur Hammerstein that, should
there be any financial problems, he, Clarence Mackay, would be
willing to make up any deficits. The older Hammerstein chose to
ignore this generous offer. Mrs. Mackay had urged her friends to
secure boxes and orchestra seats. So persuasive was she that the subscriptions for 30 to 40 per cent of these choice locations during the
seasons of 1907–1908 and 1908–1909 apparently were due to her
kind assistance. Unfortunately, Oscar Hammerstein insulted these
patrons and, in doing so, alienated their friend, Cleofonte Campanini.

On Sunday, January 10, 1909, Mrs. Mackay gave a magnificent
soirée at her Madison Avenue home for a New York debutante, Miss
Beatrice Mills, who was soon to marry the Earl of Granard. After
dinner the guests were entertained at a musicale by the young violin
virtuoso, Mischa Elman, then in the midst of his second American
season. The other rare musical treat provided for the Mackays' guests
was the entire Manhattan Opera House orchestra, under the direc-

[76] "Campanini Tells Why He Left N.Y.," *Musical America,* Vol.
X (October 2, 1909), 4.

tion of Campanini, performing a long programme of classical music. Hammerstein had given his permission for the orchestra to appear at the dinner party and told Arthur that there would be no fee. The older Hammerstein must have known of Mrs. Mackay's efforts in behalf of the company; and, in this way, he was able to reciprocate her past kindnesses.

After the brilliant musicale, glowingly recorded in the newspapers of January 11, Mrs. Mackay gave expensive gifts to those who had helped to make it possible. Campanini received a ring worth five thousand dollars. To Hammerstein, however, Mrs. Mackay did not send even a letter expressing her gratitude. Her oversight was unfortunate, but it was hardly a social error that necessitated Hammerstein's actions. He told Arthur to deliver a letter to Mrs. Mackay. What the impresario had written was that he did not want her ever again to attend a performance at his opera house. Arthur destroyed it; but several days later, when Hammerstein discovered what his son had done, he rewrote the letter and this time delivered it personally.[77] Later he brought suit against Mrs. Mackay for payment of the orchestra.

What ensued was disastrous. Campanini, the Mackays' friend, was disgusted by Hammerstein's actions; and society, loyal to its own, deserted the opera house. It required no Cassandra utterance to foretell ruin. Symbolic of society's departure was the removal of all the Grand Tier boxes at the end of the season. In the spring of 1909 Hammerstein announced that he would substitute four rows of chairs for the commodious loges. The alteration on the horseshoe began on August 25, 1909, and within ten days the work was completed.[78] The boxes in the Grand Tier at the Manhattan and what they had represented were no more. A glory had passed away.

Campanini's annual benefit was the last *Salome* of the season (March 26), followed by the Prologue to Boïto's *Mefistofele*, with Arimondi and the chorus. Afterwards many gifts were showered upon

[77] Sheean, *Oscar Hammerstein I*, 276–79.

[78] "Application for the Erection of a Theatre at 315 West 34th Street," July 26, 1909.

the venerated conductor, who had been so largely responsible for the high artistic standing of the Manhattan. Without him, the first season must have ended in bitter failure. In the two following years, he continued to work indefatigably to perfect the productions under his direction. Seemingly tireless, he conducted almost every performance after having devoted hours to the study and rehearsal of the works entrusted to him. Since he never spared himself, he would not indulge others. Superb ensembles and incandescent performances were the result. His interpretations of *Un Ballo in Maschera*, *Rigoletto*, *Aïda*, *Otello* were of the first rank; no less impressive were his readings of *Carmen*, *Faust*, *Louise*, *Pelléas et Mélisande*, *Thaïs*, *Salome*.[79]

The following evening (March 27) the New York season concluded with Tetrazzini in *Lucia*, followed by the carnival scene from *La Princesse d'Auberge*. A highlight of the gala occasion was the orchestra's playing of the waltz "Cara Mia," which Hammerstein had written for and dedicated to Tetrazzini. The impresario seemed as ebullient as ever. To a vast audience he confided:

> "When I am in good spirits I write a waltz. When I am blue I write a funeral march. The season just closed has been phenomenal. My first year's subscription amounted to $52,000. This year's to $400,000. Therefore I have written a waltz. My complete plans for next year are not ready for announcement, but I may safely promise you forty grand operas and twenty-two opera comiques in my repertory. So New York may tremble. I thank you!"[80]

The last performance at the Philadelphia Opera House occurred on Saturday, April 3, with the ever-popular Tetrazzini in *Lucia*. On this occasion, the prima donna, in an unusual gesture, sent a bouquet of sweet peas, violets, gardenias, and orchids to each box holder. In excellent voice, she dominated and electrified the entire presentation.

[79] Charles Henry Meltzer, "Opera at the Manhattan," *New York American Drama and Society Section*, March 21, 1909, p. 4.

[80] News item in *The* [New York] *Evening World*, March 29, 1909.

During the evening there were speeches, flowers for the singers, gifts to Hammerstein, and boundless enthusiasm. When the final curtain fell, Philadelphians must have been indeed proud of this extraordinary season and of the impresario. The following day the *Press* said:

> Whatever impression the presenting orators made, the audience left no room for doubt about the sincerity of the eulogistic words spoken. Each reference to Mr. Hammerstein's redeemed promise to give Philadelphia a new opera house and grand opera was cheered with overwhelming volume from the boxes, the orchestra, the balconies and the gallery, as well as the packed aisles. Each one in the audience did his best to emphasize the fact that Mr. Hammerstein has won an enviable place in Philadelphia.[81]

THE BOSTON TOUR

From March 29 to April 10 the company presented a series of performances in Boston, where the repertory consisted of the Tetrazzini showpieces: *Lucia*, *La Traviata*, *Rigoletto*; the new French operas with Garden: *Thaïs*, *Pelléas et Mélisande*, *Louise*, *Le Jongleur de Notre Dame*; and such staples as *Les Contes d'Hoffmann*, *La Bohème*, *Aïda*, *La Navarraise*, and *I Pagliacci*. Hammerstein had planned also to present *Salome*, even though there had been adverse criticism of the proposed performance. The impresario maintained, however, that he had received many letters from Boston operaphiles urging him to give the opera and that he believed it his duty to comply to their wishes. Opposition to its presentation increased. Governor Eben S. Draper, former Governor Guild, Mayor Hibbard of Boston and high dignitaries of the Protestant, Episcopalian, and Roman Catholic churches requested that the production be stopped. Faced with this formidable array, Hammerstein had no choice and withdrew the opera. Olin Downes, in *Musical America*, wrote: "It seems hardly creditable that the authorities of Boston should so belittle themselves and the reputation of a city supposed to be one of the broadest and most enlightened in the world by an exhibition of

[81] News item in *The* [Philadelphia] *Press*, April 4, 1909.

ignorance and prejudice that makes Boston the laughing stock of civilization. Unfortunately for the looks of the thing, moral coward-ice as well as the most absurd narrow-mindedness seems to have played its part in the proceedings."[82]

The short season, despite the *Salome* episode, was an unequivocal success. Boston found that the Hammerstein brand of opera meant that the "old operas were given as if they were new, the new ones as if they were old, such was the intelligence, unity of purpose and enthusi-astic co-operation of all concerned."[83] Philip Hale thought that in the past twenty years the metropolis had not seen such excellent operatic performances and praised Hammerstein for the high standard of his productions. The critic lauded the repertory, the singing actors and actresses, Campanini, and the orchestra, which he called "dramati-cally eloquent."[84]

According to Arthur Hammerstein, the company ended this third season with an enormous profit: $229,000.[85] Although the receipts for the Manhattan were not announced, Hammerstein did reveal the ones for the Philadelphia house. In the first season at the new temple of music the box-office intake was $538,000.[86] The Boston engagement had been profitable. Hammerstein said that giving opera in the Hub City would cost him $100,000;[87] at the end of the two weeks, he estimated that the receipts were between $138,000 and $140,000. The same season the Metropolitan lost $205,201.[88]

[82] Olin Downes, "Boston's Artistic Ideals and *Salomé*," *Musical America*, Vol. IX (April 10, 1909), 1.

[83] Olin Downes, "Notes and Comment upon Musical Matters," *The Boston Post Theatre Section*, April 11, 1909, p. 25.

[84] Philip Hale, "Symphony's 21st Concert of Season," *The Boston Herald Theatre Section*, April 11, 1909, p. 7.

[85] Kolodin, *The Metropolitan Opera 1883–1935*, 153.

[86] News item in the Philadelphia *Public Ledger*, April 5, 1910.

[87] Sylvester Rawling, "Hammerstein to Give Opera Comique to Prevent Musical Indigestion," *The* [New York] *Evening World Theatre Section*, March 6, 1909, p. 5.

[88] Kolodin, *The Story of the Metropolitan Opera 1883–1950*, 240.

Hammerstein had every reason to be gratified by the company's financial success, although the Philadelphia house never ceased to be a liability. Without this incubus, he might very well have produced opera in New York for several more seasons. Then, too, Hammerstein lavishly spent money on the productions, as well as on buying real estate for the chain of opera houses he envisaged throughout the United States. At various times he planned to construct theaters in Brooklyn, Washington, and Chicago. His operatic schemes were endless; his funds were not.

THE METROPOLITAN'S SEASON

During the third Manhattan season, the Metropolitan had been a center of internal dissension, a house of cross-purposes, discord, and tumult, the inevitable consequences of a divided directorship. Gatti-Casazza recalled that "intrigues were always the order of the day, ceasing scarcely for a moment."[89] One of the most publicized conflicts occurred soon after the beginning of the season. Apparently Sembrich, Eames, Farrar, Caruso, and Scotti thought their interests were best served by Dippel, who had been their colleague and knew the local situation, so they sent the directors a letter urging them to grant their friend authority equal to Gatti-Casazza's. Their pleas, however, were in vain; the executive committee of the Metropolitan (Kahn, Vanderbilt, and Griswold) replied that Dippel's position must be a subordinate one, pointedly commenting that the singers' task was to sing, not to concern themselves with administrative duties.[90]

Gatti-Casazza's and Toscanini's position seemed tenuous, however. Before coming to New York, Gatti had not been told that there would be a co-director. His wife, the soprano Frances Alda, remembered the hostility and cabals as well as her husband's dissatisfaction with Dippel.[91] Gatti also found intolerable the stars' lack of discipline, their indifference to rehearsals, and their inordinate demands.[92] Tos-

[89] *Memories of the Opera*, 165.
[90] Kolodin, *The Metropolitan Opera 1883–1935*, 150–51.
[91] Frances Alda, *Men Women and Tenors*, 119.
[92] Gatti-Casazza, *Memories of the Opera*, 169.

canini, like his friend Gatti, did not have the free rein he had enjoyed at La Scala. This very season he had wanted to direct *Tristan*, but Mahler considered this opera his "spiritual property"[93] and would not share it with any other conductor. Farrar recalled the clashes she had with the maestro at this time;[94] and Eames, who ended her long association with the Metropolitan this season, resented Toscanini's uncompromising attitude on the podium. She wrote: "Even to such as ourselves, who had an absolute respect for the music as it was written, he allowed no margin for the emotion of the moment, and his conducting was not an accompaniment but a stone wall of resistance to any personality but his own."[95] Resentment of Toscanini's methods also extended to members of the orchestra who refused to attend one of the rehearsals, having been offended by the maestro's volcanic rage and opprobrium. Later that day the solo flutist visited Toscanini to explain why the men had failed to appear and to request that he temper his remarks in the future.[96]

Even so, the presentations at the Metropolitan were more vital than they had been in years. Week after week, Toscanini's conducting, musicianship, and authority made a deeper impression on the critics and public. In his very first season he revealed what he could do with operas from the Italian, French, and German repertories. His aim was to achieve performances of the highest musical distinction, and he demanded the utmost from his associates in the service of great art. Toscanini's presence at the Metropolitan promised much for the artistic future of that institution.[97]

[93] Mahler, *Gustav Mahler* (trans. by Basil Creighton), 256.
[94] Farrar, *Such Sweet Compulsion*, 121.
[95] Emma Eames, *Some Memories and Reflections*, 299.
[96] Taubman, *The Maestro*, 114–15.
[97] Kolodin, *The Metropolitan Opera 1883–1935*, 144–45.

XVIII

Gathering Clouds, Preliminary Season
Regular Season

—·◦━◦❧❦◦━◦·—

B EFORE THE November opening of the regular 1909–10 season, Hammerstein, always the innovator, introduced at the Manhattan Opera House a preliminary "educational" series of opera performances at popular prices (50¢ to $2). His purpose was to present not cheap opera but grand opera at reduced admissions so that more New Yorkers would become interested in opera and thus would patronize the presentations at the Manhattan during the winter season. The repertory included three new productions (*Le Prophète*, *La Juive*, and *The Bohemian Girl*) as well as *Aïda*, *Carmen*, *Lucia*, *La Traviata*, *Rigoletto*, *Cavalleria Rusticana*, *I Pagliacci*, *Tosca*, *Louise*, *Il Trovatore*, *Faust*, and *Les Contes d'Hoffmann*. Hammerstein engaged a number of new artists for the principal roles, the most outstanding of these being Marguerite Sylva, Marguerite d'Alvarez, Alice Baron, Eva Grippon, Lalla Miranda, Nicola Zerola, Frederico Carasa, Jean Duffault, and William Beck. The conductors were Giuseppe Sturani, of the Philadelphia house, and Carlo Nicosia and Gaetano Scognamiglio, of the Manhattan; Jacques Coini was the stage director.

One of the new productions, Meyerbeer's *Le Prophète*, inaugurated the preliminary season on August 30, 1909. In the cast were George Lucas, formerly a secondary singer at the Metropolitan, as John of Leyden; D'Alvarez as Fidès; Walter-Villa as Bertha; and Nicolay as Zacharias, under the baton of Sturani. New York had last heard the opera six years before at the Metropolitan when Schumann-Heink, Alvarez, and Edouard de Reszke sang the leading roles. Although Hammerstein's cast certainly was not of the same vocal caliber, the standard of the ensemble was surprisingly high. Most of this was attributed to the chorus, orchestra, and staging. Of the opening night, *The New York Times* said:

> The audience last evening was large and seemed ready to be educated. It found numerous occasions for applause and enthusiasm, which indeed were not misplaced. The performance was in many ways of surprising excellence. It certainly was not to be compared with any of the offerings of opera at cheap prices that are made from time to time in this town. It had much of the flavor of the real thing in opera; there were several of the principal singers of competence and more than competence; there was a chorus, large, sonorous, and active, well trained in both singing and action on the stage. There was appropriate if not always rich or sumptuous scenery, and there were new and effective costumes.[1]

The splendour of D'Alvarez's voice was admired; and subsequent appearances as Amneris (*Aïda*) and Azucena (*Il Trovatore*) confirmed the fine impression made at her debut. Perhaps the excellent impression she continued to make was simply an instance of mind over matter. The contralto, in her autobiography, maintained that she was not at all happy appearing with the company, as she had unwillingly aroused the impresario's amatory interests, emotions which she could not reciprocate, and she stated that his attentions and solicitations created in her a loathing that very nearly had a deleterious effect on her health. Apparently Hammerstein did not understand the meaning of the word "no" in affairs of the heart, and he continued his futile pursuit of the young singer. As for D'Alvarez, she felt unbounded joy when her engagement at last came to an end and she was free to return to Europe.[2] Strangely enough, however, although the contralto protested she never again wanted to see Hammerstein, several

---

[1] *The New York Times,* August 31, 1909.
[2] Marguerite d'Alvarez, *Forsaken Altars,* 223.

seasons later she appeared under his aegis for a series of performances in London, a fact she does not mention in her memoirs.

The first performance of *La Juive*, the second novelty of the preliminary season, was on September 9 with Eva Grippon (Rachel), Jean Duffault (Eleazar), Walter-Villa (Princess), Laskin (Brogni), Nicosia conducting. Halévy's opera had not been heard in New York since 1904, when the French Company from New Orleans (Bressler-Gianoli had been with this troupe) presented it at the Casino. The opera was well produced, the chorus, orchestra, and staging being most commendable. The principals, however, were not equal to the vocal requirements of their parts. Grippon, who was extremely nervous, fainted during the second act but, quickly recovering, went on with the performance, singing in the last act with more beauty of tone than before.[3] Duffault, a Canadian tenor with a slim voice, revealed an excellent style. Hammerstein brought forward his final novelty, Balfe's *The Bohemian Girl*, on October 20, with Lalla Miranda as Arline, Maria Duchène as the Gypsy Queen, Domenico Russo as Thaddeus, and Henri Scott as Count Arnheim. Nicosia conducted. Miranda had appeared at the Théâtre de la Monnaie, Covent Garden, and the Opéra-Comique. Not a brilliant coloratura, she was, nevertheless, an artistic singer who had been heard earlier in the series as Lucia, Violetta, and Gilda. Pitts Sanborn thought the production superior to the ones usually given of this work and liked "the sweet-voiced Arline"[4] of Miranda.

As for the other new leading singers, Marguerite Sylva, a Belgian soprano who had sung in musical comedy in New York before returning to Europe for further study, made her highly successful debut as Carmen on September 1. She was an immediate favorite. Later she appeared as Santuzza, Nedda, Tosca, Marguerite (*Faust*), always to growing acclaim. Alice Baron appeared first as Aïda, singing this arduous role with "feeling and taste."[5] She was well received also for

[3] *The* [New York] *Globe and Commercial Advertiser,* September 10, 1909.

[4] *Ibid.,* October 21, 1909.

[5] *Ibid.,* September 1, 1909.

her Santuzza, Giulietta (*Les Contes d'Hoffmann*), and Louise. Apparently Hammerstein had secured Garden's permission for Baron to appear in the Charpentier opera; but when he wanted to present Sylva in *Thaïs*, Garden wired from Paris that if the opera were given, she would resign.[6] *Louise*, therefore, was the only modern French opera in the repertory. Of the tenors, Nicola Zerola was the ablest. At the beginning of the preliminary series, he was not a member of the Manhattan but was the leading dramatic tenor of a company concurrently appearing at the old Academy of Music. His two appearances there were so impressive that Hammerstein determined to engage him. Of his debut as Radames on September 23, the *New-York Daily Tribune* critic thought his voice extraordinarily powerful and "brilliant in its upper registers, which he used with greater discretion than is usually the case with modern Italian tenors."[7] The acquisition of Frederico Carasa, a young Spanish tenor, aroused much comment, since his name was similar to Caruso's. Unfortunately the comparison did not extend to his singing. Possessed of a pleasant, light voice, Carasa, like many other ambitious singers, appeared in opera too early and too often, constantly trying to make more of his vocal material than nature had intended. After his debut as Radames on August 31, he appeared as the Duke in *Rigoletto*, as Canio in *I Pagliacci*, as Cavaradossi in *Tosca* (his best role), as Turiddu in *Cavalleria Rusticana*, and as Don José in *Carmen*. William Beck, the leading baritone, was heard in a variety of parts, his outstanding achievement, perhaps, being the assumption of the three baritone roles in *Les Contes d'Hoffmann* which had hitherto been associated with Renaud.

The season ended on October 30 with a gala performance. After presenting *I Pagliacci* in its entirety, members of the company performed the fourth act of *Carmen*, the third act of *Il Trovatore*, and the Coronation Scene from *Le Prophète*. During the evening Hammerstein enlivened the proceedings by making a speech. To the crowded house he confessed:

[6] *The* [New York] *Sun*, January 2, 1910.
[7] *New-York Daily Tribune*, September 24, 1909.

"... My season of educational opera has been successful. I expected to lose $75,000, but I have lost only $50,000. I have the satisfaction of knowing that my books show that more than 150,000 persons have heard these performances. Such a work should of course be undertaken by the municipality of New York, but it appears nauseous to that body. So I am glad to do it. I shall also continue to do it. I love to pluck victory from defeat. I have learned this year some lessons that will be of advantage to me in the future, and I shall devote the fall season next year to such another season ...."[8]

The series of performances had been unique; never had New York seen better artistic opera presentations at popular prices. At times the level of excellence was so high that "one could without much difficulty imagine oneself in the full tide of the 'regular' season, and in an authentic five-dollar seat."[9]

Opera Madness

During the 1909–10 season, the production of opera in New York reached an all-time high. At the Manhattan Hammerstein scheduled a period of performances for twenty weeks of grand opera as well as *opéra comique*. He brought forward seven new grand opera productions. For the light operas, he engaged a special chorus, principal singers from Paris, and Alfred Haakman as the conductor. The Metropolitan, whose prestige and influence had been somewhat lessened as the result of Hammerstein's activities, not only undertook an equally ambitious season at the Broadway house but also conducted a series of light operas and plays at the New Theatre, on Central Park West. New York was indeed opera mad. It was possible, for instance, to see in the week of February 20, 1910, seventeen performances of opera in six days, or approximately three different operatic presentations a day. The range of the works, which were more often than not brilliantly presented, appealed to any operatic taste: *Il Maestro di*

[8] *The* [New York] *Sun*, October 31, 1909.
[9] Lawrence Gilman, "Mr. Hammerstein's New Venture," *Harper's Weekly*, Vol. LIII (October 9, 1909), 27.

Capella, Falstaff, Parsifal, Das Rheingold, Manon, Louise, Le Jongleur de Notre Dame, Les Contes d'Hoffmann, La Fille de Madame Angot, Elektra.[10] From November 8 to April 2, New Yorkers attended approximately 300 operatic performances.[11]

Furthermore, both the Manhattan and Metropolitan announced plans for extensive tours. Members of the Manhattan set out at various times in December, January, and March, while the company's *opéra comique* group left New York in December for a series of engagements in Canada and the United States. At the same time, Hammerstein weekly presented five performances of opera in New York and four in Philadelphia. The Metropolitan's tours were as long and complicated. There were no fewer than fifty-six times when the older house's schedule required concurrent performances in different areas and the "complications were so obvious and the trail so arduous that the management issued booklets showing maps of the cities visited and tabulating dates and hotels."[12] The armistice of the previous season was at an end. Warfare was to be waged in many cities and in new territory; neither force was to give quarter to the other, for the objective had become complete surrender.

That last season's quasi harmony between the Manhattan and Metropolitan had ended was indicated in August, 1909, when Hammerstein once again adopted a bellicose attitude towards the older house. The impresario had wanted the Manhattan to appear in Chicago as part of the tour he was arranging; but since the Metropolitan had a lease on the only suitable auditorium in the city, Hammerstein was unable to arrange for any appearances of the company in this Western metropolis. What particularly galled him was the fact that he had been gracious to the Metropolitan the previous spring when he had permitted Zenatello to replace the ill Caruso on the Metropolitan's annual spring tour, and that when he now requested a favour, the older house was unwilling to be of assistance.

[10] Reginald de Koven, "Banner Week of Opera . . . ," *The* [New York] *World Theatre Section,* February 27, 1910, p. 5.

[11] Quaintance Eaton, *Opera Caravan,* 131.

[12] *Ibid.,* 132.

In April, 1909, Otto Kahn asked Hammerstein whether the Metropolitan might not have the services of Zenatello for several weeks. In a conciliatory gesture and as a part of the prevailing entente, Hammerstein gave his permission provided that the programmes carried the notice that the tenor appeared with the Metropolitan through the courtesy of the Manhattan Opera House. Grateful, Dippel wrote to Hammerstein: "I wish to thank you in the name of our company for the spirit of cooperation shown, and you may rest assured that we shall heartily reciprocate whenever an occasion shall present itself."[13]

What angered Hammerstein was the Metropolitan's reluctance to extend reciprocity. And so the impresario made it clear that he would never again be beholden to his hated adversary. Furious, he threatened to sue the older house for Zenatello's services. Since Hammerstein liked going to court, no doubt he looked forward to any legal confrontation with his detested rival. That this was so is evident in a vitriolic letter he wrote to the directors of the Metropolitan several years later:

> If there is any evidence you need to create the proper time for legal proceedings immediately, it can be had from me for the asking.
>
> In other words, and as a matter of vulgar fact, I have a tumultuous desire to kick you into court, so that in time not too far distant I may experience pleasure unalloyed and joy exotic in seeing you kicked out of it, with aid of Judge impartial and jury most intelligent.
>
> In the meantime, consider yourself dismissed without a bow.[14]

As for Chicago, Hammerstein was not to be thwarted. He traveled there several times, looked about for a suitable location for an

[13] "Caruso to Sing No More This Season," *Musical America*, Vol. IX (April 17, 1909), 2.

[14] *Metropolitan Opera Company v. Oscar Hammerstein and Arthur Hammerstein*, File No. 18094–1913 (1914), p. 64.

opera house, secured a site, and announced his intentions to construct a theater in the near future.[15] The Metropolitan accepted the challenge and allied itself with the newly formed Chicago Grand Opera Company. Krehbiel has maintained that the "determinative impetus"[16] for the founding of this institution was the impresario's competition.

Even before the season was under way, there were those who realized that the coming months would witness an ultimate titanic struggle for operatic supremacy in New York as well as in the United States. Reginald de Koven, in the New York *World*, was explicit on this point: "Again without thought of quarter or relenting on either side the operatic battle is on, and, unless all signs fail, it will be fought this season to a definite end, for present conditions and indications make it financially impossible that things can continue indefinitely as they are."[17] These words, it so happens, were prophetic.

A Not So Wicked *Salome*

The Manhattan began its fourth season on Monday, November 8, 1909, with Massenet's *Hérodiade*. Although the *première* competed with the opening of the New Theatre and the Horse Show, the house held a very large audience, with an estimated 4,000 in attendance.[18] Members of New York society, however, were absent. Gone was the glitter and gold of the boxes, for when Mrs. Mackay withdrew her patronage, her friends followed in her wake. Newspapers paid scant attention to the social aspects of the opening night ceremony, while *Town Topics*, society's "official" publication, ignored it altogether. It was unfortunate that the very assistance Hammerstein should have encouraged for the continued financial well being of the company had been irrevocably cut off. From the beginning he had done very little to encourage society's attendance at the Manhattan;

[15] Edward C. Moore, *Forty Years of Opera in Chicago*, 55.

[16] *More Chapters of Opera*, 225.

[17] "Rival Opera Cohorts Gather for the Fray . . . ," *The* [New York] *World Theatre Section*, November 7, 1909, p. 5.

[18] News item in *The* [New York] *World*, November 9, 1909.

but, regardless of the impresario and his attitude, the *haut monde* had come to the house (particularly after the Melba nights of the first season) and liked what it saw and what Hammerstein was doing. Even though the Grand Tier at the Manhattan may never have possessed the prestige of the occupants of the Diamond Horseshoe, still the boxes had not been without their own special éclat and first families. In the final analysis, eminent members of society were as necessary to the Manhattan as they were to the Metropolitan. Without them, the younger house was doomed.

Hammerstein produced *Hérodiade*, one of Massenet's early works, with the hope, no doubt, that, as it concerned Salome, he might duplicate Mary Garden's tremendous success in Strauss's opera the season before. It seemed also that interest in the Judaean princess was at the high-water mark. New York and other major cities in the United States had been and were enjoying terpsichorean efforts à la Salome. On Broadway William Faversham with Olive Oliver as Salome was starring in Stephen Phillips' play *Herod*. Nor had people forgotten the banning of *Salome* at the Metropolitan in 1907, Garden's sensational triumph in the title role, and the subsequent public outcry against the presentation of the opera in Philadelphia and Boston. All was grist for the mill, and Hammerstein knew the value of publicity. Then, too, in bringing forth *Hérodiade*, he honored a composer who had contributed much to the repertory of the Manhattan and who was now, thanks to Hammerstein's efforts, very popular in New York, his operas being presented by both the Manhattan and the Metropolitan this season. It was, moreover, quite like the ingenious impresario to savor the opportunity of giving to New York yet another new work; and, this time, *mirabile dictu*, the novelty would be performed on opening night, an occasion usually reserved for operas from the standard repertory and an evening customarily associated with the social, not musical, elements. Again Hammerstein had shattered precedent. All things considered, *Hérodiade* seemed appropriate for the occasion.

As Salomé, Lina Cavalieri surprised New York critics by her vocal improvement; and, as always, her extraordinary beauty enchanted everyone. According to the New York *Sun*, the soprano "never before showed such appreciation of the beauty of continence in tone, of repose in style, of elasticity in the treatment of accentuation."[19] Dalmorès, as John the Baptist, sang as magnificently as was his wont but wore a costume which "scarcely evoked the image of one who had fed on locusts and wild honey."[20] In the role of Hérode, Renaud dominated all the scenes in which he appeared, intensely dramatic and superb in song; and, as usual, his marvelously expressive face and eyes were meaningful, unforgettable. Gerville-Réache, the Hérodiade, was less successful in her part. The conductor was Henriquez de la Fuente, the brother-in-law of Jacques Coini. Formerly he had conducted the orchestra at the opera house in Antwerp; at this performance, his first American appearance, critics considered him "a distinct acquisition."[21] He led the Manhattan orchestra with authority and consideration for the singers.

As for the opera itself, the spectacular pageantry and the two well-known arias "Il est doux, il est bon" and "Vision fugitive" were memorable; otherwise, it was dull. Hammerstein had not spared any expense in mounting and staging the work. Reginald de Koven said: "Jews, Chaldeans and Chalcedonians, dancing girls and priestesses, in picturesque garb; Roman warriors and legionaries in glittering armor formed a series of varied and ever changing stage pictures, with a background of appropriate and well executed scenery, than which anything more sumptuous, brilliant and impressive, in traditional grand opera style, has not been seen on the stage of the Manhattan. As a spectacle, and quite apart from the music, the opera is well worth while. Gorgeous is really the only word to express fittingly the festival scenes of the closing act, with its armored pageantry and sinuous and martial dances."[22] Hammerstein presented the opera eleven times, six performances being in New York and five in Philadelphia. Since then, it has been rarely performed in the United States.

[19] *The* [New York] *Sun,* November 9, 1909.
[20] *New-York Daily Tribune,* November 9, 1909.
[21] *The* [New York] *World,* November 9, 1909.
[22] *Ibid.*

A New Star

On the second night of the season, Hammerstein introduced a young tenor who was to be a great favorite at the Manhattan and later at the Metropolitan as well as one of the most successful concert artists of all time. The date was Wednesday, November 10; the opera, *La Traviata*; the glorious singer, the inimitable John McCormack, fresh from three triumphant seasons at Covent Garden. Mme Tetrazzini has implied that it was she who had urged Hammerstein to acquire the services of this artist.[23] Regardless of who recommended him, Hammerstein was prompt in getting the Irishman under contract, offering him seven hundred dollars a week for his initial season at the Manhattan.[24] Delighted with McCormack, who was twenty-five at the time of his New York debut, Hammerstein commented that he looked forward to his appearances at the opera house and that he expected to attract a new audience, since the Irish would want to hear one of their own singing Italian opera.

McCormack's presence at the Manhattan aroused much interest in the press and among his fellow countrymen in the United States. His candor, charm, and modesty were disarming. To a reporter of *The New York Herald*, he confided that he had intended to become a priest but that while preparing himself, he entered the Dublin Music Festival and won a medal for his singing, having astounded the judges by his rendition of a Handel air. He amazed them by his ability to sing an entire run of twenty bars solely on one breath. His success in the festival decided his future; he would study voice seriously. McCormack told of his early struggles:

> "I got fifty cents for my first night's work in concert, and that fifty cents looked bigger at that time than a season's earnings look now. My, but I was the proud boy that night! I got a job as a clerk and earned a dollar and a quarter a week in addition to the few dollars I picked up in concert work. I went to Milan, Italy, and studied under Signor Salatini, the dearest

[23] *My Life of Song*, 242.
[24] L. A. G. Strong, *John McCormack*, 116.

old fellow in the world. When my funds ran low and it looked as if I must give up he told me to pay him whenever I could, and it's only a few years ago that I finished paying him. He got me my first chance, and I came along rapidly after that, appearing in Covent Garden, Naples and other operatic centres in Europe. Then I was engaged to come here . . . ."[25]

He repeatedly said that he owed much to Mme Tetrazzini, who had always shown him every kindness and consideration. Calling her his "fairy godmother,"[26] McCormack was delighted that most of his operatic appearances in the United States would be with her. To another representative of the press, he said that he admired Sembrich and Caruso and admitted that he had learned much from listening to the great Italian singing.[27] No petty jealousies would mar an amiable relationship between these two men. Such frankness and humility, unusual in an opera singer, appealed to the members of the press. It is not unlikely that even before his first appearance at the Manhattan, he had won many adherents as a personality. What remained now was for him to delight and to thrill as a singer.

Countess McCormack relates in the biography of her famous husband that the tenor was suffering from a serious cold, almost the grippe, the night of his New York debut.[28] Anticipating the worst, Hammerstein had asked Zenatello to stand by in case the young Irishman was not able to appear; but by 5:30 P.M. McCormack decided that he would go on, even though his temperature was still high. It is no wonder that when the tenor first appeared on stage soon after the beginning of *La Traviata*, he seemed extremely nervous. Tetrazzini, understanding and sympathetic, went to him and gave him a pat of encouragement. Then McCormack began to sing. To the critics his voice was so beautiful that it seemed impossible he was

[25] J. A. Fitzgerald, "Mr. John McCormack-Grand Opera Tenor Whose Hobby Is Prize Fighting," *The New York Herald Theatre Section*, January 9, 1910, p. 11.

[26] *Ibid.*

[27] News item in *The New York Times*, November 1, 1909.

[28] Lily McCormack, *I Hear You Calling Me*, 57–58.

suffering from any physical affliction. The audience was immensely pleased and showed its pleasure by fervid applause. During the evening McCormack received many curtain calls, both alone and with Tetrazzini, who was delighted by her colleague's instantaneous success. Pitts Sanborn, in the New York *Globe*, commented: "The voice was beautiful in quality, and it was controlled with a skill one does not hope for nowadays from a tenor not born in Italy, and a good taste that is as rare. Such a command of mezza voce, such smoothness in legato, such fluent execution, such grace of phrase bear witness to fine schooling of fine natural gifts. And an Italian might well take pleasure in the clear enunciation of his beautiful language. If Mr. McCormack can do so much when indisposed, great things may reasonably be expected of him when he sings in restored health."[29] His costume in the first act elicited comment, as he was in a wine-colored suit of the 1840's, even though the others were in modern dress. As an actor, he left much to be desired. McCormack himself apparently liked to relate anecdotes concerning his histrionic ability. Several concern his appearances during this season at the Manhattan. Rehearsing the part of Turiddu in *Cavalleria Rusticana*, he was not passionate nor violent enough in his actions to suit his Santuzza (Carmen Melis). She implored him to be more fiery. At the public performance McCormack, remembering the soprano's pleas, hurled her so vigorously that she went crashing into the wings. She came back on stage limping but, fortunately for McCormack's peace of mind, was not hurt seriously.[30] Mariette Mazarin, also appearing as Santuzza this season, seems to have had the final word: " 'Monsieur McCormack . . . if Turiddu was like you, I should never have had to complain to his mother about my unfortunate predicament.' "[31]

As for Tetrazzini, the coloratura sang brilliantly, pouring out one luscious tone after the other. Critics marveled anew at the limpidity, freshness, velvety quality, and warmth of the voice; by all ac-

[29] *The* [New York] *Globe and Commercial Advertiser,* November 11, 1909.
[30] Strong, *John McCormack,* 128.
[31] *Ibid.,* 129.

counts she was at the peak of her career. Her skyscraping, ringing notes, portamenti, glissandi, swelling and diminishing of tones must have sent shivers of delight down the backs of her auditors. The duets with McCormack and Sammarco (Germont) were exquisite. Of less joy, however, was her first act costume, which Sanborn called "an instrument of percussion,"[32] a creation of many spangles. The conductor on this historic occasion was Oscar Anselmi, who, although not inspired, had admirable control over the forces under his baton.[33]

That McCormack's performance had pleased Hammerstein may be gleaned from the fact that he addressed the tenor at the end of the opera as "Mike,"[34] an appellation reserved for the chosen few, the men he most admired. The following day Hammerstein must have been elated when he read the reviews; and as the season continued, he had every reason to rejoice in McCormack's artistic and vocal achievements.

MAZARIN'S DEBUT AND MORE MASSENET

The other performances this first week were *Aïda* (Friday, November 12), *Thaïs* (Saturday matinee, November 13), and *Cavalleria Rusticana* and *I Pagliacci* (Saturday evening). The Aïda was of especial interest, as it was Mariette Mazarin, later in the season the creator of the title role in Strauss's *Elektra*, the last operatic *première* of historical consequence at the Manhattan Opera House. At her debut Mazarin did not do herself full justice and created what was not altogether a favorable impression. According to the *New-York Daily Tribune*, she had "a voice of greater utility than charm, much strenuous use of it having unsteadied its tones . . . ."[35] The other principals in the cast were D'Alvarez (Amneris), Zenatello (Radames), and Sammarco (Amonasro). Anselmi conducted. The following evening Mazarin fared somewhat better when she replaced Sylva as Santuzza, *The New York Herald* maintaining that she

[32] *The* [New York] *Globe and Commercial Advertiser,* November 11, 1909.

[33] *The* [New York] *World,* November 11, 1909.

[34] Strong, *John McCormack,* 122.

[35] November 13, 1909.

presented "as temperamental an impersonation of the part of this fiery Sicilian as one could wish."[36] In the afternoon's *Thaïs*, Garden and Renaud had been as musical and artistic as ever, performing with their customary assurance and making their usual telling effects.

The success of *Les Contes d'Hoffmann* may have prompted Hammerstein to introduce the series of *opéra comique* productions, or perhaps he wanted them to be counterattractions to the lighter operas the Metropolitan planned to present at the New Theatre. At any rate, in the second week Hammerstein brought forward the first of these, with Lecocq's *La Fille de Madame Angot* (Tuesday, November 16). Admission for these performances (Tuesday and Saturday evenings in New York and Wednesday and Friday evenings in Philadelphia) was $1.50 to $3. In Hammerstein's opinion the time was propitious for lighter fare: " 'Opera comique . . . is at once an antidote and a stimulant to grand opera. An unbroken diet of solid foods is not good for the stomach. A too constant hearing of the superb, lofty, inspired but heavy operas of the great composers . . . may induce musical indigestion. I shall provide the public, therefore, with a corrective in the shape of the lighter, daintier and effervescent operas that are no less the creations of genius.' "[37] After the *première* of *La Fille de Madame Angot*, many critics lauded the *opéra comique* section of the company and praised Hammerstein for his enterprise. The music was delightful; the leading singers (Delmore as Clairette, Devries as Ange Pitou, Dambrine as Pompounet) charmed; the whole production sparkled and amused. It was an excellent beginning; ostensibly Hammerstein had unearthed a gold mine in this variety of musical entertainment.

The evening following (November 17, 1909) Hammerstein presented the American *première* of *Sapho*, the second of the three Massenet novelties given this season, *Hérodiade* having been the first. The third one, *Grisélidis*, was produced after the new year, on

[36] *The New York Herald*, November 14, 1909.
[37] Sylvester Rawling, "Hammerstein to Give Opera Comique to Prevent Musical Indigestion," *The* [New York] *Evening World Theatre Section*, March 6, 1909, p. 5.

January 19, 1910. The presentations of both *Sapho* and *Grisélidis* were inspired by the presence of Garden. From having been infrequently presented before Hammerstein entered the operatic field, Massenet was now a mainstay of the Manhattan repertory. *Sapho*, however, was not the composer at his best, the work lacking inspiration. Whatever success it achieved was due to the forcible psychological study Garden gave the prostitute as Fanny Le Grand. There were those who praised her, but others thought that she was excessively vulgar in her impersonation, overdoing herself histrionically and declaiming too much of the music rather than singing it. Others in the cast were Dalmorès (Jean Gaussin), D'Alvarez (Divonne), Dufranne (Caoudal), De la Fuente conducting. There were nine performances of this opera, three being in New York, four in Philadelphia and two on tour. As for *Grisélidis*, the work itself drew high praise; Hammerstein's production and cast were superb, the *New-York Daily Tribune* critic, for one, maintaining that the impresario had excelled himself.[38] Garden's poetic interpretation of the patient Grisélidis evoked memories of her Mélisande, for she "played the part in the same spirit of half mystic subtlety and vague remoteness."[39] She sang extremely well. Others in the first American presentation were Dalmorès (Alain), Dufranne (Marquis), Huberdeau (Devil), Walter-Villa (Fiamina), Duchène (Bertrade), Villa (Prior), Scott (Gondebaud), with De la Fuente conducting. The opera was presented eight times, four performances being in New York, three in Philadelphia, and one in Boston.

AGAIN PHILADELPHIA

The evening following the opening of the Manhattan's fourth season, Hammerstein launched the second season of opera at his beautiful house in Philadelphia, where it was soon obvious that the major battles of the past year had been but minor conflicts. The date was November 9; the opera, *Aïda*, with Mazarin (Aïda), Zerola (Radames), D'Alvarez (Amneris), and Polese (Amonasro), under

[38] *New-York Daily Tribune*, January 20, 1910.
[39] *The* [New York] *World*, January 20, 1910.

the baton of Sturani, the regular conductor of the Philadelphia performances. The same evening, some blocks to the south, the Metropolitan began its regular series of performances at the Academy of Music, presenting the identical opera. In the cast were Gadski (Aïda), Caruso (Radames), Homer (Amneris) and Amato (Amonasro). Toscanini conducted. The Ramfis in each production was from Philadelphia: Henri Scott, of the Manhattan, and Allen Hinckley, of the Metropolitan. Hammerstein had wanted a direct comparison to be made; and when his rivals announced *Aïda* as the initial attraction, he immediately made known that this opera would open his new season and that the opening night would be the same date as the Metropolitan's. Unperturbed, Philadelphia rose to the occasion, completely filling the two houses with enthusiastic audiences. Members of society displayed commendable equanimity, some even attending both performances. The *Public Ledger* said: "Socially considered, one audience was quite as brilliant as the other, the actual leaders in the city's fashionable set having so divided themselves as to give to neither house an advantage in this respect over the other. Both places were filled to their capacities and the audiences in their applause were equally demonstrative."[40]

For the second performance (November 11), Hammerstein introduced Philadelphia to *Hérodiade*, with the same cast as at the New York *première* except for Egener's replacing Carew as the Slave. At the end of the third act, the audience seemed enraptured by the magnificent spectacle. Hammerstein chose this psychological moment to come before the footlights, prepared to make a speech. What he said created a sensation. For the next season Hammerstein demanded that each performance at the Philadelphia Opera House be guaranteed the same sum ($7,500) that the box holders at the Academy of Music assured the Metropolitan, which he sarcastically referred to as a " 'bunch of antidiluvian [*sic*] lemons.' "[41] Without it, he threatened that he might abandon opera in Philadelphia. He would be willing, however, to continue the performances without financial backing if the

---

[40] News item in the Philadelphia *Public Ledger,* November 10, 1909.
[41] *Ibid.,* November 12, 1909.

Metropolitan's presentations were not subsidized. He resented the inequity, his rivals being able to depend on a certain sum each time they came to Philadelphia, whereas he had to rely on popular support. What he wanted was " 'fair play, to be treated in precisely the same way.' "[42]

In issuing the pronunciamento, Hammerstein was making another strategic move in the musical war; for he believed that without a guarantee the Metropolitan would be unable to compete with him, that he would then have the field to himself. The general opinion was that Philadelphia would not or could not indefinitely continue to support two operatic enterprises of the first rank and that in the impending crisis one company would have to withdraw. Hammerstein did not intend that it would be his; he had no desire to preside over the liquidation of his operatic empire. What he must do (and the real purpose of his speech) was "to drive out his rivals."[43] For days the Metropolitan did not deign to reply. On November 23, however, Andreas Dippel, in Philadelphia with the company, issued a formal statement in which he explained the necessity for a guarantee, maintaining that it was not commensurate with the actual expense of presenting opera in Philadelphia, and that it would be more profitable if the Metropolitan added another subscription night in New York. The company, nevertheless, was not considering finances in the situation; it was "proud of and grateful for the loyalty and encouragement which it [had] always received in [Philadelphia]; and without regard to financial considerations it [would], with reciprocal loyalty, continue to give its best . . . ."[44] Dippel then made a startling statement: if Hammerstein decided to abandon the season or to quit the city, the Metropolitan would buy the Philadelphia Opera House. Should he refuse the offer, the older company intended to build a new theater or to purchase the Academy, the owners being willing, for the purpose of presenting opera there four times a week without any guarantee. When reporters rushed to Hammerstein with Dippel's proposal, the impresario, considering it briefly, then made some

[42] *Ibid.*
[43] *Ibid.*, November 13, 1909.   [44] *Ibid.*, November 24, 1909.

acrimonious comments: he did not " 'want ever to see performances such as the Metropolitan people [gave] in [his] house,' "[45] his productions in Philadelphia cost just twice as much as his rival's, and the Metropolitan's guarantee was excessive considering the quality of opera presented with the " 'little cartload of singers' "[46] from New York. The following day (November 25), Dippel, angered by the derogatory remarks, challenged and refuted what Hammerstein had said.[47] And on this note of cacophony the matter rested for a number of weeks.

There was no doubt, however, that the Metropolitan was seriously interested in buying the Philadelphia Opera House and that what Dippel had purposed coincided with a grandiose scheme contemplated by the directors of that institution, a plan to dominate the production of opera throughout the entire United States. Their policy had been indicated earlier in the month. On November 14 rumors had been circulated that Dippel would direct an opera company in Chicago the following season (1910–11) and that Campanini would be the musical director. On November 21 the Metropolitan issued an official statement that it had subscribed to stock in the Chicago Grand Opera Company and that it would have, therefore, representation in the new enterprise. The gentlemen who ultimately represented the New York house were W. K. Vanderbilt, Otto Kahn, and Clarence Mackay.[48] Any lingering doubts as to what the Metropolitan envisaged were dissipated by a later announcement (January 3, 1910) which a director (said to be Dippel) made to representatives of the press: " 'The whole proposition is a very much broader one than is generally supposed—in fact, it is of national scope; by that I mean that under the leadership of the Metropolitan Opera Company it will not be at all improbable that in time an operatic basis may be established in every principal city in the United States.' "[49] The

[45] *Ibid.*

[46] *Ibid.*

[47] *Ibid.*, November 25, 1909.

[48] News item in *The* [New York] *World*, November 21, 1909.

[49] News item in *The New York Times*, January 3, 1910.

founding of the Chicago Grand Opera Company was the " 'entering wedge to the Great West.' "[50] It was obvious that the elimination of Hammerstein from the field (and the sooner the better) could redound only to the best interests of the Metropolitan. At this time the directors undoubtedly wished for a plague on both of his opera houses.

SPARKLING PERFORMANCES AND PERFORMERS

In the meantime, the opera seasons at the Manhattan and Philadelphia Opera House were in full swing. The company had prepared two important revivals, the first of these, on November 22, being Donizetti's *La Fille du Régiment*, with Tetrazzini (Marie), McCormack (Tonio), and Gilibert (Sulpice), under the baton of Anselmi. The work was preceded by a spirited performance of *I Pagliacci* with Sylva (Nedda), Zerola (Canio), and Sammarco (Tonio). Although Tetrazzini did not look the part of a vivandière, she triumphed by her sprightly acting and sumptuous singing. At the close of the opera she interpolated the waltz from Gounod's *Mireille*. McCormack, not in especially good voice, nevertheless sang his second act aria beautifully and, responding to the tremendous applause, repeated it, much to the delight of the audience. Had it not been for Gilibert, he would not have had the ovation. The Manhattan used the Italian edition of the opera, which does not include this aria, Donizetti having added it for the French version. Fortunately Gilibert possessed a score with the melody; but since it was not translated in Italian, McCormack waxed poetical. What ensued was "Per viver vicino a Maria" and one of the tenor's greatest vocal achievements in grand opera.[51] New York had already seen Gilibert as Sulpice, since he had sung it with Sembrich at the Metropolitan in the season of 1902–1903. He was inimitable in the role, superb in his characterization.

The second revival was Hammerstein's first venture in the production of Wagner, his baptism of fire being the master's *Tannhäuser*, in a mixture of the Parisian version and the original score. The opera was presented in French, on December 10, with Zenatello as Tann-

[50] *Ibid.*

[51] Strong, *John McCormack*, 126.

häuser, Renaud as Wolfram, Mazarin as Elisabeth, Doria as Venus, and Vallier as the Landgraf, under the direction of De la Fuente. Though Zenatello was nervous and unfamiliar with the requisite style, there were moments of eloquence, the "Roman Narrative," in particular, being most artistic.[52] Vocally Mazarin was overly dramatic, her voice occasionally marred by a tremolo. Later she, too, improved, offering an affecting portrayal of the saintly Elisabeth. Renaud was the particular star of the evening, still thrilling by his superb art and voice. The sets, costumes, and staging were noteworthy. An expensive production, *Tannhäuser* was heard but two other times. Unfortunately, the omission of Wagner in the Manhattan's repertory during the past seasons was not redeemed by this presentation.

Between the first production of *La Fille du Régiment* and *Tannhäuser*, two sopranos were acclaimed for their memorable performances. The debut of an interesting singer occurred on November 26, when Carmen Melis, who had been in opera for only three years, was heard as Tosca in a cast that included Zenatello (Cavaradossi) and Renaud (Scarpia), with De la Fuente conducting. A beautiful woman, Melis sang dramatically and acted with intense realism. Of all the Toscas heard in New York, her interpretation was considered the most "redolent of the Latin temperament."[53] Later in the season she was heard as Mimi and Santuzza; and although she had wanted to sing Thaïs, Garden would not permit her to appear in the role she claimed as her exclusive property. Piqued, Melis protested against the "Thaïs trust" but to no avail. This lady is still with us, one of the very few remaining of Hammerstein's principal artists. Living in Como, Italy, she is busy teaching young operatic aspirants. One of her pupils is another great Tosca: Renata Tebaldi.

The "other" soprano delighted her many admirers and reconquered New York, simply amazing the critics in a role not associated with her career in the United States. The opera was the season's first *Faust*, on December 8; the wonderful singer (and she was vocally

[52] *The* [New York] *Evening Post*, December 11, 1909.
[53] *The* [New York] *Sun*, December 7, 1909.

resplendent!) was Mary Garden. At last the critics were hearing her in something they knew. To their surprise, they found that the quality of her tones was lovely. What some of them still did not realize was that she had, in reality, many voices; for, as always, she used her voice as a medium of dramatic expression, not just as an instrument for making beautiful sounds. She sang the "King of Thule" charmingly; the "Jewel Song" was not just a vocal showpiece, but an aria that conveyed Marguerite's innermost feelings, innocence, and delight. Her interpretation of the role was artistically complete; the innovations were well thought out and appropriate. The fact that Garden's whole performance was better than had been anticipated, as well as the fact of her having completely disarmed any would-be detractors, is apparent from the reviews. The *New-York Daily Tribune* said: "Let us be frank and state that Miss Garden disappointed many last evening, but the disappointment was a triumph for Miss Garden. She proved to the doubters that she can sing, and proved it to them where it was least expected—in the 'Jewel Song.' Miss Garden has been the authoress of many surprises, but it is doubtful if any of them was the equal of the one last night."[54]

THE MANHATTAN ON THE ROAD

On December 2, 1909, Hammerstein announced that he was abandoning the *opéra comique* productions and that the artists he had engaged for them as well as some members of the regular company would embark on an eleven-week tour of cities in Canada and in the United States after the December 11 performance of *Les Cloches de Corneville*.[55] By then, the *opéra comique* group had appeared in New York eight times: *La Fille de Madame Angot* (2); *La Mascotte* (1); *Les Dragons de Villars* (2); and *Les Cloches de Corneville* (3), while in Philadelphia there had been four performances: *La Fille de Madame Angot* (1); *La Mascotte* (2); and *Les Dragons de Villars* (1). Although critics had praised all these productions, lauding the settings, the orchestra and chorus, and the delightful principals, the operas were never successful at the box office. Perhaps

[54] *New-York Daily Tribune*, December 9, 1909.

[55] News item in *The New York Times*, December 2, 1909.

they would have been, had they been sung in English. Hammerstein thought that their failure to arouse any real interest was due to the change in public taste, since the dialogue, text, and plot were now considered outdated.

Traveling in a special train consisting of seven cars,[56] the company began its tour in Montreal on Monday, December 13, 1909, presenting here, as elsewhere, eight performances each week. Advertised as features of the entertainment were the chorus of sixty and the orchestra of forty. Among the principals were sopranos Miranda, Vicarino, Dumesnil, Delmore, Laya, Nolba; tenors Russo, Duffault, Carasa, Devries, Leroux, Dambrine; baritones Dufour, Pignataro; and bassos Nicolay, Laskin, Scott, with Alfred Haakman conducting. The repertory consisted of six light operas (*Les Cloches de Corneville, Les Dragons de Villars, La Mascotte, La Fille de Madame Angot, La Fille du Tambour-major, Le Petit Duc*) as well as *Carmen, Mignon, Lucia,* and *Faust.* In general, the company played to enthusiastic houses and to critical acclaim, although the chorus and orchestra were occasionally reproved for ragged work in the serious opera presentations, but never for their contributions to the lighter operas. *The Quebec Chronicle* said of the troupe: "Quebec has, in days gone by, heard some of the finest French opera companies which have won fame in America. From New Orleans, in particular, and, in a few rare cases, from Paris direct, there have come companies who have interpreted all that was best in light opera. There seem to be no two opinions, however, among those who were delighted by the Hammerstein troupe as to the merits of the present in comparison with the past."[57] Ultimately, however, the outcome was the same as it had been in New York and Philadelphia. On January 31, 1910, Hammerstein disbanded the group,[58] the road tour having been a financial loss of $40,000.[59] Up to that date the company had presented fifty-six per-

[56] News item in *The* [Toronto] *Globe,* January 17, 1910.

[57] January 5, 1910.

[58] "Hammerstein's Opéra Comique Company Disbanded," *Musical America,* Vol. XI (February 12, 1910), 15.

[59] Blumenthal and Menkin, *My Sixty Years in Show Business,* 126.

formances and had appeared in Montreal (December 13, 1909—January 1, 1910); Quebec (January 3–8); Ottawa (January 10–13); Hamilton (January 14–15); Toronto (January 17–22); Rochester (January 24–26); and Buffalo (January 27–29).

In addition to these peregrinations, Hammerstein sent out members of the regular company for a series of performances in Pittsburgh, Cincinnati, and Washington during December and January, and at the close of the New York season there was a spring tour to Boston. Hammerstein's purpose was to alleviate pressing financial difficulties of his opera ventures in New York and Philadelphia and to challenge his rivals in cities previously considered strongholds in Metropolitan territory. The opera war would rage in new arenas, since Hammerstein determined to infiltrate old citadels in the Metropolitan's fortifications.

Hammerstein opened the new front in Pittsburgh, where he sent a detachment of the company with an interesting repertory of the old and the new, the Tetrazzini war horses and the Garden operas. The season began with *Lucia*, on December 20, 1909. In the cast were Tetrazzini (Lucia), McCormack (Edgardo), Polese (Ashton), with Anselmi conducting. The critic of *The Pittsburgh Post*, Jennie Irene Mix, referring to the battle royal, spoke of Tetrazzini as the "standard bearer . . . who was expected to lead the invading forces to a glorious victory."[60] The coloratura, alas, did not sing as was her wont; the same critic, though admiring Tetrazzini's exquisite staccati, rich upper tones, and the warmth of her singing, found fault with the lower register, some of the trills, and scale work. She criticized also the *mise-en-scène*, costuming, chorus, and the employment of the Pittsburgh Symphony as the opera orchestra, Hammerstein not having brought one from New York. The local musicians had had but one rehearsal and without the benefit of the principals' presence. Tetrazzini's second appearance was as Violetta (December 22); and though she was scheduled to sing again in another *Lucia* (December 24), a severe sore throat prevented her from doing so, the performance then being cancelled. Renaud's Scarpia in *Tosca* (December 21)

[60] *The Pittsburgh Post*, December 21, 1909.

was admired; but it was not until Garden's appearances in *Sapho* (December 23) and in *Le Jongleur de Notre Dame* (December 25 matinee) that there was a turning point in the company's fortunes. The *Post* critic now praised where praise was due, describing *Sapho* as among the greatest presentations "not only ever seen in this city, but that could be seen on any stage in the world today . . . ,"[61] and *Le Jongleur* as "one of the most beautiful performances Pittsburgh has been privileged to hear in many a day."[62] Garden was a revelation, a much greater opera singer than had been anticipated, and, as the Juggler, brought "tears to the eyes of those long since grown stultified to the display of emotion."[63] The company concluded its engagement the evening of December 25, presenting *Cavalleria Rusticana* with Grippon (Santuzza), Russo (Turiddu) and Crabbé (Alfio) and *I Pagliacci* with Walter-Villa (Nedda), Zerola (Canio), and Polese (Tonio). The week had not been a financial success, nor had the Manhattan effaced memories of past Metropolitan productions.

Marching onward to Cincinnati, Hammerstein hoped to recoup some of the losses sustained in Pittsburgh, but, again, bad luck dogged the trail. The short engagement turned out to be a fiasco, with a variety of reasons contributing to the dismal situation. The criticisms from Pittsburgh (the small chorus, an inferior supporting company, the use of the local symphony orchestra) had circulated among Cincinnatians, who were also none too happy regarding prices ($5 top), the repertory, and the few rehearsals allowed the Cincinnati Symphony, which had been engaged for the operas.[64] Moreover, the series of performances came at an unpropitious time, since society was involved in many parties during the Christmas holiday. The principal reason for the catastrophe, however, was Tetrazzini's persistent sore throat. The attractions had been announced as *Lucia* (December 27), *Sapho* (December 28 matinee), and *La Traviata* (December 28 evening), with Tetrazzini as the star of two presentations. Unfortunately

---

[61] *Ibid.*, December 24, 1909.
[62] *Ibid.*, December 26, 1909.
[63] *Ibid.*
[64] News item in *The* [Cincinnati] *Enquirer*, December 28, 1909.

the prima donna was still indisposed and had to cancel her appearance in the Donizetti opera, which had been sold out. Hammerstein made no attempt to replace her in the cast or to present any opera at all. His hope was that Tetrazzini would be able to appear the following evening; and until late in the afternoon of the twenty-eighth, it seemed that she would perform. However, a local throat specialist stated categorically that to sing in her condition might harm her voice permanently. When the public heard that Tetrazzini was still ill, they besieged the box office, demanding their money back, even though Hammerstein had announced that there would be a performance of *La Traviata* and that Walter-Villa was to replace Tetrazzini. McCormack, who appeared as Alfredo on this occasion, always remembered it as a rare experience; for the company was singing to a practically bare auditorium.[65] The Cincinnati *Enquirer* described it this way: " . . . a gloom as thick as the proverbial London fog settled over the hall, which remained there throughout the performance in spite of the heroic efforts of the singers in the cast."[66] The only opera which took place as originally announced was the performance of *Sapho* with the indestructible Garden, whom Cincinnatians called "the operatic Sara Bernhardt."[67]

Hammerstein's next site in the campaign was Washington, where the Metropolitan had visited on many occasions, the most recent one being April, 1908.[68] In contrast to the adversities in Pittsburgh and Cincinnati, nothing but success and warm appreciation crowned the efforts of the visitors during their engagement in this beautiful city, with public and critics admiring the entire series of performances (January 10–14, 1910). Hammerstein's statement when he arrived there on Sunday, January 9, may have dismayed the Metropolitan: " ' . . . Perhaps the main reason for my coming is that I want to study the musical situation in Washington. I think that there is a

---

[65] Strong, *John McCormack*, 131–32.
[66] December 29, 1909.
[67] *Ibid.*, December 26, 1909.
[68] Eaton, *Opera Caravan*, 247–48.

splendid field for grand opera here, but I want to convince myself on that point.' "[69]

The Washington Post considered the *première* (the inevitable *Lucia* with Tetrazzini) the "most brilliant first night of grand opera that the Capital of the nation [had] ever witnessed."[70] In the boxes and orchestra stalls were leaders of society, representatives of the diplomatic corp, cabinet members, and other officials of the government. President and Mrs. Taft with their party came into the theater just before the overture; and as soon as they entered the Presidential Box, the orchestra, the regular Philadelphia Opera House ensemble, played the National Anthem. During the performance the singers seemed to outdo themselves. In the applause which thundered upon them, it was noted that the President invariably initiated the demonstration. The next evening Garden, in *Thaïs*, enthralled the sold-out house. During the morning of January 12 the President received the entire company at the White House. For years afterwards McCormack, Tetrazzini, and Garden recalled the reception. That evening the Chief Executive, his wife, and party attended the performance of *Le Jongleur de Notre Dame*. After each act Taft received many visitors, "a number of the diplomats dropping in to pay their respects, and at one time so many of the President's advisers were grouped about him that the box had the appearance of an impromptu cabinet meeting."[71] It would seem that much of the show that evening was in the audience and that for once Garden had been upstaged. At the final performance, *La Fille du Régiment* followed by *I Pagliacci* (January 14), Tetrazzini interpolated the "Polonaise" from *Mignon* in the lesson scene of the Donizetti opera, since the President had expressed a desire to hear her in this aria. Her singing pleased him, and it was observed that, again, he was the first to applaud. The rule of no encores was forgotten, for Tetrazzini sang it a second time and as brilliantly as before, tireless in her vocal efforts. According to *The*

[69] News item in *The Washington Post*, January 10, 1910.

[70] *Ibid.*, January 11, 1910.

[71] *Ibid.*, January 13, 1910.

Washington Herald, the National Capital had never had "such a remarkable and memorable season of grand opera."[72] This encomium was hardly comforting to the Metropolitan.

In Boston the two giants of grand opera locked horns, concurrently appearing during the week of March 28—April 2, 1910. It was possible to hear Garden, Tetrazzini, Mazarin, Gerville-Réache, Renaud, and McCormack at the Boston Theater, while Caruso, Farrar, Homer, Destinn, Scotti, and Gadski appeared at the Boston Opera House. The Manhattan's repertory was more interesting to those who enjoyed novelties, whereas the Metropolitan's list leaned heavily on the standard operas. Critics were generous in their praise of the various artists under Hammerstein's aegis. A few nerves at the Boston Opera House must have been unsettled by the accolades heaped upon Tetrazzini and McCormack after their performance in *Lucia* (March 29). Of McCormack's singing, *The Boston Post* said: "Not in years has a tenor voice been heard in this city so pleasing and acceptable...."[73] These words could be disconcerting to Caruso, who was sensitive to criticism and who had sung there just two nights before. Critics admired the performances of Mazarin in *Elektra* and Garden in four of her famous roles: Jongleur, Grisélidis, Mélisande, and Thaïs. David Devries acquitted himself nobly, singing the role of Pelléas (April 1) for the first time anywhere. At the end of the engagement it would have been difficult to know which of the two forces had won the battle; but Olin Downes, for one, regarded the brief season as the "greatest week of opera in the history of Boston...."[74]

To make the marathon possible, Hammerstein utilized all the resources of the company; at times he produced opera simultaneously in four cities, December 25, 1909, being an instance. On that date, while Hammerstein presented *La Tosca* and *Les Contes d'Hoffmann* in New York, Philadelphia enjoyed *Faust* and *Aïda*; and while *Le*

[72] January 15, 1910.

[73] March 30, 1910.

[74] Olin Downes, "Boston's Judgment of *Elektra*," *Musical America*, Vol. XI (April 9, 1910), 6.

Jongleur de Notre Dame, *Cavalleria Rusticana*, and *I Pagliacci* were given in Pittsburgh, Montreal enthusiastically applauded the *opéra comique* troupe in *Mignon* and *La Fille du Tambour-major*. The enormity of this gigantic undertaking is indicated by the record of performances outside New York during the season, the total being 160. What was lamentable was that with all this shuttling about, presentations at the Manhattan Opera House were below the high standard which Hammerstein had established. There was not sufficient time for rehearsals to prepare the revivals and new works. The *première* of *Grisélidis*, which had been originally announced for January 7, was postponed until January 19, and for this reason. At the beginning of the season Hammerstein had contemplated producing Victor Herbert's *Natoma*, which the composer had written for a Manhattan Opera House *première*, but by the time it was ready (January 15, 1910), the impresario was losing a great deal of money in the war with the Metropolitan and presumably did not have sufficient funds, time on the operatic schedule, or the inclination any longer to produce it. The opera was first performed in Philadelphia on February 25, 1911, by the Chicago-Philadelphia Opera Company, under the direction of Andreas Dippel. Too often the Manhattan Opera casts were without great names, since many of the leading artists were away with the peripatetic companies or making solo engagements. Tetrazzini, in addition to her appearances in opera, was on a concert tour from January 21 to February 8,[75] Hammerstein having arranged it as a desperate measure to reduce ever mounting deficits. As a result, he enfeebled the company in New York, making himself more vulnerable to attack. He was determined, however, to smash the enemy. Fire would be fought with fire.

The Metropolitan also made touring history this season, giving a total of 144 performances in various cities throughout the United States.[76] Of course, Hammerstein's competition was responsible for the expansion. Although Gatti-Casazza had advocated a less am-

[75] "Concert Tour for Tetrazzini," *The New York Clipper*, Vol. LVII (January 15, 1910), 1.
[76] Eaton, *Opera Caravan*, 132.

bitious program, Dippel's policy to increase the number of out-of-town presentations had prevailed.[77] The company again employed a double orchestra, an Italian and a German chorus, and over a hundred principals. From the few performances which the Metropolitan usually presented in Baltimore, this season the number increased to twenty; in Philadelphia it was twenty-five; in Chicago, thirty-three. Where Hammerstein was, there would the Metropolitan be also, fighting back, but at great cost.

Philadelphia had been a bitter lesson, one not to be forgotten. The Metropolitan met the challenge in Baltimore and bought the Lyric Theatre "to keep it out of the hands of Oscar Hammerstein."[78] This season the Maryland city was having too much opera, and performances had to be curtailed for lack of popular support. When Hammerstein announced that he planned to build an opera house in Brooklyn, the Metropolitan increased the number of performances in this borough, thereby decreasing, ironically enough, the attendance of Brooklynites at the Broadway house; and when he said that he would acquire land and construct an opera house in Chicago,[79] the Metropolitan again lost no time in combating Hammerstein, aligning itself with the newly formed Chicago Grand Opera Company and acquiring stock in the nascent corporation.

What the impresario did was to lay a trap for his rival. According to Arthur Hammerstein, his father planned these moves very carefully, so that the Metropolitan would overexpand. He had never been at all interested in building a theater in Baltimore or Chicago; it was all part of his tactics to ruin the enemy. Arthur maintained that "the payment of $5,000 for a sixty days' option on a piece of Chicago property, ostensibly for an opera house site, was done . . . solely to tempt the Metropolitan to do precisely what it did—jump into the Western field and prepare to invest heavily."[80] He was also

[77] Gatti-Casazza, *Memories of the Opera*, 165–66.

[78] News item in *The* [New York] *Sun*, February 13, 1910.

[79] News item in *The New York Times*, August 15, 1909.

[80] "Trap for Metropolitan," *Musical America*, Vol. XI (February 12, 1910), 18.

quoted as saying that "every move the Metropolitan makes toward extending the giving of opera outside New York will help our enterprise here . . . ."[81] The situation became more and more ludicrous. It was as if Hammerstein were a puppeteer manipulating strings, while the puppets, in this case Wall Street tycoons, danced—but to an expensive tune. A crafty strategist, Hammerstein had outguessed his rivals in operatic schemes and planning and, more often than not, outmaneuvered them in the field. A solution for such untenable operatic affairs had to be found.

[81] *Ibid.*

XIX

Shadows Fall

IN THE FIRST WEEK of January, 1910, it was announced that action was being taken to find a solution to the ruinous competition. Soon after the new year lengthy articles appeared in the New York newspapers concerning a possible merger of the Manhattan and Metropolitan forces; and though some of the information was unfounded, the ultimate settlement of the suicidal war was indicated at this time. All that transpired, however, may never be known.

According to *The New York Times* of January 1, Arthur Hammerstein said that the directors of the Metropolitan were considering a plan to secure the French forces of the Manhattan and to place the elder Hammerstein as the director of French operas.[1] The following day, however, a director of the older house emphatically stated that no such scheme was being entertained. He admitted, nevertheless, that Arthur had initiated contact with the Metropolitan sometime before and that he had offered certain proposals. When asked about this, the elder Hammerstein had little to say except that a merger would be advantageous to both companies and that he would be honored to be director of the French operas at the Metropolitan without any financial consideration.[2]

Rumors persisted, and it was said that the Metropolitan wanted to buy out Hammerstein. The impresario, however, did not seem willing to sell. He said he enjoyed being an opera director, even though it was virtually impossible to make opera remunerative under

[1] January 1, 1910.
[2] *Ibid.*, January 2, 1910.

existing conditions. At least, he had not lost his sense of humor: " 'I rather like my job; while it may not affluently keep me in bread and butter, it will certainly keep me in hot water without the expense of fuel.' "[3]

On January 4, the directors of the Metropolitan issued an official, terse statement which was released to the press at six o'clock: "The Board of Directors of the Metropolitan Opera Company states that no negotiations have been pending or are now pending between Mr. Hammerstein's Manhattan Opera Company and the Metropolitan Opera Company."[4] The names on the statement were W. K. Vanderbilt, Otto H. Kahn, Clarence H. Mackay, H. R. Winthrop, R. L. Cottenet, E. L. Baylies, George J. Gould, T. de Witt Cuyler, Frank G. Griswold, and Eliot Gregory. Two hours later Arthur Hammerstein held a press conference and gave a very detailed account of his negotiations with Otto H. Kahn, president of the board of directors at the Metropolitan.

Arthur said that he had first met Kahn at the Manhattan Opera House and that, from time to time, the financier had availed himself of the opportunity of going backstage to discuss questions germane to opera with the elder Hammerstein. Early in December, 1908, Arthur, concerned about the demands of the singers and their threats to leave one company for the other, had an interview with Kahn in order to arrange an amicable agreement between the two houses. At that meeting the banker agreed that an entente was vital to all interests. The feud between Gatti-Casazza and Dippel then being at its height, Kahn found the situation intolerable at the opera house and said that he would propose to the board of directors that Oscar Hammerstein be the sole director of the older house. He considered him " 'the only real impresario in the field.' "[5]

At a subsequent time, when Oscar and Arthur Hammerstein met with Kahn at the banker's residence, Kahn reiterated his desire to see the elder Hammerstein as the sole director of the Metropolitan. The

[3] *Ibid.*, January 3, 1910.
[4] *Ibid.*, January 5, 1910.
[5] *Ibid.*

impresario was not averse to the idea; and when Kahn presented the matter at a meeting of the board of directors, all agreed except for W. K. Vanderbilt, Sr., who, Kahn thought, would ultimately acquiesce. One tangible sign of the improved relations between the two companies was Hammerstein's permitting Zenatello to replace Caruso in the Metropolitan's spring tour of 1909.

At a later meeting, which Arthur said was on November 23, 1909, Kahn and he again discussed the singers' inordinate demands and their playing one company against the other, thereby increasing their salaries. Arthur then referred to the inducements which the Metropolitan was said to have offered to some of the Manhattan artists if they left the younger house and wondered whether Kahn, as president of the board of directors, condoned these transactions. Kahn said that he did not and again expressed his fervent desire to see some sensible resolution of the operatic affairs. What he then proposed was that the two companies join together as one operatic enterprise. The ideal person to conduct the negotiations, in his opinion, was Judge E. H. Gary, a box holder at both the Manhattan and Metropolitan and a friend of many of the directors at the older house. The following evening Arthur went to the Judge's box at the Manhattan and told him of the plan. Delighted to be of assistance, he agreed to do all that he could. His efforts, however, were to no avail. Since there still was opposition at the Metropolitan, Kahn told Arthur (December 9) that for the moment the negotiations would have to be held in abeyance; but the banker said that they were not to be abandoned.

Approximately a week later (December 15) Lee Shubert called Arthur, requesting a meeting. What he proposed (December 18) was to buy out Hammerstein, maintaining that the Metropolitan had authorized him to do so. Arthur's task was difficult; his father's life was the opera house. To sell out his interests would be unthinkable. However, in the presence of his brother William, Arthur presented the proposition to the impresario, who was, as had been anticipated, contemptuous of it.[6]

Others were asked to make comments. When Lee Shubert was

[6] *Ibid.*

interviewed by the press, he admitted that he had made some definite proposals to Arthur concerning the Manhattan. He declared, however, that he had not acted for the directors of the Metropolitan. Apparently he had discussed the operatic situation with Kahn and Dippel and directors of the New Theatre. What evolved was a plan to buy an interest in the Manhattan; but the elder Hammerstein would not agree to such a proposal.[7] The press also tried to interview Otto Kahn, but he would not make any statement.[8] In Philadelphia Harry Hammerstein, who was acting as the local manager of the opera house, acknowledged that the New York reports were true. He confirmed that the negotiations had begun more than a year before and said:

" . . . At that time it was suggested that my father join forces with the Metropolitan, and so far as Philadelphia is concerned it was said by the Metropolitan people that if the coalition were to take place, the Academy of Music would be abandoned and the performances given in the opera house at Broad and Poplar streets.

" . . . I am sure my father will not consent to any proposed affiliation if the Metropolitan management insists upon a board of directors. He wants to be the only head, or nothing at all. It was because of this point that the former discussion of the same plan came to an end."[9]

What these assertions and counter-assertions reveal is that efforts were being made to end the opera war. These efforts, in fact, were to become increasingly concerted in the following months. Correspondence in the Otto H. Kahn Collection at Princeton University discloses the fact that during the late winter and early spring there was a great deal of discussion concerning a settlement and that the directors of the older house were absolutely determined the negotiations be kept a secret.

[7] *Ibid.*
[8] *Ibid.*, January 6, 1910.
[9] News item in the Philadelphia *Public Ledger*, January 2, 1910.

A Last Great *Première*

Then, at the right moment, as he had done before when all looked portentous, Hammerstein brought forward his *pièce de résistance*, Strauss's *Elektra*, the opera sensation of the year and the company's last American *première* of historical significance. In the cast were Mariette Mazarin as Elektra, Gerville-Réache as Klytemnestra, Alice Baron as Chrysothemis, Jean Duffault as Aegisthus, and Huberdeau as Orestes, with De la Fuente conducting. Hammerstein had invested heavily in the production, paying $10,000 to the composer alone for production rights in the United States as well as $18,000 more in advance royalties.[10] The ten weeks of rehearsals cost $15,000, not to mention the expenses incurred by the additional musicians in the enlarged orchestra of 113. Regardless of expenditures, the production had to be perfect in every respect.

Much publicity preceded the first performance, and the orchestral and vocal difficulties were loudly proclaimed. Hammerstein maintained that the *Elektra* rehearsals left no time for anything else: " 'Strauss's score is so absolutely foreign to all accepted forms, so revolutionary in treatment that it upsets both my singers and my orchestra. After an exhaustive rehearsal of *Elektra* not even the certainty of extra pay has any inducement for my musicians. As for my singers, they positively refuse to think of any other music, with their minds still full of Strauss's odd, musically disconnected notes ....' "[11] In a public letter, published the day before the *première*, he exhorted opera-goers not to listen to those who considered the opera "musical rot."[12] Mazarin, who sang the title role, contributed to the much discussed subject. She said: " ' ... I am nursing all of my physical, emotional and artistic strength for Tuesday evening's premiere; I shall need every bit that I possess, for no one who has not gone

[10] Finck, *Richard Strauss*, 244.

[11] Sylvester Rawling, "Hammerstein Says Poor Performances Are Due to Preparations for *Elektra*," *The* [New York] *Evening World Theatre Section*, January 15, 1910, p. 4.

[12] Letter written by Oscar Hammerstein in *The* [New York] *Sun*, January 31, 1910, p. 7.

through the physical and emotional suffering that I have experienced during rehearsals can realize what it all means.' "[13] The public, forewarned and fascinated, responded to the publicity; and although Hammerstein doubled the prices at the initial presentation ($2.50 in the family circle to $10 in the orchestra, and $25, $50, and $100 for boxes), a very large house paid $19,700[14] for their places, ready, in the words of Henry T. Finck, "to be electrified, or, perchance, Elektracuted."[15]

From all accounts, the critics and public found the American *première* of *Elektra*, on Tuesday, February 1, 1910, an unforgettable experience. The performance was overpowering; the effect, shattering. Carl Van Vechten recalled years later that at the end of the opera roars of approval exploded from the house and that the perfervid applause was "almost hysterical in quality."[16] Critics thought the presentation one of the most remarkable in the history of music in New York. As for the work itself, however, many of them considered it disgusting and repellent from the musical standpoint. Strauss had gone the limit. W. J. Henderson of the *Sun* objected to melodies which "[spat] and [scratched] and [clawed] at each other,"[17] while Krehbiel of the *Tribune* denounced it vehemently: "Marvel as we may at the music of this lyric drama in its newest phase, there can be no other conclusion than that its brilliancy is the strongest proof of its decadence. The age of greatest technical skill—'virtuosity,' as it is called—is the age of greatest decay in really creative energy . . . . Mozart and Beethoven have not yet been dethroned, and the banishment of their music to the limbo of forgotten things is not imminent. We shall enjoy *Hänsel und Gretel* next Saturday; and be comforted."[18] De Koven, on the other hand, thought the music of *Elektra*, in com-

---

[13] Mariette Mazarin, "Mme. Mazarin on *Elektra*," *The* [New York] *World Theatre Section*, January 30, 1910, p. 1.

[14] Kolodin, *The Metropolitan Opera 1883–1935*, 158.

[15] Finck, *Richard Strauss*, 245.

[16] Van Vechten, *Interpreters and Interpretations*, 131.

[17] *The* [New York] *Sun*, February 2, 1910.

[18] *New-York Daily Tribune*, February 2, 1910.

parison to the score of *Salome*, "more straight-forward, artistically interesting, and dramatically forcible and appropriate . . . ."[19] He maintained that the concluding ten minutes of the work were "worth all the rest, in real dramatic exaltation and inspirational qualities."[20]

Many were of the opinion that had *Elektra* been sung in German, instead of in a French translation by Henri Gauthier-Villars, and that had De la Fuente's reading been more forceful, the opera would have gained immeasurably, creating the full effect that the score demanded. What was lacking was that the dynamics, the outbursts, which Strauss intended, did not receive fullest expression. Henderson wrote: "It is by no means improbable that a far different effect could be achieved were not Henriquez de la Fuente . . . so gentle and considerate in his reading of the score. What Strauss himself would say to this extremely polished version of the drama it is not difficult to imagine. He would in all likelihood ask the conductor whether he supposed that the composer wished to be mistaken for Massenet."[21]

The true glory of the occasion was the Elektra: Mariette Mazarin, the ideal interpreter of the role as an incredibly fascinating artist portraying the vengeful daughter of Agamemnon. Nothing that she had done before at the Manhattan had aroused much critical acclaim, but now every New York critic gave her the full diapason. Her whole performance was on such a high pitch of nervous energy and frenzy that the audience was swept along by her powerful portrayal, the fundamental idea of which was "diabolical ecstasy."[22] Not only did she astound by her mastery of the character, but her singing soared triumphantly over all the pitfalls and hurdles of Strauss's enormously difficult score. She sang tirelessly, with powerful tones, intensity, and glowing voice color. Her dance of triumph after the murder of her hated mother and Aegisthus was a marvelous, breathtaking climax. Apparently Mazarin had once gone to a madhouse in order to gain ideas for this dance and for her frightful interpretation of the de-

[19] *The* [New York] *World*, February 2, 1910.
[20] *Ibid.*
[21] *The* [New York] *Sun*, February 2, 1910.
[22] Van Vechten, *Interpreters and Interpretations*, 128.

mented Elektra.[23] At the end of the performance Mazarin, over-wrought by the strain of rehearsals and the *première*, tottered and fell unconscious during one of the innumerable curtain calls. Of her emotions on this evening, the soprano said:

" . . . To be truthful, outside of the character I had none. I was Elektra. I had studied her for weeks, lived with her, possessed myself of her until she possessed me and I was the mad, distraught, vengeful thing that she was, full of hate for Clytemnestra, ready to murder her when I got the chance, oblivious of all else but my purpose, my character. When I first appeared, just for a minute, through the bronze doors looking down upon the court the strained, tense faces of the audience, of which I got merely a glimpse, acted as a tonic. After that I saw nothing, felt nothing but Elektra . . . ."[24]

When Hammerstein presented the opera in Philadelphia, on February 5, 1910, the great auditorium held an enormous audience, equalled on only two other occasions: the opening night of the inaugural season and the first performance of *Salome*. The cast was the same as at the New York *première* except for three changes. Doria appeared as Klytemnestra, Gerville-Réache having renounced the role, which she declared was too taxing vocally; Devries replaced Duffault as Aegisthus; and Miranda was a serving woman in place of Milda. The score shocked the critics; but the public responded, filling the house for the other two performances. At the final presentation on Tuesday, February 15, Hammerstein invited the Saturday afternoon subscribers to be his guests; otherwise, they would have had no opportunity to see the much heralded work. Although he had originally planned to present *Elektra* four times in Philadelphia and to all his subscribers, he was unable to do so, since forty of the players in the augmented orchestra were members of the Philharmonic Orchestra

[23] *Ibid.*

[24] Sylvester Rawling, "Mazarin, Who as Elektra Has Given New York the Most Thrilling Operatic Character in Its History . . . ," *The* [New York] *Evening World Theatre Section*, February 5, 1910, p. 7.

of New York, which regularly performed on Saturday afternoons. A similar instance of Hammerstein's magnanimity was Melba's farewell of the previous season, when the impresario had invited the Saturday evening subscribers to be his guests, so that all of his patrons would hear her.

THE END OF THE SEASON

Hard on the heels of the tremendous success of *Elektra* came an announcement, on February 8, from the Metropolitan that ultimately had a profound effect on the Manhattan. The older house intended to present opera in Philadelphia next season without a guarantee "in order to give marked expression to its appreciation of the loyalty and encouragement which it [had] always received in [that] music-loving and understanding city . . . ."[25] Hammerstein retorted that, regardless of this new policy, he would not give performances in the Quaker City another year without financial assurance.[26] Hammerstein then announced that he would accept Dippel's offer of the past November and sell his Philadelphia Opera House to the Metropolitan. The older house did not make an immediate reply to this proposition. It was alleged, however, that some arrangement with Hammerstein was under consideration. Sheean maintains that at this very time positive action was being taken for a settlement of the situation since Arthur Hammerstein, with his father's permission, had resumed negotiations with the Metropolitan.[27] After a series of long conversations with Mr. Kahn, it seemed imperative to have the assistance of several lawyers: Samuel Untermyer represented the Manhattan's interests; Paul Cravath, the Metropolitan's. In due course Arthur realized that a satisfactory outcome was feasible, that the Metropolitan was serious about the entire matter. It would require considerable time, however, to consummate the issue.

Meanwhile, Hammerstein introduced a thrilling new tenor and brought forward some excellent presentations. The debut of Orville Harrold, on February 18, as Canio in *I Pagliacci* aroused much inter-

[25] News item in the Philadelphia *Public Ledger*, February 9, 1910.
[26] *Ibid.*
[27] *Oscar Hammerstein I*, 299.

est. When Hammerstein first heard the young singer at the Victoria, where he appeared as part of the variety show, the impresario knew at once that this was no ordinary voice. He arranged for Harrold to study with one of the leading teachers of the day, and after a short length of time the tenor seemed ready for his first operatic perform-ance. As Canio, he revealed a voice of beautiful quality; there was no question that he was at the beginning of a brilliant career. Many of the performances were also of uncommon interest. The house held the largest audience of the season for the *Rigoletto* of February 11 with Tetrazzini, McCormack, Renaud, and Gilibert (Monterone), Anselmi conducting. On the following day (February 12) Mazarin appeared in *Elektra* at the matinee and as Salomé in the evening's *Hérodiade*, replacing Cavalieri. For her extraordinary efforts Ham-merstein gave her a gold watch inscribed with these words: "First singer who ever volunteered to appear twice in one day."[28] On Febru-ary 19 Hammerstein revived *Otello* with Zerola (Otello), Melis (Desdemona), Polese (Iago), Venturini (Cassio), under the baton of Sturani. The opera, given only in the Philadelphia house, was not at all worthy of comparison with the *Otello* of the previous season. The revival of *Louise*, on February 23, was without its particular star. Mary Garden being ill, Alice Baron assumed the title role. On the twenty-sixth of the month, New York had the opportunity, at long last, of seeing *Le Jongleur de Notre Dame* with an all-male cast, Garden having given her permission for David Devries to assume the part of the Juggler. Apparently Hammerstein feared that with-out the glamorous prima donna in the cast, the opera itself would not attract a capacity audience. At any rate, he coupled it with *Cavalleria Rusticana*, with Melis and McCormack. Although Devries was excel-lent, Garden was missed in the role; by her genius she had made the part her own.

In the final weeks of the season, Hammerstein revived *Salome*, on March 5, with Garden, Dalmorès, Doria (Herodias), Dufranne (Jokanaan), and Devries (Narraboth), with De la Fuente con-ducting. *Pelléas et Mélisande* re-entered the repertory on the elev-

[28] *The* [New York] *Sun*, February 13, 1910.

enth with Garden, Dalmorès, Gerville-Réache, Dufranne (Golaud), Huberdeau (Ärkel), under the direction of De la Fuente. The final novelty was Delibes' *Lakmé*, first presented on March 21, with Tetrazzini (Lakmé), Duchène (Mallika), McCormack (Gerald), Huberdeau (Nilakantha), Crabbé (Frederic), Nicosia conducting. Critics wondered why Hammerstein produced this opera so late in the season. It had only one performance and must have incurred great expense. Krehbiel maintained that the impresario had given the work "a production which would have won him praise had it been made on the first night of the season . . . ."[29] Four evenings later, the Manhattan presented a grand gala performance in which almost every principal artist appeared on the stage of the opera house, either singing arias or appearing in scenes from *Les Contes d'Hoffmann*, *Hérodiade*, *Samson et Dalila*, *Roméo et Juliette* (Garden and Dalmorès were the star-crossed lovers), and *Faust*. Hammerstein also made an appearance and delivered a speech.

"At the end of each season I have the honor of being called before the curtain, very likely for the purpose of exhibiting the fact that I am still alive and that the cares and worries and exhaustions have still kept me sane and with my health not endangered. The hair on my temples has grown already whiter and the furrows in my face a little deeper.

The past season financially has been a very unfortunate one, but there has been a deluge of musical efforts and a surfeit of grand opera. While my losses have been enormous, I am proud of knowing that those of my adversaries have been much larger. My efforts in the great cause, nevertheless, will not relax, and I am again planning for next season the greatest and most sublime ojera [*sic*] for the pleasure of my audiences and for the honor of myself. Au revoir!"[30]

On March 26 the season concluded in New York with Tetrazzini in *Lucia* and in Philadelphia with a Grand Gala Performance very

[29] *New-York Daily Tribune*, March 22, 1910.
[30] News item in *The New York Herald*, March 26, 1910.

similar to the one given at the Manhattan on the previous evening. Philadelphia had particular cause to rejoice in the successful completion of the series of performances, for it had seemed several weeks before that Hammerstein might have to cease giving opera there. A streetcar strike, which began midnight of February 20, 1910, had paralyzed the city; and the impresario, faced with a mounting deficit, closed the house for the week of February 21–28, maintaining that without public transportation opera-goers would not be able to attend the presentations. Some thought this an ominous sign, for the Metropolitan, regardless of the difficulties, continued to present performances at the Academy of Music. However, on March 1, Hammerstein resumed the season, much to the pleasure of local opera lovers. Why he was able to do so was revealed on March 4, when the impresario said that once again Mr. Stotesbury had come to his aid, offering to make up personally any losses that might occur in the remaining weeks of the season. At the final gala performance Hammerstein confided to the crowded house, filled from pit to dome, that his benefactor had contributed $40,000 to cover the financial losses of the past three weeks. He also said that unless the company received a guarantee for next season, he would not and could not present opera again in the Quaker City.[31] On this portentous note the Philadelphia season ended.

From March 28–April 2, 1910, the Manhattan was in Boston for a week of opera that was highly successful in artistic terms. At the termination of this series of performances, the company disbanded, the principal artists returning to Europe for a well-deserved rest or for engagements at various opera houses. Hammerstein, however, delayed his departure for the continent, one reason being that he wanted to know positively whether he would obtain the guarantee for the Philadelphia season of 1910–11. On April 4 he and his son Harry met with representatives of the box holders and subscribers at the Philadelphia Opera House in order to discuss plans for financial assistance. For the season just completed, the gross receipts had been $425,000 (the first season the gross receipts were $538,000); and

[31] News item in the Philadelphia *Public Ledger*, March 27, 1910.

the deficit for the second season, according to Hammerstein, was $103,000.[32] What the impresario demanded, if he were to give opera there another year, was a guarantee of $7,500 for each of three performances a week (Tuesday and Thursday evenings, and the Saturday matinee), or $450,000 covering sixty presentations out of the season's eighty. He did not require a subsidy for the Saturday evening operas, since these had been invariably profitable.[33] At the meeting a committee of five composed of E. T. Stotesbury, J. Gardner Cassatt, Thomas Leaming, Joseph B. Bailey, and Ellis A. Gimbel was appointed to solicit the local opera-goers in order to determine whether Philadelphia would be willing to guarantee the next season.

On April 11 Hammerstein met with the members of the committee at Mr. Stotesbury's office. What they requested was more time to secure the necessary financial assurance, for their efforts thus far had been futile. Apparently Philadelphia was no longer in the mood to subsidize grand opera, whether the company be the Manhattan or the Metropolitan. Hammerstein was indignant, although he realized that the failure to secure a guarantee was not due to any lack of effort on the part of the committee. Afterward he said: " 'Time, time, time! .... Time is all that I ever hear Philadelphia ask for. I have no time to give them. I am leaving for Europe . . . and there is nothing to do but take this matter into my own hands.' "[34] He then announced that next season the company would present but two performances a week in Philadelphia (Tuesday and Thursday evenings), that the local chorus and orchestra were to be dismissed, and that there would be an increase in the subscription cost.[35]

All Readied for the Settlement

Four days later (April 15) Hammerstein signed a document which gave his son Arthur his power of attorney. That the younger Hammerstein had brought the negotiations between the Manhattan and Metropolitan to a very advanced stage is indicated by the terms to which his father agreed: Arthur might enter into a contract that

[32] *Ibid.*, April 5, 1910. [33] *Ibid.*

[34] *Ibid.*, April 12, 1910. [35] *Ibid.*

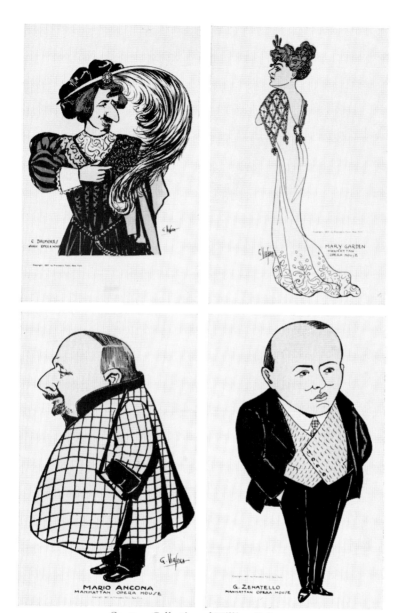

Courtesy Collection of William P. Sears

Charles Dalmorès (upper left); Mary Garden (upper right);
Mario Ancona (lower left); Giovanni Zenatello (lower right).

Courtesy Collection of William P. Sears

Fernando Gianoli-Galletti (upper left); Amedeo Bassi (upper
right); Francesco Daddi (lower left); Giannina Russ
(lower right).

Courtesy Collection of William P. Sears

Adamo Didur (upper left); Maurice Renaud (upper right);
Mario Sammarco (lower left); Eleanora de Cisneros
(lower right).

Courtesy Collection of William P. Sears

Oscar Hammerstein (upper left); Clotilde Bressler-Gianoli
(upper right); Mlle Alice Zeppilli (lower left); Cleofonte
Campanini (lower right).

would keep the impresario out of the production of grand opera for ten years from the date of the agreement with the purchaser. The document under Oscar Hammerstein's name was specific on this point:

> ... I hereby authorize and empower my said attorney to enter into an agreement in writing, under seal, with such purchaser, in a form satisfactory to my said attorney-in-fact, to the effect that I will not for the term of ten years from the date of any such agreement engage in or be directly or indirectly connected, either as owner, partner, officer, director, stockholder or otherwise, in any business, partnership or corporation that may during said term be or become engaged in the business of producing opera in any part of the United States of America ...
>
> I further authorize my said attorney to alter the form and purport of such covenant as he may see fit, hereby ratifying all that he may do in such agreement . . . .[36]

The next day (April 16) Hammerstein sailed for Europe. To the representatives of the press at the pier he seemed his old ebullient self, unperturbed by the vicissitudes of the past season. As usual, he was good copy. When one reporter inquired where he intended to go while abroad, Hammerstein replied without a moment's hesitation: " 'To Cairo. I understand there is a great singer there with two heads and two voices, contralto and soprano, and I want to engage her so that I can get the two voices for one salary.' "[37]

Although his jaunty manner had not left him and though he talked confidently of the coming season, Hammerstein knew full well that the days of the Manhattan Opera Company were numbered. When he returned, New York would again have but one opera company of the first rank. A glorious period in operatic history would be at an end.

[36] *Metropolitan Opera Company* v. *Oscar Hammerstein and Arthur Hammerstein*, File No. 18094–1913 (1914), p. 58.

[37] "To Search Europe for More Singers," *Musical America*, Vol. XI (April 23, 1910), 1.

XX

The Covenant and the Passing
of the Manhattan Opera Company

—◦◦✠◦◦—

T EN DAYS LATER, on April 26, 1910, at the New York residence of
Otto Kahn, Arthur Hammerstein, using his father's power of attorney, sold Oscar Hammerstein's operatic interests to representatives
of the Metropolitan. The contract was signed in the presence of
Samuel Untermyer, Hammerstein's counsel, and E. B. Root. Paul
Cravath was counsel for the older house. In the transaction, Edward
T. Stotesbury, represented by Kahn, was the nominal purchaser of
the entire enterprise *except* for the Manhattan Opera House. Arthur
transferred to Stotesbury the title to the Philadelphia Opera House
as well as the scenery, stage furnishings, costumes, librettos, and
scores to all operas in the Manhattan repertory. Also included in the
transaction were Hammerstein's exclusive rights to a number of operas (among these were *Salome, Elektra, Thaïs, Louise, Le Jongleur,
Sapho, Grisélidis, Hérodiade, Pelléas et Mélisande,* and *Samson et
Dalila*), together with the contracts of Tetrazzini, Garden, Renaud,
McCormack, Dalmorès, and Gilibert, with an option on Mazarin's
contract in case Garden refused to accept the new situation. The purchaser required that these artists "sing in New York, Philadelphia,
Chicago and Boston, and wherever the Metropolitan Opera Company or its affiliated companies may require, and will consent to the
elimination from his or her contract of any unusual provision or provisions which would be inapplicable in view of the changed conditions."[1] The contracts of Lyle D. Andrews, the business manager of

[1] *Metropolitan Opera Company* v. *Oscar Hammerstein and Arthur
Hammerstein,* File No. 18094–1913 (1914), p. 42.

the Manhattan, and William J. Guard, the press representative of the company, were also assigned to the purchaser. It was further agreed that neither Oscar nor Arthur Hammerstein would engage in the production of grand opera for ten years from the date of the agreement in New York, Philadelphia, Boston, or Chicago:

> [Oscar Hammerstein or Arthur Hammerstein] will not, nor will either of them, at any time hereafter within ten years from the date hereof, be or become, directly or indirectly, engaged or interested in or connected with, either alone or as a member or members of any firm or partnership, or in conjunction with others, or as an officer, director, manager, stockholder, employee of any corporation that may be or become engaged in any such business, or as an employee or in any other capacity whatsoever, in the cities of New York, Boston, Philadelphia or Chicago, in the business of producing grand opera ... in any language or any opera, operetta or comic opera that has ever been produced at the Metropolitan Opera House or the Manhattan Opera House in the City of New York, or any operetta or comic opera that may at any time hereafter have been first given at the Metropolitan Opera House or at any opera house in the City of New York, and that no opera, operetta or comic opera of the character described will be permitted or suffered to be produced upon the premises now occupied by the Manhattan Opera House within five years from the date hereof, nor will [Oscar Hammerstein or Arthur Hammerstein] be connected in any business that interferes with or encroaches upon the field now occupied by the Metropolitan Opera Company ....[2]

Although it was said at the time that the purchase price was more than $2,000,000, the actual amount was less. What Hammerstein received was $1,200,000.[3] Stotesbury absorbed half of this, as he had loaned the elder Hammerstein $600,000, holding a $400,000

[2] *Ibid.*, 44–45.
[3] *Ibid.*, 48.

mortgage on the Philadelphia Opera House and a second mortgage on the Manhattan Opera House.[4] In addition to the $400,000 which Hammerstein had originally obtained from Stotesbury in January, 1909, the impresario later borrowed $200,000 more from the financier. Hammerstein received the remaining $600,000 in monthly installments which ended October 15, 1910.

The question arises as to who contributed the $1,200,000. For years it was a well-guarded secret. According to Kolodin's study of the Metropolitan, published in 1936, Arthur Hammerstein declared that one director of the older house had given part of it for the sole purpose of getting rid of Lina Cavalieri, whose presence at the Manhattan had been untenable, since the director's son had become infatuated with the glamorous singer.[5] In a later history of the Metropolitan, published in 1953, Kolodin said that the sum had come from "various sources."[6] Then, in 1956, Sheean, in his biography of Oscar Hammerstein, theorized that the entire amount came from Otto Kahn and that his generosity was motivated by altruism. Sheean wrote: "My own view is that the motives of self-interest played a small part in the matter, where Kahn was concerned. They may have existed, but they did not determine the result. No doubt he was quite pleased to assume the attitude of St. George after the extinction of the dragon. As an extremely intelligent human being, just the same, he must have known all along that the dragon was dead before the battle began."[7] Seven years later (1963) Kahn's biographer Mary Jane Matz confirmed Sheean's speculation that it indeed was Kahn who provided the $1,200,000 which eliminated Hammerstein from the New York operatic scene.[8] She also said that throughout the opera war, Kahn and W. K. Vanderbilt had contributed heavily to the coffers of the Metropolitan so that the company could "sustain its losses without failing."[9]

[4] *Ibid.*, 46–47.
[5] *The Metropolitan Opera 1883–1935*, 166.
[6] *The Story of the Metropolitan Opera 1883–1950*, 255.
[7] *Oscar Hammerstein I*, 302.
[8] *The Many Lives of Otto Kahn*, 91. [9] *Ibid.*, 90.

As a result of the settlement, the Metropolitan stood to gain a great deal, the acquisition of Hammerstein's operatic interests fitting in very well with the older house's plans of aggrandizement. The inchoate Chicago Grand Opera Company needed sets, stage properties, costumes, scores, and exclusive rights to opera productions, and all of this was already available in Hammerstein's operatic enterprise. Hammerstein had under contract some of the greatest artists in the world; by the settlement of the difficulties they could appear with other companies in the United States. The Philadelphia Opera House was a magnificent structure that provided a far better setting for opera productions than the venerable Academy of Music. And with the Chicago Grand Opera Company and the Boston Opera, the Metropolitan had an interlinking directorate which assured cooperation in operatic affairs in the United States.

On April 28, 1910, the settlement was publicly announced. At the same time Stotesbury issued a statement that in the future, grand opera would be presented in Philadelphia not only by the Metropolitan but also by the Chicago Grand Opera Company, which after a series of performances at its home base was to present a ten-week season of opera at the Philadelphia Opera House, renamed the Metropolitan Opera House.[10] The company also was scheduled to appear as a welcome guest at New York's Metropolitan one evening a week during the winter season. Thus was the genesis of the Chicago-Philadelphia Grand Opera Company, under the aegis of Dippel, who retired from his duties in New York. Campanini was appointed musical director. For several years it regularly performed in Philadelphia at the opera house Hammerstein had constructed, and on Tuesday evenings at the Metropolitan. However, it ultimately withdrew from Philadelphia as a result of financial difficulties, once again leaving the Metropolitan as the sole source of organized opera in the Quaker City. The company concluded its appearances at the Metropolitan Opera House in New York at the end of the 1913–14 season, thereafter appearing in that metropolis as a competitor.

In many ways the Chicago-Philadelphia Opera carried on Ham-

[10] News item in the Philadelphia *Public Ledger*, April 28, 1910.

merstein's policies for a number of years. With some leading singers from his company (Garden, Dalmorès, Sammarco, Dufranne, Cavalieri, Tetrazzini, and McCormack among the more effulgent) and operas in the repertory formerly associated with the Manhattan, it seemed that the New York company had not disbanded but had merely transferred its center of activity. What the impresario had created therefore endured for some time in the Chicago-Philadelphia Opera Company, until it disbanded in 1913–14 and the Chicago Opera Company emerged as the sole inheritor of the Hammerstein tradition.

As for the impresario, he could not help being torn by mixed emotions. When he received the terms of the settlement, he said that he was both happy and sorry, a comment characteristic of the man. To a representative of the press, he commented:

> "I believe that operagoers will be the gainers by the new arrangement . . . . I believe that the existing unbusinesslike conditions and oversupply of opera which have made possible the boundless exactions of artists will be effectually stopped, but that at the same time European stars will continue to sing in America, despite a reduction in salaries. The Metropolitan, which will now be in a position to make a profit, will not, I feel certain, permit the high standard set for opera in the United States to be lowered.

> "Reports of my own losses have been exaggerated. I always made money, with the exception of last year. Personally, I am not ashamed to say that I retire with sadness and regret, although the Metropolitan Opera Company made most satisfactory financial arrangements with me. I have worked hard to give the public something uplifting and beneficial, and I had wished to end my career with a record of success as a producer of grand opera. But I am tired and I need rest badly.

> "I cannot say now what I will do after the next few months of rest, but I will do something. I could not stand idleness . . . ."[11]

[11] "Sweeping Effects of Giant Merger," *Musical America*, Vol. XI (May 7, 1910), 2.

What Hammerstein ultimately elected to do, of course, was to produce grand opera again, for it was such an obsession that he could not give it up. His new venture was in London, where for many years the Royal Opera at Covent Garden had reigned supreme. On November 13, 1911, he opened his London Opera House with a brilliant performance of Jean Noguès' *Quo Vadis*, with Renaud and Mlle Aline Vallandri. It was an auspicious beginning; but the weeks that followed must have been bitter ones, as the presentations at the beautiful new theater were not well attended. On July 15, 1912, at the end of the spring season, which had been financially disastrous, there seemed to be no recourse open to Hammerstein except to abandon the entire enterprise. Returning to the United States, he expressed a desire to present opera again at his Manhattan Opera House, the scene of so many former triumphs, but, of course, he was prevented from doing so by the terms of the agreement with the Metropolitan. Thwarted, he said he looked forward to the termination of the hated contract, on April 26, 1920, when he could legally return to the production of grand opera. And months before this date there were persistent rumors that the impresario, who was now in his early seventies, was involved in preparations to compete once more against the Metropolitan. The old warrior, however, was never again to challenge that institution. Oscar Hammerstein died on August 1, 1919.

Epilogue

—··◦❧❦☙◦··—

Few PERIODS in the history of opera in New York (or in the United States for that matter) have been so thrilling and vital as the four seasons in which the Manhattan Opera Company existed. The life-and-death struggle between the Manhattan and Metropolitan, two titans of grand opera, created a tremendous interest and excitement in operatic matters and contributed to making Americans more opera-conscious, Hammerstein's avowed purpose when he entered the field in 1906. Above all, the healthy competition resulted in productions that were extraordinary for their high standard of excellence.

The repertory of the Manhattan Opera Company was unusual for its emphasis on contemporary works. Hammerstein presented in the United States for the first time such masterpieces as *Louise*, *Pelléas et Mélisande*, and *Elektra*, the last two being considered milestones in twentieth-century music. His production of *Salome* was memorable, a revival which required considerable fortitude after the scandal of the Metropolitan *première*. The impresario offered many of Massenet's operas: *La Navarraise*, *Hérodiade*, *Le Jongleur de Notre Dame*, *Thaïs*, *Sapho*, *Grisélidis*, the last four of these receiving their first production in the United States under his aegis. With so many of them in the repertory and as a result of their success at the box office, it often seemed that opera-goers suffered from what the critics called "Massenetitis" and that the Manhattan Opera House might well have been called the Opéra-Massenet. Offenbach's *Les Contes d'Hoffmann* and Saint-Saëns' *Samson et Dalila* were other superb presentations, operatic novelties that had been heard infrequently in New York until Hammerstein popularized them. There were also the productions of Berlioz's *La Damnation de Faust*, Giordano's *Siberia* and *Andrea Chénier* and Blockx's *La Princesse d'Auberge*.

The Manhattan provided an abundance of riches in the traditional repertory, works superlatively interpreted under the baton of Campanini, who was largely responsible for the high musical standard of the institution during his three years with the company. Among these glories were *Aïda, Carmen, Otello, Rigoletto, Un Ballo in Maschera, Tosca,* and *Il Barbiere di Siviglia.* Palpably lacking in the list of operas, however, were the music dramas of Wagner, not a happy circumstance for a major opera company and the one area in which the Manhattan could not challenge the Metropolitan. Hammerstein's sole excursion into the Wagnerian domain was his production of *Tannhäuser*, presented in French, during the last season. It was not an achievement of artistic distinction.

Hammerstein was fortunate in his singers, some of whom seemed ideal interpreters of their roles, as Garden's Mélisande, Louise, Jongleur, and Thaïs; Dalmorès' Julien (*Louise*); Mazarin's Elektra; Renaud's Don Giovanni; Bressler-Gianoli's Carmen; Trentini's Musetta; Gerville-Réache's Dalila; and Gilibert's many inimitable portrayals. The artistry and magnificent voices of Melba, Tetrazzini, McCormack, Zenatello, Bonci, and Sammarco contributed much to the success of the company. What was especially remarkable was the unflagging devotion of the singers to the Manhattan, to Hammerstein, and to the art which they ennobled. In May, 1963, Mme Pauline Donalda wrote: "We all had the greatest admiration for [Hammerstein's] pluck and courage and we all stood by him firmly for his artistic endeavors."[1] As a consequence, critics and public alike marveled at the company's *esprit de corps*, a factor which contributed to the exhilaration and polish of the performances.

Hammerstein, it is generally agreed, was one of the greatest impresarios in the history of opera. He was ahead of his time when he insisted that the opera houses he constructed should have the stage

[1] Letter to the author from Pauline Donalda, May 15, 1963.

as the central focus of the auditorium, with each patron's having adequate sight lines, whether the price of the seat was five dollars or one dollar. The Manhattan and Philadelphia Opera Houses were built for all the patrons, not just for the box holders. Hammerstein did much to democratize grand opera in the United States. He had the adventurousness and foresight to present novelties that were musical as well as dramatic revelations, subsequently demonstrating that first-rate productions of these contemporary works could be as much a magnet to fill an opera house as illustrious names bejeweling the casts of operas from the standard repertory. His accomplishments in this sphere virtually revolutionized operatic production in New York. His policy of assembling singers for a particular presentation and then keeping them together contributed to splendid ensemble performances; the artistic value of this innovation was readily apparent in the Garden vehicles, which invariably included the same casts. He opened the doors of his opera houses to native-born American singers who had had no previous European experience, a virtually unheard of practice at that time. Orville Harrold and Alice Gentle were two such artists Hammerstein encouraged and materially assisted at the outset of their careers. He developed a chorus unlike any that New York had ever heard or seen before. He insisted on the verisimilitude of the stage direction, the historical accuracy of the *mise-en-scène*, realistic settings with natural objects, appropriate costuming and furnishings, with expense being no object. Jacques Coini, the Manhattan's stage director, said of this largesse: " 'I have never known another impresario like him in this respect, and I have served under a great many directors in my twenty-five years of experience.' "[2] Hammerstein had a flair for publicity, an asset that kept him and the Manhattan Opera Company constantly before the public eye. Above all, his greatness as an impresario lay in his ability to engender in others the desire to give of their very best, as he himself gave of his best, his industry, personality, and presence exerting a profound influ-

[2] "Real Grand Opera Czar Is the Stage Manager," *The* [Philadelphia] *North American Theatre Section*, February 28, 1909, p. 5.

ence. He kept the members of the Manhattan on their mettle. And, after all, the company was but the lengthened shadow of this man.

At the same time, Hammerstein was not without his faults as an impresario. He did not plan his seasons sufficiently in advance, seemingly unaware of or unconcerned with the numerous details entailed in running an opera house. In the first season, having engaged a minimum number of leading singers, he had no replacements for certain roles, as Mme Russ was the only dramatic soprano, Bonci the sole lyric tenor, and Bassi the one dramatic tenor. Whether, in 1908, he had formulated his plans carefully before announcing his decision to run two opera houses concurrently is a moot question. He failed to secure the services of a conductor comparable to Campanini, a factor which proved catastrophic to the artistic quality of the institution in the last season. He lavished money on operas that were unworthy of presentation or that he offered only a few times, as the expensive productions of *Andrea Chénier* and *Lakmé*, which were given only one time each at the Manhattan Opera House. An empire-builder, he overstretched himself and his financial resources in constructing and operating the Philadelphia Opera House. Had it not been for this liability, the Manhattan might have endured for several seasons longer. He alienated some of the company's principal supporters and personnel, not placing the best interests of the Manhattan first. No doubt his age and ego, as well as years of overwork, were determining factors during the final two seasons, when the impresario's unfortunate actions did so much to destroy what he had created.

Still, what Hammerstein and the Manhattan Opera accomplished was and is an inspiration. Competing against a formidable array of millionaires, the impresario, alone in his endeavors, fought on and on, surmounting adversities, overcoming obstacles, untiring in his efforts to produce great opera regardless of opposition, expense, time, and personal sacrifices, ever determined to make his company a resounding success. That he did so reflects his genius. The competition he provided benefited the musical public and opera itself. Forced out of a rut, the Metropolitan had to assume a responsibility to opera-goers and to art, which, at times in the past, had been conspicuously lacking. No longer did the wealthy, complacent directors of the Metropolitan adopt the attitude that the public be damned. Hammerstein had destroyed their monopoly. In the end, of course, the smaller treasury had to give way to the larger. Nevertheless, when Hammerstein conceded to the Metropolitan, he retired from the field with laurels and the consolation that he had been faithful to the mission of grand opera, now diademed by his achievement.

Today, as many Americans turn their attention to the construction of cultural centers throughout the length and breadth of the United States, they would do well to remember the herculean tasks of Oscar Hammerstein, who persevered against a sea of troubles to succeed ultimately in rejuvenating and revitalizing opera in this country. At the same time, the nation might recall the Manhattan, a glorious institution that transformed Hammerstein's dream into reality, a superb ensemble which rightly took its place among the foremost opera companies in the world.

It was a memorable achievement, a potent force, and a guiding light in the cause of culture in this republic, the brilliance of which remains undimmed as the years accumulate. The place of the Manhattan Opera Company in the annals of opera, therefore, is significant and secure.

Appendix I

Manhattan Opera Casts
for Performances at the
Manhattan Opera House, 1906–10

—◦◦✦❦✦◦◦—

THIS MATERIAL is based on official Manhattan Opera Company programmes, newspaper advertisements, and reviews. Where there was a
doubt as to whether a performer appeared in a given cast or when it
was impossible to verify certain members in a performance, the author
has inserted a question mark in the list of dramatis personae. The
abbreviation "c" has been used for conductor.

The Sunday evening concerts, regularly performed at the Manhattan Opera House from 1906–10 by members of the company and
guests, have not been included in these annals. Only the operatic presentations and benefit concerts given during the week are listed. Nor
are the performances on tour of the *opéra comique* part of the company included in these annals. It was impossible to ascertain all the
casts for this group when it was on the road in 1909–10.

1906–1907 Season

Personnel

Male Artists
Altchevsky, Ivan
Ancona, Mario
Arimondi, Vittorio
Bassi, Amadeo
Bonci, Alessandro
Brag, Hermann
Daddi, Francesco
Dalmorès, Charles
Fossetta, Nicolo

Gianoli-Galletti,
 Fernando
Gilibert, Charles
Minolfi, Renzo
Mugnoz, Luigi
Occellier, Victor
Renaud, Maurice
Reschiglian, Vincenzo
Romolo, Sig.
Sammarco, Mario

Seveilhac, Paul
Tecchi, Giuseppe
Venturini, Emilio

Female Artists
Arta, Regina
Bressler-Gianoli,
 Clotilde
Calvé, Emma
Cisneros, Eleanora de

Donalda, Pauline
Donnelle, Mme.
Giacomini, Emma
Giaconia, Guissepppina
Ingenoff, Mme.
Lejeune, Gabrielle
Melba, Nellie
Pinkert, Regina
Russ, Giannina

Severina, Gina
Trentini, Emma
Zaccaria, Emma
Zeppilli, Alice

Ballet
Belle Dazie
  (Prima Ballerina)

Chorus Master
Gaetano Merola

Conductors
Bendix, Max
Companari, Leandro
Campanini, Cleofonte
Tanara, Fernando

1906–1907 Season

December 3
I Puritani
  Campanini (c)
Lord Walton : Mugnoz
Sir George : Arimondi
Elvira : Pinkert
Henrietta : Zaccaria
Lord Arthur : Bonci
Sir Richard : Ancona
Sir Bruno : Venturini

December 5
Rigoletto
  Campanini (c)
Duke : Bonci
Rigoletto : Renaud
Gilda : Pinkert
Sparafucile : Arimondi
Maddalena : Giaconia
Giovanna : Severina
Monterone : Mugnoz
Marullo : Fossetta
Borsa : Venturini
Ceprano : Reschiglian
Countess : Zaccaria

December 7
Faust
  Campanini (c)

Faust : Dalmorès
Marguerite : Donalda
Méphistophélès :
  Arimondi
Valentin : Seveilhac
Siébel : Giaconia
Marthe : Donnelle
Wagner : Fossetta

December 8 (mat.)
I Puritani
Same cast as Dec. 3
  except:
Sir George : Mugnoz
Lord Walton : Brag

December 8
Faust
  Campanari (c)
Same cast as Dec. 7
  except:
Faust : Altchevsky

December 10
Rigoletto
Same cast as Dec. 5
  except:
Rigoletto : Ancona

December 12
Don Giovanni
  Campanini (c)
Don Giovanni :
  Ancona
Donna Anna : Russ
Donna Elvira : Arta
Zerlina : Donalda
Commendatore :
  Mugnoz
Don Ottavio : Bonci
Leporello : Brag
Masetto : Gilibert

December 14
Carmen
  Campanini (c)
Carmen : Bressler-
  Gianoli
Don José : Dalmorès
Micaëla : Donalda
Escamillo : Ancona
Zuniga : Brag
Morales : Reschiglian
Frasquita : Trentini
Mercédès : Giaconia
Dancaïre : Gilibert
Remendado : Daddi

December 15 (mat.)
Don Giovanni
Same cast as Dec. 12
except:
Don Giovanni :
  Renaud
Donna Elvira :
  Lejeune

December 15
Carmen
Same cast as Dec. 14
except:
Micaëla : Lejeune
Escamillo : Seveilhac

December 17
Don Giovanni
Same cast as Dec. 15

December 19
Aïda
  Campanini (c)
King : Mugnoz
Amneris : De Cisneros
Aïda : Russ
Radames : Bassi
Amonasro : Ancona
Ramfis : Arimondi
Messenger : Tecchi

December 21
Lucia di Lammermoor
  Tanara (c)
Lucia : Pinkert
Alisa : Severina
Edgardo : Bonci
Ashton : Minolfi

Raimondo : Mugnoz
Arturo : Venturini
Normanno : Tecchi

December 22 (mat.)
Carmen
Same cast as Dec. 14
except:
Micaëla : Lejeune
Escamillo : Renaud
Zuniga : Mugnoz

December 22
Faust
Same cast as Dec. 7
except:
Faust : Altchevsky
Valentin : Ancona
Marthe : Lejeune

December 24
Lucia di Lammermoor
Same cast as Dec. 21
except:
Ashton : Seveilhac

December 25
Aïda
Same cast as Dec. 19

December 26
Carmen
Same cast as Dec. 22

December 28
Faust
Same cast as Dec. 7
except:

Faust : Altchevsky
Marthe : Lejeune

December 29 (mat.)
Rigoletto
Same cast as Dec. 5
except:
Maddalena :
  Giacomini

December 29
Aïda
Same cast as Dec. 19

December 31
Aïda
Same cast as Dec. 19

January 1
Il Trovatore
  Tanara (c)
Leonora : Russ
Manrico : Dalmorès
Count di Luna :
  Seveilhac
Azucena :
  De Cisneros
Inez : Zaccaria
Ferrando : Mugnoz
Ruiz : Tecchi

January 2
La Traviata
  Campanini (c)
Violetta : Melba
Alfredo : Bassi
Germont : Renaud
Flora : Zaccaria

Annina : Severina
Gastone : Venturini
Baron Douphol :
 Fossetta
Marquis d'Obigny :
 Reschiglian
Dr. Grenvil :
 Gilibert

January 4
Carmen
Same cast as Dec. 14
 except:
Escamillo : Renaud
Zuniga : Mugnoz

January 5 (mat.)
L'Elisir d'Amore
 Campanini (c)
Adina : Pinkert
Gianetta : Trentini
Nemorino : Bonci
Belcore : Seveilhac
Dulcamara : Gilibert

January 5
La Traviata
Same cast as Jan. 2
 except:
Violetta : Donalda

January 7
Il Trovatore
Same cast as Jan. 1

January 9
L'Elisir d'Amore
Same cast as Jan. 5

January 11
Rigoletto
Same cast as Dec. 5
 except:
Gilda : Melba
Maddalena :
 Giacomini

January 12 (mat.)
Aïda
Same cast as Dec. 19

January 12
Carmen
Same cast as Dec. 14
 except:
Escamillo : Seveilhac
Zuniga : Mugnoz

January 14
Faust
Same cast as Dec. 7
 except:
Valentin : Ancona
Marthe : Lejeune

January 16
Don Giovanni
Same cast as Dec. 15

January 18
Les Huguenots
 Campanini (c)
Marguerite : Pinkert
St. Bris : Seveilhac
Valentine : Russ

Nevers : Ancona
Cossé : Daddi
Tavannes : Venturini
Retz : Fossetta
Raoul : Bassi
Marcel : Arimondi
Urbain : De Cisneros
Maurevert : Mugnoz
Bois Rosé : ?
Ladies of Honor :
 Arta, Severina

January 19 (mat.)
La Traviata
Same cast as Jan. 2
 except:
Germont : Ancona

January 19
Il Trovatore
Same cast as Jan. 1

January 21
Il Barbiere di Siviglia
 Campanini (c)
Almaviva : Bonci
Dr. Bartolo : Gilibert
Rosina : Pinkert
Figaro : Ancona
Don Basilio : Mugnoz
Berta : Trentini
Fiorello : Venturini

January 23
Les Huguenots
Same cast as Jan. 18
 except:

Marcel : Mugnoz
Maurevert : ?

January 25
La Sonnambula
  Tanara (c)
Adina : Pinkert
Elvino : Bonci
Rodolfo : Mugnoz
Alessio : Reschiglian
Notary : Tecchi
Lisa : Trentini
Teresa : Severina

January 26 (mat.)
Carmen
Same cast as Jan. 12

January 26
Aïda
Same cast as Dec. 19

January 28
Lucia di Lammermoor
Same cast as Dec. 24
  except:
Lucia : Melba

January 30
Carmen
Same cast as Dec. 14
  except:
Micaëla : Arta
Escamillo : Seveilhac
Zuniga : Mugnoz

January 31
Rigoletto
Same cast as Jan. 11
  except:
Rigoletto : Ancona

February 1
Cavalleria Rusticana
  Campanini (c)
Santuzza : Russ
Turiddu : Dalmorès
Lola : Giacomini
Alfio : Seveilhac
Lucia : Severina

I Pagliacci
  Campanini (c)
Nedda : Donalda
Canio : Bassi
Tonio : Sammarco
Beppe : Venturini
Silvio : Seveilhac

February 2 (mat.)
Il Barbiere di Siviglia
Same cast as Jan. 21
  except:
Don Basilio : Arimondi

February 2
Les Huguenots
Same cast as Jan. 18
  except:
Marguerite : Zeppilli

February 4
Carmen
Same cast as Jan. 12

February 6
Cavalleria Rusticana
Same cast as Feb. 1
  except:
Lola : De Cisneros

I Pagliacci
Same cast as Feb. 1

February 7
Mignon
  Campanini (c)
Mignon : Bressler-
  Gianoli
Philine : Pinkert
Wilhelm : Bonci
Lothario : Arimondi
Laerte : Gilibert
Jarno : Mugnoz
Frederic : Giaconia

February 8
Faust
Same cast as Dec. 7
  except:
Marguerite : Melba
Valentin : Ancona
Siébel : Trentini
Marthe : Ingenoff

February 9 (mat.)
Mignon
Same cast as Feb. 7

February 9
Aïda
Same cast as Dec. 19

February 11

Cavalleria Rusticana
Same cast as Feb. 1
except:
Lola : Giaconia

I Pagliacci
Same cast as Feb. 1

February 12
La Sonnambula
Same cast as Jan. 25

February 13
Les Huguenots
Same cast as Feb. 2

February 14
Rigoletto
Same cast as Dec. 5
except:
Rigoletto : Sammarco
Gilda : Melba

February 15
Aïda
Same cast as Dec. 19

February 16 (mat.)
Lucia di Lammermoor
Same cast as Dec. 21
except:
Lucia : Melba
Ashton : Sammarco

February 16
Il Trovatore
Same cast as Jan. 1

February 18
Mignon
Same cast as Feb. 7

February 20
Dinorah
Campanini (c)
Dinorah : Pinkert
Goatherds : Trentini,
Giaconia
Corentino :
Altchevsky
Harvester : Venturini
Huntsman : Mugnoz
Hoel : Ancona

February 22 (mat.)
Carmen
Same cast as Dec. 14
except:
Micaëla : Lejeune
Zuniga : Mugnoz

February 22
Cavalleria Rusticana
Same cast as Feb. 1
except:
Turiddu : Venturini
Lola : Giaconia

I Pagliacci
Same cast as Feb. 1

February 23 (mat.)
La Traviata
Same cast as Jan. 2
except:

Germont : Sammarco
Gaston : ?

February 23
Lucia di Lammermoor
Same cast as Dec. 24

February 25
Rigoletto
Same cast as Dec. 5
except:
Rigoletto : Ancona
Gilda : Melba

February 27
Un Ballo in Maschera
Campanini (c)
Riccardo : Bassi
Renato : Sammarco
Amelia : Russ
Ulrica : De Cisneros
Oscar : Zeppilli
Silvano : Reschiglian
Sam : Arimondi
Tom : Mugnoz

February 28
Carmen
Same cast as Dec. 14
except:
Zuniga : Mugnoz
Frasquita : Lejeune

March 1
La Bohème
Tanara (c)

Rodolfo : Bonci
Marcello : Sammarco
Schaunard : Gilibert
Colline : Arimondi
Mimi : Melba
Musetta : Trentini
Benoit, Alcindoro :
  Gianoli-Galletti
Parpignol : Tecchi

March 2 (mat.)

Un Ballo in Maschera
Same cast as Feb. 27

March 2

Mixed Bill
  Campanini (c)
Cavalleria Rusticana
Same cast as Feb. 11
Second Act of *Dinorah*
Dinorah : Pinkert
Goatherd : Giaconia
Corentino :
  Altchevsky
Hoel : Ancona

Last Act of *Faust*
Faust : Dalmorès
Marguerite : Donalda
Méphistophélès :
  Occellier

March 4

La Sonnambula
Same cast as Jan. 25
  except:
Rodolfo : Arimondi

I Pagliacci
Same cast as Feb. 1

March 5

Carmen
Same cast as Feb. 28

March 6

La Bohème
Same cast as Mar. 1

March 8

Fra Diavolo
  Campanini (c)
Fra Diavolo : Bonci
Milord : Gilibert
Pamela : Giaconia
Lorenzo : Venturini
Matteo : Fossetta
Zerline : Pinkert
Beppo : Gianoli-
  Galletti
Giacomo : Arimondi

March 9 (mat.)

Carmen
Same cast as Mar. 5
  except:
Escamillo : Seveilhac

March 9

Aïda
Same cast as Dec. 19

March 11

La Bohème
Same cast as Mar. 1

March 13

Fra Diavolo
Same cast as Mar. 8

March 15

L'Elisir d'Amore
  Tanara (c)
Same cast as Jan. 5
  except:
Gianetta : Severina

March 16 (mat.)

Cavalleria Rusticana
Same cast as Feb. 1
  except:
Turiddu : Venturini
Lola : Zaccaria

I Pagliacci
Same cast as Feb. 1

March 16

Carmen
  Tanara (c)
Same cast as Dec. 14
  except:
Micaëla : Zeppilli
Escamillo : Occellier
Zuniga : Mugnoz
Frasquita : Lejeune
Mercédès : Severina

March 18

Fra Diavolo
  Tanara (c)
Same cast as Mar. 8

March 20
Rigoletto
Same cast as Feb. 25

March 22
Faust
Same cast as Dec. 7
  except:
Faust : Bassi
Marguerite : Russ
Valentin : Sammarco
Siébel : Zeppilli
Marthe : Severina

March 23 (mat.)
Martha
  Tanara (c)
Harriet : Donalda
Nancy : De Cisneros
Lionel : Bonci
Plunkett : Arimondi
Tristan : Gianoli-
  Galletti

March 23
Il Trovatore
Same cast as Jan. 1
  except:
Azucena : Bressler-
  Gianoli

March 25
La Bohème
Same cast as Mar. 1

March 27
Carmen
Same cast as Dec. 14
  except:

Carmen : Calvé
Zuniga : Mugnoz

March 29
Manzoni Requiem
  Campanini (c)
Soloists : Russ, De
  Cisneros, Bassi,
  Arimondi

March 30 (mat.)
Cavalleria Rusticana
Same cast as Feb. 1
  except:
Santuzza : Calvé
Lola : Giaconia

I Pagliacci
Same cast as Feb. 1

March 30
Fra Diavolo
Same cast as Mar. 8

April 1
Carmen
Same cast as Dec. 14
  except:
Carmen : Calvé
Zuniga : Mugnoz
Frasquita : Lejeune
Mercédès : Severina

April 3
Martha
Same cast as Mar. 23

April 5
Carmen
Same cast as Apr. 1
  except:
Micaëla : Zeppilli
Escamillo : Seveilhac
Mercédès : Giaconia

April 6 (mat.)
Aïda
Same cast as Dec. 19

April 6
Rigoletto
Same cast as Dec. 5
  except:
Rigoletto : Sammarco
Sparafucile : Mugnoz
Monterone : Gilibert

April 8
Martha
Same cast as Mar. 23

April 9
Aïda
Same cast as Dec. 19

April 10
I Pagliacci
Same cast as Feb. 1

La Navarraise
  Campanini (c)
Anita : Calvé
Garrido : Arimondi

Araguil : Dalmorès
Ramon : Altchevsky
Bustamente : Gilibert
Remigio : Seveilhac

April 11
Lucia di Lammermoor
  Max Bendix (c)
Same cast as Dec. 21
  except:
Ashton : Seveilhac

April 12
I Pagliacci
Same cast as Feb. 1

Cavalleria Rusticana
Same cast as Mar. 30

April 13 (mat.)
Rigoletto
Same cast as Apr. 6

April 13
Les Huguenots
Same cast as Feb. 2

April 15
Rigoletto
Same cast as Dec. 5
  except:
Rigoletto : Sammarco
Sparafucile : Mugnoz
Monterone :
  Reschiglian
Ceprano : Romolo

April 16
Carmen
Same cast as Dec. 14
  except:
Carmen : Calvé
Micaëla : Lejeune
Escamillo : Seveilhac
Zuniga : Mugnoz

April 17
Martha
  Bendix (c)
Same cast as Mar. 23

April 18
I Pagliacci
Same cast as Feb. 1
  except:
Nedda : Zeppilli
Tonio : Ancona
Silvio : Reschiglian

La Navarraise
Same cast as April 10
  except:
Remigio : Gianoli-
  Galletti

April 19
Campanini Night
Il Trovatore (Act I,
  Second Scene)
Leonora : Russ
Manrico : Dalmorès
Count di Luna :
  Seveilhac
Inez : Severina

Aria—*Der Freischütz* :
  Arta

Duet—*La Favorita* :
  Bressler-Gianoli,
  Altchevsky

Duet—*Les Dragons
  de Villars* : Lejeune,
  Gilibert

Duet—*Don Pasquale* :
  Zeppilli, Gianoli-
  Galletti

Rigoletto (Act IV)
Duke : Bonci
Rigoletto : Ancona
Gilda : Pinkert
Sparafucile : Mugnoz
Maddalena : De
  Cisneros

Mefistofele (Pro-
  logue) :
  Arimondi and
  Chorus

I Pagliacci (Act I)
Same cast as Feb. 1

April 20 (mat.)
Carmen
Same cast as Dec. 14
  except:
Carmen : Calvé
Micaëla : Zeppilli
Zuniga : Mugnoz

April 20
Aïda
Same cast as Dec. 19
  except:
Amonasro : Sammarco

1907–1908 Season

Personnel

Male Artists
Albani, Carlo
Ancona, Mario
Arimondi, Vittorio
Bassi, Amadeo
Cacici, Sig.
Cazauran, Leon
Crabbé, Armand
Daddi, Francesco
Dalmorès, Charles
Didur, Adamo
Dufranne, Hector
Fossetta, Nicolo
Gianoli-Galletti,
  Fernando
Gilibert, Charles
Giussani, Sig.
Mugnoz, Luigi
Périer, Jean
Pierucci, Sig.
Renaud, Maurice
Reschiglian, Vincenzo
Sammarco, Mario
Venturini, Emilio
Zaini, Sig.

Zenatello, Giovanni

Female Artists
Agostinelli, Adelina
Borello, Camille
Bregnac, Miss de
Bressler-Gianoli,
  Clotilde
Calvé, Emma
Cisneros, Eleanora de
Davis, Miss
Francisca, Fannie
Garden, Mary
Gerville-Réache,
  Jeanne
Giaconia, Guisseppina
Hayes, Lillian
Hume, Julie
Inman, Grace
Johnston, Miss
Jomelli, Jeanne
Koèlling, Helene
Laurie, Annie
Loubet, Mlle.
Morichini, Mauricia

Nordica, Lillian
Russ, Giannina
Schumann-Heink,
  Ernestine
Severina, Gina
Sigrist, Ludmilla
Tetrazzini, Luisa
Tetrazzini-Campa-
  nini, Eva
Trentini, Emma
Valliere, Atala
Zaccaria, Emma
Zeppilli, Alice

Ballet
Anita Malinverni
  (Prima Ballerina)

Chorus Master
Josiah Zuro

Conductors
Campanini, Cleofonte
Charlier, Marcel
Parelli, Attilio

1907–1908 Season

November 4

La Gioconda
  Campanini (c)
La Gioconda : Nordica
Laura : De Cisneros
Alvise : Didur
La Cieca : Gerville-
  Réache

Enzo : Zenatello
Barnaba : Ancona
Zuane : Fossetta
Isepo : Venturini

November 5

Carmen
  Campanini (c)

Carmen : Bressler-
  Gianoli
Don José : Dalmorès
Micaëla : Zeppilli
Escamillo : Crabbé
Zuniga : Mugnoz
Morales : Reschiglian
Frasquita : Trentini
Mercédès : Giaconia

Dancaïre : Gilibert
Remendado : Daddi

November 6
*La Damnation de
Faust*
  Campanini (c)
Marguerite : Jomelli
Faust : Dalmorès
Brander : Crabbé
Méphistophélès :
  Renaud

November 8
La Gioconda
Same cast as Nov. 4

November 9 (mat.)
Carmen
Same cast as Nov. 5
  except:
Micaëla : Borello

November 9
Il Trovatore
  Parelli (c)
Leonora : Jomelli
Manrico : Albani
Count di Luna :
  Fossetta
Azucena : De
  Cisneros
Inez : Zaccaria
Ferrando : Mugnoz
Ruiz : Venturini

November 11
Aïda
  Campanini (c)
King : Mugnoz
Amneris : De Cisneros
Aïda : Nordica
Radames : Zenatello
Amonasro : Ancona
Ramfis : Arimondi
Messenger : Venturini

November 13
Carmen
Same cast as Nov. 5
  except:
Carmen : Gerville-
  Réache
Escamillo : Ancona

November 15
*Les Contes
  d'Hoffmann*
  Campanini (c)
Olympia : Zeppilli
Giulietta : Jomelli
Antonia : Francisca
Hoffmann : Dalmorès
Nicklausse : De
  Cisneros
Coppelius, Dapertutto,
  Miracle : Renaud
Cochenille, Pitichi-
  naccio : Daddi
Luther : Fossetta
Nathanael :
  Venturini

Hermann :
  Reschiglian
Spalanzani, Crespel :
  Gilibert
Lindorf, Schlemil :
  Crabbé
Franz : Gianoli-
  Galletti
A Voice : Giaconia

November 16 (mat.)
La Gioconda
Same cast as Nov. 4

November 16
Carmen
Same cast as Nov. 5
  except:
Micaëla : Koèlling

November 18
*Les Contes
  d'Hoffmann*
Same cast as Nov. 15
  except:
Antonia : Trentini

November 20
Aïda
Same cast as Nov. 11

November 22
*Les Contes
  d'Hoffmann*
Same cast as Nov. 18

November 23 (mat.)

Aïda
Same cast as Nov. 11

November 23

Il Trovatore
Same cast as Nov. 9
except:
Azucena : Bressler-
Gianoli

November 25

Thaïs
Campanini (c)
Thaïs : Garden
Nicias : Dalmorès
Athanaël : Renaud
Palemon : Mugnoz
Crobyle : Trentini
Myrtale, Albine :
Giaconia
Servant : Reschiglian

November 27

*Les Contes
d'Hoffmann*
Same cast as Nov. 18

November 28 (mat.)

Carmen
Same cast as Nov. 16

November 28

Faust
Campanini (c)
Faust : Zenatello

Marguerite : Zeppilli
Méphistophélès :
Didur
Valentin : Crabbé
Siébel : Giaconia
Marthe : Severina
Wagner : Fossetta

November 29

Faust
Same cast as Nov. 28
except:
Valentin : Ancona

November 30 (mat.)

Thaïs
Same cast as Nov. 25

November 30

Aïda
Same cast as Nov. 11
except:
Aïda : Russ

December 2

*Les Contes
d'Hoffmann*
Same cast as Nov. 18
except:
Giulietta : Morichini

December 4

Thaïs
Same cast as Nov. 25
except:
Crobyle : Koèlling

December 6

Aïda
Same cast as Nov. 30

December 7 (mat.)

*Les Contes
d'Hoffmann*
Same cast as Nov. 15
except:
Giulietta : Morichini
Antonia : Borello

December 7

Faust
Same cast as Nov. 29
except:
Siébel : ?
Marthe : ?
Wagner : ?

December 9

La Navarraise
Campanini (c)
Anita : Gerville-
Réache
Garrido : Arimondi
Araguil : Dalmorès
Ramon : Crabbé
Bustamente : Gianoli-
Galletti

I Pagliacci
Campanini (c)
Nedda : Zeppilli
Canio : Bassi
Tonio : Sammarco
Beppe : Venturini
Silvio : Crabbé

December 11

Ernani
Parelli (c)
Elvira : Russ
Giovanna : Zaccaria
Ernani : Bassi
Don Carlo : Ancona
Don Ruy Gomez :
  Arimondi
Iago : Reschiglian
Don Riccardo :
  Venturini

December 13

Thaïs
Same cast as Nov. 25
  except:
Palemon : ?
Servant : ?

December 14 (mat.)

La Navarraise
Same cast as Dec. 9

I Pagliacci
Same cast as Dec. 9

December 14

La Gioconda
  Parelli (c)
Same cast as Nov. 4
  except: *
La Gioconda : Russ
Zuane : ?
Isepo : ?

December 16

Carmen
Same cast as Nov. 5
  except:
Escamillo : Ancona
Zuniga : ?
Morales : ?
Frasquita : ?
Mercédès : ?
Remendado : ?

December 18

La Navarraise
Same cast as Dec. 9

I Pagliacci
Same cast as Dec. 9

December 20

Rigoletto
  Campanini (c)
Duke : Bassi
Rigoletto : Sammarco
Gilda : Zeppilli
Sparafucile : Arimondi
Maddalena : Giaconia
Giovanna : Severina
Monterone : Gilibert
Marullo : Fossetta
Borsa : Venturini
Ceprano : Reschiglian
Countess : Zaccaria

December 21 (mat.)

Faust
Same cast as Nov. 28
  except:

Faust : Bassi
Marguerite : Agosti-
  nelli
Marthe : Zaccaria

December 21

*Les Contes
  d'Hoffmann*
Same cast as Dec. 7

December 23

*La Damnation de
  Faust*
Same cast as Nov. 6

December 25 (mat.)

*Les Contes
  d'Hoffmann*
Same cast as Dec. 7

December 25

Aïda
Same cast as Nov. 11
  except:
Aïda : Agostinelli
Amonasro : Sammarco
Ramfis : Didur
High Priestess : Hume

December 26

La Navarraise
Same cast as Dec. 9

I Pagliacci
Same cast as Dec. 9
  except:

* Giaconia replaced Gerville-Réache after the latter fainted at the end
of the first act.

Nedda : Agostinelli
Beppe : ?

December 27
Un Ballo in Maschera
 Campanini (c)
 Riccardo : Zenatello
 Renato : Sammarco
 Amelia : Russ
 Ulrica : De Cisneros
 Oscar : Zeppilli
 Silvano : Reschiglian
 Sam : Arimondi
 Tom : Mugnoz
 Judge : Venturini

December 28 (mat.)
Don Giovanni
 Campanini (c)
 Don Giovanni :
 Renaud
 Donna Anna : Russ
 Donna Elvira : Jomelli
 Zerlina : Zeppilli
 Commendatore :
 Mugnoz
 Don Ottavio :
 Cazauran
 Leporello : Didur
 Masetto : Gilibert

December 28
Carmen
Same cast as Nov. 5
 except:
 Micaëla : Koèlling
 Zuniga : ?
 Morales : ?

Frasquita : ?
Remendado : ?

December 30
Don Giovanni
Same cast as Dec. 28

December 31
Cavalleria Rusticana
 Campanini (c)
 Santuzza : Russ
 Lola : Giaconia
 Turiddu : Dalmorès
 Alfio : Crabbé
 Lucia : Severina

I Pagliacci
Same cast as Dec. 26

January 1
Un Ballo in Maschera
Same cast as Dec. 27
 except:
 Ulrica : Bressler-
 Gianoli
 Oscar : Trentini

January 2
*Les Contes
 d'Hoffmann*
Same cast as Nov. 15
 except:
 Antonia : Bordello
 Hoffmann : Cazauran
 Nicklausse : Giaconia

January 3
Louise
 Campanini (c)

Louise : Garden
Julien : Dalmorès
Mother : Bressler-
 Gianoli
Father : Gilibert
Irma : Zeppilli
Camille : Morichini
Gertrude : Giaconia
Apprentice : Sigrist
Elsie, A Street
 Sweeper : Severina
Blanche, Milk
 Woman : Zaccaria
Suzanne : Koèlling
Forewoman : Inman
Marguerite : Laurie
Painter, Second
 Philosopher :
 Fossetta
First Philosopher,
 Sculptor : Crabbé
Poet, Old Clothes
 Man : Daddi
Student : Pierucci
Song Writer, Rag
 Picker : Reschiglian
King of Fools :
 Venturini
Junk Man : Mugnoz
Street Arab : Trentini
Madeleine : Hume
Bird Food Vendor :
 Valliere
Chair Mender : Davis
Artichoke Vendor :
 Hayes
Street Pedler : John-
 ston

First Policeman :
  Zaini
Second Policeman :
  Giussani
Apprentice : De
  Bregnac

January 4 (mat.)
Rigoletto
Same cast as Dec. 20
  except:
Rigoletto : Renaud
Monterone : Mugnoz

January 4
Cavalleria Rusticana
  Parelli (c)
Same cast as Dec. 31

I Pagliacci
  Parelli (c)
Same cast as Dec. 9
  except:
Nedda : Agostinelli
Canio : Zenatello

January 6
Un Ballo in Maschera
Same cast as Jan. 1

January 8
Louise
Same cast as Jan. 3
  except:
Camille : Trentini

January 9
Aïda
Same cast as Nov. 11
  except:

Aïda : Agostinelli
Radames : Bassi

January 10
Don Giovanni
Same cast as Dec. 28

January 11 (mat.)
Louise
Same cast as Jan. 3
  except:
Rag Picker : Gianoli-
  Galletti

January 11
Il Trovatore
Same cast as Nov. 9
  except:
Leonora : Russ
Manrico : Zenatello
Count di Luna :
  Sammarco
Ferrando : Arimondi

January 13
Louise
Same cast as Jan. 11

January 15
La Traviata
  Campanini (c)
Violetta : Tetrazzini
Alfredo : Bassi
Germont : Ancona
Flora : Zaccaria
Annina : Severina
Gastone : Venturini

Baron Douphol :
  Fossetta
Marquis d'Obigny :
  Reschiglian
Dr. Grenvil : Gilibert

January 16
*La Damnation de
  Faust*
Same cast as Nov. 6

January 17
Thaïs
Same cast as Nov. 25

January 18 (mat.)
La Traviata
Same cast as Jan. 15

January 18
Un Ballo in Maschera
  Parelli (c)
Same cast as Dec. 27
  except:
Oscar : Trentini

January 20
Lucia di Lammermoor
  Campanini (c)
Lucia : Tetrazzini
Ashton : Sammarco
Edgardo : Zenatello
Alisa : Severina
Raimondo : Arimondi
Arturo : Venturini
Normanno : Daddi

January 22
Louise
Same cast as Jan. 11

January 24
Lucia di Lammermoor
Same cast as Jan. 20

January 25 (mat.)
Thaïs
Same cast as Nov. 25

January 25
Aïda
Same cast as Nov. 30
except:
King : ?
Messenger : ?

January 27
Il Trovatore
Same cast as Jan. 11
except:
Azucena : Schumann-
Heink
Ferrando : Mugnoz
Inez : ?
Ruiz : ?

January 29
Rigoletto
Same cast as Dec. 20
except:
Rigoletto : Renaud
Gilda : Tetrazzini
Maddalena : De
Cisneros

January 31
Louise
Same cast as Jan. 11

February 1 (mat.)
Rigoletto
Same cast as Jan. 29
except:
Rigoletto : Sammarco
Maddalena : Giaconia
Monterone : Mugnoz

February 1
*Les Contes
d'Hoffmann*
Charlier (c)
Same cast as Nov. 18

February 3
Thaïs
Same cast as Nov. 25

February 4
*Les Contes
d'Hoffmann*
Charlier (c)
Same cast as Nov. 18
except:
Nicklausse :
Giaconia

February 5
Siberia
Campanini (c)
Stephana : Agostinelli
La Fanciulla :
Trentini
Nikona : Zaccaria
Vassili : Zenatello
Gleby : Sammarco
Walitzin : Crabbé

Alexis : Cazauran
Ivan, Sergeant :
Venturini
Captain : Mugnoz
Invalid : Gianoli-
Galletti
Miskinsky :
Reschiglian
L'Ispravnick, Cossack,
Inspector : Fossetta

February 7
La Traviata
Same cast as Jan. 15
except:
Alfredo : Zenatello

February 8 (mat.)
Louise
Same cast as Jan. 3
except:
Rag Picker : Gianoli-
Galletti

February 8
Cavalleria Rusticana
Same cast as Dec. 31
except:
Santuzza : Agostinelli
Lola : De Cisneros
Turiddu : Bassi
Alfio : Ancona

I Pagliacci
Same cast as Dec. 9
except:
Canio : Zenatello

February 10
La Traviata
Same cast as Feb. 7

February 12
Lucia di Lammermoor
Same cast as Jan. 20

February 14
Siberia
Same cast as Feb. 5
  except:
Vassili : Bassi

February 15 (mat.)
Lucia di Lammermoor
Same cast as Jan. 20

February 15
Carmen
  Charlier (c)
Same cast as Nov. 5
  except:
Escamillo : Ancona
Mercédès : Severina

February 17
Rigoletto
Same cast as Dec. 20
  except:
Gilda : Tetrazzini
Sparafucile : Mugnoz
Maddalena : De
  Cisneros

February 19
Pelléas et Mélisande
  Campanini (c)

Mélisande : Garden
Geneviève : Gerville-
  Réache
Little Yniold : Sigrist
Pelléas : Périer
Golaud : Dufranne
Ärkel : Arimondi
Physician : Crabbé

February 21
Lucia di Lammermoor
Same cast as Jan. 20

February 22 (mat.)
Pelléas et Mélisande
Same cast as Feb. 19

February 22
Siberia
Same cast as Feb. 14

February 24
Louise
Same cast as Jan. 11
  except:
Irma : Koèlling
Street Arab : Sigrist

February 26
Dinorah
  Campanini (c)
Dinorah : Tetrazzini
Goatherds : Trentini,
  Giaconia
Corentino : Daddi
Harvester : Venturini
Huntsman : Mugnoz
Hoel : Ancona

February 28
Pelléas et Mélisande
Same cast as Feb. 19

February 29 (mat.)
Lucia di Lammermoor
Same cast as Jan. 20

February 29
Aïda
Same cast as Nov. 11
  except:
Aïda : Russ
Radames : Bassi

March 2
Pelléas et Mélisande
Same cast as Feb. 19

March 4
Pelléas et Mélisande
Same cast as Feb. 19

March 6
Crispino e la Comare
  Campanini (c)
Crispino : Gianoli-
  Galletti
Annetta : Tetrazzini
Dr. Fabrizio :
  Sammarco
Mirabolano : Arimondi
Count del Fiore :
  Venturini
Don Asdrubale :
  Fossetta
Comare : Zaccaria
Bartolo : Pierucci

March 7 (mat.)
Louise
Same cast as Jan. 11

March 7
Il Trovatore
Same cast as Jan. 11
except:
Azucena : Gerville-
Réache
Ferrando : Mugnoz

March 9
Crispino e la Comare
Same cast as Mar. 6

March 10
Cavalleria Rusticana
Same cast as Feb. 8
except:
Alfio : Crabbé

I Pagliacci
Same cast as Feb. 8

March 11
Lucia di Lammermoor
Same cast as Jan. 20

March 13
Carmen
Same cast as Nov. 5
except:
Carmen : Calvé
Escamillo : Dufranne
Dancaïre : Gianoli-
Galletti

March 14 (mat.)
Pelléas et Mélisande
Same cast as Feb. 19

March 14
La Navarraise
Same cast as Dec. 9

I Pagliacci
Same cast as Dec. 9
except:
Nedda : Agostinelli

March 16
Carmen
Same cast as March 13
except:
Dancaïre : Gilibert

March 18
Louise
Same cast as Jan. 3
except:
Father : Dufranne
Rag Picker : Gianoli-
Galletti

March 20
Pelléas et Mélisande
Same cast as Feb. 19

March 21 (mat.)
Crispino e la Comare
Same cast as Mar. 6

March 21
Carmen
Same cast as Mar. 16

March 23
La Traviata
Same cast as Jan. 15
except:
Dr. Grenvil : Crabbé

March 25
Lucia di Lammermoor
Parelli (c)
Same cast as Jan. 20

March 27
Andrea Chénier
Campanini (c)
Andrea Chénier :
Bassi
Maddalena : Eva
Tetrazzini-Cam-
panini
Countess di Coigny :
Giaconia
Carlo Gérard :
Sammarco
Bersi : Zeppilli
Fléville : ?
Abbé : Daddi
Madelon : De Cisneros
Mathieu : Gianoli-
Galletti
Spy : Venturini
Fouquier : Arimondi
Dumas : Mugnoz
Roucher : Crabbé
Schmidt : Fossetta
Majordomo :
Reschiglian

March 28 (mat.)
Louise
Same cast as Jan. 11
except:
Father : Dufranne

March 28
Gala Performance
Campanini (c)
La Traviata (Act I)
Violetta : Tetrazzini
Alfredo : Bassi
Flora : Zaccaria
Gastone : Venturini

Baron Douphol :
Fossetta
Marquis d'Obigny :
Reschiglian
Dr. Grenvil : Gilibert

I Pagliacci (Act I)
Same cast as Dec. 9
except:
Nedda : Agostinelli
Canio : Zenatello

Faust (Act II)
Faust : Dalmorès

Marguerite : Garden
Méphistophélès :
Arimondi
Siébel : Zeppilli
Marthe : Loubet

Lucia di Lammermoor
(Mad scene)
Lucia : Tetrazzini

Aïda (Second Act)
Same cast as Nov. 11
except:
Aïda : Russ
Radames : Bassi

1908–1909 Season

Personnel

Male Artists
Agosti, Sig.
Arimondi, Vittorio
Cacici, Sig.
Cernusco, Sig.
Collin, M.
Constantino, Florencio
Crabbé, Armand
Daddi, Francesco
Dalmorès, Charles
Deutz, M.
Dufranne, Hector
Elia, Santa
Fossetta, Nicolo
Franzini, Rocco
Gherkier, M.
Gianoli-Galletti,
Fernando
Gilibert, Charles
Giussani, Sig.

Gogny, Jules
Grazia, Giuseppe de
Malfatti, Sig.
Montanari, Sig.
Parola, Angelo
Pierucci, Sig.
Polese, Giovanni
Renaud, Maurice
Reschiglian, Vincenzo
Sammarco, Mario
Sampieri, Michele
Segurola, Andrés de
Sellav, M.
Taccani, Giuseppe
Tronconi, Sig.
Vallès, Andrien
Venturini, Emilio
Vieuille, Félix
Zaini, Sig.
Zenatello, Giovanni

Zuro, Louis

Female Artists
Agostinelli, Adelina
Aldrich, Mariska
Avezza, Maria
Boyd, Miss
Cavalieri, Lina
Doria, Augusta
Egener, Minnie
Engel, Charlotte
Espinasse, Jeanne
Garden, Mary
Gentle, Alice
Gerville-Réache,
Jeanne
Hayes, Lillian
Hume, Julie
Inman, Grace
Johnston, Miss

Keenan, Beth
Kerf, Christine
Koèlling, Helene
Labia, Maria
Laurie, Annie
Melba, Nellie
Ponzano, Adele
Severina, Gina
Tancredi, Sybil
Tetrazzini, Luisa

Trentini, Emma
Valliere, Atala
Zeppilli, Alice

Ballet
Malinverni, Anita
Valéry, Odette

Chorus Masters
Nepoti, Pietro

Zuro, Josiah

Conductors
Campanini, Cleofonte
Charlier, Marcel
Parelli, Attilio
Scognamiglio, Gaetano
  (Guest Conductor)
Sturani, Giuseppe

1908–1909 Season

November 9

Tosca

Campanini (c)
Tosca : Labia
Cavaradossi : Zenatello
Scarpia : Renaud
Angelotti : De
  Grazia
Sacristan : Gilibert
Spoletta : Montanari
Sciarrone : Fossetta
Jailer : Reschiglian
Shepherd : Severina

November 11

Thaïs

Campanini (c)
Thaïs : Garden
Nicias : Dalmorès
Athanaël : Renaud
Palemon : Vieuille
Crobyle : Trentini
Myrtale, Albine :
  Ponzano
Servant : Reschiglian

November 13

Samson et Dalila

Campanini (c)
Dalila : Gerville-
  Réache
Samson : Dalmorès
High Priest : Dufranne
Abimelech : Crabbé
Old Hebrew : Vieuille
Messenger : Venturini
Philistines : Monta-
  nari, Reschiglian

November 14 (mat.)

Tosca
Same cast as Nov. 9

November 14

Il Barbiere di Siviglia

Campanini (c)
Almaviva : Parola
Dr. Bartolo :
  Gilibert
Rosina : Tetrazzini
Figaro : Sammarco

Don Basilio : De
  Segurola
Berta : Trentini
Fiorello : Venturini
Sergeant : Fossetta

November 16

Il Barbiere di Siviglia
Same cast as Nov. 14

November 18

Lucia di Lammermoor
Campanini (c)
Lucia : Tetrazzini
Alisa : Severina
Edgardo : Taccani
Ashton : Polese
Raimondo : De
  Grazia
Arturo : Venturini
Normanno : Monta-
  nari

November 20

Les Huguenots
Campanini (c)

Marguerite : Zeppilli
St. Bris : De Segurola
Valentine : Agostinelli
Nevers : Sammarco
Bois Rosé, Tavannes :
　Venturini
Meru : De Grazia
Raoul : Zenatello
Marcel : Arimondi
Urbain : Aldrich
Ladies of Honor :
　Severina, Avezza

November 21 (mat.)
Samson et Dalila
Same cast as Nov. 13
　except:
Philistine : Malfatti
　(for Montanari)

November 21
Thaïs
Same cast as Nov. 11
　except:
Nicias : Vallès

November 23
Les Huguenots
Same cast as Nov. 20

November 25
Samson et Dalila
Same cast as Nov. 13

November 26
Carmen
　Charlier (c)
　Carmen : Labia

Don José : Vallès
Micaëla : Zeppilli
Escamillo : Crabbé
Zuniga : De Grazia
Morales : Reschiglian
Frasquita : Trentini
Mercédès : Ponzano
Dancaïre : Gilibert
Remendado : Daddi

November 27
*Le Jongleur de Notre
　Dame*
　Campanini (c)
Jean : Garden
Boniface : Renaud
Prior : Dufranne
Monk Poet : Vallès
Monk Painter : De
　Segurola
Monk Sculptor :
　Vieuille
Monk Musician :
　Crabbé
Jovial Fellow :
　Gherkier
Drunken Man : Zuro
Knight : Pierucci

November 28 (mat.)
Il Barbiere di Siviglia
Same cast as Nov. 14
　except:
Fiorello : Montanari

November 28
Tosca
Same cast as Nov. 9
　except:

Cavaradossi : Taccani
Angelotti : Sampieri
Sacristan : Gianoli-
　Galletti

November 30
Samson et Dalila
Same cast as Nov. 13

December 2
*Le Jongleur de Notre
　Dame*
Same cast as Nov. 27

December 4
Cavalleria Rusticana
　Campanini (c)
Santuzza : Labia
Turiddu : Taccani
Lola : Aldrich
Alfio : Polese
Lucia : Severina

La Chair
　(Operatic Panto-
　mime by Georges
　Wagues)
　Charlier (c)
Wife : Valéry
Lover : Kerf
Husband : Montanari

I Pagliacci
　Campanini (c)
Nedda : Espinasse
Canio : Zenatello
Tonio : Sammarco

Beppe : Venturini
Silvio : Crabbé

December 5 (mat.)

Le Jongleur de Notre Dame
Same cast as Nov. 27

December 5

Rigoletto
  Campanini (c)
Duke : Constantino
Rigoletto :
  Sammarco
Gilda : Tetrazzini
Sparafucile :
  Arimondi
Maddalena : Ponzano
Giovanna : Severina
Monterone : Fossetta
Marullo : Sampieri
Borsa : Pierucci
Ceprano : Cacici
Countess : Egener

December 7

Le Jongleur de Notre Dame
Same cast as Nov. 27

December 9

Cavalleria Rusticana
  Parelli (c)
Same cast as Dec. 4

La Chair
  (Operatic Pantomime

by Georges Wagues)
  Parelli (c)
Same cast as Dec. 4

I Pagliacci
  Parelli (c)
Same cast as Dec. 4

December 11

Lucia di Lammermoor
Same cast as Nov. 18
except:
Raimondo : Arimondi

December 12 (mat.)

Thaïs
Same cast as Nov. 21
except:
Palemon : De Grazia
Servant : Fossetta

December 12

La Traviata
  Campanini (c)
Violetta : Tetrazzini
Alfredo : Constantino
Germont : Sammarco
Flora : Egener
Annina : Severina
Gastone : Malfatti
Baron Douphol :
  Fossetta
Marquis d'Obigny :
  Sampieri
Dr. Grenvil : Cacici

December 14

La Bohème
  Campanini (c)
Rodolfo : Zenatello
Marcello : Sammarco
Schaunard : Gilibert
Colline : De Segurola
Mimi : Melba
Musetta : Trentini
Benoit, Alcindoro :
  Gianoli-Galletti
Parpignol : Venturini

December 16

Les Contes d'Hoffmann
  Charlier (c)
Olympia : Zeppilli
Giulietta : Espinasse
Antonia : Trentini
Hoffmann : Dalmorès
Nicklausse : Doria
Coppelius, Dapertutto,
  Miracle : Renaud
Cochenille, Pitichinac-
  cio : Daddi
Luther : Fossetta
Nathanael : Venturini
Hermann :
  Reschiglian
Spalanzani, Crespel :
  Gilibert
Lindorf, Schlemil :
  Crabbé
Franz : Gianoli-
  Galletti
A Voice : Aldrich

December 18
Tosca
Same cast as Nov. 9
 except:
Cavaradossi :
 Constantino
Scarpia : Sammarco
Sacristan : Gianoli-
 Galletti

December 19 (mat.)
La Bohème
Same cast as Dec. 14
 except:
Rodolfo :
 Constantino

December 19
*Le Jongleur de Notre
 Dame*
Same cast as Nov. 27

December 21
*Les Contes
 d'Hoffmann*
Same cast as Dec. 16

December 23
La Bohème
Same cast as Dec. 14

December 25
Otello
 Campanini (c)
Otello : Zenatello
Desdemona : Melba
Iago : Sammarco
Emilia : Doria
Cassio : Venturini

Roderigo :
 Montanari
Lodovico : De
 Segurola
Montano : Crabbé
Herald : Zuro

December 26 (mat.)
Lucia di Lammermoor
Same cast as Nov. 18
 except:
Edgardo : Constantino
Ashton : Sammarco
Raimondo : Arimondi
Normanno : Daddi

December 26
Samson et Dalila
Same cast as Nov. 13

December 28
Thaïs
Same cast as Nov. 21

December 30
Rigoletto
Same cast as Dec. 5
 except:
Marullo : Reschiglian
Borsa : Venturini
Countess : Avezza
Page : Egener

December 31
*Les Contes
 d'Hoffmann*
Same cast as Dec. 16
 except:
Luther : Zuro

January 1
La Traviata
Same cast as Dec. 12
 except:
Alfredo : Taccani
Gastone : Montanari

January 2 (mat.)
Otello
Same cast as Dec. 25

January 2
Lucia di Lammermoor
Same cast as Nov. 18
 except:
Alisa : Hume
Edgardo :
 Constantino
Raimondo : Arimondi

January 4
Otello
Same cast as Dec. 25

January 6
Pelléas et Mélisande
 Campanini (c)
Mélisande : Garden
Geneviève : Gerville-
 Réache
Little Yniold :
 Trentini
Pelléas : Dalmorès
Golaud : Dufranne
Ärkel : Vieuille
Physician : Crabbé

January 8
*Les Contes
 d'Hoffmann*
Same cast as Dec. 31
 except:
Nathanael : ?
Hermann : ?

January 9 (mat.)
Pelléas et Mélisande
Same cast as Jan. 6

January 9
Crispino e la Comare
 Campanini (c)
Crispino : Gianoli-
 Galletti
Annetta : Tetrazzini
Dr. Fabrizio :
 Sammarco
Mirabolano :
 Arimondi
Count del Fiore :
 Venturini
Don Asdrubale :
 Fossetta
Comare : Severina
Bartolo : Pierucci
La Mort de Cléopâtre
 (Ballet) : Valéry
 Parelli (c)

January 11
Rigoletto
Same cast as Dec. 5
 except:
Rigoletto : Renaud
Gilda : Melba

Monterone : Gilibert
Marullo : Cacici
Borsa : Venturini
Ceprano :
 Reschiglian
Countess : Hayes

January 13
Crispino e la Comare
 Parelli (c)
Same cast as Jan. 9

I Pagliacci
 Parelli (c)
Same cast as Dec. 4

January 15
Pelléas et Mélisande
Same cast as Jan. 6

January 16 (mat.)
La Traviata
Same cast as Dec. 12
 except:
Alfredo : Taccani
Flora : Koèlling
Gastone : Montanari
Baron Douphol :
 Sampieri
Marquis d'Obigny :
 Reschiglian
Dr. Grenvil : De
 Grazia

January 16
Otello
Same cast as Dec. 25
 except:
Desdemona : Labia

Lodovico : De Grazia
Montano : Sampieri

January 18
Lucia di Lammermoor
 Parelli (c)
Same cast as Nov. 18
 except:
Raimondo : Arimondi
Arturo : ?
Normanno : ?

January 20
La Traviata
Same cast as Dec. 12
 except:
Alfredo : Taccani
Flora : Koèlling
Gastone : Venturini
Baron Douphol,
 Dr. Grenvil : Cacici
Marquis d'Obigny :
 Reschiglian

January 22
Thaïs
Same cast as Nov. 21
 except:
Servant : ?

January 23 (mat.)
Carmen
Same cast as Nov. 26
 except:
Carmen : Gerville-
 Réache
Don José :
 Constantino

Zuniga : ?
Morales : ?
Remendado : ?

January 23
Pelléas et Mélisande
Same cast as Jan. 6

January 25
Tosca
Same cast as Nov. 9
except:
Tosca : Cavalieri
Scarpia : Sammarco
Shepherd : Avezza

January 27
Otello
Same cast as Jan. 16

January 28
Salome
 Campanini (c)
Herod : Dalmorès
Herodias : Doria
Salome : Garden
Jokanaan : Dufranne
Narraboth : Vallès
Page : Severina
Two Nazarenes : De
 Segurola, Malfatti
Five Jews : Sellav,
 Venturini, Montanari,
 Daddi, Collin
Two Soldiers : Crabbé
 De Grazia
Cappadocian : Fossetta
Slave : Tancredi

January 29
Rigoletto
Same cast as Dec. 5
except:
Rigoletto : Renaud
Sparafucile : De
 Segurola
Marullo :
 Reschiglian
Borsa : Venturini
Countess, Page :
 Hayes

January 30 (mat.)
Salome
Same cast as Jan. 28

January 30
Cavalleria Rusticana
 Scognamiglio (c)
Same cast as Dec. 4
except:
Santuzza :
 Agostinelli
Turiddu :
 Constantino
Alfio : Crabbé

I Pagliacci
 Scognamiglio (c)
Same cast as Dec. 4
except:
Nedda : Zeppilli
Canio : Taccani
Beppe : ?

La Mort de Cléopâtre
 (Ballet) : Valéry

February 1
Cavalleria Rusticana
 Parelli (c)
Same cast as Dec. 4
except:
Turiddu :
 Constantino
Alfio : Crabbé

Crispino e la Comare
 Parelli (c)
Same cast as Jan. 9

February 3
Salome
Same cast as Jan. 28

February 5
Salome
Same cast as Jan. 28

February 6 (mat.)
La Bohème
Same cast as Dec. 14
except:
Rodolfo : Constantino
Schaunard : Fossetta
Mimi : Cavalieri
Musetta : Zeppilli

February 6
*Les Contes
 d'Hoffmann*
Same cast as Dec. 16
except:
Nicklausse : Aldrich
Luther : Franzini

February 8

Salome
Same cast as Jan. 28

February 10

Aïda
  Campanini (c)
King : De Grazia
Amneris : Doria
Aïda : Agostinelli
Radames : Zenatello
Amonasro : Sammarco
Ramfis : Arimondi
Messenger :
  Venturini

February 12

Lucia di Lammermoor
Same cast as Nov. 18

February 13 (mat.)

*Les Contes
  d'Hoffmann*
Same cast as Dec. 31
  except:
Nicklausse : Aldrich

February 13

La Sonnambula
  Parelli (c)
Adina : Tetrazzini
Elvino : Parola
Rodolfo : De Segurola
Alessio : Reschiglian
Notary : Pierucci
Lisa : Trentini
Teresa : Severina

February 15

*Le Jongleur de Notre
  Dame*
Same cast as Nov. 27

February 17

La Bohème
Same cast as Dec. 14
  except:
Mimi : Cavalieri

February 19

Louise
  Campanini (c)
Louise : Garden
Julien : Dalmorès
Mother : Doria
Father : Gilibert
Irma : Zeppilli
Camille : Tancredi
Gertrude : Avezza
Apprentice, Street
  Arab : Trentini
Elsie, A Street
  Sweeper : Severina
Blanche, Milk
  Woman : Ponzano
Suzanne : Koëlling
Forewoman : ?
Marguerite : ?
Painter : ?
First Philosopher,
  Sculptor : Crabbé
Poet, Old Clothes
  Man : Daddi
Song Writer :
  Reschiglian

Rag Picker : Gianoli-
  Galletti
King of Fools :
  Venturini
Junk Man : Zuro
(The rest of this pro-
  gramme is lost.)

February 20 (mat.)

La Sonnambula
Same cast as Feb. 13
  except:
Teresa : Avezza

February 20

Salome
Same cast as Jan. 28

February 22 (mat.)

Louise
Same cast as Feb. 19
  except:
Father : Vieuille
Forewoman : Inman
Marguerite : Laurie
Madeleine : Hume
Student : Montanari
Song Writer :
  Reschiglian
Street Peddler :
  Johnston
First Policeman :
  Zaini
Second Policeman :
  Giussani
Junk Man : Zuro
Bird Food Vendor :
  Valliere

Artichoke Vendor :
Hayes
Chair Mender :
Gentle

February 22
La Sonnambula
Same cast as Feb. 20
Cavalleria Rusticana
Parelli (c)
Same cast as Dec. 4
except:
Alfio : Crabbé
Lucia : Avezza

February 24
Louise
Same cast as Feb. 22

February 26
I Puritani
Campanini (c)
Lord Walton : De
Grazia
Sir George : De
Segurola
Elvira :
Tetrazzini
Henrietta : Severina
Lord Arthur :
Constantino
Sir Richard : Polese
Sir Bruno : Venturini

February 27 (mat.)
Salome
Same cast as Jan. 28

February 27
Aïda
Same cast as Feb. 10
except:
Amneris : Gerville-
Réache
Amonasro : Polese
Ramfis : De
Segurola
Messenger :
Montanari

March 1
Il Trovatore
Sturani (c)
Leonora :
Agostinelli
Manrico : Zenatello
Count di Luna :
Sammarco
Azucena : Gerville-
Réache
Inez : Avezza
Ferrando : De Grazia
Ruiz : Zaini

March 3
*Les Contes
d'Hoffmann*
Same cast as Dec. 16
except:
Luther : Franzini

March 5
Otello
Same cast as Dec. 25
except:
Desdemona : Labia

March 6 (mat.)
Louise
Same cast as Feb. 22
except:
Apprentice : Engel

March 6
*Le Jongleur de Notre
Dame*
Same cast as Nov. 27

March 8
Rigoletto
Same cast as Jan. 29
except:
Sparafucile :
Arimondi
Monterone : Gilibert
Ceprano : De Grazia

March 10
*La Princesse
d'Auberge*
Campanini (c)
Rita : Labia
Katelyne : Gerville-
Réache
Reinilde : Zeppilli
Merlyn : Vallès
Marcus : Crabbé
Bluts : Gilibert
Rabo : Dufranne
Student : Venturini
Three Sisters of Rita :
Koèlling, Tancredi,
Severina
Old Peasant :
Reschiglian

Young Peasant :
  Montanari
Old Servant : Hume
Citizen : Fossetta
Bluts's Companions :
  Zuro, Daddi

March 12
Thaïs
Same cast as Nov. 21
  except:
Crobyle : Koèlling

March 13 (mat.)
*La Princesse
  d'Auberge*
Same cast as March 10

March 13
Salome
Same cast as Jan. 28

March 15
Louise
Same cast as Mar. 6

March 17
I Puritani
  Parelli (c)
Same cast as Feb. 26

March 19
*La Princesse
  d'Auberge*
Same cast as Mar. 10

March 20 (mat.)
La Navarraise
  Campanini (c)
Anita : Gerville-
  Réache
Garrido : Dufranne
Araguil : Vallès
Ramon : Crabbé
Bustamente : Gianoli-
  Galletti
Remigio : Vieuille

I Pagliacci
  Parelli (c)
Same cast as Dec. 4
  except:
Nedda : Labia

March 20
Salome
Same cast as Jan. 28

March 22
*Thaïs**
Same cast as Nov. 21

March 24
La Traviata
Same cast as Dec. 12
  except:
Flora : Koèlling
Gastone : Montanari
Marquis d'Obigny :
  Reschiglian

Dr. Grenvil : De
  Grazia

March 26
Salome
Same cast as Jan. 28

Prologue to
  Mefistofele :
  Arimondi and Chorus

March 27 (mat.)
Samson et Dalila
Same cast as Nov. 13

March 27
*Lucia di
  Lammermoor***
Same cast as Dec. 26
  except:
Normanno :
  Montanari
*La Princesse
  d'Auberge*
  (Carnival Scene)
Rita : Labia
Merlyn : Gogny
Bluts : Gilibert
Rabo : Dufranne
Three Sisters of Rita :
  Koèlling, Tancredi,
  Severina
Student : Venturini

* The young Mischa Elman played the "Meditation" with the orchestra
at this performance.
** During an intermission, Campanini conducted a new waltz written
by Hammerstein. It was "Cara Mia," composed for Tetrazzini.

Preliminary Season (August–October, 1909)

Personnel

Male Artists
Beck, William
Bernardo, Giuseppe di
Carasa, Frederico
Chapman, M.
Contesso, Sig.
Dauche, M.
Davies, Harry
Duffault, Jean
Fossetta, Nicolo
Franzini, Rocco
Grazia, Giuseppe de
Laskin, Henry
Leroux, Pierre
Lucas, George
Nicolay, Constantin
Pignataro, Enrico
Roger, M.
Russo, Domenico
Scott, Henri

Shields, George
Venturini, Emilio
Villa, Gaston
Zano, Sig.
Zerola, Nicola
Zuro, Louis

Female Artists
Alvarez, Marguerite d'
Baron, Alice
Carew, Charlotte
Combe, Ernestine de
De Rosa, Miss
Desmond, Mary
Duchène, Maria
Engel, Charlotte
Engel, Josephine
Gentle, Alice
Grippon, Eva
Johnston, Miss

Keenan, Beth
Lango, Tati
Miranda, Lalla
Morris, Denise
Rivers, Annie
Severina, Gina
Soyer, Berthe
Sylva, Marguerite
Valliere, Atala
Vicarino, Regina
Walter-Villa, Mme

Chorus Master
Josiah Zuro

Conductors
Nicosia, Carlo
Scognamiglio, Gaetano
Sturani, Giuseppe

Preliminary Season (August–October, 1909)

August 30

Le Prophète
  Sturani (c)
John of Leyden :
  Lucas
Fidès : D'Alvarez
Bertha : Walter-
  Villa
Jonas : Leroux
Mathisen : Villa
Zacharias : Nicolay
Oberthal : Laskin
Soldier : ?

Peasant : ?

August 31

Aïda
  Sturani (c)
King : De Grazia
Amneris : Soyer
Aïda : Baron
Radames : Carasa
Amonasro : Pignataro
Ramfis : Scott
Messenger :
  Venturini

Priestess : Gentle

September 1

Carmen
  Nicosia (c)
Carmen : Sylva
Don José : Lucas
Micaëla : Walter-
  Villa
Escamillo : Laskin
Zuniga : De Grazia
Morales : Fossetta
Frasquita : Lango

Mercédès : Duchène
Dancaïre : Nicolay
Remendado : Leroux

September 2
Lucia di Lammermoor
 Sturani (c)
Lucia : Miranda
Alisa : Severina
Edgardo : Russo
Ashton : Pignataro
Raimondo : ?
Arturo : Venturini
Normanno : De Grazia

September 3
Aïda
Same cast as Aug. 31

September 4 (mat.)
La Traviata
 Nicosia (c)
Violetta : Miranda
Alfredo : Di Bernardo
Germont : Beck
Flora : Gentle
Annina : Severina
Gastone : Venturini
Baron Douphol :
 Fossetta
Marquis d'Obigny :
 Roger
Dr. Grenvil : De
 Grazia

September 4
Le Prophète
Same cast as Aug. 30

September 6
Carmen
Same cast as Sept. 1
 except:
Micaëla : Vicarino
Escamillo : Beck
Mercédès : Gentle

September 7
La Traviata
Same cast as Sept. 4

September 8
Le Prophète
Same cast as Aug. 30

September 9
La Juive
 Nicosia (c)
Rachel : Grippon
Princess : Walter-
 Villa
Eleazar : Duffault
Brogni : Laskin
Leopold : Russo
Ruggiero : Villa
Albert : De Grazia

September 10
Rigoletto
 Sturani (c)
Duke : Carasa
Rigoletto : Beck
Gilda : Miranda
Sparafucile : Scott
Maddalena : Gentle
Giovanna : Severina

Monterone : De
 Grazia
Marullo : Franzini
Borsa : Zano
Ceprano : Fossetta
Countess : Johnston

September 11 (mat.)
Carmen
Same cast as Sept. 1

September 11
La Juive
Same cast as Sept. 9

September 13
Aïda
Same cast as Aug. 31
 except:
Amonasro : ?

September 14
Carmen
Same cast as Sept. 1

September 15
Rigoletto
Same cast as
 Sept. 10 (?)

September 16
Le Prophète
Same cast as Aug. 30

September 17
Cavalleria Rusticana
 Sturani (c)

Santuzza : Sylva
Turiddu : Lucas
Lola : Gentle
Alfio : Beck
Lucia : Severina

I Pagliacci
 Sturani (c)
Nedda : Sylva
Canio : Carasa
Tonio : Laskin
Beppe : Venturini
Silvio : Fossetta

September 18 (mat.)
La Juive
Same cast as Sept. 9

September 18
Tosca
 Sturani (c)
Tosca : Grippon
Cavaradossi : Carasa
Scarpia : Beck
Angelotti : De
 Grazia
Sacristan : Nicolay
Spoletta : Venturini
Sciarrone : Fossetta
Shepherd : Severina

September 20
Rigoletto
Same cast as Sept. 10
 except:
Duke : Di
 Bernardo

Marullo : ?
Borsa : ?

September 21
Cavalleria Rusticana
Same cast as Sept. 17
 except:
Lola : Desmond
Alfio : Pignataro

I Pagliacci
Same cast as Sept. 17

September 22
Tosca
Same cast as Sept. 18
 except:
Tosca : Sylva

September 23
Aïda
Same cast as Aug. 31
 except:
Amneris : D'Alvarez
Aïda : Grippon
Radames : Zerola

September 24
Louise
 Nicosia (c)
Louise : Baron
Julien : Duffault
Mother : Duchène
Father : Beck
Irma : Vicarino
Camille : Lango

Gertrude : Gentle
Apprentice : Engel, C.
Elsie, Street Sweeper :
 Severina
Blanche : Desmond
Suzanne : De Rosa
Forewoman :
 Johnston
Marguerite : Carew
Madeleine : Morris
Painter, First
 Philosopher :
 Fossetta
Sculptor : Venturini
Poet, Old Clothes
 Man : Leroux
Student : Villa
Song Writer : ?
Newspaper Girl : ?
Rag Picker : Nicolay
Milk Woman : Gentle
Coal Picker : ?
King of Fools :
 Venturini
First Policeman :
 Contesso
Second Policeman :
 Dauche
Junk Man : Zuro
Street Arab :
 Engel, J.
Bird Food Vendor :
 Rivers
Artichoke Vendor :
 Coombs
Chair Mender :
 Keenan
Carrot Vendor : ?

September 25

Il Trovatore

Sturani (c)
Leonora : Grippon
Manrico : Zerola
Count di Luna :
  Pignataro
Azucena : D'Alvarez
Inez : Gentle
Ferrando : De Grazia
Ruiz : Venturini

September 27

Louise

Same cast as Sept. 24
except:
Apple Woman : Custer

September 28

Il Trovatore

Same cast as Sept. 25
except:
Count di Luna :
  Fossetta

September 29

Carmen

Same cast as Sept. 1

September 30

Aïda

Same cast as Aug. 31
except:
Amneris : D'Alvarez
Radames : Zerola

October 1

Faust

Nicosia (c)
Faust : Duffault
Marguerite : Sylva
Méphistophélès :
  Laskin
Valentin : Beck
Siébel : Lango
Marthe : Duchène
Wagner : De Grazia

October 2 (mat.)

Louise

Same cast as Sept. 24

October 2

Cavalleria Rusticana

Same cast as Sept. 17
except:
Santuzza : Baron
Turiddu : Carasa

I Pagliacci

Same cast as Sept. 17
except:
Nedda : Walter-
  Villa
Canio : Zerola

October 4

Tosca

Same cast as Sept. 18
except:
Tosca : Baron

October 5

Cavalleria Rusticana

Same cast as Sept. 17
except:
Santuzza : Baron
Turiddu : Carasa
Alfio : Pignataro

I Pagliacci

Same cast as Sept. 17
except:
Nedda : Walter-
  Villa
Canio : Zerola

October 6

Faust

Same cast as Oct. 1
except:
Valentin : Villa

October 7

Aïda

Same cast as Sept. 30
except:
Aïda : Grippon

October 8

*Les Contes
  d'Hoffmann*

Nicosia (c)
Olympia, Antonia :
  Walter-Villa
Giulietta : Baron
Hoffmann : Lucas
Nicklausse : Gentle
Lindorf, Schlemil :
  De Grazia

Coppelius, Dapertutto,
  Miracle : Beck
Cochenille, Pitichinac-
  cio, Franz : Leroux
Luther : Zuro
Nathanael : Venturini
Hermann : Fossetta
Spalanzani : Nicolay
Crespel : Villa
Voice : Duchène

October 9 (mat.)
Carmen
Same cast as Sept. 1
  except:
Don José : Carasa

October 9
Louise
Same cast as Sept. 24

October 11
Le Prophète
Same cast as Aug. 30

October 12
Cavalleria Rusticana
Same cast as Oct. 2
  except:
Alfio : Pignataro

I Pagliacci
Same cast as Sept. 17
  except:
Canio : Zerola
Silvio : Beck

October 13
*Les Contes
  d'Hoffmann*
Same cast as Oct. 8

October 14
Il Trovatore
Same cast as Sept. 25
  except:
Count di Luna :
  Fossetta
Inez : ?

October 15
Louise
Same cast as
  Sept. 24 (?)

October 16 (mat.)
*Les Contes
  d'Hoffmann*
Same cast as Oct. 8

October 16
Aïda
Same cast as Oct. 7

October 18
Cavalleria Rusticana
Same cast as Sept. 17
  except:
Turiddu : Carasa
Alfio : Pignataro

I Pagliacci
Same cast as Sept. 17
  except:
Canio : Zerola

Silvio : Beck

October 19
*Les Contes
  d'Hoffmann*
Same cast as Oct. 8

October 20
The Bohemian Girl
  Nicosia (c)
Arline : Miranda
Gypsy Queen :
  Duchène
Buda : Coombs
Thaddeus : Russo
Count Arnheim :
  Scott
Florestein : Davies
Devilshoof : Shields
Captain : Chapman
Officer : Dauche

October 21
Carmen
Same cast as Oct. 9

October 22
Aïda
Same cast as Oct. 7

October 23 (mat.)
The Bohemian Girl
Same cast as Oct. 20

October 23
*Les Contes
  d'Hoffmann*
Same cast as Oct. 8

October 25
Tosca
  Scognamiglio (c)
Same cast as Sept. 22

October 26
The Bohemian Girl
Same cast as Oct. 20

October 27
Cavalleria Rusticana
Same cast as Oct. 2
  except:
Alfio : Pignataro

I Pagliacci
Same cast as Oct. 18

October 28
Rigoletto
  Scognamiglio (c)
Same cast as Sept. 10
  except:

Marullo : Fossetta
Borsa : Venturini
Ceprano : Zano

October 29
The Bohemian Girl
Same cast as Oct. 20

October 30 (mat.)
Les Contes
  d'Hoffmann
Same cast as Oct. 8

October 30
Gala Performance
I Pagliacci
  Scognamiglio (c)
Same cast as Oct. 18
  except:
Tonio : Laskin (?)
Silvio : Beck (?)
Carmen (Act IV)
  Nicosia (c)

Carmen : Sylva
Don José : Carasa
Escamillo : Beck
Frasquita : Lango
Mercédès : Duchène

Il Trovatore (Act III)
  Scognamiglio (c)
Same cast as Sept. 25
  except:
Count di Luna :
  Fossetta

Le Prophète
  (Coronation Scene)
  Scognamiglio (c)
John of Leyden :
  Lucas
Fidès : D'Alvarez
Jonas : Leroux
Mathisen : Villa
Zacharias : Nicolay

1909–10 Season
Personnel

Male Artists

Beck, William
Carasa, Frederico
Contesso, Sig.
Crabbé, Armand
Daddi, Francesco
Dalmorès, Charles
Dambrine, Alfred
Dauche, M.
D'Axtimo, Sig.
Delparte, Jean

Devries, David
Domenico, M.
Duffault, Jean
Dufour, Michel
Dufranne, Hector
Duvernois, M.
Fossetta, Nicolo
Franzini, Rocco
Gilibert, Charles
Gogny, Jules
Grazia, Giuseppe de

Grenier, M.
Harrold, Orville
Huberdeau, Gustave
Keyser, Jean de
Laskin, Henry
Leroux, Pierre
Lucas, George
Lucas, Oliver
Malfatti, Sig.
McCormack, John
Michaloff, M.

Moyroud, M.
Nemo, Sig.
Nicolay, Constantin
Pierucci, Sig.
Pignataro, Enrico
Polese, Giovanni
Renaud, Maurice
Renier, M.
Russo, Domenico
Sammarco, Mario
Sampieri, Michele
Scott, Henri
Vallès, Andrien
Vallier, Jean
Venturini, Emilio
Villa, Gaston
Zaini, Sig.
Zano, Sig.
Zenatello, Giovanni
Zerola, Nicola
Zuro, Louis
Zwieback, M.

Female Artists

Alvarez, Marguerite d'
Baron, Alice
Blondel, Elizabeth
Carew, Charlotte
Cavalieri, Lina

Custer, Miss
Delmore, Henriette
Desmond, Mary
Doria, Augusta
Dubois, Marianne
Duchène, Maria
Dumesnil, Suzanne
Egener, Minnie
Engel, Charlotte
Engel, Josephine
Garden, Mary
Gentle, Alice
Gerville-Réache,
 Jeanne
Govain, Mlle
Grippon, Eva
Hayes, Lillian
Johnston, Miss
Keenan, Beth
Lango, Tati
Laurie, Annie
Laya, Rachel
Mazarin, Mariette
Melis, Carmen
Merly, Mlle
Milda, Mlle
Miranda, Lalla
Morris, Denise
Nolba, Mlle

Renny, Miss
Rivers, Annie
Schaesser, Barbara
Severina, Gina
Soyer, Berthe
Sylva, Marguerite
Tetrazzini, Luisa
Trentini, Emma
Vicarino, Regina
Walter-Villa, Mme

Ballet

Mlle Galimberti
 (Prima ballerina)

Chorus Masters

Nepoti, Pietro
Zuro, Josiah

Conductors

Anselmi, Oscar
Charlier, Marcel
De la Fuente,
 Henriquez
Haakman, Alfred
Nicosia, Carlo
Sturani, Giuseppe

1910–10 Season

November 8
Hérodiade
 De la Fuente (c)
Salomé : Cavalieri
Hérodiade : Gerville-
 Réache

Slave : Carew
Jean : Dalmorès
Hérode : Renaud
Vitellius : Crabbé
Phanuel : Vallier
High Priest : Nicolay

Voice : Venturini

November 10
La Traviata
 Anselmi (c)
Violetta : Tetrazzini

Alfredo : McCormack
Germont : Sammarco
Flora, Annina :
  Severina
Gastone : Venturini
Baron Douphol :
  Fossetta
Marquis d'Obigny :
  Zano
Dr. Grenvil :
  Pierucci

November 12
Aïda
  Anselmi (c)
King : De Grazia
Amneris : D'Alvarez
Aïda : Mazarin
Radames : Zenatello
Amonasro : Sammarco
Ramfis : Vallier
Messenger : Venturini

November 13 (mat.)
Thaïs
  De la Fuente (c)
Thaïs : Garden
Nicias : Vallès
Athanaël : Renaud
Palemon : Scott
Crobyle : Trentini
Myrtale, Albine :
  Duchène
Servant : Fossetta

November 13
Cavalleria Rusticana
  Anselmi (c)

Santuzza : Mazarin
Turiddu : Lucas
Lola : Duchène
Alfio : Crabbé
Lucia : Severina

I Pagliacci
  Anselmi (c)
Nedda : Cavalieri
Canio : Zenatello
Tonio : Sammarco
Beppe : Venturini
Silvio : Beck

November 15
Lucia di Lammermoor
  Anselmi (c)
Lucia : Tetrazzini
Alisa : Severina
Edgardo : McCor-
  mack
Ashton : Sammarco
Raimondo : De Grazia
Arturo : Venturini
Normanno : Daddi

November 16
*La Fille de Madame
  Angot*
  Haakman (c)
Ange Pitou : Devries
Pompounet :
  Dambrine
Larivaudiere :
  Blondel
Trénitz : Leroux
Louchard : Nicolay
Cadet : Moyroud

Clairette : Delmore
Mlle Lange : Nolba
Amarante : Laya
Mme Herbelin :
  Govain
Mme Ducoudray :
  Dumesnil
Babet : Merly
Mme Delaunay :
  Lango
Hersilie : ?

November 17
Sapho
  De la Fuente (c)
Fanny Le Grand :
  Garden
Jean Gaussin :
  Dalmorès
Divonne : D'Alvarez
Irène : Walter-
  Villa
Caoudal : Dufranne
Césaire Gaussin :
  Leroux
Innkeeper : Villa

November 19
La Traviata
Same cast as Nov. 10

November 20 (mat.)
Hérodiade
Same cast as Nov. 8
  except:
Hérodiade : Doria
Slave : Duchène
Jean : Duffault

November 20
La Fille de Madame Angot
Same cast as Nov. 16

November 22
I Pagliacci
Same cast as Nov. 13
except:
Nedda : Sylva
Canio : Zerola
Silvio : Crabbé

La Fille du Régiment
Anselmi (c)
Marie : Tetrazzini
Marquise : Duchène
Tonio :
   McCormack
Sulpice : Gilibert
Hortentius : ?
Corporal : Nicolay

November 23
La Mascotte
   Haakman (c)
Bettina : Delmore
Fiametta : Nolba
Lorenzo XVII :
   Blondel
Pippo : Dufour
Prince Frederic :
   Dambrine
Rocco : Moyroud

November 24
Hérodiade
Same cast as Nov. 8

November 25
Carmen
   De la Fuente (c)
Carmen : Cavalieri
Don José : Zenatello
Micaëla : Miranda
Escamillo : Dufranne
Zuniga : De Grazia
Morales : Venturini
Frasquita : Lango
Mercédès : Gentle
Dancaïre : Nicolay
Remendado : Leroux

November 26
La Tosca
   De la Fuente (c)
Tosca : Melis
Cavaradossi :
   Zenatello
Scarpia : Renaud
Angelotti : De
   Grazia
Sacristan : Gilibert
Spoletta : Venturini
Sciarrone : Fossetta
Shepherd : Severina

November 27 (mat.)
Sapho
Same cast as Nov. 17
except:
Divonne : Soyer
Innkeeper : ?

November 27
Les Dragons de Villars
   Haakman (c)

Rose Friquet : Walter-
   Villa
Georgette : Dumesnil
Sylvain : Devries
Belamy : Dufour
Thibaut : Dambrine
Clergyman : Nicolay
Lieutenant : Renier
Dragoon : Moyroud

November 29
Sapho
Same cast as Nov. 27

November 30
Les Dragons de Villars
Same cast as Nov. 27
except:
Clergyman : Nemo (?)

December 1
La Fille du Régiment
Same cast as Nov. 22

I Pagliacci
Same cast as Nov. 22
except:
Nedda : Trentini

December 3
Hérodiade
Same cast as Nov. 8
except:
Jean : Duffault

December 4 (mat.)
*Le Jongleur de
Notre Dame*
De le Fuente (c)

Jean : Garden
Boniface : Renaud
Prior : Dufranne
Monk Poet : Lucas
Monk Painter :
Laskin
Monk Sculptor :
Huberdeau
Monk Musician :
Crabbé
Jovial Fellow : ?
Drunken Man : ?
Knight : ?

December 4
*Les Cloches de
Corneville*
Haakman (c)
Serpolette :
Delmore
Germaine : Nolba
Henri : Crabbé
Jean : Leroux
Gaspard : Blondel
Bailli : Dambrine

December 6
La Tosca
Same cast as Nov. 26

December 7
*Les Cloches de
Corneville*
Same cast as Dec. 4
except:
Henri : Dufour

December 8
Faust
De la Fuente (c)
Faust : Dalmorès
Marguerite : Garden
Méphistophélès :
Vallier
Valentin : Dufranne
Siébel : Vicarino
Marthe : Duchène
Wagner : Villa

December 10
Tannhäuser
De la Fuente (c)
Hermann : Vallier
Tannhäuser :
Zenatello
Wolfram : Renaud
Walther : Lucas
Biterolf : Huberdeau
Heinrich :
Venturini
Reinmar : Scott
Elisabeth : Mazarin
Venus : Doria
Shepherd : Duchène

December 11 (mat.)
Faust
Same cast as Dec. 8
except:
Méphistophélès :
Huberdeau

December 11
*Les Cloches de
Corneville*
Same cast as Dec. 7

December 13
Tannhäuser
Same cast as Dec. 10

December 15
*Le Jongleur de
Notre Dame*
Same cast as Dec. 4
except:
Monk Painter : Scott

December 17
Thaïs
Same cast as Nov. 13
except:
Nicias : Dalmorès
Servant : Villa

December 18 (mat.)
Lucia di Lammermoor
Same cast as Nov. 15

December 20
*Le Jongleur de Notre
Dame*
Same cast as Dec. 4
except:
Boniface : Gilibert
Monk Painter : Scott

December 22
Tannhäuser
Same cast as Dec. 10

December 24
Carmen
Same cast as Nov. 25
except:
Don José : Carasa

Micaëla : Vicarino
Escamillo : Laskin
Frasquita : Trentini
Mercédès : Duchène
Dancaïre : Gilibert

December 25 (mat.)
La Tosca
Same cast as Nov. 26
except:
Cavaradossi : Carasa
Scarpia :
    Sammarco
Sacristan : Nicolay
Shepherd : Vicarino

December 25
*Les Contes
    d'Hoffmann*
    De la Fuente (c)
Olympia, Antonia :
    Trentini
Giulietta : Cavalieri
Hoffmann : Dalmorès
Nicklausse : Gentle
Coppelius, Dapertutto,
    Miracle : Renaud
Cochenille, Pitichi-
    naccio, Franz :
    Leroux
Luther : Zuro
Nathanael : Venturini
Hermann : Fossetta
Spalanzani, Crespel :
    Gilibert
Lindorf, Schlemil :
    De Grazia

December 27
Carmen
Same cast as Dec. 24
except:
Don José : Zenatello

December 29
*Les Contes
    d'Hoffmann*
Same cast as Dec. 25
except:
Hoffmann : Lucas

December 31
*Le Jongleur de
    Notre Dame*
Same cast as Dec. 4
except:
Monk Musician : Scott
Boniface : Gilibert

January 1 (mat.)
La Fille du Régiment
Same cast as Nov. 22

I Pagliacci
Same cast as Nov. 13
except:
Nedda : Trentini
Canio : Lucas
Silvio : Crabbé

January 1
Hérodiade
Same cast as Nov. 8
except:

Hérodiade :
    D'Alvarez
Slave : Duchène
Jean : Duffault

January 3
Thaïs
Same cast as Dec. 17
except:
Servant : Nicolay

January 5
Lucia di Lammermoor
Same cast as Nov. 15

January 7
Faust
Same cast as Dec. 8
except:
Méphistophélès :
    Huberdeau
Siébel : Lango

January 8 (mat.)
Thaïs
Same cast as Nov. 13
except:
Nicias : Lucas
Servant : Nicolay

January 8
Il Trovatore
    Anselmi (c)
Leonora : Grippon
Manrico : Zerola
Count di Luna :
    Sammarco

Azucena : D'Alvarez
Inez : Gentle
Ferrando : De Grazia
Ruiz : Daddi

January 10
Aïda
Same cast as Nov. 12
  except :
Amneris : Doria
Radames : Zerola
Amonasro : Crabbé
Priestess : Gentle

January 12
Carmen
Same cast as Nov. 25
  except:
Carmen : Mazarin
Don José : Lucas
Micaëla : Walter-
  Villa
Escamillo : Laskin
Frasquita : Trentini
Mercédès : Duchène
Remendado : Daddi

January 14
La Bohème
  Anselmi (c)
Rodolfo : Duffault
Marcello : Polese
Schaunard : Fossetta
Colline : Huberdeau
Mimi : Melis
Musetta : Trentini
Benoit, Alcindoro :
  Daddi

Parpignol :
  Pierucci

January 15 (mat.)
*Les Contes
d'Hoffmann*
Same cast as Dec. 25
  except:
Giulietta : Duchène
Cochenille,
  Pitichinaccio :
  Daddi
Franz, Hermann :
  Fossetta

January 15
Cavalleria Rusticana
Same cast as Nov. 13
  except:
Santuzza : Baron
Lola : Gentle

I Pagliacci
Same cast as Nov. 13
  except:
Nedda : Walter-
  Villa
Canio : Zerola
Silvio : Crabbé

January 17
La Bohème
Same cast as Jan. 14
  except:
Rodolfo :
  McCormack
Marcello : Sammarco
Schaunard : Gilibert

January 19
Grisélidis
  De la Fuente (c)
Grisélidis : Garden
Fiamina : Walter-
  Villa
Bertrade : Duchène
Marquis : Dufranne
Alain : Dalmorès
Devil : Huberdeau
Prior : Villa
Gondebaud : Scott

January 21
*Les Contes
d'Hoffmann*
Same cast as Dec. 25
  except:
Hoffmann : Lucas
Cochenille, Pitichinac-
  cio : Daddi
Spalanzani : Nicolay
Crespel : Villa
Lindorf, Schlemil :
  Crabbé

January 22 (mat.)
La Bohème
Same cast as Jan. 17
  except:
Colline : Laskin
Parpignol : Franzini

January 22
Aïda
Same cast as Nov. 12
  except:
King : ?

Radames : Zerola
Amonasro : Crabbé
Priestess : Gentle
Messenger : ?

January 24
Grisélidis
Same cast as Jan. 19

January 26
La Bohème
Same cast as Jan. 17
except:
Schaunard :
   Huberdeau
Colline : Gilibert
Mimi : Cavalieri
Parpignol :
   Michaloff

January 28
Samson et Dalila
   De la Fuente (c)
Dalila : Gerville-
   Réache
Samson : Dalmorès
High Priest : Dufranne
Abimelech : Crabbé
Old Hebrew : Vallier
Messenger : Venturini
Philistines : Fossetta,
   Venturini, Dauche

January 29 (mat.)
Grisélidis
Same cast as Jan. 19

January 29
Il Trovatore
Same cast as Jan. 8
   except:
Leonora : Baron
Di Luna : Pignataro
Azucena : Doria
Inez : Severina
Ferrando : Nicolay
Ruiz : Venturini

January 31
*Les Contes
   d'Hoffmann*
Same cast as Dec. 25
   except:
Hoffmann : Lucas
Cochenille, Pitichinac-
   cio : Daddi
Lindorf, Schlemil :
   Crabbé

February 1
Elektra
   De la Fuente (c)
Klytemnestra :
   Gerville-Réache
Elektra : Mazarin
Chrysothemis : Baron
Aegisthus : Duffault
Orestes : Huberdeau
Guardian of Orestes :
   Nicolay
Confidant : Desmond
Trainbearer :
   Johnston
Young Servant :
   Venturini

Old Servant : Scott
Overseer of Servants :
   Lango
Serving Women :
   Gentle, Severina,
   Milda, Walter-Villa,
   Duchène

February 2
Thaïs
Same cast as Nov. 13
   except:
Nicias : Lucas

February 4
Grisélidis
Same cast as Jan. 19

February 5 (mat.)
Samson et Dalila
   Sturani (c)
Same cast as Jan. 28
   except:
Dalila : D'Alvarez
Samson : Gogny
Old Hebrew : Laskin
Messenger :
   Malfatti

February 5
La Bohème
Same cast as Jan. 17
   except:
Schaunard :
   Fossetta
Colline : Nicolay
Parpignol :
   Franzini

February 7 (mat.)

Grand Operatic
Concert
(Benefit of Paris
Flood Sufferers)
Program arranged by
Mary Garden
De la Fuente (c)

Roméo et Juliette
(Act IV)
Juliette : Garden
Gertrude : Duchène
Roméo : Dalmorès
Capulet : Dufranne
Friar Laurence :
Huberdeau

Songs : Trentini,
Sammarco, Gerville-
Réache

Tosca (Act II)
Tosca : Cavalieri
Cavaradossi :
McCormack
Scarpia : Renaud
Spoletta : Venturini
Sciarrone : Fossetta

Songs : Tetrazzini

Thaïs
(Meditation and Act
II, Scene 1)
Thaïs : Garden
Nicias : Lucas
Athanaël : Renaud

Hérodiade (Act III)
Hérodiade :
D'Alvarez
Phanuel : Vallier

Song : Zerola

Manon
(St. Sulpice Scene)
Manon : Garden
Des Grieux :
Dalmorès
Count Des Grieux :
Huberdeau

February 7

Elektra
Same cast as Feb. 1
except:
Klytemnestra :
Doria
Aegisthus : Devries

February 9

La Traviata
Same cast as Nov. 10
except:
Flora : Gentle
Marquis d'Obigny :
Nemo

February 11

Rigoletto
Anselmi (c)
Duke : McCormack
Rigoletto : Renaud
Gilda : Tetrazzini

Sparafucile :
Vallier
Maddalena : Gentle
Giovanna : Severina
Monterone : Gilibert
Marullo : Fossetta
Borsa : Venturini
Ceprano : Nemo
Countess :
Johnston
Page : Keenan

February 12 (mat.)

Elektra
Same cast as Feb. 7
except:
Serving Woman :
Vicarino (for Milda)

February 12

Hérodiade
Same cast as Nov. 8
except:
Salomé : Mazarin
Hérodiade :
D'Alvarez
Jean : Lucas
Vitellius : Dufour

February 14

La Traviata
Same cast as Feb. 9

February 16

Elektra
Same cast as Feb. 7

February 18
Cavalleria Rusticana
Same cast as Nov. 13
except:
Turiddu :
McCormack

I Pagliacci
Same cast as Nov. 13
except:
Canio : Harrold
Silvio : Crabbé

February 19 (mat.)
Lucia di Lammermoor
Same cast as Nov. 15

February 19
Carmen
Same cast as Nov. 25
except:
Don José : Dalmorès
Morales : Villa
Frasquita : Trentini
Mercédès : Duchène
Dancaïre : Gilibert

February 21
Rigoletto
Same cast as Feb. 11

February 22 (mat.)
Elektra
Same cast as Feb. 12

February 22
*Les Contes
  d'Hoffmann*
Same cast as Dec. 25
except:
Hoffmann : Devries

February 23
Louise
  De la Fuente (c)
Louise : Baron
Julien : Dalmorès
Mother : Doria
Father : Gilibert
Irma : Walter-
  Villa
Camille : Vicarino
Gertrude : Gentle
Apprentice : Dumesnil
Elsie : Severina
Blanche : Desmond
Suzanne : Lango
Forewoman :
  Johnston
Marguerite : Laurie
Madeleine : Morris
Painter : Fossetta
Philosopher : Villa
Sculptor : Villa
Student : Daddi
Song Writer : Nemo
Street Peddler :
  Custer
Street Sweeper :
  Severina
Young Rag Picker :
  Rivers
Milk Woman: Gentle

King of Fools :
  Venturini
First Policeman :
  Dauche
Second Policeman :
  Contesso
Rag Picker :
  Nicolay
Junk Man : Zuro
Street Arab :
  Dumesnil
Old Clothes Man :
  Daddi
Bird Food Vendor :
  Carew
Artichoke Vendor :
  Renney
Chair Mender :
  Keenan

February 25
Lucia di Lammermoor
Same cast as Nov. 15

February 26 (mat.)
Louise
Same cast as Feb. 23
except:
Louise : Mazarin
Father : Dufranne

February 26
*Le Jongleur de Notre
  Dame*
  Anselmi (c)
Same cast as Dec. 4
except:
Jean : Devries

Boniface : Dufranne
Prior : Huberdeau
Monk Sculptor : Scott

Cavalleria Rusticana
Same cast as Nov. 13
  except:
Santuzza : Melis
Turiddu :
  McCormack

February 28
La Navarraise
  De la Fuente (c)
Anita : Gerville-
  Réache
Garrido : Dufranne
Araguil : Dalmorès
Ramon : Crabbé
Bustamente : Nicolay
Remigio : Huberdeau

I Pagliacci
  Anselmi (c)
Same cast as Feb. 18

March 2
Rigoletto
Same cast as Feb. 11
  except:
Monterone : De
  Grazia

March 4
Elektra
Same cast as Feb. 12

March 5 (mat.)
Salome
  De la Fuente (c)
Herod : Dalmorès
Herodias : Doria
Salome : Garden
Jokanaan : Dufranne
Narraboth : Devries
Page : Severina
Nazarenes : Dufour,
  Vallier
Five Jews : Duvernois,
  Venturini, Daddi,
  Delparte, Leroux
Soldiers : De Grazia,
  Scott
Cappadocian :
  Fossetta
Slave : Vicarino

March 5
*Les Contes
  d'Hoffmann*
  Charlier (c)
Same cast as Feb. 22

March 7
Lucia di Lammermoor
Same cast as Nov. 15

March 9
Salome
Same cast as Mar. 5

March 11
Pelléas et Mélisande
  De la Fuente (c)

Mélisande : Garden
Geneviève :
  Gerville-Réache
Little Yniold :
  Trentini
Pelléas : Dalmorès
Golaud : Dufranne
Ärkel : Huberdeau
Physician : Crabbé

March 12 (mat.)
Rigoletto
Same cast as Feb. 11
  except:
Duke : Harrold
Rigoletto :
  Sammarco
Sparafucile : Scott
Monterone : De
  Grazia
Borsa : Zaini
Countess : Laurie

March 12
Carmen
Same cast as Nov. 25
  except:
Don José : Devries
Escamillo : Crabbé
Morales : Villa
Frasquita : Trentini
Dancaïre : Gilibert
Remendado : Daddi

March 14
Salome
Same cast as Mar. 5

March 16
Pelléas et Mélisande
Same cast as Mar. 11

March 18
La Fille du Régiment
Same cast as Nov. 22

Cavalleria Rusticana
Same cast as Nov. 13
except:
Santuzza : Melis

March 19 (mat.)
*Les Contes
d'Hoffmann*
Same cast as Feb. 22

March 19
La Navarraise
Same cast as Feb. 28
except:
Araguil : Devries

I Pagliacci
Same cast as Feb. 18
except:
Nedda : Trentini

March 21
Lakmé
  Nicosia (c)
Lakmé : Tetrazzini
Mallika : Duchène
Ellen : Trentini
Rose : Vicarino
Mrs. Benson :
  Severina

Gerald :
  McCormack
Nilakantha :
  Huberdeau
Frederic : Crabbé
Hadji : Russo

March 23
Thaïs
Same cast as Nov. 13
except:
Nicias : Lucas
Servant : Nicolay

March 24 (mat.)
Elektra
Same cast as Feb. 12

March 24
Salome
Same cast as Mar. 5
except:
Page : Gentle
Slave : Dumesnil

March 25
Grand Gala
  Performance
*Les Contes
  d'Hoffmann*
  (Act II)
Charlier (c)
Giulietta : Cavalieri
Hoffmann : Devries
Nicklausse : Gentle
Dapertutto : Renaud
Pitichinaccio :
  Leroux
Schlemil : De Grazia

I Pagliacci
(Prologue) :
Sammarco
Anselmi (c)

Hérodiade (Act III,
  Scene 1)
De la Fuente (c)
Hérodiade :
  D'Alvarez
Phanuel : Vallier

Aria : *Le Cid* :
  Gilibert
Charlier (c)

Samson et Dalila
  (Act II)
De la Fuente (c)
Dalila : Gerville-
  Réache
Samson : Dalmorès
High Priest :
  Dufranne

Aria : *Madama
  Butterfly* : Trentini
Anselmi (c)

Irish Air : Mc-
  Cormack

Aria: *Le Prophète*:
  Doria

Roméo et Juliette
  (Chamber Scene)
De la Fuente (c)
Juliette : Garden
Gertrude : Duchène

Roméo : Dalmorès
Capulet : Dufranne
Friar Laurence :
 Huberdeau

Song : Crabbé

Aria : *Sigurd* :
 Mazarin
 Charlier (c)

Hérodiade (Act I)
 Nicosia (c)

Salomé : Cavalieri
Hérodiade :
 D'Alvarez
Jean : Lucas
Hérode : Renaud
Phanuel : Vallier

Arias : Harrold
 Anselmi (c)

Faust (Final Scene)
 Nicosia (c)

Faust : Dalmorès
Marguerite : Garden
Méphistophélès :
 Huberdeau

March 26 (mat.)
Pelléas et Mélisande
Same cast as March 11

March 26
Lucia di Lammermoor
Same cast as Nov. 15

Appendix II

Manhattan Opera Casts for Performances at the Philadelphia Opera House, 1908–10

November 17
Carmen
  Campanini (c)
  Carmen : Labia
  Don José : Dalmorès
  Micaëla : Zeppilli
  Escamillo : De
    Segurola
  Zuniga : Vieuille
  Morales : Reschiglian
  Frasquita : Trentini
  Mercédès : Ponzano
  Dancaïre : Gilibert
  Remendado : Daddi

November 19
Samson et Dalila
  Sturani (c)
  Dalila : Gerville-
    Réache
  Samson : Dalmorès
  High Priest :
    Dufranne
  Abimelech : Crabbé
  Old Hebrew :
    Vieuille

Messenger :
  Venturini
Philistines :
  Montanari,
  Reschiglian

November 21 (mat.)
*Il Barbiere di
  Siviglia*
  Sturani (c)
  Almaviva : Parola
  Dr. Bartolo : Gilibert
  Rosina : Tetrazzini
  Figaro : Polese
  Don Basilio : De
    Segurola
  Berta : Severina
  Fiorello : Montanari
  Sergeant : ?

November 21
Tosca
  Sturani (c)
  Tosca : Labia
  Cavaradossi :
    Zenatello

Scarpia :
  Sammarco
Angelotti : De
  Grazia
Sacristan : Gianoli-
  Galletti
Spoletta : Montanari
Sciarrone : Sampieri
Shepherd : Severina

November 24
Thaïs
  Campanini (c)
  Thaïs : Garden
  Nicias : Vallès
  Athanaël : Renaud
  Palemon : Vieuille
  Crobyle : Trentini
  Myrtale, Albine :
    Ponzano
  Servant :
    Reschiglian

November 26
Lucia di Lammermoor
  Sturani (c)

Lucia : Tetrazzini
Alisa : Severina
Edgardo : Taccani
Ashton : Polese
Raimondo : Arimondi
Arturo : Venturini
Normanno :
Montanari

November 28 (mat.)
Samson et Dalila
Same cast as Nov. 19
except:
Dalila : Doria
Philistine : Malfatti
(for Montanari)

November 28
Les Huguenots
Sturani (c)
Marguerite : Zeppilli
St. Bris : De Grazia
Valentine :
Agostinelli
Nevers : Polese
Tavannes, Bois Rosé :
Venturini
Meru : Cacici
Raoul : Zenatello
Marcel : Arimondi
Urbain : Aldrich
Ladies of Honor :
Severina, Avezza

December 1
Rigoletto
Sturani (c)
Duke : Constantino

Rigoletto : Sammarco
Gilda : Tetrazzini
Sparafucile : Arimondi
Maddalena : Ponzano
Giovanna : Severina
Monterone : Gilibert
Marullo : Fossetta
Borsa : Venturini
Ceprano : Reschiglian
Countess : Egener

December 3
*Le Jongleur de Notre
Dame*
Campanini (c)
Jean : Garden
Boniface : Renaud
Prior : Dufranne
Monk Poet : Vallès
Monk Painter : De
Segurola
Monk Sculptor :
Vieuille
Monk Musician :
Crabbé
Jovial Fellow :
Gherker
Drunken Man :
Zuro
Knight : Pierucci

December 5 (mat.)
Carmen
Sturani (c)
Same cast as Nov. 17
except:
Carmen : Gerville-
Réache

Zuniga : De Grazia
Mercédès : Avezza

December 5
Cavalleria Rusticana
Sturani (c)
Santuzza : Labia
Turiddu : Taccani
Lola : Ponzano
Alfio : Polese
Lucia : Avezza

La Chair (Operatic
Pantomime by
Georges Wagues)
Charlier (c)
Wife : Valéry
Lover : Kerf
Husband : Montanari

I Pagliacci
Sturani (c)
Nedda : Espinasse
Canio : Zenatello
Tonio : Polese
Beppe : Venturini
Silvio : Reschiglian

December 8
Lucia di Lammermoor
Same cast as Nov. 26
except:
Edgardo : Constantino

December 10
*Les Contes
d'Hoffmann*
Charlier (c)

Olympia : Zeppilli
Giulietta :
  Espinasse
Antonia : Trentini
Hoffmann : Dalmorès
Nicklausse : Doria
Lindorf, Schlemil,
  Cochenille : Crabbé
Coppelius, Daper-
  tutto, Miracle :
  Renaud
Franz : Gianoli-
  Galletti
Pitichinaccio :
  Daddi
Luther : Fossetta
Nathanael : Venturini
Hermann : Reschiglian
Spalanzani, Crespel :
  Gilibert
Voice : Aldrich

December 12 (mat.)
Cavalleria Rusticana
Same cast as Dec. 5
except:
Lola : Aldrich

La Chair (Operatic
  Pantomime by
  Georges Wagues)
Same cast as Dec. 5

I Pagliacci
Same cast as Dec. 5
except:
Silvio : Crabbé

December 12
Samson et Dalila
Same cast as Nov. 19

December 15
*Le Jongleur de Notre
  Dame*
Same cast as Dec. 3

December 17
La Bohème
  Sturani (c)
Rodolfo : Zenatello
Marcello : Polese
Schaunard :
  Reschiglian
Colline : De Segurola
Mimi : Melba
Musetta : Trentini
Benoit, Alcindoro :
  Gianoli-Galletti
Parpignol : Malfatti

December 19 (mat.)
Il Trovatore
  Sturani (c)
Leonora : Agostinelli
Manrico : Zenatello
Count di Luna :
  Fossetta
Azucena : Doria
Inez : Avezza
Ferrando : De Grazia
Ruiz : Montanari

December 19
La Traviata
  Campanini (c)
Violetta : Tetrazzini

Alfredo : Taccani
Germont : Polese
Flora : Egener
Annina : Avezza
Gastone : Montanari
Baron Douphol, Dr.
  Grenvil : Sampieri
Marquis d'Obigny :
  Franzini

December 22
La Traviata
  Sturani (c)
Same cast as Dec. 19
  except:
Alfredo : Constantino
Gastone : Malfatti

December 24
*Le Jongleur de Notre
  Dame*
Same cast as Dec. 3
  except:
Boniface : Gilibert

December 25
Cavalleria Rusticana
Same cast as Dec. 5
  except:
Turiddu : Parola
Lola : Aldrich

La Chair (Operatic
  Pantomime by
  Georges Wagues)
Parelli (c)
Same cast as Dec. 5
  except:
Husband : Elia

I Pagliacci
Same cast as Dec. 5
 except:
Canio : Taccani
Beppe : Malfatti

December 26 (mat.)
Tosca*
Same cast as Nov. 21
 except:
Cavaradossi : Taccani
Scarpia : Polese

December 26
Thaïs
 Charlier (c)
Same cast as Nov. 24
 except:
Palemon : De Grazia
Servant : Fossetta

December 29
La Bohème
Same cast as Dec. 17
 except:
Schaunard : Gilibert

December 31
Tosca
Same cast as Dec. 26
 except:
Sacristan : Fossetta
Shepherd : Avezza

La Chair (Operatic
 Pantomime by
 Georges Wagues)
Same cast as Dec. 25

January 1
Les Huguenots
Same cast as Nov. 28
 except:
St. Bris : De Segurola
Tavannes :
 Montanari
Bois Rosé : Malfatti
Meru : Franzini
Raoul : Constantino
Lady of Honor :
 Ponzano (for
 Severina)

January 2 (mat.)
Thaïs
 Charlier (c)
Same cast as Nov. 24

January 2
Carmen
 Sturani (c)
Same cast as Nov. 17
 except:
Escamillo :
 Dufranne
Zuniga : De Grazia

January 5
Cavalleria Rusticana
Same cast as Dec. 5
 except:
Santuzza : Agostinelli
Lola : Aldrich

I Pagliacci
Same cast as Dec. 5

January 7
Rigoletto
Same cast as Dec. 1
 except:
Monterone :
 Fossetta
Marullo :
 Reschiglian
Borsa : Malfatti
Ceprano : Franzini
Page : Egener

January 9 (mat.)
La Traviata
 Sturani (c)
Same cast as Dec. 19
 except:
Violetta : Melba
Annina : Severina

January 9
La Bohème
Same cast as Dec. 17
 except:
Schaunard : Gilibert
Mimi : Agostinelli
Musetta : Zeppilli
Benoit, Alcindoro :
 Reschiglian

January 12
*Les Contes
 d'Hoffmann*
Antonia : Koèlling
Luther : Franzini

* Late arrival of the scenery delayed the opera an hour and fifteen minutes.

January 14
Otello
Sturani (c)
Otello : Zenatello
Desdemona : Labia
Iago : Polese
Emilia : Doria
Cassio : Venturini
Roderigo : Montanari
Lodovico : De
  Segurola
Montano : Crabbé
Herald : Franzini

January 16 (mat.)
La Bohème
Same cast as Dec. 17
  except:
Rodolfo : Constantino
Schaunard : Fossetta
Mimi : Zeppilli
Benoit, Alcindoro
  Reschiglian

January 16
*Le Jongleur de Notre
  Dame*
Sturani (c)
Same cast as Dec. 24

January 19
Samson et Dalila
Same cast as Nov. 19

January 21
Il Trovatore
Same cast as Dec. 19
  except:

Count di Luna :
  Polese
Azucena : Gerville-
  Réache

January 23 (mat.)
Crispino e la Comare
Parelli (c)
Crispino : Gianoli-
  Galletti
Annetta : Tetrazzini
Dr. Fabrizio : Sam-
  marco
Mirabolano : Ari-
  mondi
Count del Fiore :
  Venturini
Don Asdrubale :
  Fossetta
Comare : Severina
Bartolo : Pierucci

La Mort de Cléopâtre
(Ballet with Music
  by Louis Gannes) :
  Valéry

January 23
Otello
Same cast as Jan. 14
  except:
Montano : Fossetta

January 26
Rigoletto
Same cast as Dec. 1
  except:
Rigoletto : Polese
Giovanna : Avezza

Marullo : Sampieri
Borsa : Malfatti
Page : Egener

January 28
Faust
Sturani (c)
Faust : Constantino
Marguerite :
  Cavalieri
Méphistophélès :
  Arimondi
Valentin : Polese
Siébel : Zeppilli
Marthe : Avezza
Wagner : Sampieri

January 30 (mat.)
Otello
Same cast as Jan. 14
  except:
Emilia : Ponzano
Cassio : Agosti
Roderigo : Zaini
Lodovico : Cernusco
Montano : Sampieri

January 30
La Sonnambula
Parelli (c)
Adina : Tetrazzini
Elvino : Parola
Rodolfo : Arimondi
Alessio : Gianoli-
  Galletti
Notary : Sampieri
Lisa : Trentini
Teresa : Avezza

February 2
Tosca
Same cast as Nov. 21
 except:
Tosca : Cavalieri
Scarpia : Renaud
Sciarrone :
 Fossetta
Shepherd : Avezza

February 4
Crispino e la Comare
Same cast as Jan. 23

Cavalleria Rusticana
Same cast as Dec. 5
 except:
Turiddu :
 Constantino
Lola : Aldrich

February 6 (mat.)
La Sonnambula
Same cast as Jan. 30
 except:
Alessio : Sampieri
Notary : Deutz

February 6
Il Trovatore
Same cast as Dec. 19
 except:
Count di Luna : Polese

February 9
Pelléas et Mélisande
 Campanini (c)
Mélisande : Garden

Geneviève : Gerville-
 Réache
Little Yniold :
 Trentini
Pelléas : Dalmorès
Golaud : Dufranne
Ärkel : Vieuille
Physician : Crabbé

February 11
Salome
 Campanini (c)
Herod : Dalmorès
Herodias : Doria
Salome : Garden
Jokanaan : Dufranne
Narraboth : Vallès
Page : Severina
Nazarenes : De
 Segurola, Malfatti
Jews : Sellav, Ven-
 turini, Daddi,
 Montanari, Collin
Soldiers : Crabbé,
 De Grazia
Cappadocian :
 Fossetta
Slave : Tancredi

February 13 (mat.)
Faust
Same cast as Jan. 28
 except:
Siébel : Koèlling

February 13
Aïda
 Sturani (c)

King : Sampieri
Amneris : Doria
Aïda : Agostinelli
Radames : Zenatello
Amonasro :
 Sammarco
Ramfis : De Grazia
Messenger :
 Montanari

February 16
Salome
Same cast as Feb. 11

February 18
Rigoletto
Same cast as Dec. 1
 except:
Rigoletto : Renaud
Giovanna : Avezza
Monterone :
 Sampieri
Borsa : Malfatti
Page : Egener
Maddalena : Aldrich

February 20 (mat.)
Aïda
Same cast as Feb. 13
 except:
King : De Grazia
Ramfis : Arimondi

February 20
La Bohème
Same cast as Dec. 17
 except:
Rodolfo : Constantino

Schaunard : Gilibert
Colline : Arimondi
Mimi : Labia
Musetta : Zeppilli

February 22
Il Trovatore
Same cast as Dec. 19
  except:
Count di Luna :
  Polese
Azucena : Gerville-
  Réache
Inez : Egener
Ruiz : Malfatti

February 23
Otello
Same cast as Jan. 14
  except:
Iago : Sammarco
Emilia : Ponzano
Montano : Sampieri

February 25
Thaïs
  Charlier (c)
Same cast as Nov. 24
  except:
Palemon : De Grazia

February 27 (mat.)
Tosca
Same cast as Nov. 21
  except:
Cavaradossi :
  Taccani

Scarpia : Renaud
Angelotti : Gianoli-
  Galletti
Sacristan : Gilibert
Spoletta : Tronconi

February 27
Crispino e la Comare
Same cast as Jan. 23

Cavalleria Rusticana
Same cast as Dec. 5
  except:
Santuzza : Espinasse
Turiddu : Parola
Alfio : Crabbé
Lucia : Severina

March 1
Salome
Same cast as Feb. 11

March 2
Aïda
Same cast as Feb. 13
  except:
Amonasro : Polese
Ramfis : Arimondi

March 4
La Sonnambula
Same cast as Jan. 30
  except:
Rodolfo : De
  Segurola
Alessio : Sampieri

Notary : Deutz

Cavalleria Rusticana
  Parelli (c)
Same cast as Dec. 5
  except:
Santuzza :
  Agostinelli
Lola : Aldrich

March 6 (mat.)
Lucia di Lammermoor
Same cast as Nov. 26
  except:
Alisa : Egener
Edgardo : Constantino
Raimondo : De
  Grazia
Arturo : Malfatti

March 6
Un Ballo in Maschera
  Sturani (c)
Riccardo : Zenatello
Renato :
  Sammarco
Amelia :
  Agostinelli
Ulrica : Aldrich
Oscar : Trentini
Silvano : Sampieri
Sam : Arimondi
Tom : De Grazia

March 9
Un Ballo in Maschera
Same cast as Mar. 6

March 11
Lucia di Lammermoor
Same cast as Nov. 26
except:
Alisa : Egener

March 13 (mat.)
Un Ballo in Maschera
Same cast as Mar. 6
except:
Silvano : Pierucci
Sam : De Grazia
Tom : Sampieri

March 13
I Puritani
Parelli (c)
Lord Walton :
Sampieri
Sir George :
Arimondi
Elvira : Tetrazzini
Henrietta : Avezza
Lord Arthur :
Constantino
Sir Richard : Polese
Sir Bruno : Zaini

March 16
Le Jongleur de Notre Dame
Sturani (c)
Same cast as Dec. 3
except:
Boniface : Gilibert
Jovial Fellow :
Cernusco

Drunken Man :
Franzini
Knight : Malfatti

March 18
Louise
Charlier (c)
Louise : Garden
Julien : Dalmorès
Mother : Doria
Father : Vieuille
Irma : Zeppilli
Camille : Tancredi
Gertrude : Avezza
Apprentice, Street
Arab : Trentini
Elsie, Street Sweeper :
Severina
Blanche, Milk
Woman : Ponzano
Suzanne : Koèlling
Forewoman : Inman
Madeleine : Hume
Painter : Fossetta
Philosopher,
Sculptor : Crabbé
Poet, Old Clothes
Man : Daddi
Student : Montanari
Song Writer, Second
Policeman :
Reschiglian
Newspaper Girl : ?
Rag Vendor : ?
Coal Picker : ?
King of Fools :
Venturini
First Policeman :
Zaini

Rag Picker : Gianoli-
Galletti
Junk Man : Zuro
Bird Food Vendor :
Boyd
Artichoke Vendor :
Hayes
Chair Mender :
Keenan
Carrot Vendor : ?

March 20 (mat.)
Rigoletto
Same cast as Dec. 1
except:
Duke : Parola
Rigoletto : Renaud
Sparafucile :
De Grazia
Giovanna : Avezza
Monterone : Fossetta
Marullo : Franzini
Borsa : Malfatti

March 20
Faust
Same cast as Jan. 28
except:
Marguerite :
Agostinelli
Siébel : Koèlling
Wagner : Reschiglian

March 23
Louise
Same cast as Mar. 18
except:
Father : Gilibert

Second Policeman :
  Giussani
Bird Food
  Vendor : Valliere
Chair Mender :
  Gentle

March 25
La Navarraise
  Charlier (c)
Anita : Gerville-
  Réache
Garrido : Dufranne
Araguil : Vallès
Ramon : Crabbé
Bustamente : Gianoli-
  Galletti
Remigio : Vieuille

I Pagliacci
Same cast as Dec. 5
  except:
Nedda : Labia
Silvio : Crabbé

November 9
Aïda
  Sturani (c)
King : De Grazia
Amneris : D'Alvarez
Aïda : Mazarin
Radames : Zerola
Amonasro : Polese
Ramfis : Scott
Messenger : Venturini
Priestess : Egener

March 27 (mat.)
Il Trovatore
Same cast as Dec. 19
  except:
Count di Luna: Polese
Inez : Egener
Ruiz : Malfatti

March 27
Thaïs
  Charlier (c)
Same cast as Nov. 24
  except:
Thaïs : Espinasse
Palemon : De
  Grazia
Servant : Fossetta

March 30
Samson et Dalila
Same cast as Nov. 19
  except:
Messenger : Malfatti

1909–10 Season

November 11
Hérodiade
  Nicosia (c)
Salomé : Cavalieri
Hérodiade : Gerville-
  Réache
Slave : Egener
Jean : Dalmorès
Hérode : Renaud
Vitellius : Crabbé
Phanuel : Vallier

April 1
Aïda
Same cast as Feb. 13
  except:
Amonasro : Polese
Ramfis : De
  Segurola
Messenger : Malfatti

April 3 (mat.)
*Le Jongleur de Notre
  Dame*
Same cast as Mar. 16

April 3
Lucia di Lammermoor
Same cast as Nov. 26
  except:
Alisa : Egener
Raimondo :
  Sampieri
Arturo : Montanari
Normanno : Malfatti

High Priest :
  Nicolay
Voice : Venturini

November 13 (mat.)
Lucia di Lammermoor
  Sturani (c)
Lucia : Tetrazzini
Alisa : Egener
Edgardo : Mc-
  Cormack

Ashton : Polese
Raimondo : Scott
Arturo : Russo
Normanno : De
  Grazia

November 13

Carmen
  Nicosia (c)
Carmen : Sylva
Don José : Carasa
Micaëla : Walter-
  Villa
Escamillo : Laskin
Zuniga : De
  Grazia
Morales : Fossetta
Frasquita : Lango
Mercédès : Gentle
Dancaïre : Nicolay
Remendado : Leroux

November 16

Hérodiade
Same cast as Nov. 11
  except:
Jean : Duffault
High Priest : De
  Grazia

November 17

*La Fille de Madame
  Angot*
  Haakman (c)
Ange Pitou : Devries
Pompounet :
  Dambrine

Larivaudiere :
  Blondel
Trénitz : Leroux
Louchard : Nicolay
Cadet : Moyroud
Guillaume : ?
Buteux :?
Officer : ?
Incroyable : ?
Clairette : Delmore
Mlle Lange : Nolba
Amarante : Laya
Javotte : ?
Thérèse : ?
Babet : Merly
Mme Delaunay :
  Lango
Hersilie : ?

November 18
Aïda
Same cast as Nov. 9

November 19
La Mascotte
  Haakman (c)
Bettina : Delmore
Fiametta : Nolba
Lorenzo XVII :
  Dambrine
Pippo : Blondel
Prince Frederic :
  Leroux
Rocco : Moyroud

November 20 (mat.)
Sapho
  Nicosia (c)

Fanny Le Grand :
  Garden
Jean Gaussin :
  Dalmorès
Divonne :
  D'Alvarez
Irène : Walter-
  Villa
Caoudal :
  Dufranne
Césaire Gaussin :
  Huberdeau
La Borderie :
  Leroux
Innkeeper : Villa

November 20
Cavalleria Rusticana
  Sturani (c)
Santuzza : Mazarin
Turiddu : Carasa
Lola : Duchène
Alfio : Polese
Lucia : Severina

I Pagliacci
  Sturani (c)
Nedda : Sylva
Canio : Zenatello
Tonio : Polese
Beppe : Venturini
Silvio : Crabbé

November 22
La Mascotte
Same cast as Nov. 19
  except:
Pippo : Dufour

November 23
Sapho
Same cast as Nov. 20

November 25
I Pagliacci
Same cast as Nov. 20
except:
Nedda : Trentini
Canio : Zerola
Beppe : Malfatti

La Fille du Régiment
Sturani (c)
Marie : Tetrazzini
La Marquise :
Duchène
Tonio :
McCormack
Sulpice : Gilibert
Hortentius : Fossetta
Corporal : ?

November 26
Les Dragons de Villars
Haakman (c)
Rose Friquet :
Walter-Villa
Georgette :
Dumesnil
Sylvain : Devries
Belamy : Dufour
Thibaut : Dambrine
Clergyman : Nicolay
Lieutenant : Renier
Dragoon : Moyroud

November 27 (mat.)
Carmen
Same cast as Nov. 13
except:
Carmen : Mazarin
Don José : Lucas
Micaëla : Miranda
Escamillo : Crabbé
Dancaïre : Leroux
Remendado :
De Keyser

November 27
Aïda
Same cast as Nov. 9
except:
Amneris : Doria
Aïda : Baron
Radames : Zenatello

November 30
Carmen:
Same cast as Nov. 13
except:
Carmen : Cavalieri
Don José :
Zenatello
Micaëla : Miranda
Escamillo : Crabbé
Frasquita : Trentini

December 2
Sapho
Same cast as Nov. 20
except:
Divonne : Soyer

December 4 (mat.)
La Fille du Régiment
Same cast as Nov. 25
except:
Hortentius : Nicolay

I Pagliacci
Same cast as Nov. 20
except:
Nedda : Trentini
Canio : Carasa
Silvio : Fossetta

December 4
Il Trovatore
Sturani (c)
Leonora : Grippon
Manrico : Zerola
Count di Luna :
Sammarco
Azucena : Gerville-
Réache
Inez : Egener
Ferrando : De Grazia
Ruiz : Venturini

December 7
La Traviata
Sturani (c)
Violetta : Tetrazzini
Alfredo : McCormack
Germont : Sammarco
Flora : Gentle
Annina : Egener
Gastone : Venturini

Baron Douphol :
Fossetta
Marquis d'Obigny :
Zano
Dr. Grenvil :
De Grazia

December 9
*Le Jongleur de Notre
Dame*
Sturani (c)
Jean : Garden
Boniface : Gilibert
Prior : Dufranne
Monk Poet : Lucas,
O.
Monk Sculptor :
Huberdeau
Monk Musician :
Crabbé
Jovial Fellow : ?
Drunken Man : ?
Knight : ?

December 11 (mat.)
Tosca
Sturani (c)
Tosca : Melis
Cavaradossi :
Carasa
Scarpia : Polese
Angelotti : De
Grazia
Sacristan : Nicolay
Spoletta : Venturini
Sciarrone : Fossetta
Shepherd : Egener

December 11
Hérodiade
Same cast as Nov. 11
except:
Jean : Duffault

December 14
La Fille du Régiment
Same cast as Dec. 4

I Pagliacci
Same cast as Nov. 20
except:
Nedda : Trentini
Canio : Zerola
Tonio : Sammarco
Silvio : Fossetta

December 16
Tosca
Same cast as Dec. 11
except:
Cavaradossi :
Zenatello
Scarpia :
Sammarco
Sacristan : Gilibert

December 18 (mat.)
Il Trovatore
Same cast as Dec. 4
except:
Leonora : Mazarin
Count di Luna :
Polese
Azucena : Doria
Ferrando : Nicolay

Ruiz : Malfatti

December 18
*Le Jongleur de Notre
Dame*
Same cast as Dec. 9
except:
Monk Painter : Scott

December 21
Samson et Dalila
Sturani (c)
Dalila : Gerville-
Réache
Samson : Dalmorès
High Priest :
Dufranne
Abimelech : Crabbé
Old Hebrew :
Vallier
Messenger : Villa
Philistines :
Dauche, Malfatti

December 23
Il Trovatore
Same cast as Dec. 4
except:
Leonora : Mazarin
Azucena :
D'Alvarez
Ruiz : Malfatti

December 25 (mat.)
Faust
Sturani (c)
Faust : Duffault
Marguerite : Baron

Méphistophélès :
  Laskin
Valentin : Villa
Siébel : Egener
Marthe : Duchène
Wagner : Franzini

December 25
Aïda
Same cast as Nov. 9
  except:
King : Laskin
Amneris : Doria
Radames :
  Zenatello
Amonasro :
  Pignataro
Ramfis : Vallier
Messenger : Malfatti

December 28
Tosca
Same cast as Dec. 11
  except:
Scarpia :
  Sammarco
Shepherd :
  Schaesser

December 30
Samson et Dalila
Same cast as Dec. 21
  except:
Messenger :
  Venturini
Philistine :
  Sampieri
  (for Dauche)

December 31
*Les Contes
  d'Hoffmann*
Charlier (c)
Olympia, Antonia :
  Trentini
Giulietta : Baron
Hoffmann : Lucas, O.
Nicklausse : Gentle
Lindorf, Schlemil :
  De Grazia
Coppelius, Dapertutto,
  Miracle : Renaud
Cochenille, Franz,
  Pitichinaccio : Leroux
Luther : Franzini
Nathanael : Venturini
Hermann : Fossetta
Spalanzani : Nicolay
Crespel : Villa
Voice : Duchène

January 1 (mat.)
Aïda
Same cast as Nov. 27
  except:
King : Laskin
Radames : Zerola
Messenger : Malfatti

January 1
Sapho
Same cast as Dec. 2

January 4
Il Trovatore
Same cast as Dec. 18
  except:
Ferrando : De Grazia

January 6
Lucia di Lammermoor
Anselmi (c)
Same cast as Nov. 13
  except:
Alisa : Severina
Ashton : Sammarco
Raimondo : Malfatti
Arturo : Venturini

January 8 (mat.)
Rigoletto
Sturani (c)
Duke : McCormack
Rigoletto : Polese
Gilda : Tetrazzini
Sparafucile :
  Huberdeau
Maddalena : Soyer
Giovanna : Severina
Monterone : Gilibert
Marullo : Malfatti
Borsa : Zaini
Ceprano : Fossetta
Countess, Page :
  Egener

January 8
Samson et Dalila
Same cast as Dec. 30

January 11
Cavalleria Rusticana
Anselmi (c)
Same cast as Nov. 20
  except:
Santuzza : Melis

Turiddu : Lucas
Lola : Gentle
Alfio : Crabbé

I Pagliacci
Anselmi (c)
Same cast as Nov. 20
except:
Nedda : Cavalieri
Canio : Zerola

January 13
Carmen
De la Fuente (c)
Same cast as Nov. 13
except:
Carmen : Mazarin
Don José : Lucas
Escamillo : Dufranne
Zuniga : Huberdeau
Morales : Villa
Mercédès : Duchène
Remendado : Daddi

January 15 (mat.)
*Le Jongleur de Notre
Dame*
Same cast as Dec. 9
except:
Boniface : Dufranne
Prior : Huberdeau
Monk Poet : ?
Monk Sculptor :
Duvernois

January 15
La Bohème
Sturani (c)

Rodolfo : McCormack
Marcello : Polese
Schaunard : Fossetta
Colline : Huberdeau
Mimi : Melis
Musetta : Trentini
Benoit : Nicolay
Parpignol : Pierucci
Alcindoro : Daddi

January 18
*Les Contes
d'Hoffmann*
Nicosia (c)
Same cast as Dec. 31
except:
Giulietta : Cavalieri

January 20
Faust
Nicosia (c)
Same cast as Dec. 25
except:
Faust : Dalmorès
Marguerite : Garden
Méphistophélès :
Huberdeau
Valentin : Dufranne
Siébel : Gentle
Wagner : Villa

January 22 (mat.)
Grisélidis
Nicosia (c)
Grisélidis : Garden
Fiamina : Walter-
Villa

Bertrade : Duchène
Marquis : Dufranne
Alain : Dalmorès
Devil : Huberdeau
Prior : Villa
Gondebaud : Scott

January 22
Lucia di Lammermoor
Same cast as Nov. 13
except:
Alisa : Severina
Edgardo : Carasa
Arturo : Venturini
Normanno : Scott

January 25
Thaïs
Nicosia (c)
Thaïs : Garden
Nicias : Lucas
Athanaël : Renaud
Palemon : Scott
Crobyle : Trentini
Myrtale, Albine :
Duchène
Servant : Fossetta

January 27
La Bohème
Same cast as Jan. 15
except:
Marcello :
Sammarco
Schaunard : Gilibert
Benoit : Daddi
Parpignol : Franzini

January 29 (mat.)

Tosca

Same cast as Dec. 11
  except:
Cavaradossi :
  McCormack
Scarpia : Sammarco

January 29

*Les Contes
  d'Hoffmann*
Nicosia (c)
Same cast as Dec. 31
  except:
Giulietta : Cavalieri
Cochenille, Franz,
  Pitichinaccio : Crabbé
Luther : Zuro
Spalanzani, Crespel :
  Gilibert

February 1

Faust

Same cast as Jan. 20
  except:
Méphistophélès :
  Vallier
Siébel : Trentini
Marthe : Egener

February 3

Hérodiade

Same cast as Nov. 11
  except:
Hérodiade :
  D'Alvarez
Slave : Carew

Jean : Duffault
Vitellius : Villa

February 5 (mat.)

*Les Contes
  d'Hoffmann*
Charlier (c)
Same cast as Jan. 29
  except:
Antonia : Walter-
  Villa

February 5

Elektra
De la Fuente (c)
Klytemnestra : Doria
Elektra : Mazarin
Chrysothemis : Baron
Aegisthus : Devries
Orestes : Huberdeau
Guardian of Orestes :
  Nicolay
Confidant : Desmond
Trainbearer :
  Johnston
Young Servant :
  Venturini
Old Servant : Scott
Overseer of Servants :
  Lango
Serving Women :
  Gentle, Severina,
  Miranda, Walter-
  Villa, Duchène

February 8

Grisélidis
Same cast as Jan. 22

February 10

Elektra

Same cast as Feb. 5

February 12 (mat.)

Samson et Dalila

Same cast as Dec. 21
  except:
Old Hebrew :
  Laskin
Messenger :
  Venturini
Philistines :
  Sampieri
  (for Dauche)

February 12

Rigoletto

Same cast as Jan. 8
  except:
Rigoletto :
  Sammarco
Gilda : Miranda
Sparafucile : Scott
Maddalena : Gentle
Marullo : Fossetta
Borsa : Malfatti
Ceprano : Zaini

February 15

Elektra

Same cast as Feb. 5

February 17

Grisélidis

Same cast as Jan. 22

February 19 (mat.)
Thaïs
Same cast as Jan. 25
  except:
Servant : Nicolay

February 19
Otello
  Sturani (c)
Otello : Zerola
Desdemona : Melis
Iago : Polese
Emilia : Gentle
Cassio : Venturini
Roderigo : Malfatti
Lodovico : Vallier
Montano : Sampieri
Herald : Franzini

(Hammerstein closed
the opera house after
this performance, not
opening until a strike
involving public trans-
portation was settled.)

March 1
*Le Jongleur de Notre
  Dame*
  Nicosia (c)
Same cast as Dec. 9

March 3
La Fille du Régiment
Same cast as Dec. 4

La Navarraise
  Nicosia (c)

Anita : Gerville-
  Réache
Garrido : Huberdeau
Araguil : Lucas
Ramon : Crabbé
Bustamente : Nicolay
Remigio : Sampieri

March 5 (mat.)
La Navarraise
Same cast as Mar. 3

I Pagliacci
Same cast as Nov. 20
  except:
Nedda : Walter-
  Villa
Canio : Harrold
Tonio : Sammarco
Beppe : Malfatti

March 5
La Traviata
Same cast as Dec. 7
  except:
Germont : Polese
Flora : Egener
Annina : Severina
Baron Douphol :
  Sampieri
Marquis d'Obigny :
  Franzini
Dr. Grenvil : Scott

March 8
La Navarraise
Same cast as Mar. 3

I Pagliacci
Same cast as Mar. 5
  except:
Tonio : Polese

March 10
Otello
Same cast as Feb. 19
  except:
Cassio : Russo
Herald : Zaini

March 12 (mat.)
Hérodiade
Same cast as Nov. 11
  except:
Salomé : Mazarin
Slave : Carew
Jean : Lucas
Vitellius : Villa

March 12
Louise
  Nicosia (c)
Louise : Garden
Julien : Dalmorès
Mother : Doria
Father : Dufranne
Irma : Walter-Villa
Camille : Vicarino
Gertrude : Duchène
Apprentice : Engel, C.
Elsie : Severina
Blanche : Desmond
Suzanne : Lango

Forewoman :
  Johnston
Marguerite : Laurie
Madeleine : Morris
Painter, First
  Philosopher :
  Fossetta
Second Philosopher : ?
Sculptor : ?
Poet : Leroux
Student : ?
Song Writer : Nemo
Street Sweeper : ?
Newspaper Girl : ?
Young Rag Picker :
  Rivers
Milk Woman :
  Duchène
Coal Picker : ?
King of Fools :
  Venturini
First Policeman :
  Dauche
Second Policeman :
  Contesso
Rag Picker : Nicolay
Junk Man : Zuro
Street Arab :
  Dumesnil
Old Clothes Man :
  Daddi
Bird Food Vendor :
  Carew
Artichoke Vendor :
  Hayes
Chair Mender :
  Keenan
Carrot Vendor : ?

March 15
Otello
Same cast as Feb. 19
  except:
Iago : Sammarco
Herald : Zaini

March 16
Carmen
Same cast as Nov. 13
  except:
Carmen : Mazarin
Don José : Devries
Micaëla : Miranda
Morales : Villa
Mercédès : Duchène
Frasquita : Dumesnil
Dancaïre : Gilibert
Remendado : Daddi

March 17
Thaïs
Same cast as Feb. 19

March 19 (mat.)
Faust
Same cast as Jan. 20
  except:
Méphistophélès :
  Vallier
Valentin : Dufour
Siébel : Vicarino

March 19
Gala Performance

Il Trovatore
  (Act II)
  Sturani (c)

Manrico : Zerola
Azucena : Doria

Carmen
  (Act IV)
  Nicosia (c)
Carmen : Sylva
Don José : Lucas
Escamillo : Dufour

Cavalleria Rusticana
  Sturani (c)
Same cast as Nov. 20
  except:
Santuzza : Melis
Turiddu : Lucas

Aïda
  (Act II)
  Sturani (c)
Amneris : Doria
Aïda : Mazarin
Radames : Zerola
Amonasro : Polese
Ramfis : Scott

March 21
Louise
  Charlier (c)
Same cast as Mar. 12
  except:
Father : Gilibert

March 22
Pelléas et Mélisande
  De la Fuente (c)
Mélisande : Garden
Geneviève : Gerville-
  Réache

Little Yniold :
 Trentini
Pelléas : Dalmorès
Golaud : Dufranne
Ärkel : Huberdeau
Physician : Crabbé

March 24
Lakmé
 Nicosia (c)
Lakmé : Tetrazzini
Mallika : Duchène
Ellen : Trentini
Rose : Vicarino
Mrs. Benson :
 Severina
Gerald :
 McCormack
Nilakantha :
 Huberdeau
Frederic : Crabbé
Hadji : Russo

March 26 (mat.)
Rigoletto
Same cast as Jan. 8
 except:
Duke : Harrold
Gilda : Miranda

Sparafucile :
 Vallier
Maddalena : Gentle
Monterone : Sampieri
Marullo : Fossetta
Borsa : Malfatti
Ceprano : Franzini
Page : ?
March 26
Gala Performance
 Sturani (c)

I Pagliacci
 (Prologue) :
 Polese

*Les Contes
 d'Hoffmann*
 (Act III)
Giulietta :
 Cavalieri
Hoffmann : Devries
Nicklausse : Gentle
Dapertutto : Renaud
Schlemil : Crabbé

Arias : Gilibert,
 Miranda, Zerola,
 Trentini

Samson et Dalila
 (Act II)
Dalila : Doria
Samson : Dalmorès
High Priest :
 Dufranne

Roméo et Juliette
 (Act III)
Juliette : Garden
Gertrude : Duchène
Roméo : Dalmorès
Capulet : Dufranne
Friar Laurence :
 Huberdeau

Hérodiade (Act I)
Salomé : Cavalieri
Hérodiade :
 D'Alvarez
Jean : Lucas
Hérode : Renaud
Phanuel : Vallier

Aria : Harrold

Faust (Final Scene)
Faust : Dalmorès
Marguerite : Garden
Méphistophélès :
 Vallier

Appendix III
Manhattan Opera Tour Casts, 1908–10

1907–1908 Season

PHILADELPHIA

March 19, 1908
(Academy of Music)
Lucia di Lammermoor
Campanini (c)
Lucia : Tetrazzini
Alisa : Severina
Edgardo : Zenatello
Ashton : Sammarco
Raimondo : Arimondi
Arturo : Venturini
Normanno : Daddi

March 26, 1908
(Academy of Music)
Louise
Campanini (c)
Louise : Garden
Julien : Dalmorès

Mother : Bressler-
  Gianoli
Father : Gilibert
Irma : Zeppilli
Camille : Morichini
Gertrude : Giaconia
Apprentice : Sigrist
Elsie : ?
Blanche : Zaccaria
Suzanne : Koèlling
Forewoman : Inman
Marguerite : Laurie
Madeleine : Hume
Painter : Fossetta
First Philosopher :
  Crabbé
Second Philosopher :
  Fossetta
Poet : Daddi

Student : Pierucci
Song Writer :
  Reschiglian
King of Fools :
  Venturini
First Policeman :
  Zaini
Second Policeman :
  Giussani
Rag Picker : Gianoli-
  Galletti
Old Clothes Man :
  Daddi
Bird Food Vendor :
  Valliere
Artichoke Vendor :
  Hayes
Chair Mender :
  Davis

1908–1909 Season

BALTIMORE

January 4, 1909
Lucia di Lammermoor
Sturani (c)

Lucia : Tetrazzini
Alisa : Severina
Edgardo : Constantino

Ashton : Polese
Raimondo : Arimondi
Arturo : Malfatti

Normanno : Daddi

January 11, 1909

La Traviata
Sturani (c)

Violetta : Tetrazzini
Alfredo : Taccani
Germont : Polese
Flora : Egener
Annina : Avezza
Gastone : Montanari

Baron Douphol :
Sampieri
Marquis d'Obigny :
Franzini
Dr. Grenvil :
De Grazia

BOSTON

March 29, 1909
Lucia di Lammermoor
Campanini (c)
Same cast as Jan. 4
except:
Raimondo : De
Grazia
Arturo : Venturini
Normanno :
Montanari

March 30, 1909
Thaïs
Campanini (c)
Thaïs : Garden
Nicias : Vallès
Athanaël : Renaud
Palemon : De Grazia
Crobyle : Trentini
Myrtale, Albine :
Ponzano
Servant : Fossetta

March 31, 1909
La Traviata
Campanini (c)
Same cast as Jan. 11
except:
Alfredo :

Constantino
Germont : Sammarco
Flora : Koèlling
Annina : Severina
Gastone : Venturini
Baron Douphol :
Fossetta
Marquis d'Obigny :
Reschiglian

April 1, 1909
Pelléas et Mélisande
Campanini (c)
Mélisande : Garden
Geneviève : Gerville-
Réache
Little Yniold :
Trentini
Pelléas : Dalmorès
Golaud : Dufranne
Ärkel : Vieuille
Physician : Crabbé

April 2, 1909
*Les Contes
d'Hoffmann*
Charlier (c)
Olympia, Giulietta :
Zeppilli
Antonia : Trentini

Hoffmann :
Dalmorès
Nicklausse : Doria
Lindorf, Schlemil :
Crabbé
Coppelius, Dapertutto,
Miracle : Renaud
Cochenille, Pitichinac-
cio : Daddi
Franz : Gianoli-
Galletti
Luther : Zuro
Nathanael : Venturini
Hermann :
Reschiglian
Spalanzani, Crespel :
Gilibert

April 3, 1909 (mat.)
La Bohème
Campanini (c)
Rodolfo :
Constantino
Marcello :
Sammarco
Schaunard : Fossetta
Colline : De
Segurola
Mimi : Labia
Musetta : Trentini

Benoit, Alcindoro :
Gianoli-Galletti
Parpignol : Venturini

April 3, 1909
Aïda
Campanini (c)
King : De Grazia
Amneris : Gerville-
Réache
Aïda : Agostinelli
Radames : Zenatello
Amonasro :
Sammarco
Ramfis : De
Segurola
Messenger :
Venturini

April 5, 1909
Louise
Campanini (c)
Louise : Garden
Julien : Dalmorès
Mother : Doria
Father : Gilibert
Irma : Zeppilli
Blanche, Camille :
Tancredi
Gertrude : Ponzano
Apprentice : Trentini
Elsie : Severina
Suzanne : Koèlling
Forewoman : Gentle
Marguerite : Laurie
Madeleine : Hume
Painter : Fossetta

First Philosopher,
Sculptor : Crabbé
Poet : Daddi
Student : Montanari
Song Writer :
Reschiglian
Street Sweeper :
Severina
King of Fools :
Venturini
First Policeman :
Zaini
Second Policeman :
Giussani
Rag Picker :
Gianoli-Galletti
Junk Man : Zuro
Street Arab : Trentini
Old Clothes Man :
Daddi
Bird Food Vendor :
Valliere
Artichoke Vendor :
Laurie
Chair Mender :
Gentle
Milk Woman :
Ponzano

April 6, 1909
Rigoletto
Campanini (c)
Duke : Constantino
Rigoletto : Renaud
Gilda : Tetrazzini
Sparafucile : De
Segurola
Maddalena : Ponzano

Giovanna : Severina
Monterone : Gilibert
Marullo : Fossetta
Borsa : Venturini
Ceprano :
Reschiglian
Countess : Laurie

April 7, 1909
Pelléas et Mélisande
Same cast as April 1

April 8, 1909 (mat.)
La Navarraise
Campanini (c)
Anita : Gerville-
Réache
Garrido : Dufranne
Araguil : Vallès
Ramon : Crabbé
Bustamente : Gianoli-
Galletti
Remigio : Vieuille

I Pagliacci
Campanini (c)
Nedda : Zeppilli
Canio : Zenatello
Tonio : Sammarco
Beppe : Venturini
Silvio : Crabbé

April 8, 1909
La Traviata
Same cast as Mar. 31
except:

Alfredo : Taccani

April 9, 1909

Le Jongleur de Notre Dame
Campanini (c)
Jean : Garden
Boniface : Gilibert
Prior : Dufranne
Monk Poet : Vallès

Monk Painter : De
  Segurola
Monk Sculptor :
  Vieuille
Monk Musician :
  Crabbé
Jovial Fellow :
  Gherkier
Drunken Man : Zuro
Knight : Pierucci

April 10, 1909 (mat.)

Thaïs
Same cast as Mar. 30

April 10, 1909

Lucia di Lammermoor
Same cast as Mar. 29
  except:
Ashton : Sammarco

1909–10 Season

PITTSBURGH

December 20, 1909

Lucia di Lammermoor
Anselmi (c)
Lucia : Tetrazzini
Alisa : Severina
Edgardo :
  McCormack
Ashton : Polese
Raimondo : De
  Grazia
Arturo : Domenico
Normanno : Pierucci

December 21, 1909

Tosca
Anselmi (c)
Tosca : Melis
Cavaradossi : Carasa
Scarpia : Renaud
Angelotti : De
  Grazia
Sacristan : Nicolay
Spoletta : Domenico
Sciarrone : Fossetta
Shepherd : Severina

December 22, 1909

La Traviata
Anselmi (c)
Violetta : Tetrazzini
Alfredo :
  McCormack
Germont : Polese
Flora : Egener
Annina : Severina
Gastone : Domenico
Baron Douphol :
  Fossetta
Marquis d'Obigny :
  Zwieback
Dr. Grenvil : De
  Grazia

December 23, 1909

Sapho
Nicosia (c)
Fanny Le Grand :
  Garden
Jean Gaussin :
  Dalmorès

Divonne Gaussin :
  Soyer
Irène : Walter-
  Villa
Caoudal : Dufranne
Césaire Gaussin :
  Huberdeau
La Borderie : Leroux
Innkeeper : Villa

**December 25, 1909
(mat.)**

Le Jongleur de Notre Dame
Nicosia (c)
Jean : Garden
Boniface : Dufranne
Prior : Huberdeau
Monk Poet : Lucas
Monk Painter : Scott
Monk Sculptor :
  Duvernois
Monk Musician :
  Crabbé
Jovial Fellow : ?

Drunken Man : ?
Knight : ?

December 25, 1909
Cavalleria Rusticana
Anselmi (c)
Santuzza : Grippon

Lola : Desmond
Turiddu : Russo
Alfio : Crabbé
Lucia : Severina

I Pagliacci
Anselmi (c)

Nedda : Walter-
Villa
Canio : Zerola
Tonio : Polese
Beppe : Russo
Silvio : Crabbé

CINCINNATI

December 28, 1909
(mat.)
Sapho
Same cast as Dec. 23
except:
Césaire Gaussin :
Laskin

December 28, 1909
La Traviata
Same cast as Dec. 22
except:
Violetta : Walter-
Villa

Baron Douphol :
Zwieback

Marquis d'Obigny :
Nemo

Dr. Grenvil : Scott

WASHINGTON

January 10, 1910
Lucia di Lammermoor
Sturani (c)
Same cast as Dec. 20
except:
Raimondo : Scott
Normanno : Malfatti

January 11, 1910
Thaïs
Nicosia (c)
Thaïs : Garden
Nicias : Dalmorès
Athanaël : Renaud
Palemon : Scott
Crobyle : Trentini
Myrtale, Albine :
Duchène
Servant : Nicolay

January 12, 1910
(mat.)
La Traviata
Same cast as Dec. 22
except:
Germont : Sammarco
Marquis d'Obigny :
Franzini
Dr. Grenvil :
Sampieri

January 12, 1910
*Le Jongleur de Notre
Dame*
Same cast as Dec. 25

January 13, 1910
*Les Contes
d'Hoffmann*
Nicosia (c)

Olympia, Giulietta,
Antonia : Trentini
Hoffmann : Dalmorès
Nicklausse : Gentle
Lindorf, Schlemil :
De Grazia
Coppelius, Dapertutto,
Miracle : Renaud
Cochenille, Pitichinac-
cio, Franz : Leroux
Luther : Franzini
Nathanael : Venturini
Hermann : Sampieri
Spalanzani, Crespel :
Gilibert
Voice : Gentle

January 14, 1910
La Fille du Régiment
Sturani (c)

Marie : Tetrazzini
Marquise : Duchène
Tonio : Mc-
 Cormack
Sulpice : Gilibert

Hortentius : Fossetta
Corporal : Nicolay

I Pagliacci
Sturani (c)

Same cast as Dec. 25
 except:
Tonio : Sammarco
Beppe : Venturini

BOSTON

March 28, 1910
Elektra
 De la Fuente (c)
Klytemnestra : Doria
Elektra : Mazarin
Chrysothemis : Baron
Aegisthus : Devries
Orestes : Huberdeau
Guardian of Orestes :
 Nicolay
Confidant : Desmond
Trainbearer :
 Johnston
Young Servant :
 Venturini
Old Servant : Scott
Overseer of Servants :
 Carew
Serving Women :
 Gentle, Severina,
 Vicarino, Walter-
 Villa, Duchène

March 29, 1910
Lucia di Lammermoor
Same cast as Dec. 20
 except:
Arturo : Venturini
Normanno : De
 Grazia

March 30, 1910
(mat.)
*Le Jongleur de Notre
 Dame*
 De la Fuente (c)
Same cast as Dec. 25
 except:
Boniface : Renaud
Monk Painter : Laskin
Monk Sculptor :
 Scott

March 30, 1910
Grisélidis
 De le Fuente (c)
Grisélidis : Garden
Fiamina : Walter-
 Villa
Bertrade : Duchène
Marquis : Dufranne
Alain : Devries
Devil : Huberdeau
Prior : Villa
Gondebaud : Scott

March 31, 1910
(mat.)
*Les Contes
 d'Hoffmann*
 De la Fuente (c)

Same cast as Jan. 13
 except:
Giulietta : Duchène
Hoffmann : Devries
Lindorf, Schlemil :
 Crabbé
Luther : Zuro
Hermann : Fossetta
Voice : Dubois

March 31, 1910
La Navarraise
 De la Fuente (c)
Anita : Gerville-
 Réache
Garrido : Dufranne
Araguil : Lucas
Ramon : Crabbé
Bustamente : Nicolay
Remigio : Huberdeau

La Fille du Régiment
Anselmi (c)
Same cast as Jan. 14

April 1, 1910
Pelléas et Mélisande
 De la Fuente (c)
Mélisande : Garden
Genéviève : Gerville-
 Réache

Little Yniold : Tren-
tini
Pelléas : Devries
Golaud : Dufranne
Ärkel : Huberdeau
Physician : Crabbé

April 2, 1910 (mat.)
La Traviata
Same cast as Dec. 22
  except:
Flora : Gentle
Gastone : Venturini

April 2, 1910
Thaïs
  De la Fuente (c)
Same cast as Jan. 11
  except:
Nicias : Lucas

Appendix IV

The Manhattan-Metropolitan Contract of April 26, 1910, and the Power of Attorney Granted to Arthur Hammerstein

Exhibit A.

AN AGREEMENT, made and entered into as of this 26th day of April, in the year one thousand nine hundred and ten, between OSCAR HAMMERSTEIN, of the City of New York (hereinafter called the "Vendor"), party of the first part; ARTHUR HAMMERSTEIN, of the same place, party of the second part, and EDWARD T. STOTESBURY, of the City of Philadelphia, in the State of Pennsylvania, (hereinafter called the "Purchaser"), party of the third part:

The Vendor is now engaged in the business of producing Grand Opera at the Manhattan Opera House, in the City of New York, and at the Philadelphia Opera House, in the City of Philadelphia. He owns the real property, together with the buildings and appurtenances, of the Philadelphia Opera House property, and also owns the scenery and costumes connected with the said business, and the exclusive rights to produce in America certain operas hereinafter enumerated. Said properties, scenery and costumes are stored partly at the Manhattan Opera House and the remainder at a storage house at Forty-fourth Street and Eleventh Avenue, in the City of New York.

The party of the second part is actually engaged with the Vendor in said business, and his participation in this agreement is essential to secure the good-will to the Purchaser.

It has been arranged between the Vendor and the Purchaser that the Purchaser shall acquire the real property known as the Philadelphia Opera House, together with all its appurtenances and improvements, and all the aforesaid properties, costumes and scenery, and the rights of the Vendor in the operas hereinafter enumerated, together with the good-will of the business of the Vendor connected with the conduct of the business of producing opera, and that he and the party of the second part shall enter into such covenants and assurances as will assure to the Purchaser the good-will to be sold.

The Vendor has entered into agreements with artists, composers and publishers upon the terms hereinafter referred to, part of which are to be assigned to the Purchaser as hereinafter provided.

The Metropolitan Opera Company and other persons and corporations are interested with the Purchaser in the acquisition of the real and personal property and good-will herein described, and are willing to participate in such purchase only upon condition that they shall share in the acquisition of said good-will and shall be entitled to enforce each and all of the covenants of the Vendor and of the party of the second part hereinafter set forth.

The Vendor controls the Manhattan Opera House in the City of New York, and is in a position to determine the uses to which such Opera House shall be put and the character of the productions to be made therein for a period of five years from the date hereof.

Now, THEREFORE, in consideration of the sum of One hundred thousand dollars ($100,000), this day in hand paid on account of this contract by the Purchaser to the Vendor and the party of the second part, the receipt whereof is hereby acknowledged, and for other good and valuable considerations, IT IS AGREED between the parties hereto as follows:

FIRST: The Vendor hereby sells and the Purchaser hereby agrees to purchase:

(a) The title in fee simple to the premises at the corner of Broad and Poplar Streets, in the City of Philadelphia, covering a lot two hundred and forty (240) feet or thereabouts on Broad and Carlisle Streets and one hundred and sixty (160) feet or thereabouts on Poplar Street, known as the Philadelphia Opera House, together with all the improvements thereon erected, and all the fixtures, chairs, carpets, hangings and other property therein contained or therewith connected, subject to a mortgage now an existing lien upon said property in the sum of Four hundred thousand dollars ($400,000), bearing interest at the rate of five and four-tenths per cent. (5 4/10%) per annum, now held by the Purchaser.

(b) All the scenery, properties and costumes and the score and libretto of the music of all operas that are included in the repertoire of operas enumerated in Schedule "A," constituting what is known as the music library of the Vendor, and all other appurtenances connected with the business of the Vendor in the production of opera, part of which properties, costumes, scenery, music score and appurtenances are now in and upon the premises known as the Manhattan Opera House, at Number 315 West 34th Street, in the City of New York, and the balance of which are now stored at the storage house of the Vendor at Forty-fourth Street and Eleventh Avenue, in the City of New York. Attached hereto, marked "A" and forming part hereof, is a list of the operas constituting the repertoire of the Vendor, in connection with which said properties, scenery, costumes and music scores have been used.

The Vendor hereby represents that the aforesaid properties, costumes, scenery and music scores at the Manhattan Opera House and at the said storage warehouse, constitute all the properties, costumes, scenery and music scores that are in use by him in his said business of producing opera, the intention hereof being that all property, scenery, costumes and music scores that have been so used and that are still in existence and owned by him, wherever located, shall be deemed to be transferred to the Purchaser hereunder.

(c) All existing contracts with artists that are shown upon the Schedule hereto annexed, marked "B," are hereby assigned to the Purchaser or his nominees, and the latter hereby assumes the obligations of all such contracts, which are herewith produced for the inspection of the Purchaser; provided, however, that the Purchaser shall become obligated only upon such contracts as are by their terms assignable, or as to which the artists consent to the assignment and actually enter upon the performance of such contracts; and, further provided,

(1) That the Purchaser will assume the contract with Renaud for twenty-four (24) performances only;

(2) That the Purchaser will assume the contract with Mazarin only in case Mary Garden declines to assent to the assignment of her contract to the Purchaser;

(3) That the Purchaser shall not be obligated to assume the contracts of any of the artists named in said schedule unless the contract

of such artist contains the customary concert clause or such artist agrees to sing also in concert as part of his or her guaranteed performances;

(4) The Purchaser shall not be obligated to assume the contract of any artist unless such artist will agree to sing in New York, Philadelphia, Chicago and Boston, and wherever the Metropolitan Opera Company or its affiliated companies may require, and will consent to the elimination from his or her contract of any unusual provision or provisions which would be inapplicable in view of the changed conditions.

The Vendor further covenants with respect to said contracts: (1) That no obligation is imposed for a term longer than one year; (2) that as to the artists named in said schedule who are paid for each performance, the Vendor is not obligated for any greater number of performances than appears upon the said schedule, nor for any salary or compensation for each performance longer than therein stated; (3) that as to the artists who are therein represented as employed under contract providing for payment in weekly salaries, but all of said artists are so employed on the terms as stated and at the salaries appearing on said list, and for no longer terms or at larger salaries; and (4) that said contracts are now in full force and effect and constitute lawful and binding obligations of the respective artists on the terms therein stated.

(d) All the rights of the Vendor, all of which are represented to be exclusive rights for production in this country, to produce the following named operas from year to year upon giving notice prior to June 15, 1910, and upon compliance with the other terms stated in the contracts, all of which are hereby assigned to the Purchaser or his nominees:

Name of Opera:	*General Description of Terms:*
"SALOME"	$500 for each performance, provided six performances are given during each year;
"ELEKTRA"	$800 for each performance, provided there shall be at least six performances during each year;
"THAIS" "LOUISE" "LE JONGLEUR" "SAPPHO" "GRISELIDIS" "HERODIADE"	On payment of 3,000 francs as to each of such operas for each season in which any production of such operas is given, and an additional sum of 500 francs for each performance;

"Pelleas et Melisande"	On payment of $400 for each season in which opera is given, and an additional sum of $100 per performance;
"Samson et Dellilah"	$100 for each performance.

The Vendor herewith produces and exhibits to the Purchaser the original contracts for said operas for more accurate information as to the details thereof.

(e) All rights and options owned or held by the Vendor or in which he may be interested for the production of new operas, all of which are to be assured to the Purchaser.

(f) Assignments of the existing contracts between the Vendor and his business manager, Lyle D. Andrews, and his press agent, U. J. Guard.

(g) The undertaking and good-will of the Vendor in and to said business of producing operas.

SECOND: For the purpose of assuring the good-will of said business unto the Purchaser and his assigns, the Vendor and the party of the second part hereby jointly and severally covenant with the Purchaser and his assigns and with the Metropolitan Opera Company and its assigns, and will covenant with such other persons or corporations (not exceeding two) as the Purchasers shall designate, that they will not, nor will either of them, at any time hereafter within ten years from this date hereof, be or become, directly or indirectly, engaged or interested in or connected with, either alone or as a member or members of any firm or partnership, or in conjunction with others, or as an officer, director, manager, stockholder, employee of any corporation that may be or become engaged in any such business, or as an employee or in any other capacity whatsoever, in the cities of New York, Boston, Philadelphia or Chicago, in the business of producing grand opera or any of the operas named in Schedule "A" hereto annexed, in any language or any opera, operetta or comic opera that has ever been produced at the Metropolitan Opera House or the Manhattan Opera House in the City of New York, or any operetta or comic opera that may at any time hereafter have been first given at the Metropolitan Opera House or at any opera house in the City of New York, and that no opera, operetta or comic opera of the character described will be permitted or suffered to be produced upon the premises now occupied by the Manhattan Opera House within five years from the date hereof, nor will the Vendor or the party of the second part be connected in any business that interferes with or encroaches upon the field now occupied by the Metropolitan Opera Company; it being understood that the prohibition herein contained is co-extensive only with the good-will hereby sold, and that the same does not exceed in limitation of territory or in any of its other provisions the good-will so sold, and that such prohibition is necessary to assure such good-will to the Purchaser.

The Vendor, who owns in fee the Manhattan Opera House, subject to a first mortgage of Three hundred and fifty thousand dollars ($350,000), and to the mortgage held by the Purchaser, will enter into an agreement describing said property with particularity and containing effective covenants which shall run with the land, to the effect that during said period of five years from the date hereof the Manhattan Opera House shall not be used or permitted to be used for any of the purposes hereinbefore specified, such agreement to be in such form that it may be recorded as an instrument affecting said real estate.

Nothing herein contained shall, however, be construed to prevent the Vendor or the party of the second part from engaging in the business of producing musical comedies, or of producing comic opera in the sense in which that term is used in the United States, as distinguished from the term "opera comique" as used in France, except as above restricted; provided, however, that in any such venture the Vendor will not advertise, solicit or accept season or part season subscriptions for seats for any such performance, but will conduct such business in the sale of seats in the manner in which the ordinary theatrical ventures are conducted in the City of New York.

THIRD: No announcement of or interview, news or other statement or information with respect to the transaction evidenced by this agreement shall be made or issued by the Vendor or the party of the second part, except in a form approved by the parties hereto, or by their counsel.

FOURTH: The Purchaser will pay to the Vendor and the party of the second part for the real and personal property, assets, effects, rights, contracts, undertakings and good-will hereby sold and for the covenants herein contained, the sum of One million two hundred thousand dollars ($1,200,000), as follows:

$100,000   The sum of One hundred thousand dollars ($100,000) in cash at the time of the execution and delivery hereof, the receipt whereof is hereby acknowledged, at which time the deed of conveyance of the Philadelphia real property (without Mrs. Hammerstein's signature) shall be deposited with the purchaser in escrow, and the title and possession of the personal property, rights and contracts hereinbefore described shall be vested in the Purchaser, with the right meantime to use the same, as security for the full performance of this contract by the Vendor.

$400,000   The sum of Four hundred thousand dollars ($400,000) by accepting the deed of conveyance of the Philadelphia Opera House property, subject to a mortgage now an existing lien thereon for the sum of Four hundred thousand dollars ($400,000) held by the Purchaser, which mortgage is, however, not to be or become merged in the deed of conveyance to the Purchaser unless he shall hereafter so elect, but the Vendor shall be held and kept harmless from any personal liability on the bond given by him to secure said mortgage. The interest upon said mortgage shall be adjusted as of the date of the delivery of the final deed, and any overdue or accrued interest shall be deducted from the payment due May 30, 1910.

$100,000   The sum of One hundred thousand dollars ($100,000) on the thirtieth day of May, 1910, by crediting that amount on account of a debt of Two hundred thousand dollars ($200,000) owing by the Vendor to the Purchaser, which is secured by a second mortgage on the Manhattan Opera House property, and by the deposit with the Purchaser of the entire share capital of One hundred thousand dollars ($100,000) par value of the Hammerstein Amusement Company.

$200,000   The sum of One hundred thousand dollars ($100,000) in cash on the fifteenth day of July, 1910, and the remaining One hundred thousand dollars ($100,000) of said payment by crediting that amount in payment of the balance due on said last mentioned mortgage of Two hundred thousand dollars ($200,000), at which time the said mortgage shall be cancelled and satisfied of record; on the payment to the Purchaser of the interest then accrued on said loan, the Purchaser will surrender said stock and will satisfy the said mortgage.

$200,000   The sum of Two hundred thousand dollars ($200,000) in cash on the thirtieth day of August, 1910.

$200,000   The balance of Two hundred thousand dollars ($200,000) of the purchase money on the fifteenth day of October, 1910.

$1,200,000

None of said payments, except said first payment of $100,000, shall be payable, nor the notes representing the same deliverable, until the Vendor and the party of the second part shall have executed and delivered the various papers mentioned in Paragraph Fifth hereof, as therein provided.

FIFTH: The deferred cash payments shall be represented and secured by the negotiable promissory notes of a corporation to be organized by the Purchaser, payable at the times and in the amounts above specified. Said corporation shall be organized under the laws of Pennsylvania, New York or New Jersey. It will have a capital stock of $800,000, of which $400,000 shall be paid in in cash on or before the consummation of this agreement, and the remaining $400,000 shall be subscribed for by responsible subscribers to be approved by the Purchaser, whose subscriptions shall be payable in such instalments that the proceeds thereof shall be received within such period as shall be necessary to enable the Company to pay said promissory notes. The said notes shall be made payable to the order of the Vendor, and shall be delivered at the office of Mr. Samuel Untermyer, Number 37 Wall Street, in the City of New York, on the 25th day of May, 1910, at eleven o'clock in the forenoon, or sooner on a previous notice of five days from the Vendor stating the time and place, at which the Vendor shall execute and deliver to the Purchaser (1) a further confirmatory deed with full covenants af warranty, in which his wife shall join, conveying unto the Purchaser or his nominee a good and indefeasible title in and to the Philadelphia Opera House property, fixtures and improvements, free and clear of all liens, claims and encumbrances, other than the mortgage above mentioned, and the Vendor shall at said time furnish and deliver at his own expense to the

Purchaser the policy of a responsible title company of the City of Philadelphia certifying to the validity of said title in the Vendor at the time of transfer, that the property is then free and clear of all liens and encumbrances, except as above stated, and that the deed of conveyance to the Purchaser will vest in him a good, indefeasible title to said property free from all liens and encumbrances, except said mortgage; (2) separate bills of sale vesting and confirming in the Purchaser or his nominees the title to the personal property contained in the Philadelphia Opera House, and the title to the properities, scenery, costumes and music scores above described, accompanied by agreements containing covenants assuring the good-will of the business to the Purchaser, the Metropolitan Opera Company and other persons or corporations as above provided, and said agreement respecting the Manhattan Opera House; (3) assignments of the rights in and to the ten (10) operas above mentioned, and of all contracts and options held by the Vendor for other operas, and (4) assignments of the contracts with the artist enumerated in Schedule "B" hereto annexed, and such other instruments as may be necessary to carry out the intent hereof.

SIXTH: This Agreement shall bind the legal representatives of the parties hereto. It is understood that the Metropolitan Opera Company is interested with the Purchaser in the subject-matter of this agreement, that all the covenants hereof on the part of the Vendor and the party of the second part are intended to enure to the benefit of the Metropolitan Opera Company, and may be enforced by it as though it were named herein as a party hereto.

IN WITNESS WHEREOF, the parties hereto have hereunto set their respective hands and seals the day and year first above written.

In presence of
EDWIN B. ROOT,
SAML. UNTERMYER.

OSCAR HAMMERSTEIN (L.S.),
by ARTHUR HAMMERSTEIN, his Attorney in Fact.

EDWARD T. STOTESBURY (L.S.),
by OTTO H. KAHN, his Attorney in Fact.

ARTHUR HAMMERSTEIN (L.S.)
EDWIN B. ROOT, as to A. H.

SCHEDULE A.

"Herodiade"
"Aida"
"Thais"
"Cavallieria Rusticana"
"Pagliacci"
"Lucia di Lammermoor"
"Sappho"
"Daughter of the Regiment"
"Le Jongleur"
"Tannhauser"
"Carmen"
"Tales of Hoffman"
"Mephistopheles"
"Puritani"
"Otello"
"Crispino La Comare"
"The Huguenots"
"Elise d'Amour"
"Don Giovanni"
"Traviata"

"Mignon"
"Trovatore"
"Boheme"
"Faust"
"Grisiledis"
"Samson and Delilah"
"Elektra"
"Rigoletto"
"Louise"
"Salome"
"Pelleas et Melisande"
"Lakme"
"La Sonnambula"
"Princess d'Auberge"
"Navarraise"
"La Tosca"
"Barber of Seville"
"La Giaconda"
"Damnation of Faust"
"Dinora"

SCHEDULE B.

Name of Artist	Price per Performance	No. of Performances
Tetrazzini	$1,500	40
Mary Garden	1,400	20
Renaud	1,000	40*
Dalmores	600	50
Mazarin	457.50 per week	20 weeks**
McCormack	800 " "	20 "
Gilibert	750 " "	20 "

*To be assumed for twenty-four only.
**To be assumed only as provided in contract.

Exhibit B.

An Agreement made as of the twenty-sixth day of April, 1910, between Oscar Hammerstein, of the City of New York, party of the first part; ARHUR HAMMERSTEIN, of the City of New York, party of the second part; and METROPOLITAN OPERA COMPANY, a corporation of the State of New York, party of the third part.

The parties of the first and second part have entered into a contract with Edward T. Stotesbury (therein and herein called the Purchaser), dated April 26, 1910, which provides in general for the sale for a valuable consideration of the business of producing grand opera heretofore carried on by the parties of the first and second part, and in particular, among other things, for the assignment of the undertaking and good-will of the parties of the first and second part in and to the business of producing opera. By the terms of said contract the parties of the first and second part are to execute and deliver further instruments, of which this is one, in order fully to effectuate said contract.

Said contract recites that the party of the third part is interested with the Purchaser in the acquisition of the real and personal property and good-will therein described, and is willing to participate in such purchase only upon condition that it shall share in the acquisition of said good-will and shall be entitled to enforce each and all of the covenants of the parties of the first and second part hereto in said contract contained. The party of the third part is engaged in the business of producing opera in the Cities of New York and Boston and elsewhere, and it has been agreed between the Purchaser and the party of the third part that it should be entitled to and should be assured the undertaking and good-will of the parties of the first and second part in respect of the Cities of New York and Boston.

NOW, THEREFORE, THIS AGREEMENT WITNESSETH that, in consideration of the premises and of the covenants on the part of the Purchaser in said contract and of the sum of one dollar to each of them in hand paid by the party of the third part, the receipt of which is hereby acknowledged, and for other valuable consideration:

I.   The parties of the first and second part hereby sell, assign, transfer and set over unto the party of the third part all the undertaking and good-will of the parties of the first and second part, and of each of them, in and to the business of producing opera in the Cities of New York and Boston.

II.   For the purpose of assuring said good-will to the party of the third part, the parties of the first and second part further jointly and severally covenant and agree that neither of them, at any time hereafter within ten years from the date hereof, either alone or as a member of any firm or partnership or in conjunction with others, or as an officer, director, stockholder, manager, or employee of any corporation or association that may be or become engaged in any such business, or as an employee of any person or persons, or in any other capacity whatsoever, will be or become directly or indirectly engaged or interested in, or connected with, the business of producing, or any instance or instances of producing, in the Cities of New York and Boston, or in either of such Cities, in any language, grand opera, or any of the operas named in Schedule A hereto annexed, or any opera, operetta or comic opera that has ever been produced at the Metropolitan Opera House or at the Manhattan Opera House in the City of New York, or any opera, operetta or comic opera that may at any time hereafter have first been produced at the Metropolitan Opera House or at any other opera house in the City of New York, and in general will not be or become connected with any business that may interfere with or encroach upon the field now occupied by the party of the third part in the Cities of New York and Boston; it being understood that the prohibition herein contained is co-extensive only with the good-will hereby assigned, and that such prohibition shall not be taken to exceed in limitation of territory or in any of its other provisions the good-will so assigned, and that such prohibition is necessary to assure such good-will to the party of the third part.

III.   Nothing herein contained, however, shall be construed to prevent the parties of the first and second part, or either of them, from engaging in the Cities of New York and Boston in the business of producing musical comedies, or of producing comic opera in the sense in which that term is used in the United States as distinguished from the term "opera comique," as used in France, except as above restricted; provided, however, that in any such venture the parties of the first and second part will not, nor will either of them, advertise, solicit, or accept season or part season subscriptions for seats for any performance, but they and each of them will conduct the sale of seats in such business in the manner in which the ordinary theatrical ventures are conducted in the Cities of New York and Boston.

In witness whereof, the parties of the first and second part have respectively hereunto set their hands and seals the day and year first above written.

Witness: OSCAR HAMMERSTEIN (L.S.)
  EDWIN B. ROOT,   by ARTHUR HAMMERSTEIN,
  WARREN A. SCHENCK.   His Attorney-in-Fact.
    ARTHUR HAMMERSTEIN (L.S.)

SCHEDULE A.

"Herodiade"	"Mignon"
"Aida"	"Trovatore"
"Thais"	"Boheme"
"Cavallieria Rusticana"	"Faust"
"Pagliacci"	"Grisiledis"
"Lucia di Lammermoor"	"Samson and Delilah"
"Sappho"	"Elektra"
"Daughter of the Regiment"	"Rigoletto"
"Le Jongleur"	"Louise"
"Tannhauser"	"Salome"
"Carmen"	"Pelleas et Melisande"
"Tales of Hoffman"	"Lakme"
"Mephistopheles"	"La Sonnambula"
"Puritani"	"Princess d'Auberge"
"Otello"	"Navarraise"
"Crispino La Comare"	"La Tosca"
"The Huguenots"	"Barber of Seville"
"Elise d'Amour"	"La Giaconda"
"Don Giovanni"	"Damnation of Faust"
"Traviata"	"Dinora"

Exhibit C.

KNOW ALL MEN BY THESE PRESENTS, that I, OSCAR HAMMERSTEIN, of the Borough of Manhattan, City, County and State of New York, have made, constituted and appointed, and by these presents do make, constitute and appoint my son, Arthur Hammerstein, of the same place, my true and lawful attorney, for me and in my name, place and stead, to lease my lands, tenements or hereditaments of which I may be seized or possessed, or in which I may have an estate or interest, wherever the same may be situate, to such person or persons, and for such a term or number of years, or for life or lives, and at and under such yearly and other rents as he shall think fit; or otherwise to sell and dispose of the same absolutely in fee simple; for such price or sum of money, and upon such terms as to cash, credit, security and otherwise, and to such person or persons, as he shall think fit and convenient; and also for me, and in my name, and as my act and deed, to sign, seal, execute and deliver such deeds and conveyances for the leasing or for the absolute sale and disposal thereof, or of any part thereof, with such clauses, covenants and agreements to be therein contained as my said attorney shall think fit and expedient; and also to bargain, sell, grant and convey any and all fixtures and personal property, of any kind or description, which I may own, or in which I may have an interest capable of being sold and conveyed, including theatrical properties and scenery, furniture and fittings, musical and operatic scores, contracts with singers, performers, composers and music publishers, contracts, patents, copyrights and trademarks, licenses and royalty agreements, electrical devices and other theatrical equipments, and in connection with the sale of my property and businesses in the production of opera in the United States to sell and convey the good-will thereof; and to execute any and all releases from and assignments of and licenses under any of the said contracts, patents, copyrights, trade-marks, licenses and royalty agreements, at such prices or sums of money and upon such terms as to cash, credit, security and otherwise, as my said attorney shall think fit and expedient; also for me, and in my name, place and stead, to ask, demand, sue for or upon, recover and receive all moneys, debts, demands, negotiable instruments or other choses in action, which may become due or payable to me, or which I may be entitled to receive as the proceeds or consideration of any of the conveyances of real or personal property made by my said attorney by virtue of this power of attorney; and to have, use and take all lawful ways and means, in my name or otherwise, for the recovery thereof, by any legal process, and to compound, arbitrate and agree for the same, and to give acquittances and other sufficient discharges for the same.

I hereby undertake for myself, my legal representatives and assigns, that my said attorney, Arthur Hammerstein, may agree to and with any person or corporation that may become the purchaser of the property, business, assets, effects and good-will used in and connected with the business of conducting operatic performances now being conducted by me in the cities of New York, Philadelphia and elsewhere, to assure to such purchaser his or its legal representatives, successors or assigns, the good-will so to be sold. For the purpose of vesting in and assuring such good-will to the said purchaser, his or its legal representatives, successors or assigns, I hereby authorize and empower my said attorney to enter into an agreement in writing, under seal, with such purchaser, in a form satisfactory to my said attorney-in-fact, to the effect that I will not for the term of ten years from the date of any such agreement engage in or be directly or indirectly connected, either as owner, partner, officer, director, stockholder or otherwise, in any business, partnership or corporation that may during said term be or become engaged in the business of producing opera in any part of the United States of America; it being understood that the good-will of the business so to be sold in the event of a sale thereof by my said attorney extends throughout the United States and that the prohibition to be contained in said agreement is coextensive only with the good-will so to be sold and does not exceed in limitation of territory or otherwise such good-will.

I further authorize my said attorney to alter the form and purport of such covenant as he may see fit, hereby ratifying all that he may do in such agreement.

The purchaser shall not in any event be required to see to the disposition of the proceeds of any sale or any part thereof.

And for me, and in my name, to make, seal and deliver all documents and papers and do all lawful acts and things whatsoever concerning the premises, as fully in every respect as I myself might or could do were I personally present; hereby ratifying and confirming, and by these presents allowing whatsoever my said attorney shall, in my name, lawfully do or cause to be done in and about the premises by virtue of these presents.

IN WITNESS WHEREOF, I have hereunto set my hand and seal the 15th day of April, nineteen hundred and ten.

O. HAMMERSTEIN (L. S.)

Witness:

WARREN A. SHENKOWITZ.

Bibliography

In such scholarly works as Henry Edward Krehbiel's *Chapters of Opera* and *More Chapters of Opera*, Irving Kolodin's histories of the Metropolitan Opera, and various biographies and autobiographies, there are some sections and allusions to the Manhattan Opera Company. Prior to this book, however, there has been no complete study of this very important organization and its profound influence, the details of which were recorded in daily newspapers and obscure legal documents.

One of the most difficult research problems was the compilation of the annals of the performances with the casts and conductors. Listing, generally speaking, was based on the official Manhattan Opera Company programs, which are scattered in different institutions in New York, Philadelphia, Washington, and Princeton. Where there was an omission in the official programs, *Musical America,* a weekly concerning the world of music, or New York and Philadelphia daily newspapers supplied the necessary information. In some instances there is a discrepancy between the official program and the entry in the annals, since the scheduled artists did not always appear at the performance. As for the lists of the singers and important personnel of each season, the names in these rosters differ somewhat from the official Manhattan Opera Company prospectuses, for they include the actual participants in a series of performances. Some of the individuals announced in a prospectus subsequently never appeared with the company, while others were added once a season had begun. Luisa Tetrazzini's name, for example, is not on the official Manhattan Opera Company prospectus of 1907–1908; yet after she joined the company in January, 1908, she became a star of the first magnitude, often referred to as a second Adelina Patti. Thus, each list is composed of those who actually appeared at the Manhattan; and as often as possible, full names are given, although at that time the Manhattan Opera Company prospectuses and programs rarely supplied the first names of all the artists and personnel. Newspapers and periodicals of this period are also lacking in this respect.

Of the related literature used in this history, certain works were of inestimable value. Henry Edward Krehbiel's *Chapters of Opera* and *More Chapters of Opera,* William H. Seltsam's *Metropolitan Opera Annals,* and Irving Kolodin's histories of the Metropolitan Opera were Golcondas, scholarly sources of information concerning the presentation of opera in New York prior to 1906 and the atmosphere there which prompted Oscar Hammerstein in December, 1906, to produce opera in competition with the entrenched Metropolitan Opera Company. John Curtis's unpublished history "One Hundred Years of Grand Opera in Philadelphia" and Quaintance Eaton's *Opera Caravan* provided factual information of the operatic activities in Philadelphia prior to 1908, the year Hammerstein constructed an opera house in the Quaker City as a part of the opera war between the Manhattan and Metropolitan. Donald J. Grout's *A Short History of Opera,* as well as Wallace Brockway and Herbert Weinstock's *The Opera* are authoritative histories of European operatic movements, which, just prior to 1906, generated innovations in the repertory and productions of the Manhattan Opera Company. Finally, Ernest Newman's three volume *Stories of the Grand Operas,* Alfred Loewenberg's two volume *Annals of Opera 1597–1940,* and *Kobbé's Complete Opera Book* (ed. by the Earl of Harewood) contain analyses of the texts and the music of many of the operas identified with the Manhattan. Needless to say, operas and composers that were critically reviewed in New York and Philadelphia newspapers and in such periodicals as *Musical Courier, Musical America, Harper's Weekly,* and *The Theatre Magazine* revealed the opinions of competent music critics concerning the productions given by Hammerstein's company. These varying materials are the highlights of the related literature used in this study.

As for the source materials in this investigation, Krehbiel's *Chapters of Opera* and *More Chapters of Opera,* Kolodin's histories of the Metropolitan Opera, Seltsam's *Metropolitan Opera Annals,* Eaton's *Opera Caravan,* and Curtis's "One Hundred Years of Grand Opera in Philadelphia" provided information concerning opera in New York and Philadelphia during the years of the Manhattan Opera Company's activity. Many details germane to the history of the Manhattan and its relation to the Metropolitan are revealed in the biographies of Oscar Hammerstein and Heinrich Conried, general manager of the Metropolitan from 1903–1908, and in the autobiography of Giulio Gatti-Casazza, director of the Metropolitan who was Conried's successor. Of the artists who appeared at the Manhattan Opera House from 1906–10 and at Hammerstein's Philadelphia Opera House from 1908–10, the autobiographies of Nellie Melba, Luisa Tetrazzini, Marguerite d'Alvarez, and Mary Garden, as well as the biographies of John McCormack and Lillian Nordica devote pages to the Manhattan Opera Company and to Oscar Hammerstein.

Unfortunately these various autobiographies and biographies have many errors. *Mary Garden's Story* is but one example of an autobiography that states inaccuracies concerning the company. She writes that Hammerstein presented Strauss's *Salome* in Philadelphia without meeting any opposition from the press, the moralists, or the police: "There was no fuss over our performances in . . . Philadelphia. No scandal, no wild talk, no anything; just a brilliant success. There was never any question of padlocking the opera."[1] Contrary to what Miss Garden says, the clergy and many of the laity in Philadelphia were violently opposed to the presentation of *Salome*.[2] After a third performance Hammerstein withdrew it from the repertory, as there had been "a strong undercurrent of dissension among the established clientele of the [Philadelphia] Opera House as to the propriety of presenting this opera."[3] Still, even though from time to time these works contain inaccurate statements, they are nevertheless of great assistance in revealing reminiscences otherwise unavailable, material worthy of inclusion in the history of this company.

Source material also included the New York and Philadelphia daily newspapers of this period, the critical reviews for the performances being taken from such New York papers as the *Globe, Sun, Times, Herald, Daily-Tribune, The World, The Evening World, Press, American, The Evening Post, The Evening Journal,* and such Philadelphia dailies as the *Public Ledger, The North American,* and *Inquirer.* Reviews of eminent music critics in *Musical Courier, Musical America,* and *Harper's Weekly* were of great assistance.

Finally, invaluable information was provided in Oscar Hammer-

[1] Garden and Biancolli, *Mary Garden's Story,* 127.
[2] [Philadelphia] *Public Ledger,* February 8, 1909.
[3] *Ibid.,* February 18, 1909.

stein's letters concerning opera production and the company, as well as in the contract between the Manhattan and the Metropolitan by which Hammerstein sold his interests in the Manhattan and by which he was eradicated from opera production in New York, Philadelphia, Boston, and Chicago for ten years from the date of the covenant on April 26, 1910.

Alda, Frances. *Men Women and Tenors*. Boston, Houghton Mifflin Co., 1937.

Aldrich, Richard. "A New Opera House Worthy of Support," *The New York Times Theatre Section*, December 30, 1906, p. 5.

———. "Apropos of Close of Opera Season," *The New-York Times Theatre Section*, March 5, 1905, p. 6.

———. "Close of Another Year of Opera," *The New-York Times Theatre Section*, March 18, 1906, p. 3.

———. "First Week of Opera by Mr. Hammerstein," *The New York Times Theatre Section*, December 9, 1906, p. 5.

———. "Tetrazzini's Reception Almost Unparalleled in New York's Operatic History . . . ," *The New York Times Theatre Section*, January 19, 1908, p. 4.

———. "*Traviata* at Last Properly Costumed," *The New York Times Theatre Section*, January 6, 1907, p. 5.

Alvarez, Marguerite d'. *Forsaken Altars*. London, Hupert Hart-Davis, 1954.

"An Epoch for America," *Musical America*, Vol. X (July 24, 1909), 14.

Apel, Willi. *Harvard Dictionary of Music*. Cambridge, Harvard University Press, 1944.

"Application for the Erection of a Theatre at 315 West 34th Street," September 5, 1902; September 23, 1907; July 26, 1909 (New York, Bureau of Buildings for the Borough of Manhattan).

Armstrong, William. *The Romantic World of Music*. New York, E. P. Dutton, 1922.

Aronson, Rudolph. *Theatrical and Musical Memoirs*. New York, McBride, Nast and Co., 1913.

"At the Opera," *The Theatre Magazine*, Vol. VII (January, 1907), ix–x, 8–9.

Blom, Eric (ed.). *Grove's Dictionary of Music and Musicians*. Fifth edition. 9 vols. London, Macmillan & Co. Ltd., 1954.

Blumenthal, George, and Arthur H. Menkin. *My Sixty Years in Show Business*. New York, Frederick C. Osberg, Publisher, 1936.

"*Boheme* for Hammerstein," *Musical Courier*, Vol. LIV (January 9, 1907), 23–24.

Brockway, Wallace, and Herbert Weinstock. *The Opera*. New York, Simon and Schuster, 1941.

Buffalo Express, January 28–30, 1910.

"Building a Grand Opera Chorus from Native Material," *The New York Herald Magazine Section*, August 19, 1906, p. 2.

Calvé, Emma. *My Life*. Trans. by Rosamond Gilder. New York, D. Appleton and Co., 1922.

"Campanini Tells Why He Left N.Y.," *Musical America*, Vol. X (October 2, 1909), 4.

Carré, Albert. *Souvenirs de Théâtre*. Paris, Librairie Plon, 1950.

"Caruso to Sing No More This Season," *Musical America*, Vol. IX (April 17, 1909), 2.

Chaliapin, Feodor. *Man and Mask*. Trans. by Phyllis Mégroz. London, Victor Gollancz Ltd., 1932.

"Changes Planned at the Manhattan," *Musical America*, Vol. V (March 23, 1907), 13.

Colson, Percy. *Melba*. London, Grayson & Grayson, 1932.

"Concert Tour for Tetrazzini," *The New York Clipper*, Vol. LVII (January 15, 1910), 1.

Curtis, John. "One Hundred Years of Grand Opera in Philadelphia." 7 vols. Unpublished MS, The Historical Society of Pennsylvania, Philadelphia [n.d.].

Cushing, Mary Watkins. *The Rainbow Bridge*. New York, G. P. Putnam's Sons, 1954.

Dalmorès, Charles. "Well Known Singer Tells Story of Rise to Operatic Fame," *The New York Times Theatre Section*, December 29, 1907, p. 7.

Darnton, Charles. "Oscar Hammerstein Believes He Was Born for Grand Opera," *The* [New York] *Evening World Magazine Section*, December 15, 1906, p. 9.

Donalda, Pauline. Letters to the author, May 15, 1963, and June 5, 1963.

Downes, Olin. "Boston's Artistic Ideals and *Salomé*," *Musical America*, Vol. IX (April 10, 1909), 1, 29.

———. "Boston's Judgment of *Elektra*," *Musical America*, Vol. XI (April 9, 1910), 6.

———. "Notes and Comment upon Musical Matters," *The Boston Post Theatre Section*, April 11, 1909, p. 25.

Eames, Emma. *Some Memories and Reflections*. New York, D. Appleton and Co., 1927.

Earl of Harewood (ed.). *Kobbé's Complete Opera Book*. New York, G. P. Putnam's Sons, 1954.

Eaton, Quaintance. *Opera Caravan*. New York, Farrar, Straus and Cudahy, 1957.

Eaton, Walter Prichard. "Oscar Hammerstein A Boy Who Never Grew Up," *The American Magazine*, Vol. LXIV (May, 1907), 32–34.

Ewen, David. *Encyclopedia of the Opera*. New York, A. A. Wyn, Inc., 1955.

Farrar, Geraldine. Letter to the author, April 20, 1961.

———. *Such Sweet Compulsion*. New York, The Greystone Press, 1938.

Finck, Abbie H. C. "Maurice Renaud," *The Century Illustrated Monthly Magazine*, Vol. LXXVII (February, 1909), 614.

Finck, Henry T. "Mary Garden," *The Century Illustrated Monthly Magazine*, Vol. LXXVI (May, 1908), 148–51.

———. *Massenet and His Operas*. New York, John Lane Co., 1910.

———. *My Adventures in the Golden Age of Music*. New York, Funk & Wagnalls Co., 1926.

———. *Richard Strauss*. Boston, Little, Brown, and Co., 1917.

———. *Success in Music and How It Is Won*. New York, Charles Scribner's Sons, 1913.

Fitzgerald, J. A. "Mr. John McCormack—Grand Opera Tenor Whose Hobby Is Prize Fighting," *The New York Herald Theatre Section*, January 9, 1910, p. 11.

Franko, Sam. *Chords and Discords*. New York, The Viking Press, 1938.

Garden, Mary. "My Life," *Hearst's International*, Vol. XLV (January-February, 1924), 58–59, 73–74, 130–32, 151–52.

———. "The Heights," *Ladies' Home Journal*, Vol. XLVII (June, 1930), 12–13, 115–18.

———. "The Opera Singer and the Public," *The American Magazine*, Vol. LXXVIII (August, 1914), 30–33, 73–78.

————, and Louis Biancolli. *Mary Garden's Story*. New York, Simon and Schuster, 1951.

Gatti-Casazza, Giulio. *Memories of the Opera*. New York, Charles Scribner's Sons, 1941.

Gerson, Robert A. *Music in Philadelphia*. Philadelphia, Theodore Presser Co., 1940.

Gilman, Lawrence. "Concerning an Epoch-Making Score," *Harper's Weekly*, Vol. LII (March 21, 1908), 25.

————. "Giordano's *Siberia*," *Harper's Weekly*, Vol. LII (February 22, 1908), 25.

————. "Mr. Hammerstein's New Venture," *Harper's Weekly*, Vol. LIII (October 9, 1909), 27.

————. "What Heinrich Conried Has Done for Opera," *Harper's Weekly*, Vol. XLIX (April 15, 1905), 548.

Glackens, Ira. *Yankee Diva*. New York, Coleridge Press, 1963.

Grout, Donald Jay. *A Short History of Opera*. 2 vols. New York, Columbia University Press, 1947.

Hale, Philip, "Symphony's 21st Concert of Season," *The Boston Herald Theatre Section*, April 11, 1909, p. 7.

Hammerstein, Arthur. "Builder Tells How the Speed Record Was Made," *The* [Philadelphia] *North American Grand Opera Edition*, November 17, 1908, p. 9.

"Hammerstein Happy at Big Success Here," *The* [Philadelphia] *North American Drama Section*, March 14, 1909, p. 7.

"Hammerstein Loses Luise Tetrazzini," *Musical America*, Vol. IV (August 18, 1906), 1.

Hammerstein, Oscar. "The Artistic Temperament in the Aviary with the Song-Birds," *The Saturday Evening Post*, 181 (January 2, 1909), 3–4.

————. "The Mission of Grand Opera," *The* [Philadelphia] *North American Grand Opera Edition*, November 17, 1908, p. 1.

————. "Waiting for the First Rap of the Baton," *The* [New York] *Evening Telegram Theatre Section*, December 1, 1906, p. 13.

"Hammersteiniana," *Musical Courier*, Vol. XXII (June 3, 1891), 578.

"Hammerstein's Opéra Comique Company Disbanded," *Musical America*, Vol. XI (February 12, 1910), 15.

"Hammerstein's Plans for Grand Opera," *The Theatre Magazine*, Vol. VI (April, 1906), *vii*, 108–109.

Hanson, Henry (ed.), *The World Almanac and Book of Facts 1961*. New York, New York *World–Telegram* and *The Sun*, 1961.

Henderson, W. J. "A Dream of Two Singers," *The* [New York] *Sun Theatre Section*, January 6, 1907, p. 6.

———. "Mr. Hammerstein's Production of *Siberia*," *The* [New York] *Sun Theatre Section*, February 9, 1908, p. 8.

———. "Mr. Hammerstein's Season," *The* [New York] *Sun Theatre Section*, March 29, 1908, p. 8.

———. "New York the Greatest Opera City in the World," *The World Book*, Vol. XVII (April, 1909), 11,435–41.

———. "Opera and Opera Singers," *The* [New York] *Sun Theatre Section*, December 23, 1906, p. 6.

———. "Opera Season Reviewed," *The* [New York] *Sun Theatre Section*, March 5, 1905, p. 8.

———. *The Art of Singing*. New York, The Dial Press, 1938.

———. "The Record of the Year," *The* [New York] *Sun Theatre Section*, December 29, 1907, p. 8.

———. "The Season of Grand Opera," *Harper's Weekly*, Vol. XXXIX (February 16, 1895), 158–59.

———. "Walter Damrosch on the French *Tristan et Yseult*," *The* [New York] *Sun Theatre Section*, December 15, 1907, p. 8.

"His Double Opera Life," *The* [New York] *Sun Magazine Section*, October 25, 1908, p. 2.

"How Impresario Was Led to Build Opera House Here," *The* [Philadelphia] *North American Grand Opera Edition*, November 17, 1908, p. 8.

Huneker, James Gibbons. *Bedouins*. New York, Charles Scribner's Sons, 1920.

———. *Steeplejack*. 2 vols. New York, Charles Scribner's Sons, 1921.

J.B.C. "*Trilby* in Grand Opera Form Will Be Reginald De Koven's Next Task," *Musical America*, Vol. X (July 24, 1909), 3.

"Kahn, Morgan, and *Salome*," *Saturday Review*, Vol. XLVII (May 30, 1964), 60.

Kahn, Otto H. Manuscript letters for the year 1910, in the Kahn manuscripts and letters in the Princeton University Library.

Klein, Herman, *Great Women-Singers of My Time*. New York, E. P. Dutton & Co., 1931.

————. *Unmusical New York*. London, John Lane The Bodley Head, 1910.

Kolodin, Irving. *The Metropolitan Opera 1883–1935*. New York, Oxford University Press, 1936.

————. *The Story of the Metropolitan Opera 1883–1950*. New York, Alfred A. Knopf, 1953.

Koven, Reginald de. "Banner Week of Opera . . . ," *The* [New York] *World Theatre Section*, February 27, 1910, p. 5.

————. "New Flemish Opera . . . ," *The* [New York] *World Theatre Section*, March 14, 1909, p. 3.

————. "Rival Opera Cohorts Gather for the Fray . . .," *The* [New York] *World Theatre Section*, November 7, 1909, p. 5.

Krehbiel, Henry Edward. *Chapters of Opera*. New York, Henry Holt and Co., 1908.

————. *More Chapters of Opera*. New York, Henry Holt and Co., 1919.

Lahee, Henry C. *The Grand Opera Singers of To-Day*. Boston, L. C. Page and Co., 1912.

La [Montreal] *Presse*, December 14, 1909–January 2, 1910.

Lathrop, Elsie. " 'Each Time I Sing a Rôle I See New Possibilities . . .' " *Musical America*, Vol. IX (December 26, 1908), 3.

Lawton, Mary. *Schumann-Heink, The Last of the Titans*. New York, The Macmillan Co., 1928.

Le Figaro, April, 1900–March, 1907.

Lehmann, Lilli. *My Path Through Life*. Trans. by Alice Benedict Seligman. New York, G. P. Putnam's Sons, 1914.

Leiser, Clara. *Jean de Reszke and the Great Days of Opera*. London, Gerald Howe Ltd., 1933.

Lippincott, Horace Mather. "Edward T. Stotesbury." Paper read at the Old York Road Historical Association, Jenkintown, Pennsylvania, November 19, 1941.

Loewenberg, Alfred. *Annals of Opera 1597–1940*. Second ed. 2 vols. Genève, Societas Bibliographica, 1955.

[London] *Pall Mall Gazette*, July, 1902–December, 1906.

"Lure of the Footlights as Felt by a Manager's Daughter," *The New York Times Magazine Section*, May 31, 1908, p. 6.

Mahler, Alma. *Gustav Mahler*. Trans. by Basil Creighton. New York, The Viking Press, 1946.

Manhattan Opera Company Programmes and Prospectuses, 1906–1910.

"Manhattan Opera House," *Architectural Record*, Vol. XXI (February, 1907), 148–52.

Marek, George R. *Puccini*. New York, Simon and Schuster, 1951.

Massenet, Jules. *My Recollections*. Trans. by H. Villiers Barnett. Boston, Small, Maynard and Co., 1919.

Matz, Mary Jane. *The Many Lives of Otto Kahn*. New York, The Macmillan Company, 1963.

Mazarin, Mariette. "Mme. Mazarin on *Elektra*," *The* [New York] *World Theatre Section*, January 30, 1910, p. 1.

McC., R. L. "Taking Our Readers for a Glance Through New York's Brand-New Opera-House," *The* [New York] *World Theatre Section*, December 2, 1906, p. 2.

McCormack, Lily. *I Hear You Calling Me*. Milwaukee, The Bruce Publishing Co., 1949.

Melba, Nellie. *Melodies and Memories*. London, Thornton Butterworth, Ltd., 1925.

———. "Singers Born, Not Made, Says Melba," *The* [Philadelphia] *North American Grand Opera Edition*, November 17, 1908, p. 1.

Meltzer, Charles Henry. "Opera at the Manhattan," *New York American Drama and Society Section*, March 21, 1909, p. 4.

———. "Smart Singers and Others," *New York American Drama and Society Section*, January 12, 1908, p. 4.

———. "The Operatic Outlook," *New York American Drama and Society Section*, December 29, 1907, p. 3.

Metropolitan Opera Company. Minutes of the Board of Directors for the years 1908–1929, in the Metropolitan Opera Archives.

Metropolitan Opera Company v. Oscar Hammerstein and Arthur Hammerstein, File No. 18094–1913 (1914).

"Miss Mary Garden Talks about Her American Operatic Debut," *The New York Herald Society and Drama Section*, December 1, 1907, p. 12.

"Monsieur Hammerstein Tells in Nobody's Words but His Own How He Engaged Songbird Melba," *The* [New York] *World Theatre Section*, May 6, 1906, p. 2.

Moore, Edward C. *Forty Years of Opera in Chicago*. New York, Horace Liveright, 1930.

Moses, Montrose J. *The Life of Heinrich Conried.* New York, Thomas Y. Crowell Co., 1916.

"Mr. Heinrich Conried Says the Most Highly Educated Opera Audiences in the World Are Right Here in New York," *The New York Herald Society and Drama Section,* January 5, 1908, p. 12.

Murphy, Agnes G. *Melba: A Biography.* New York, Doubleday, Page & Co., 1909.

Musical Courier, Vol. XXII (June 3, 1891), 577.

Newman, Ernest. *Stories of the Great Operas.* 3 vols. Garden City, Garden City Publishing Co., Inc., 1948.

New York American, March, 1899–April, 1910.

New-York Daily Tribune, September, 1889–April, 1910.

"New York Opera Season Begins," *The New York Herald Society and Drama Section,* November 8, 1908, p. 9.

"New York's $2,000,000 Season of Grand Opera," *The New York Times Magazine Section,* March 29, 1908, p. 4.

Norris, G. Heide. "New Opera House Makes This a Socially United City and Center of Art," *The* [Philadelphia] *North American Grand Opera Edition,* November 17, 1908, p. 1.

O'Connor, Harvey. *The Astors.* New York, Alfred A. Knopf, 1941.

Odell, George C. D. *Annals of the New York Stage.* 15 vols. New York, Columbia University Press, 1927–49.

"Oscar Inspects Operas from His Seat in Wings," *The* [Philadelphia] *North American Theatre Section,* December 20, 1908, p. 8.

[Philadelphia] *Public Ledger,* August, 1907–April, 1910.

" 'Poverty, the Madhouse and Untimely Death Have Been the Reward of Operatic Management,' " *The* [New York] *World Theatre Section,* January 17, 1909, p. 2.

"Production of *Salome* Is a Costly Work," Philadelphia *Public Ledger Magazine Section,* January 24, 1909, p. 5.

Rawling, Sylvester. "Hammerstein Says Poor Performances Are Due to Preparations for *Elektra,*" *The* [New York] *Evening World Theatre Section,* January 15, 1910, p. 4.

————. "Hammerstein to Give Opera Comique to Prevent Musical Indigestion," *The* [New York] *Evening World Theatre Section,* March 6, 1909, p. 5.

————. "Mazarin, Who as Elektra Has Given New York the Most Thrilling Operatic Character in Its History . . . ," *The* [New York] *Evening World Theatre Section,* February 5, 1910, p. 7.

————. "What Opera Singers Really Are Paid Told Frankly by Arthur Hammerstein," *The* [New York] *Evening World,* May 7, 1910, p. 4.

"Real Grand Opera Czar Is the Stage Manager," *The* [Philadelphia] *North American Theatre Section,* February 28, 1909, p. 5.

Richardson, Anne Steese. " 'I'm the Little Man,' says Hammerstein, 'Who'll Provide Grand Opera for the Masses,' " *The* [New York] *World Theatre Section,* January 21, 1906, p. 2.

[Rochester] *Democrat and Chronicle,* January 23–27, 1910.

[Rochester] *Post Express,* January 23–27, 1910.

Rosenthal, Harold. *Two Centuries of Opera at Covent Garden.* London, Putnam, 1958.

Scholes, Percy A. *The Oxford Companion to Music.* Ninth ed. London, Oxford University Press, 1955.

S.E.E. "Cornerstone Laid in Philadelphia," *Musical America,* Vol. VIII (July 4, 1908), 5.

Seligman, Vincent. *Puccini Among Friends.* London, Macmillan & Co. Ltd., 1938.

Seltsam, William H. *Metropolitan Opera Annals.* New York, The H. W. Wilson Co., 1947.

"Serious Students of Music in Manhattan Opera Chorus," *Musical America,* Vol. V (April 6, 1907), 14.

Seroff, Victor I. *Debussy Musician of France.* New York, G. P. Putnam's Sons, 1956.

Sheean, Vincent. *Oscar Hammerstein I.* New York, Simon and Schuster, 1956.

Sohn, Joseph. "Opera in New York," *The Forum,* Vol. XXXVIII (April, 1907), 507–25.

Stokes, I. N. Phelps. *The Iconography of Manhattan Island.* 6 vols. New York, Robert H. Dodd, 1915–28.

Stoullig, Edmond. *Les Annales du Théâtre et de la Musique.* 41 vols. Paris, Charpentier et Cie, 1876–96 and P. Ollendorff, 1897–1918.

Strauss, Richard. "*Salome's* Composer on the Duties of Music Critics," *New York American Drama and Society Section,* March 28, 1909, p. 5.

Strong, L. A. G. *John McCormack*. New York, The Macmillan Co., 1941.

Sullivan, Mark. *The Turn of the Century, 1900–1904* (Vol. I of *Our Times; the United States, 1900–1925*. 6 vols.) New York, Charles Scribner's Sons, 1926–35.

"Sweeping Effects of Giant Merger," *Musical America*, Vol. XI (May 7, 1910), 2–3.

Taubman, Howard. *The Maestro*. New York, Simon and Schuster, 1951.

Tetrazzini, Luisa. *My Life of Song*. Philadelphia, Dorrance and Co., Inc., 1922.

The [Baltimore] *Sun*, January 5–12, 1909.

The Boston Daily Globe, March 29–April 10, 1909, and March 28–April 12, 1910.

The Boston Herald, March 29–April 10, 1909, and March 28–April 12, 1910.

The Boston Journal, March 29–April 10, 1909, and March 28–April 12, 1910.

The Boston Post, March 29–April 10, 1909, and March 28–April 12, 1910.

The [Cincinnati] *Enquirer*, December 26–29, 1909.

The Hamilton [Canada] *Spectator*, January 13–17, 1910.

"The Inauguration of the Manhattan Opera House," *The New York Herald Society and Drama Section*, October 21, 1906, p. 5.

The [London] *Times*, July, 1902–December, 1907.

"The Longest Wig in the World," *The* [New York] *World Magazine Section*, February 16, 1908, p. 5.

"The Manhattan Opera House Opens Its Season of 1907–08," *The New York Herald Society and Drama Section*, November 3, 1907, p. 12.

The Montreal Daily Star, December 14, 1909–January 2, 1910.

The [New York] *Evening Mail*, February, 1906–April, 1910.

The [New York] *Evening Post*, February, 1906–April, 1910.

The [New York] *Evening Sun*, February, 1906–April, 1910.

The [New York] *Evening Telegram*, February, 1906–April, 1910.

The [New York] *Evening World*, February, 1906–May, 1910.

The [New York] *Globe and Commercial Advertiser*, February, 1906–April, 1910.

The New York Herald, February, 1906–April, 1910.

The [New York] *Morning Telegraph*, July 21, 1906.

The New York Press, February, 1906–April, 1910.

The [New York] *Sun*, September, 1889–April, 1910.

The New York Times, September, 1889–April, 1910.

The [New York] *World*, February, 1906–April, 1910.

"The Opera Season," *Musical America*, Vol. III (March 24, 1906), 8.

The [Ottawa] *Citizen*, January 4–13, 1910.

The [Philadelphia] *Evening Bulletin*, November, 1908–April, 1910.

The [Philadelphia] *Evening Telegraph*, August, 1907–April, 1910.

The Philadelphia Inquirer, August, 1907–April, 1910.

The [Philadelphia] *North American*, August, 1907–April, 1910.

The [Philadelphia] *Press*, November, 1908–April, 1910.

The Philadelphia Record, November, 1908–April, 1910.

The Pittsburgh Post, December 21–26, 1909.

The Quebec Chronicle, January 3–11, 1910.

"The Raconteur," *Musical Courier*, Vol. XXI (October 15, 1890), 380.

The Rochester Union and Advertiser, January 25–27, 1910.

The [Toronto] *Daily Mail and Empire*, January 15–24, 1910.

The [Toronto] *Globe*, January 15–24, 1910.

The Washington Herald, January 10–16, 1910.

The Washington Post, January 10–16, 1910.

The Washington Times, January 10–16, 1910.

Thompson, Oscar. *The American Singer*. New York, The Dial Press, Inc., 1937.

————, (ed.). *The International Cyclopedia of Music and Musicians*. 7th ed. New York, Dodd, Mead and Co., 1956.

"To Search Europe for More Singers," *Musical America*, Vol. XI (April 23, 1910), 1, 29.

Town Topics, December, 1906–April, 1910.

"Trap for Metropolitan," *Musical America*, Vol. XI (February 12, 1910), 18.

Unidentified clipping, New York, early April, 1907.

Van Vechten, Carl. *Interpreters and Interpretations*. New York, Alfred A. Knopf, 1917.

————. *In the Garret*. New York, Alfred A. Knopf, 1920.

————. *The Merry-Go-Round*. New York, Alfred A. Knopf, 1918.

Wagenknecht, Edward. *Seven Daughters of the Theater*. Norman, University of Oklahoma Press, 1964.

Wagnalls, Mabel. *Stars of the Opera*. New York and London, Funk & Wagnalls, 1907.

Washington Journal, January 10–16, 1910.

Waters, Edward N. *Victor Herbert*. New York, The Macmillan Co., 1955.

Wechsberg, Joseph. *Red Plush and Black Velvet*. Boston, Little, Brown and Co., 1961.

Index

Oscar Hammerstein's Manhattan Opera Company
has been set on the Linotype in 11½-point Caslon Old Face,
a faithful rendering of the original types
of William Caslon.

This book is printed on paper bearing
the watermark of the University of Oklahoma Press
and designed for an effective life of
at least three hundred years.

University of Oklahoma Press
Norman